Chapter 6

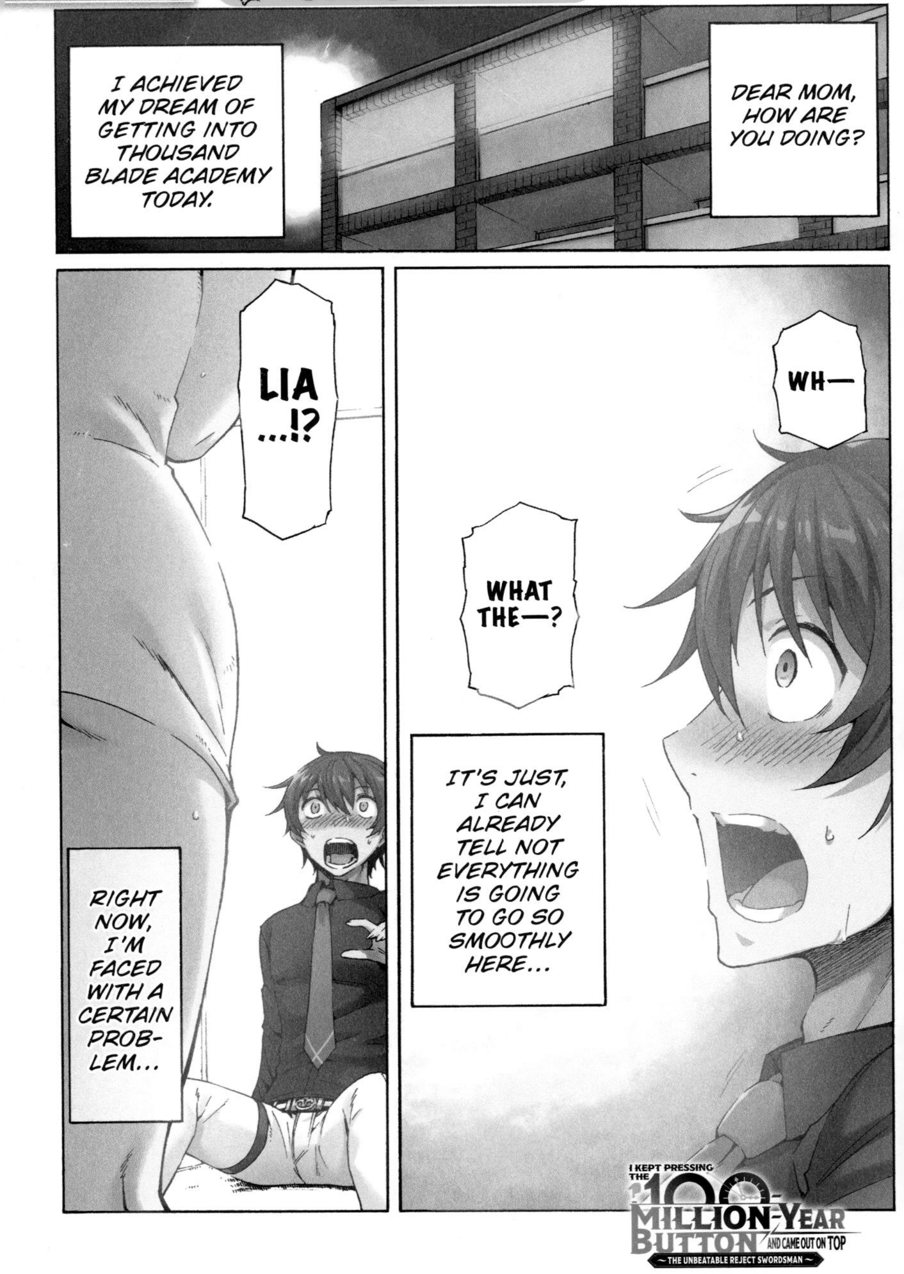
DEAR MOM, HOW ARE YOU DOING?
I ACHIEVED MY DREAM OF GETTING INTO THOUSAND BLADE ACADEMY TODAY.
WH—
WHAT THE—?
IT'S JUST, I CAN ALREADY TELL NOT EVERYTHING IS GOING TO GO SO SMOOTHLY HERE…
LIA …!?
RIGHT NOW, I'M FACED WITH A CERTAIN PROB- LEM…

I KEPT PRESSING THE 100-MILLION-YEAR BUTTON AND CAME OUT ON TOP
~THE UNBEATABLE REJECT SWORDSMAN~

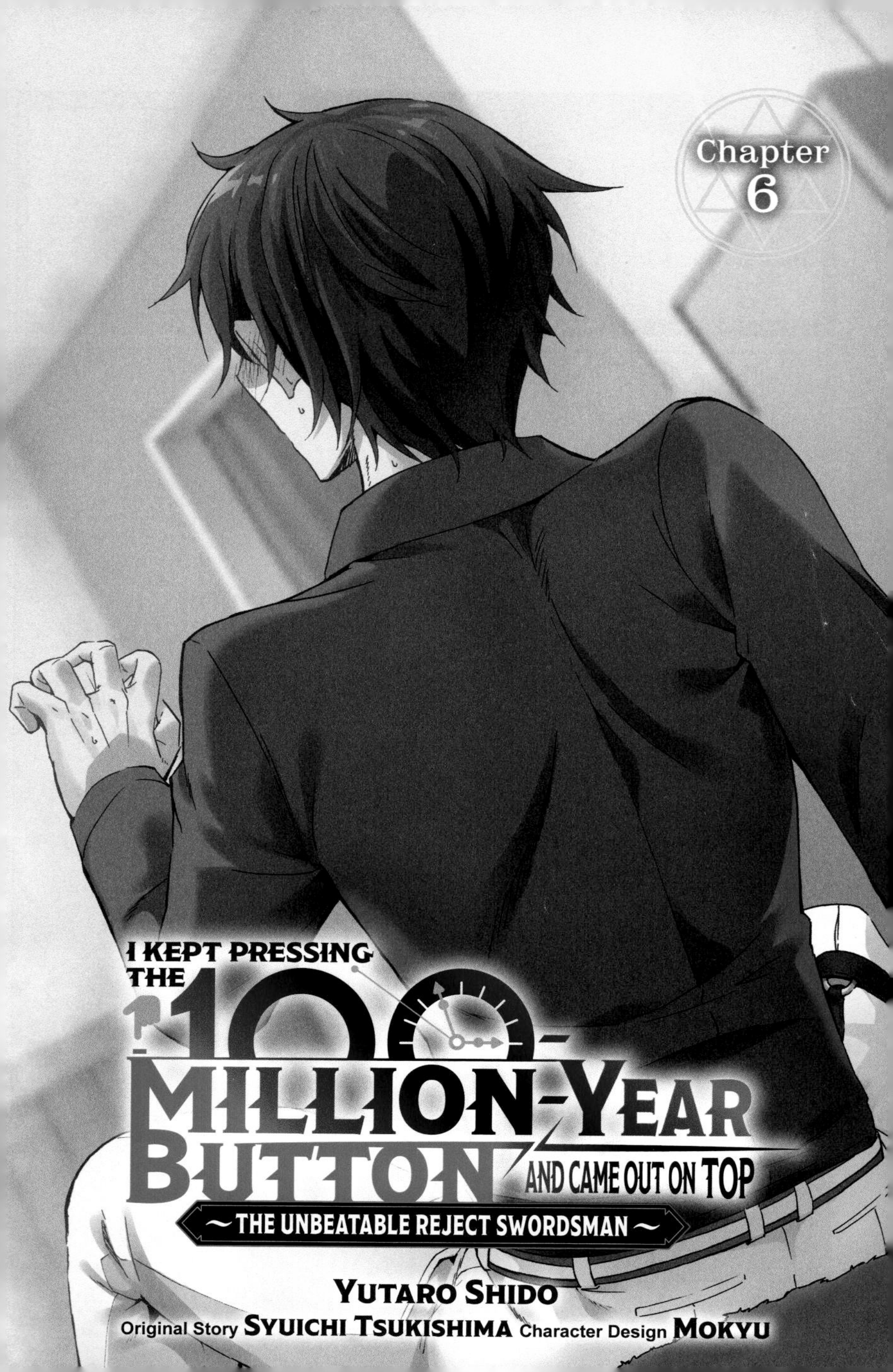
Chapter 6
I KEPT PRESSING THE 100-MILLION-YEAR BUTTON AND CAME OUT ON TOP
~THE UNBEATABLE REJECT SWORDSMAN~
YUTARO SHIDO
Original Story SYUICHI TSUKISHIMA Character Design MOKYU

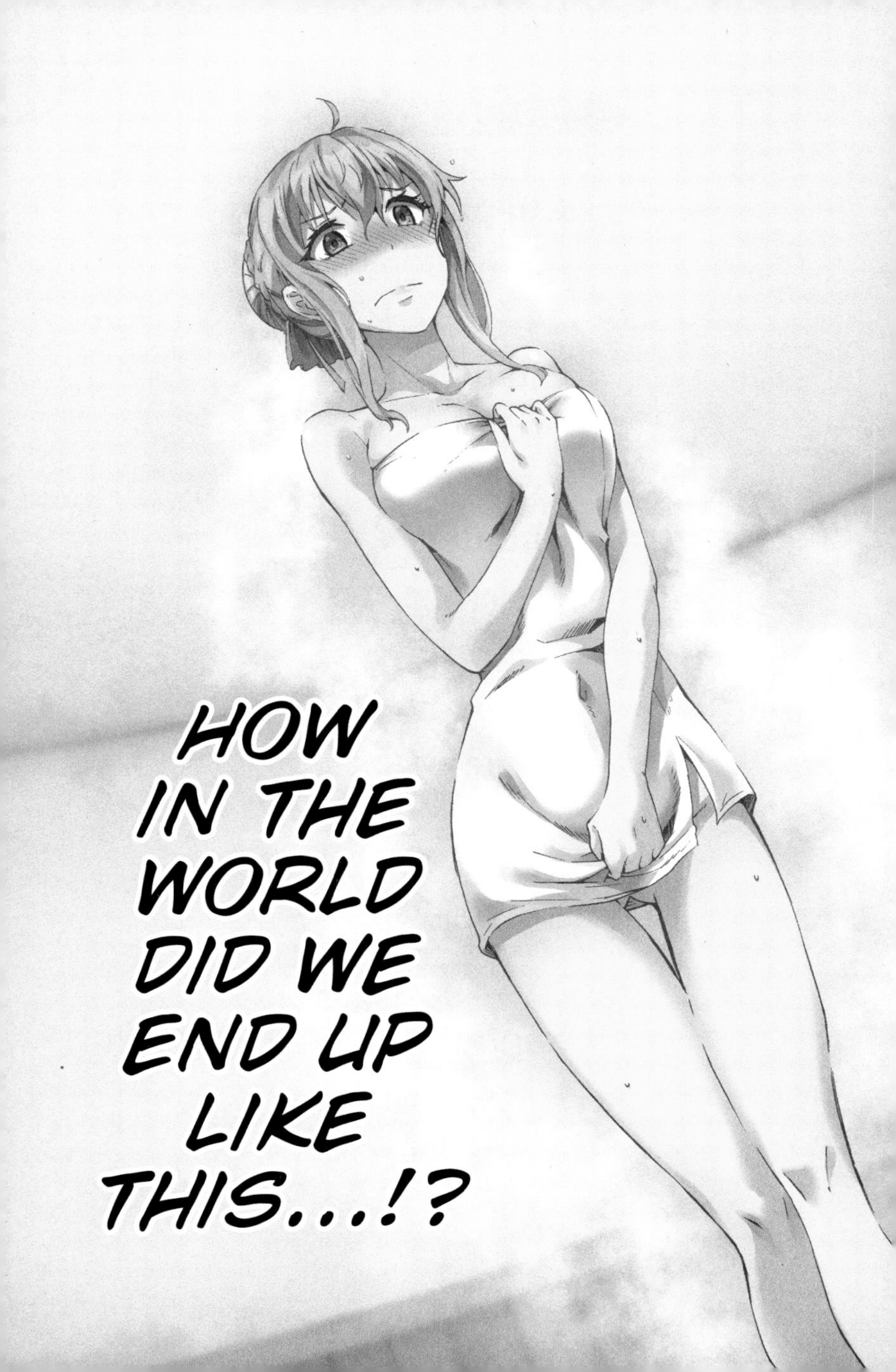
HOW IN THE WORLD DID WE END UP LIKE THIS...!?

CONTENTS

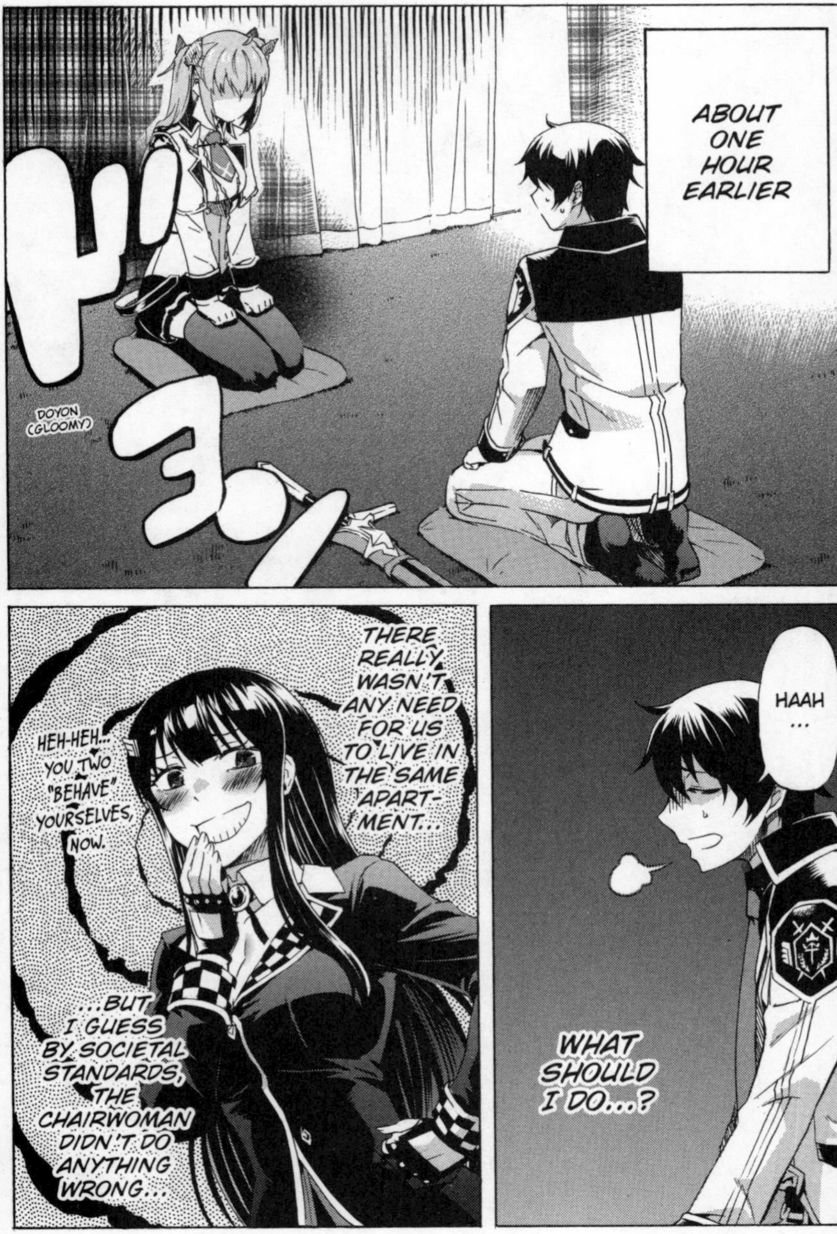

ABOUT ONE HOUR EARLIER
DOYON (GLOOMY)
HAAH...
WHAT SHOULD I DO...?
THERE REALLY WASN'T ANY NEED FOR US TO LIVE IN THE SAME APARTMENT...
HEH-HEH... YOU TWO "BEHAVE" YOURSELVES, NOW.
...BUT I GUESS BY SOCIETAL STANDARDS, THE CHAIRWOMAN DIDN'T DO ANYTHING WRONG...

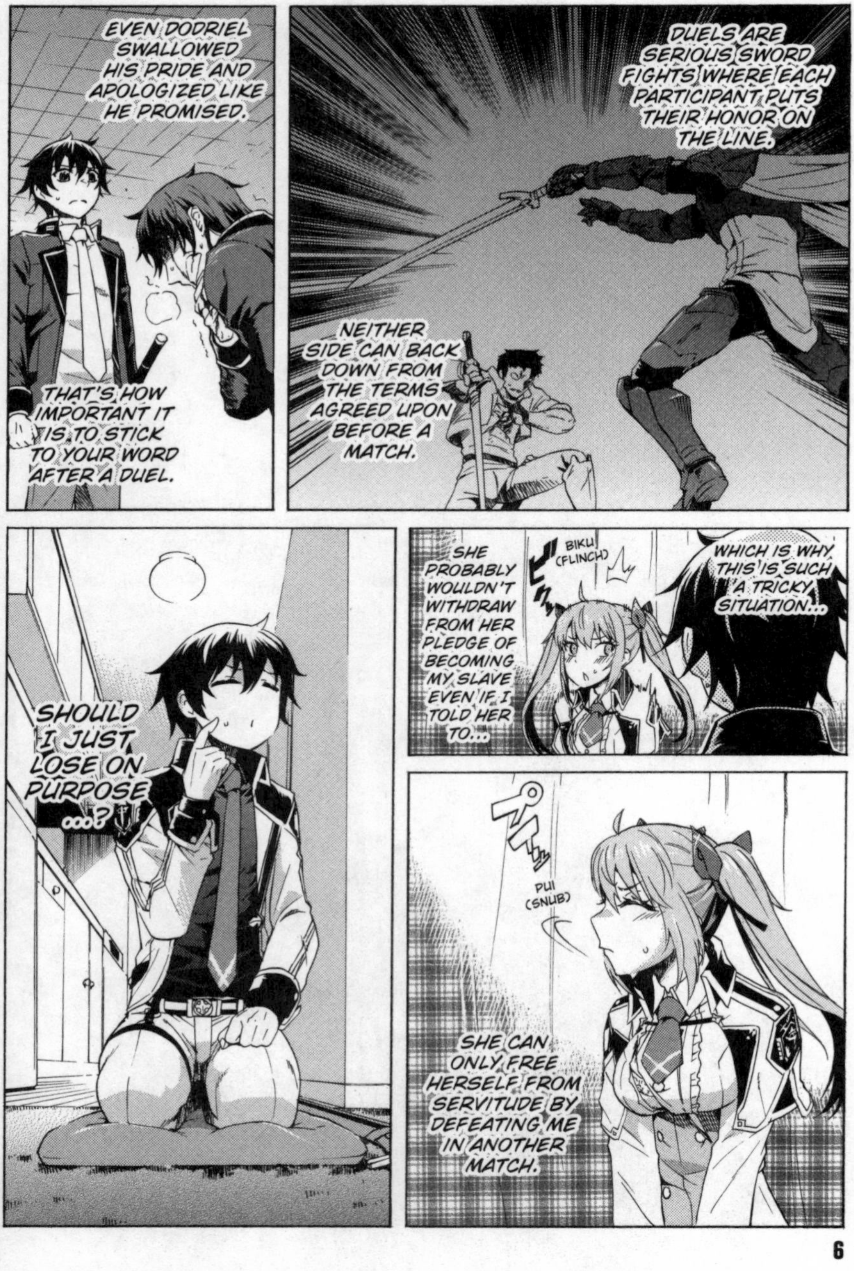
DUELS ARE SERIOUS SWORD FIGHTS WHERE EACH PARTICIPANT PUTS THEIR HONOR ON THE LINE.
NEITHER SIDE CAN BACK DOWN FROM THE TERMS AGREED UPON BEFORE A MATCH.
EVEN DODRIEL SWALLOWED HIS PRIDE AND APOLOGIZED LIKE HE PROMISED.
THAT'S HOW IMPORTANT IT IS TO STICK TO YOUR WORD AFTER A DUEL.
WHICH IS WHY THIS IS SUCH A TRICKY SITUATION...
BIKU (FLINCH)
SHE PROBABLY WOULDN'T WITHDRAW FROM HER PLEDGE OF BECOMING MY SLAVE EVEN IF I TOLD HER TO...
PUI (SNUB)
SHE CAN ONLY FREE HERSELF FROM SERVITUDE BY DEFEATING ME IN ANOTHER MATCH.
SHOULD I JUST LOSE ON PURPOSE ...?

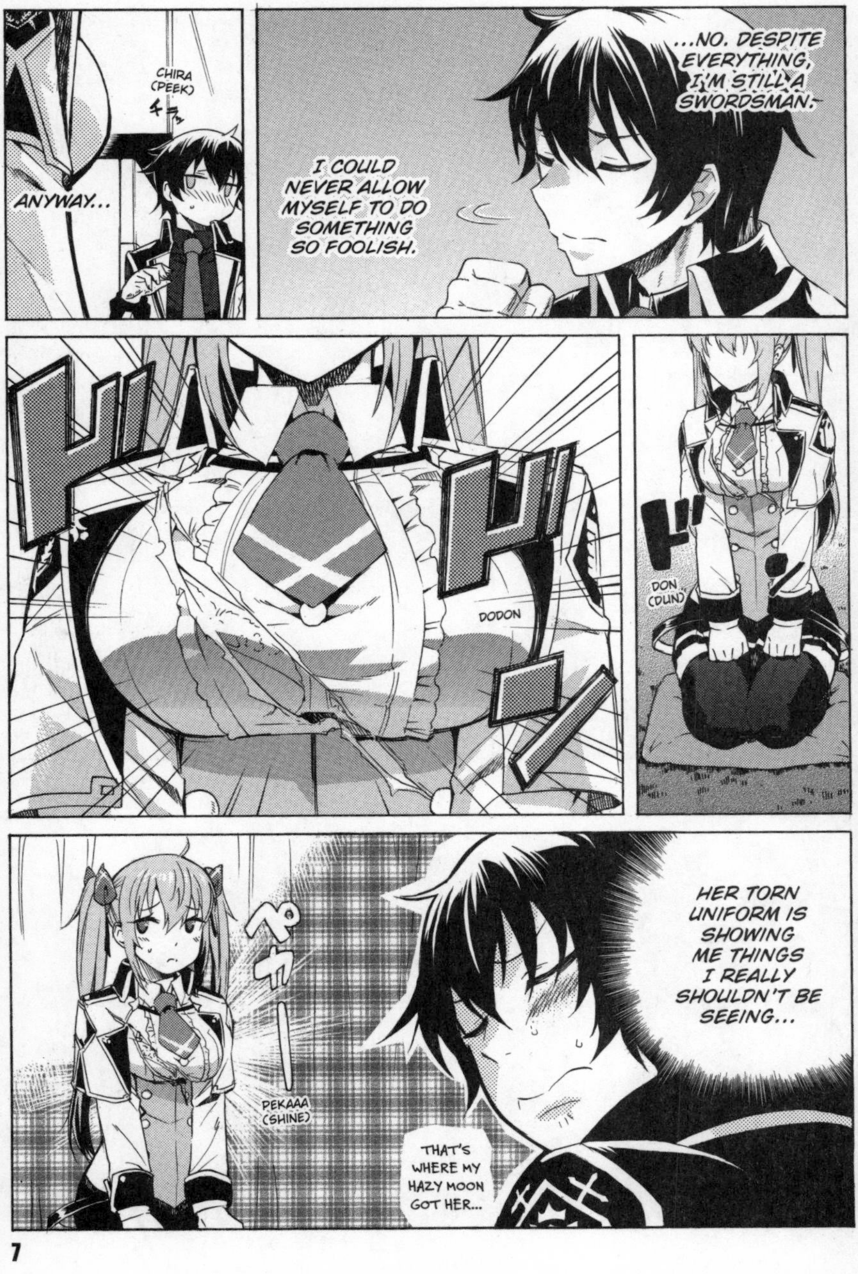
...NO. DESPITE EVERYTHING, I'M STILL A SWORDSMAN.
I COULD NEVER ALLOW MYSELF TO DO SOMETHING SO FOOLISH.
CHIRA (PEEK)
ANYWAY...
DON (DUN)
DODON
HER TORN UNIFORM IS SHOWING ME THINGS I REALLY SHOULDN'T BE SEEING...
THAT'S WHERE MY HAZY MOON GOT HER...
PEKAAA (SHINE)

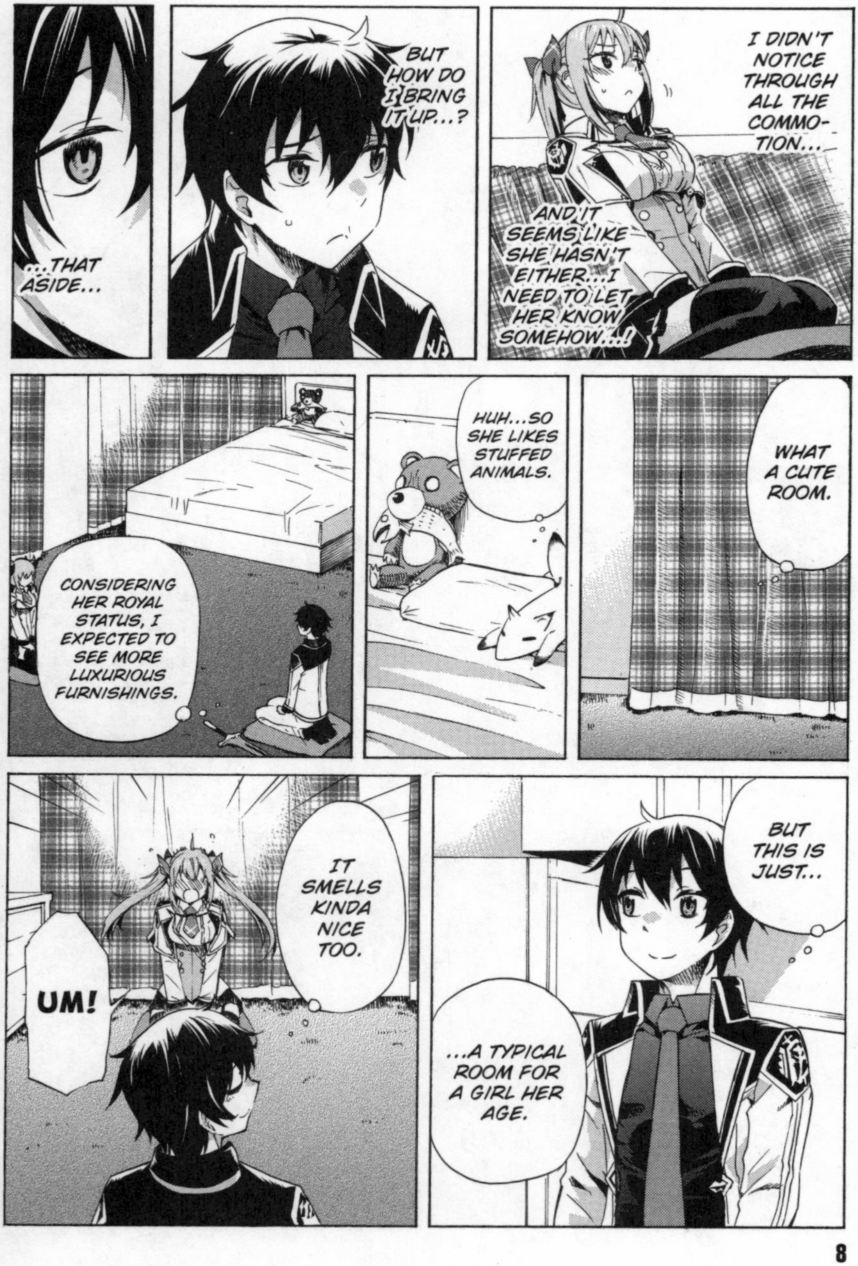
I DIDN'T NOTICE THROUGH ALL THE COMMOTION...
AND IT SEEMS LIKE SHE HASN'T EITHER...I NEED TO LET HER KNOW SOMEHOW...!
BUT HOW DO I BRING IT UP...?
...THAT ASIDE...
WHAT A CUTE ROOM.
HUH...SO SHE LIKES STUFFED ANIMALS.
CONSIDERING HER ROYAL STATUS, I EXPECTED TO SEE MORE LUXURIOUS FURNISHINGS.
BUT THIS IS JUST...
...A TYPICAL ROOM FOR A GIRL HER AGE.
IT SMELLS KINDA NICE TOO.
UM!

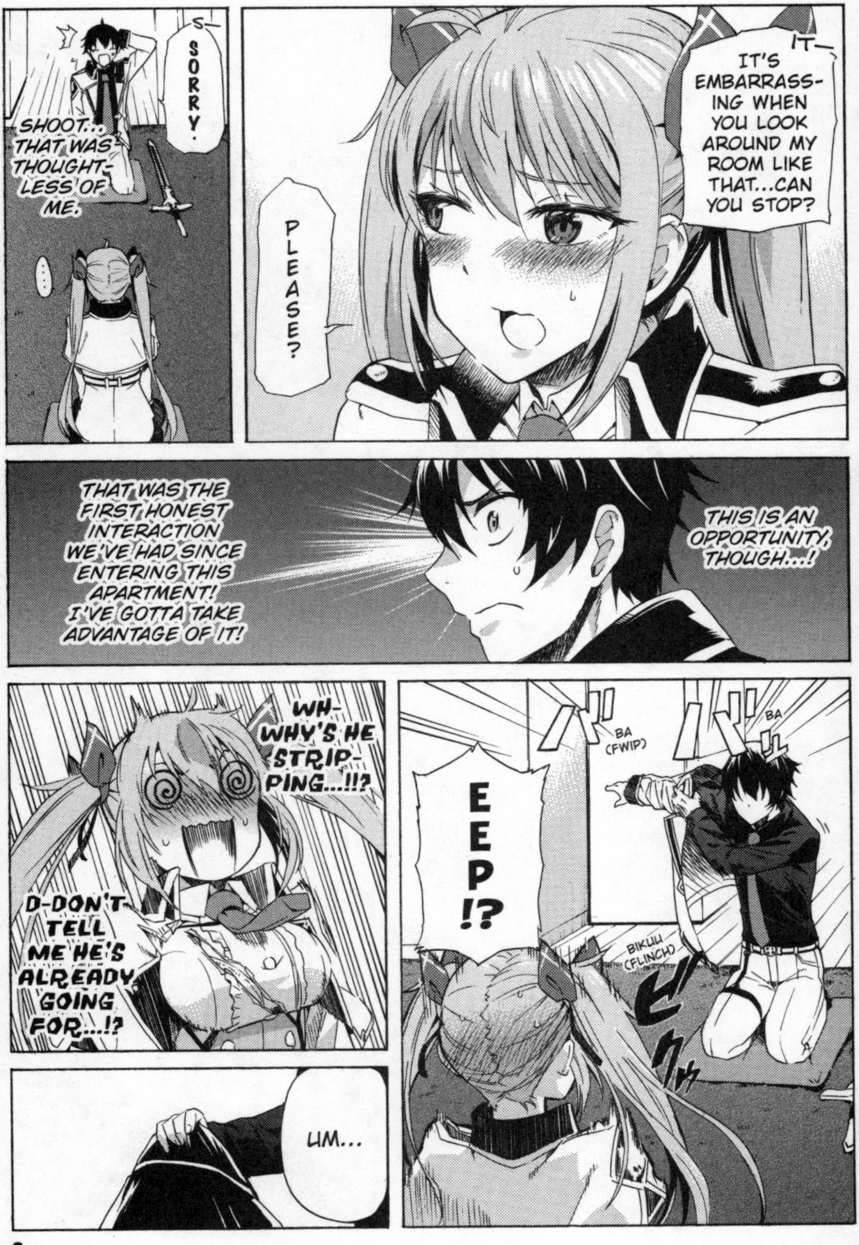

IT—
IT'S EMBARRASSING WHEN YOU LOOK AROUND MY ROOM LIKE THAT...CAN YOU STOP?
PLEASE?
S—SORRY.
SHOOT... THAT WAS THOUGHTLESS OF ME.
...
THIS IS AN OPPORTUNITY, THOUGH...!
THAT WAS THE FIRST HONEST INTERACTION WE'VE HAD SINCE ENTERING THIS APARTMENT! I'VE GOTTA TAKE ADVANTAGE OF IT!
BA
BA (FWIP)
EEP!?
BIKUU (FLINCH)
WH-WHY'S HE STRIPPING...!!?
D-DON'T TELL ME HE'S ALREADY GOING FOR...!?
UM...

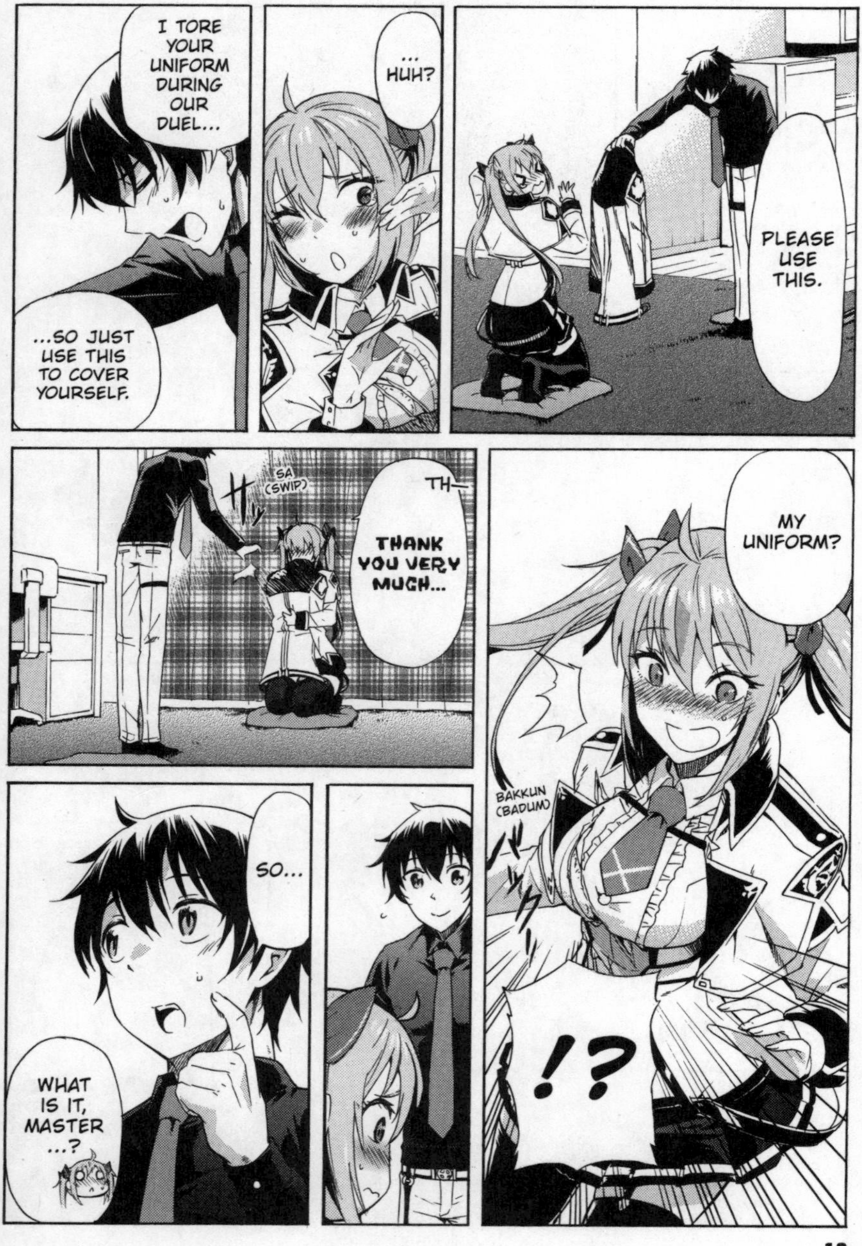
PLEASE USE THIS.
... HUH?
I TORE YOUR UNIFORM DURING OUR DUEL...
...SO JUST USE THIS TO COVER YOURSELF.
MY UNIFORM?
BAKKUN (BADUM)
!?
SA (SWIP)
TH—
THANK YOU VERY MUCH...
SO...
WHAT IS IT, MASTER ...?

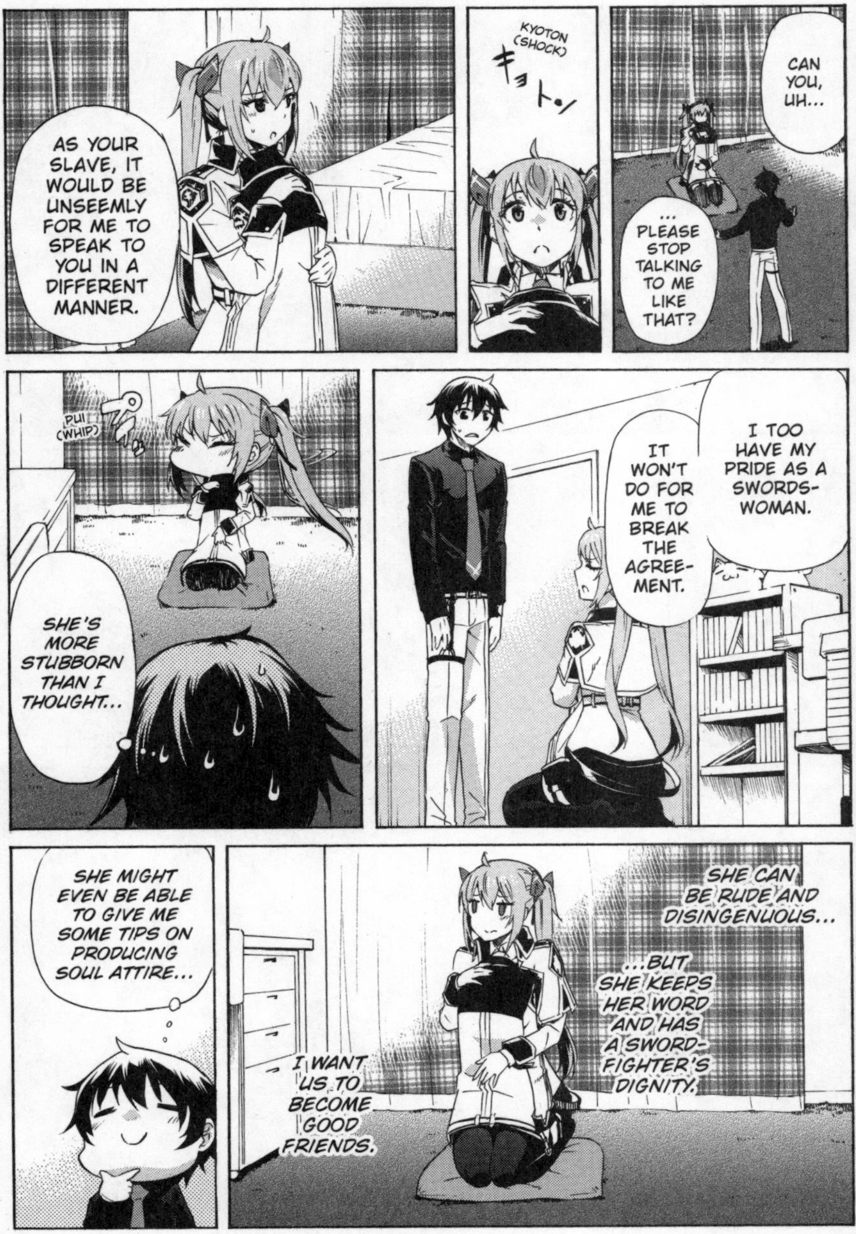
CAN YOU, UH...
...PLEASE STOP TALKING TO ME LIKE THAT?
KYOTON (SHOCK)
キョトン
AS YOUR SLAVE, IT WOULD BE UNSEEMLY FOR ME TO SPEAK TO YOU IN A DIFFERENT MANNER.
I TOO HAVE MY PRIDE AS A SWORDS-WOMAN.
IT WON'T DO FOR ME TO BREAK THE AGREE-MENT.
PUI (WHIP)
SHE'S MORE STUBBORN THAN I THOUGHT...
SHE CAN BE RUDE AND DISINGENUOUS...
...BUT SHE KEEPS HER WORD AND HAS A SWORD-FIGHTER'S DIGNITY.
I WANT US TO BECOME GOOD FRIENDS.
SHE MIGHT EVEN BE ABLE TO GIVE ME SOME TIPS ON PRODUCING SOUL ATTIRE...

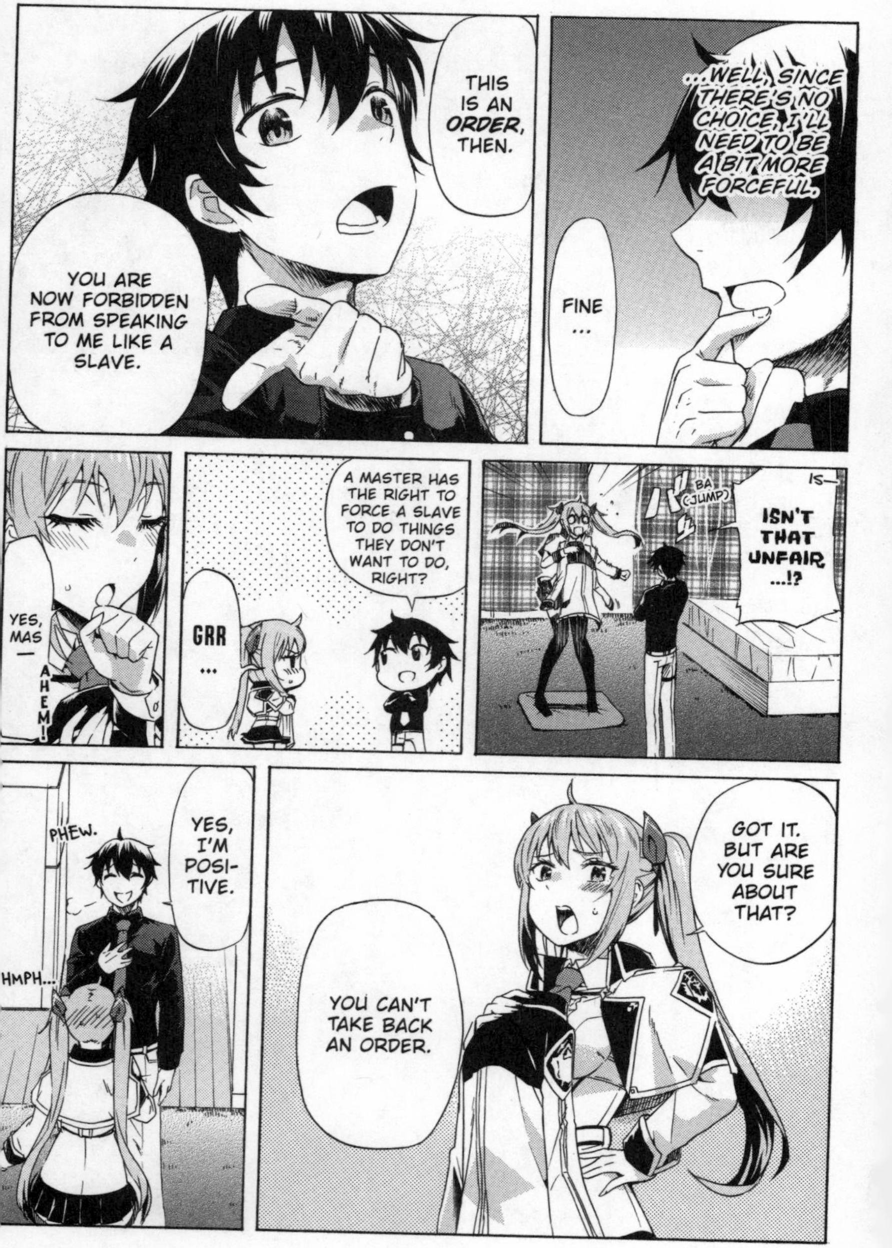
...WELL, SINCE THERE'S NO CHOICE, I'LL NEED TO BE A BIT MORE FORCEFUL.
FINE...
THIS IS AN ORDER, THEN.
YOU ARE NOW FORBIDDEN FROM SPEAKING TO ME LIKE A SLAVE.
IS—
BA (JUMP)
ISN'T THAT UNFAIR...!?
A MASTER HAS THE RIGHT TO FORCE A SLAVE TO DO THINGS THEY DON'T WANT TO DO, RIGHT?
GRR...
YES, MAS—
AHEM!
GOT IT. BUT ARE YOU SURE ABOUT THAT?
YOU CAN'T TAKE BACK AN ORDER.
YES, I'M POSI-TIVE.
PHEW.
HMPH...

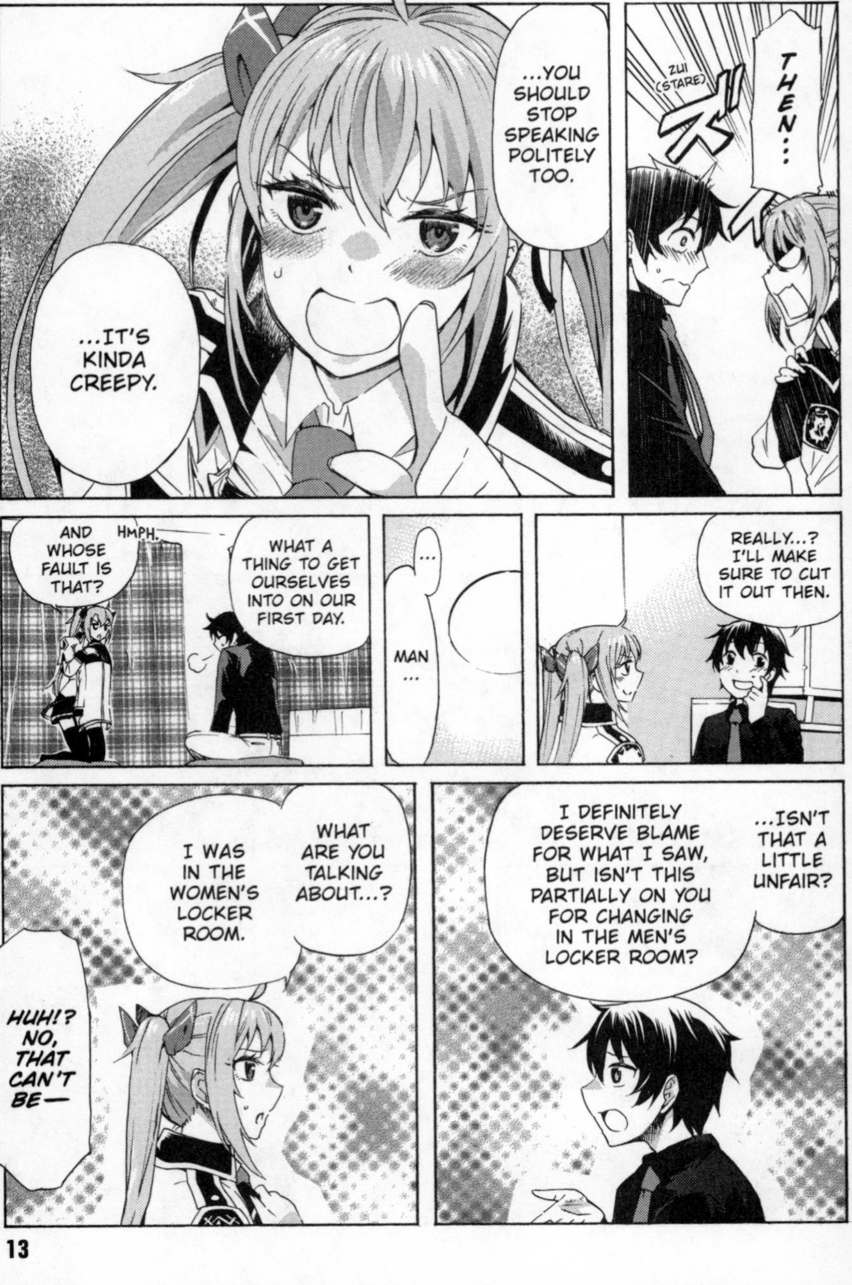
THEN...
ZUI (STARE)
...YOU SHOULD STOP SPEAKING POLITELY TOO.
...IT'S KINDA CREEPY.
REALLY...? I'LL MAKE SURE TO CUT IT OUT THEN.
...
MAN...
WHAT A THING TO GET OURSELVES INTO ON OUR FIRST DAY.
HMPH.
AND WHOSE FAULT IS THAT?
...ISN'T THAT A LITTLE UNFAIR?
I DEFINITELY DESERVE BLAME FOR WHAT I SAW, BUT ISN'T THIS PARTIALLY ON YOU FOR CHANGING IN THE MEN'S LOCKER ROOM?
WHAT ARE YOU TALKING ABOUT...?
I WAS IN THE WOMEN'S LOCKER ROOM.
HUH!? NO, THAT CAN'T BE—

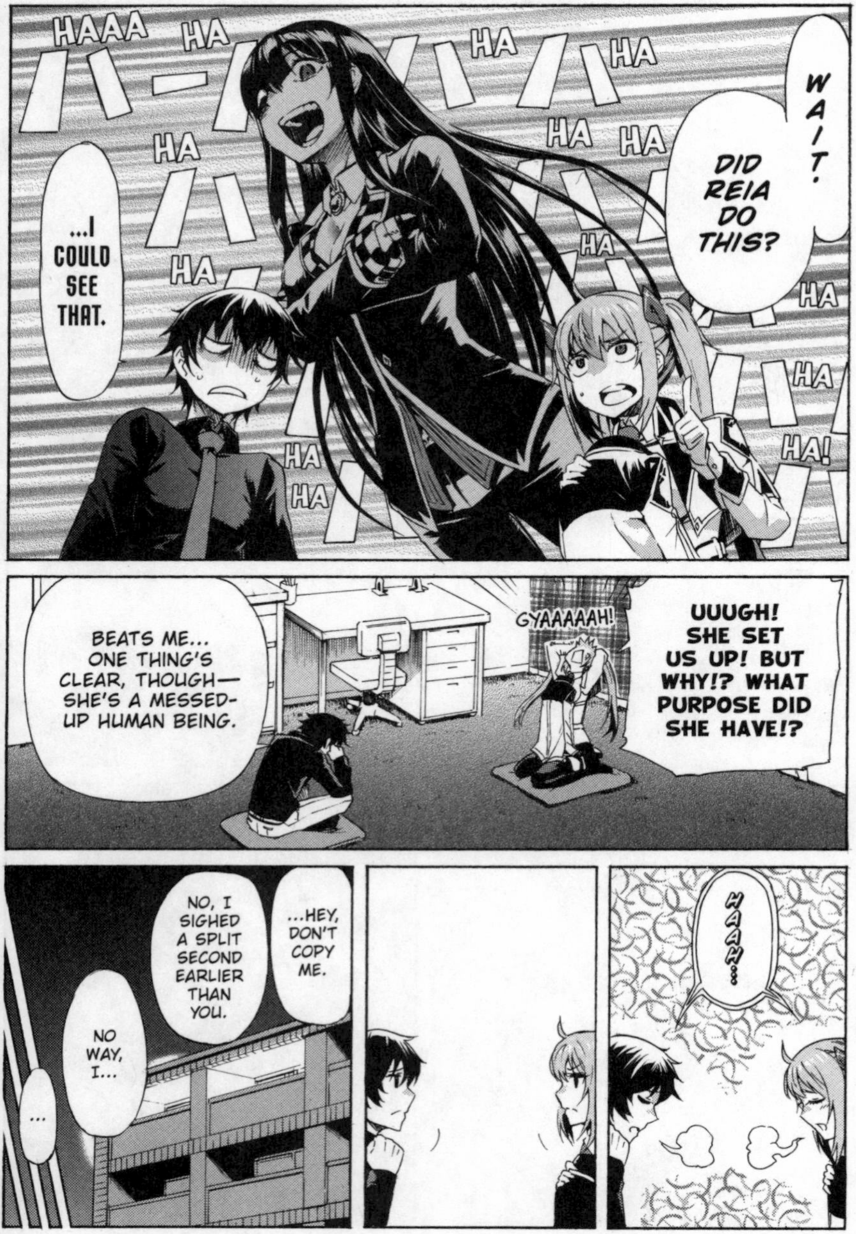
WAIT.
DID REIA DO THIS?
HAAAA HA HA HA HA HA HA HA HA HA HA HA HA! HA HA
...I COULD SEE THAT.
UUUGH! SHE SET US UP! BUT WHY!? WHAT PURPOSE DID SHE HAVE!?
GYAAAAAH!
BEATS ME... ONE THING'S CLEAR, THOUGH—SHE'S A MESSED-UP HUMAN BEING.
HAAAH..
...HEY, DON'T COPY ME.
NO, I SIGHED A SPLIT SECOND EARLIER THAN YOU.
NO WAY, I...
...

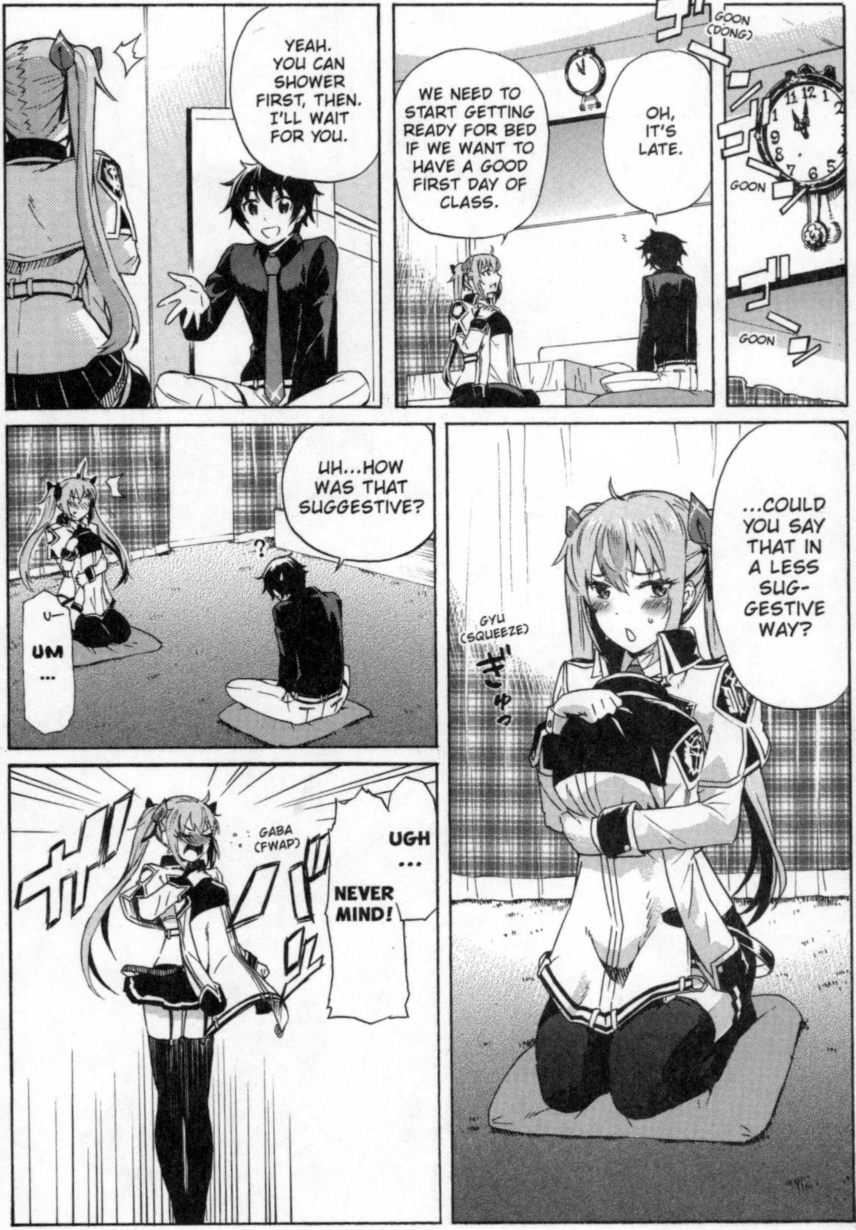

GOON (DONG)
GOON
GOON
OH, IT'S LATE.
WE NEED TO START GETTING READY FOR BED IF WE WANT TO HAVE A GOOD FIRST DAY OF CLASS.
YEAH. YOU CAN SHOWER FIRST, THEN. I'LL WAIT FOR YOU.
...COULD YOU SAY THAT IN A LESS SUG-GESTIVE WAY?
GYU (SQUEEZE)
UH...HOW WAS THAT SUGGESTIVE?
U- UM ...
GABA (FWAP)
UGH ... NEVER MIND!

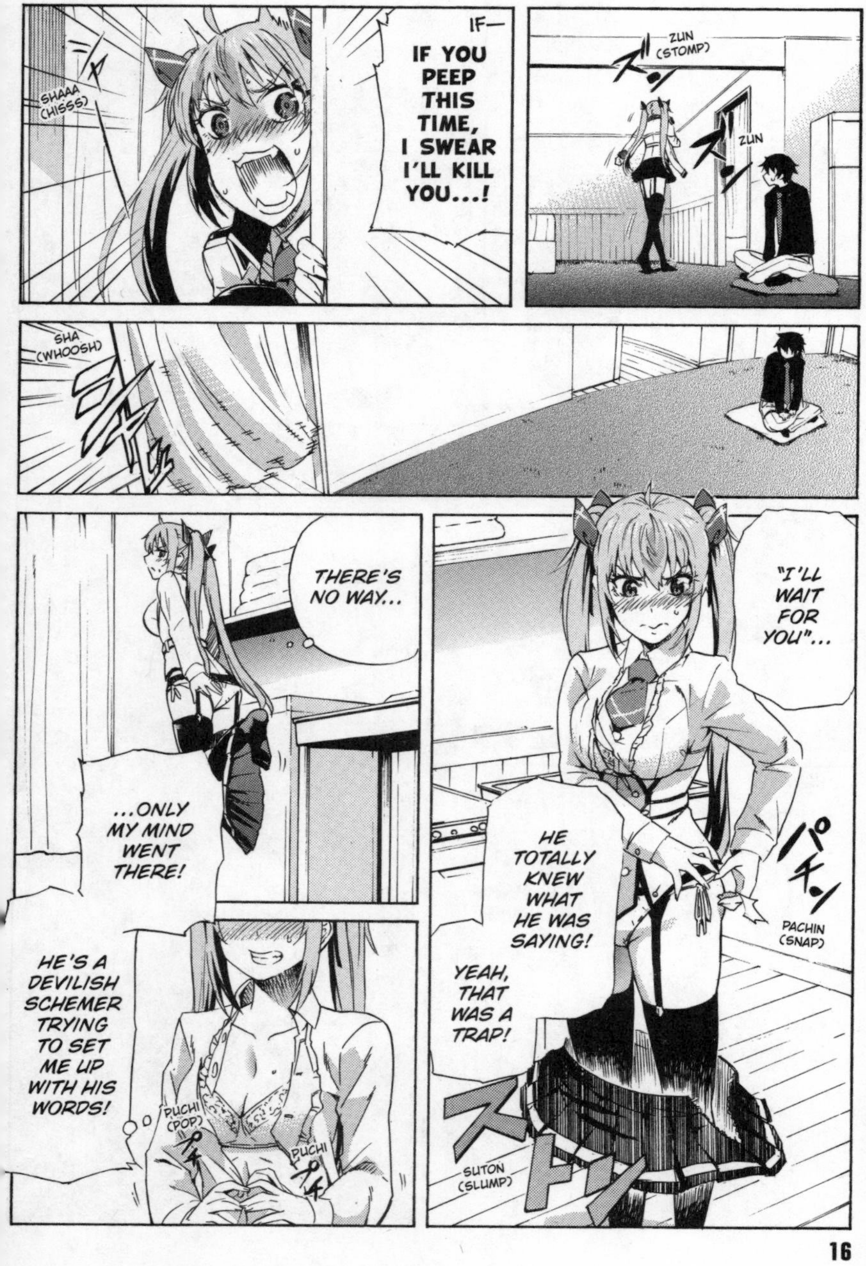
ZUN (STOMP)
ZUN
IF—
IF YOU PEEP THIS TIME, I SWEAR I'LL KILL YOU...!
SHAAA (HISSS)
SHA (WHOOSH)
"I'LL WAIT FOR YOU"...
HE TOTALLY KNEW WHAT HE WAS SAYING!
YEAH, THAT WAS A TRAP!
PACHIN (SNAP)
SUTON (SLUMP)
THERE'S NO WAY...
...ONLY MY MIND WENT THERE!
HE'S A DEVILISH SCHEMER TRYING TO SET ME UP WITH HIS WORDS!
PUCHI (POP)
PUCHI

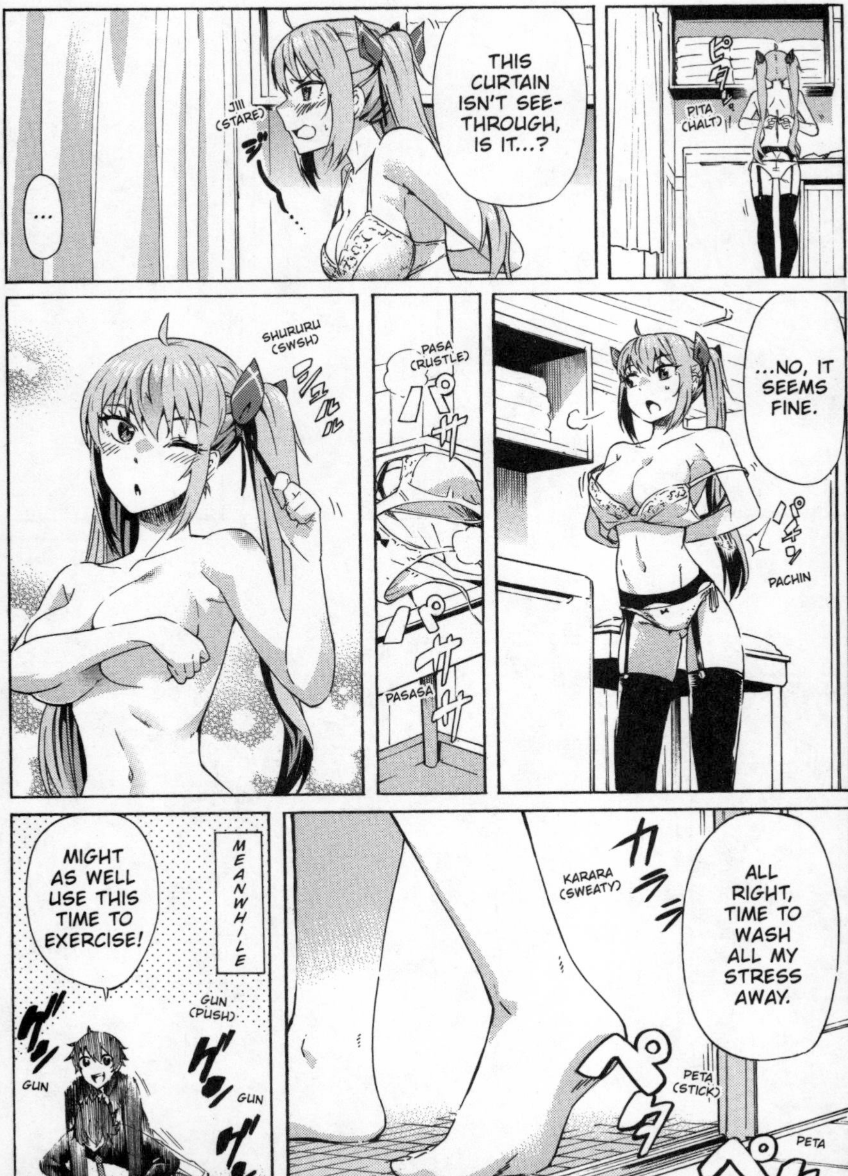
PITA (HALT)
THIS CURTAIN ISN'T SEE-THROUGH, IS IT...?
JIII (STARE)
...
...NO, IT SEEMS FINE.
PACHIN
PASA (RUSTLE)
PASASA
SHURURU (SWSH)
ALL RIGHT, TIME TO WASH ALL MY STRESS AWAY.
KARARA (SWEATY)
PETA (STICK)
PETA
MEANWHILE
MIGHT AS WELL USE THIS TIME TO EXERCISE!
GUN (PUSH)
GUN
GUN

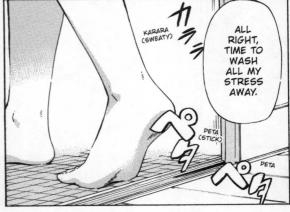

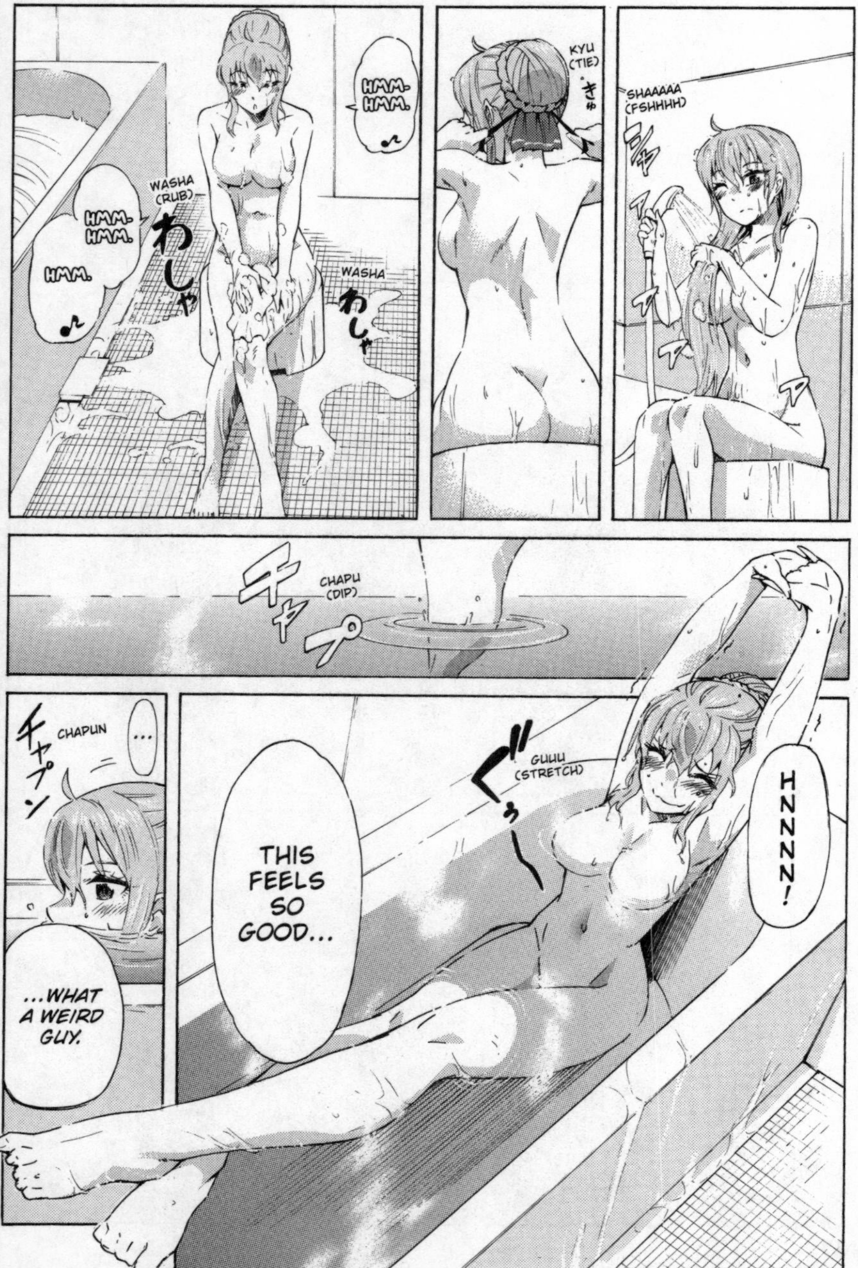
SHAAAAA (FSHHHH)
KYU (TIE)
きゅ
HMM-HMM. ♪
WASHA (RUB)
わしゃ
HMM-HMM. HMM. ♪
WASHA
わしゃ
チャプ
CHAPU (DIP)
HNNNN!
GUUU (STRETCH)
ぐぅ
THIS FEELS SO GOOD...
...
チャプン
CHAPUN
...WHAT A WEIRD GUY.

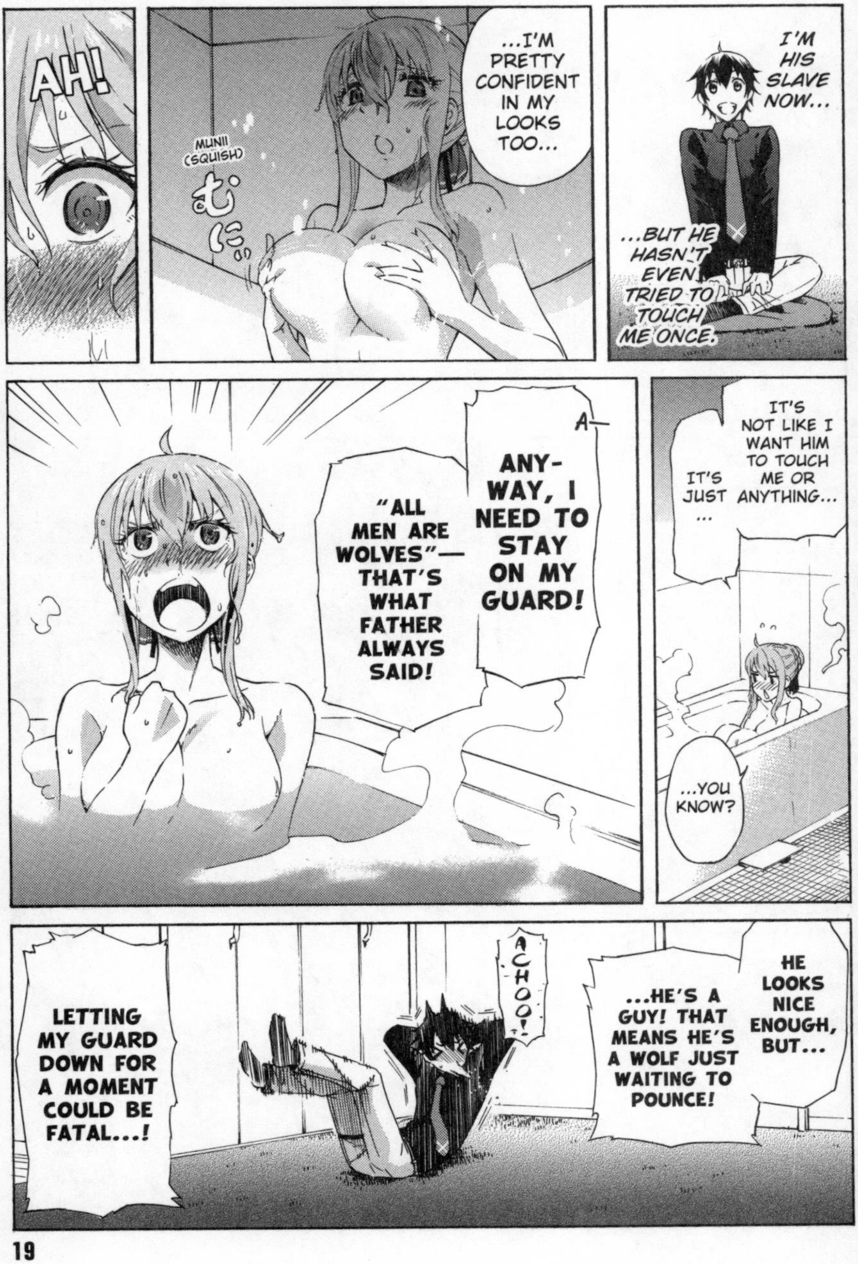
I'M HIS SLAVE NOW...
...BUT HE HASN'T EVEN TRIED TO TOUCH ME ONCE.
...I'M PRETTY CONFIDENT IN MY LOOKS TOO...
MUNII (SQUISH)
むに
AH!
IT'S NOT LIKE I WANT HIM TO TOUCH ME OR ANYTHING...
IT'S JUST...
...YOU KNOW?
A—
ANY-WAY, I NEED TO STAY ON MY GUARD!
"ALL MEN ARE WOLVES"—THAT'S WHAT FATHER ALWAYS SAID!
HE LOOKS NICE ENOUGH, BUT...
...HE'S A GUY! THAT MEANS HE'S A WOLF JUST WAITING TO POUNCE!
ACHOO!
LETTING MY GUARD DOWN FOR A MOMENT COULD BE FATAL...!

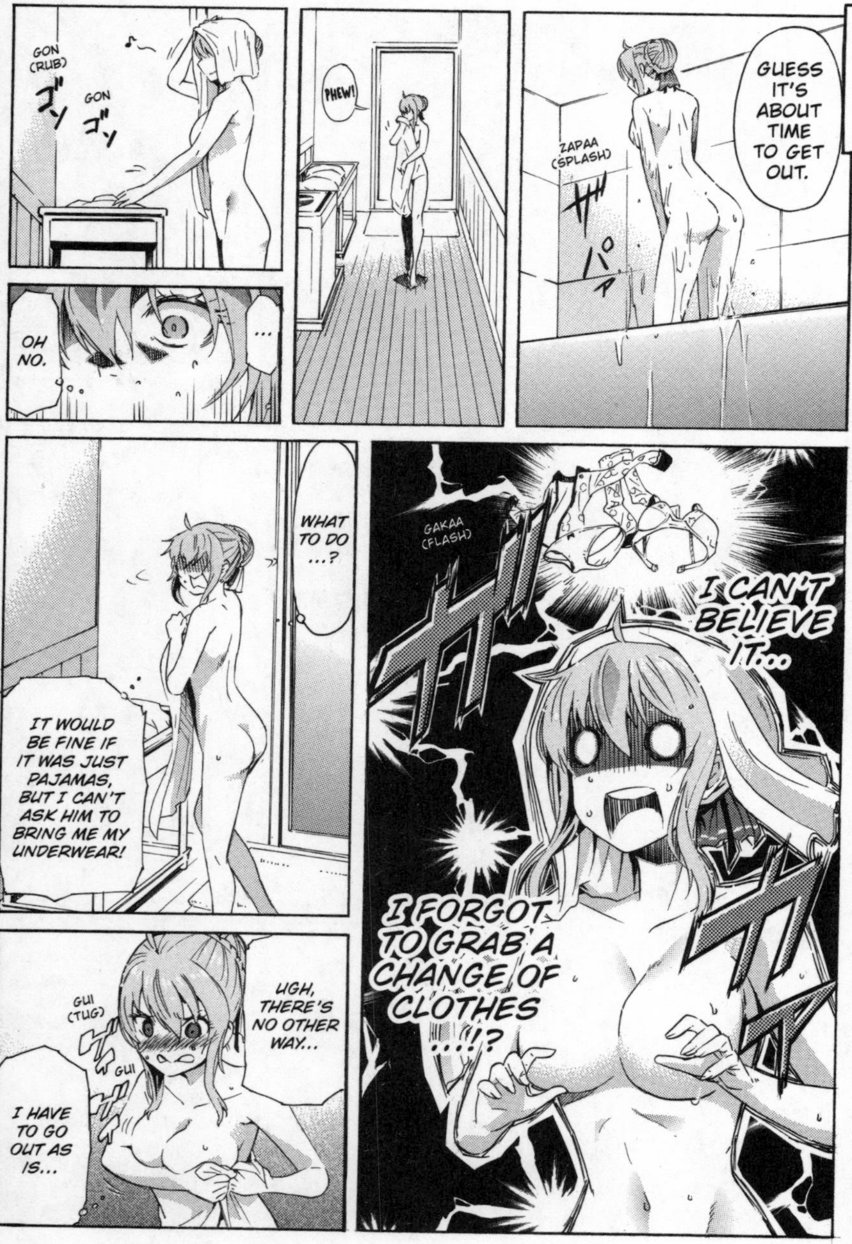
GUESS IT'S ABOUT TIME TO GET OUT.
ZAPAA (SPLASH)
PHEW!
GON (RUB)
GON
OH NO.
...
GAKAA (FLASH)
I CAN'T BELIEVE IT...
I FORGOT TO GRAB A CHANGE OF CLOTHES ...!?
WHAT TO DO ...?
IT WOULD BE FINE IF IT WAS JUST PAJAMAS, BUT I CAN'T ASK HIM TO BRING ME MY UNDERWEAR!
UGH, THERE'S NO OTHER WAY...
GUI (TUG)
GUI
I HAVE TO GO OUT AS IS...

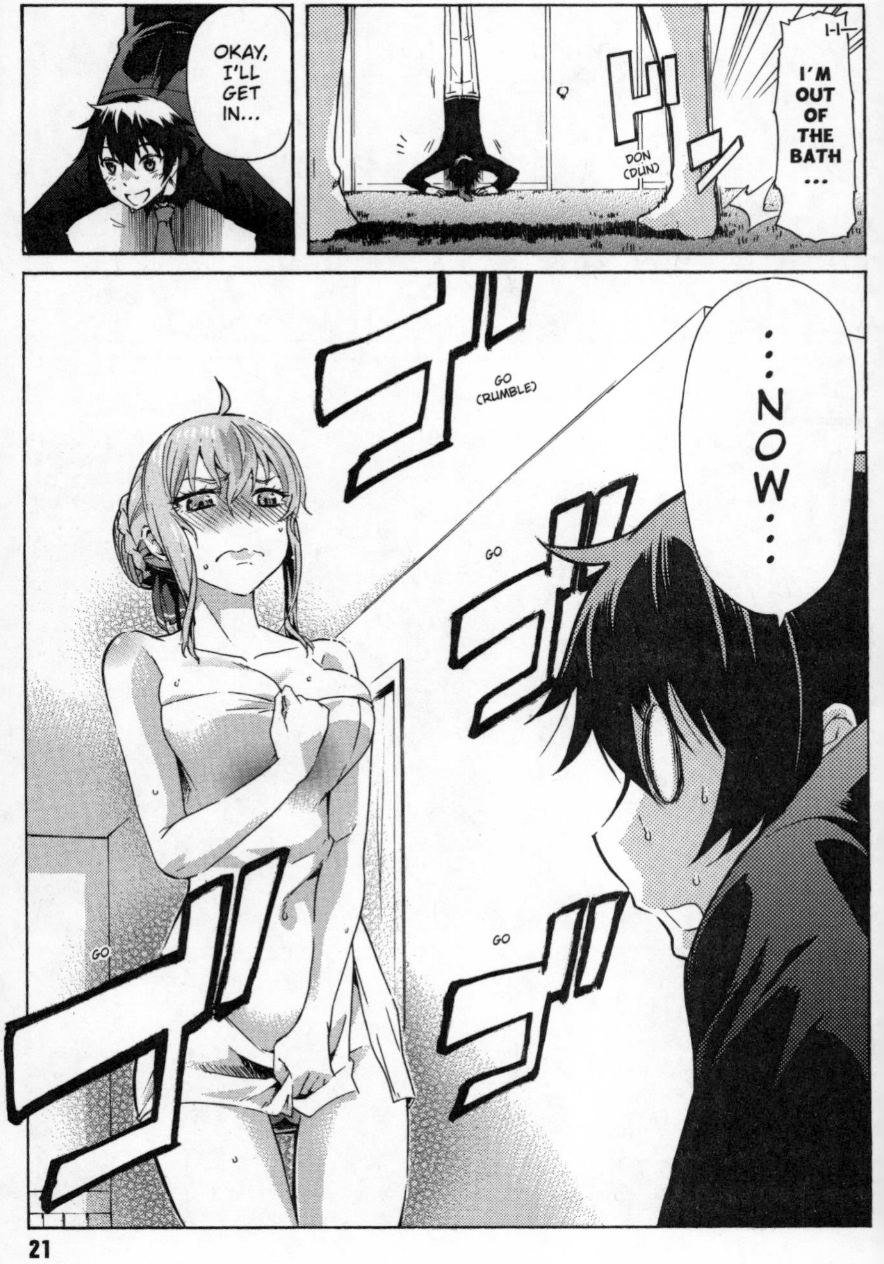
I-I—
I'M OUT OF THE BATH...
DON (DUN)
OKAY, I'LL GET IN...
...NOW...
GO (RUMBLE)
GO
GO
GO

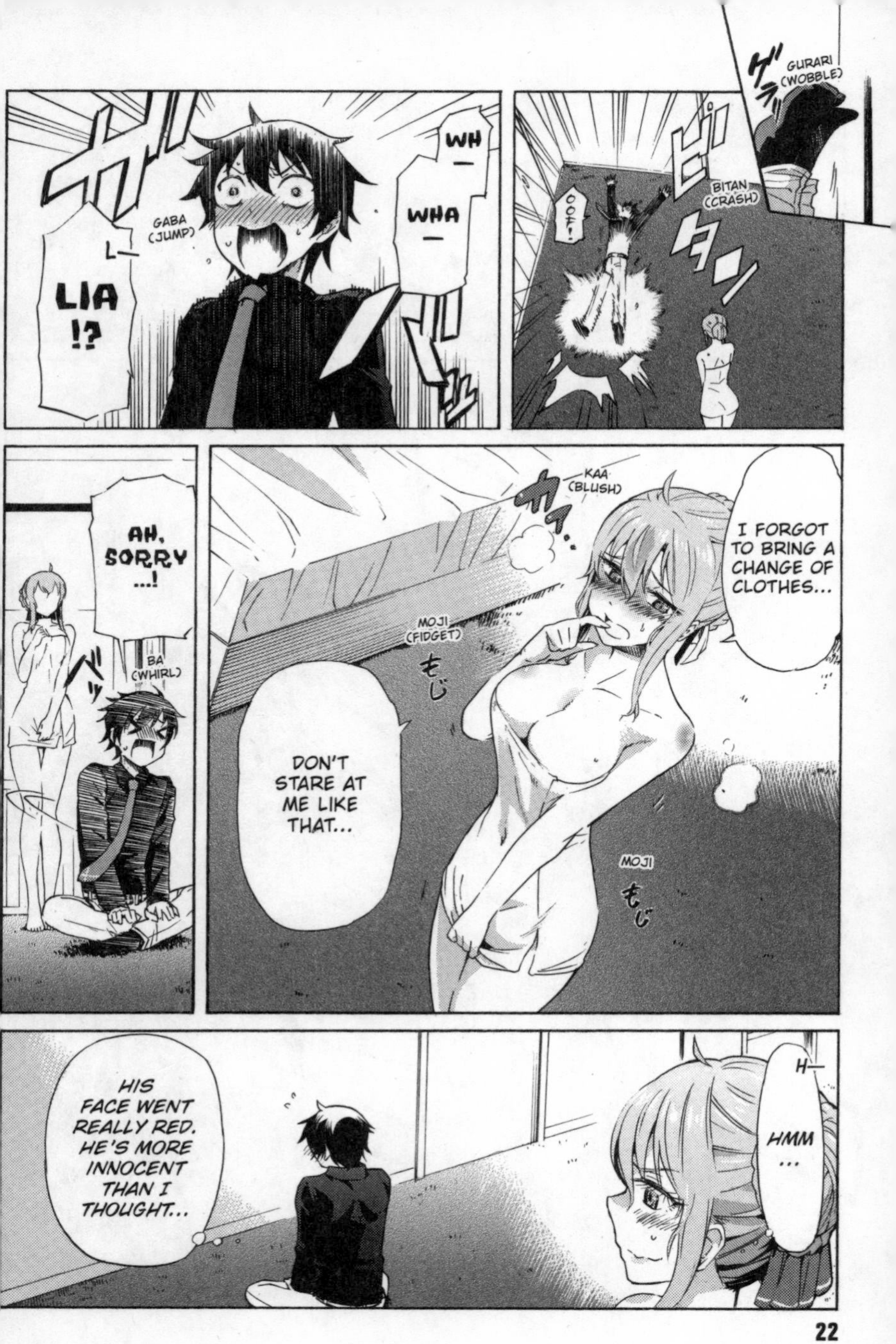
GURARI (WOBBLE)
BITAN (CRASH)
OOF!
WH— WHA—
GABA (JUMP)
L— LIA!?
I FORGOT TO BRING A CHANGE OF CLOTHES...
KAA (BLUSH)
MOJI (FIDGET)
DON'T STARE AT ME LIKE THAT...
MOJI
AH, SORRY...!
BA (WHIRL)
H— HMM...
HIS FACE WENT REALLY RED. HE'S MORE INNOCENT THAN I THOUGHT...

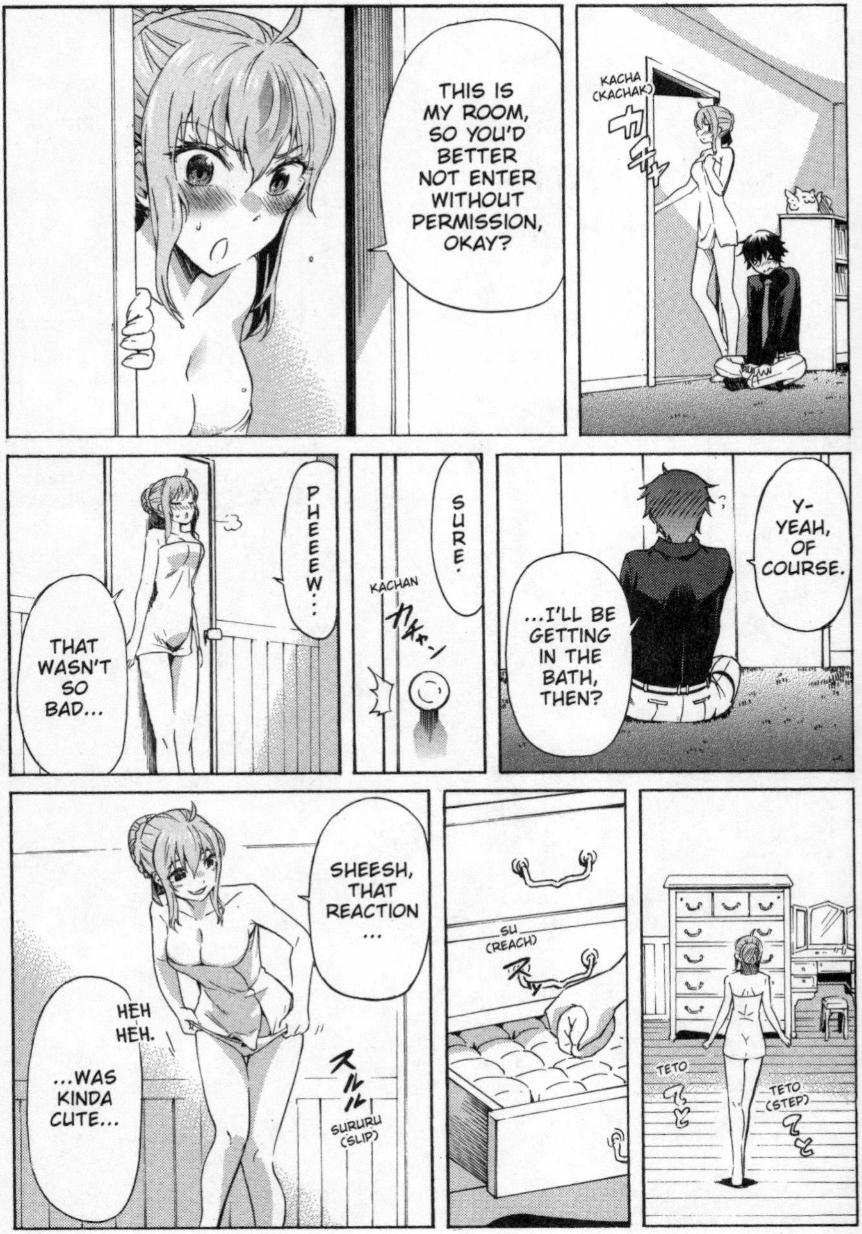
KACHA (KACHAK)
THIS IS MY ROOM, SO YOU'D BETTER NOT ENTER WITHOUT PERMISSION, OKAY?
Y-YEAH, OF COURSE.
...I'LL BE GETTING IN THE BATH, THEN?
SURE.
KACHAN
PHEEEW...
THAT WASN'T SO BAD...
TETO (STEP)
TETO
SU (REACH)
SHEESH, THAT REACTION ...
HEH HEH.
...WAS KINDA CUTE...
SURURU (SLIP)

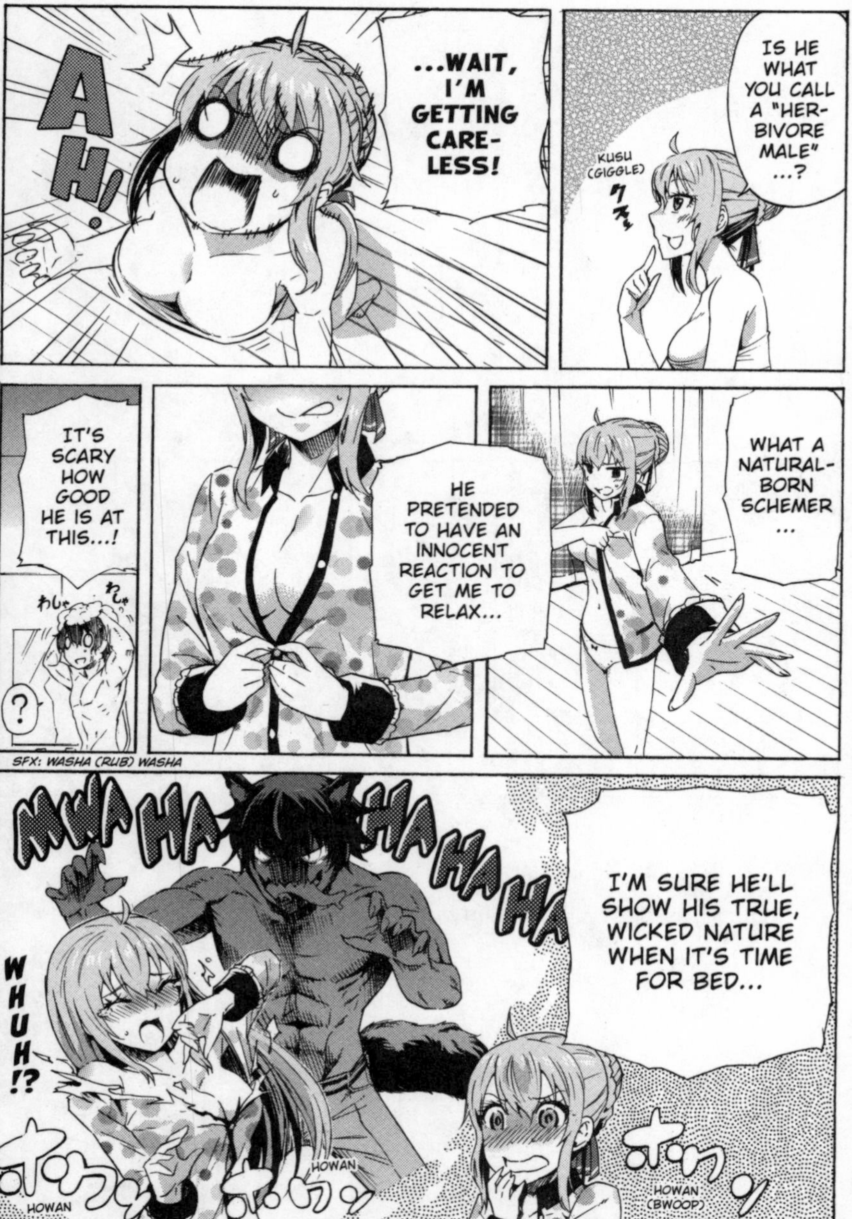
IS HE WHAT YOU CALL A "HER-BIVORE MALE" ...?
KUSU (GIGGLE)
クス
...WAIT, I'M GETTING CARE-LESS!
AH!
WHAT A NATURAL-BORN SCHEMER ...
HE PRETENDED TO HAVE AN INNOCENT REACTION TO GET ME TO RELAX...
IT'S SCARY HOW GOOD HE IS AT THIS...!
わしゃ
わしゃ
?
SFX: WASHA (RUB) WASHA
I'M SURE HE'LL SHOW HIS TRUE, WICKED NATURE WHEN IT'S TIME FOR BED...
MWAHAHAHAHAHA
WHUH!?
HOWAN (BWOOP)
HOWAN
HOWAN

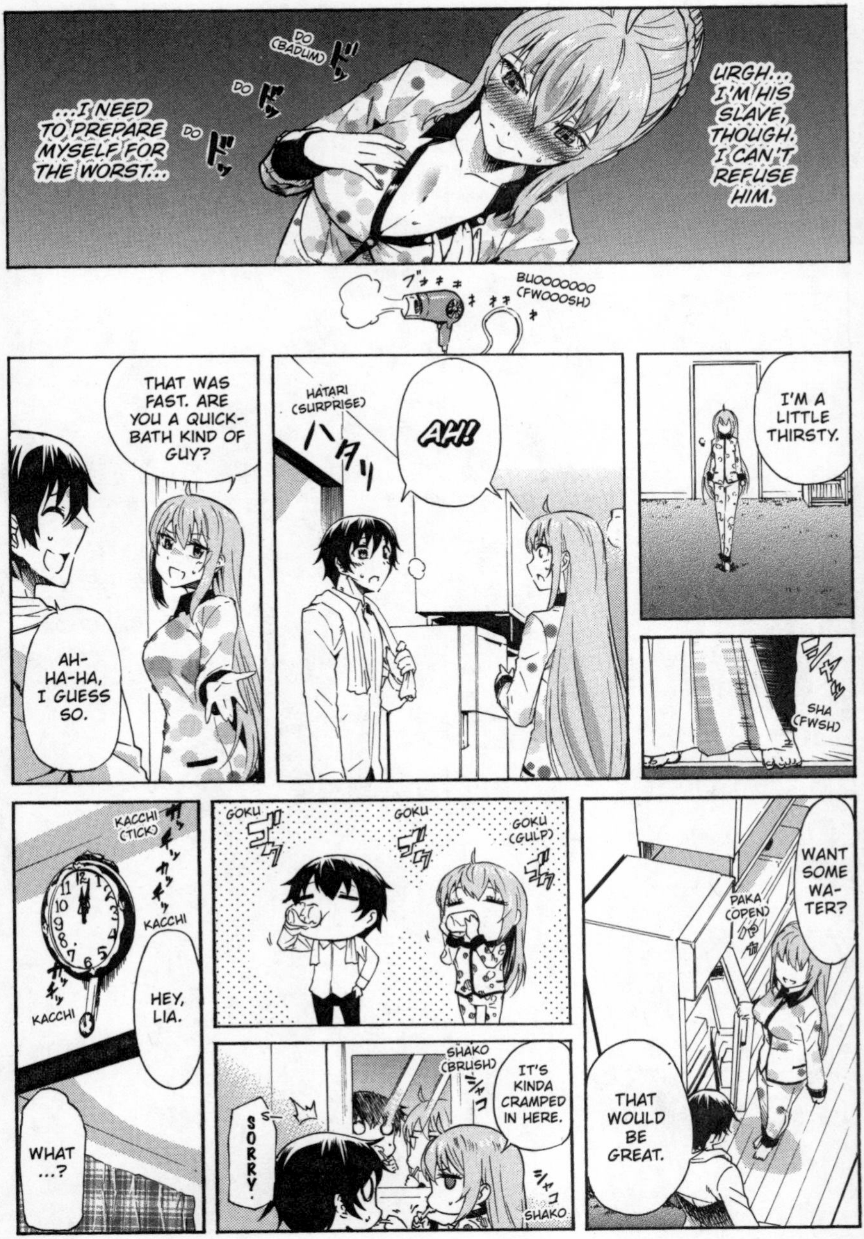
URGH... I'M HIS SLAVE, THOUGH. I CAN'T REFUSE HIM.
DO (BADUM)
DO
DO
...I NEED TO PREPARE MYSELF FOR THE WORST...
BUOOOOOOO (FWOOOSH)
I'M A LITTLE THIRSTY.
SHA (FWSH)
HATARI (SURPRISE)
AH!
THAT WAS FAST. ARE YOU A QUICK-BATH KIND OF GUY?
AH-HA-HA, I GUESS SO.
WANT SOME WA-TER?
PAKA (OPEN)
THAT WOULD BE GREAT.
GOKU (GULP)
GOKU
GOKU
SHAKO (BRUSH)
IT'S KINDA CRAMPED IN HERE.
S-
SORRY.
SHAKO
KACCHI (TICK)
KACCHI
KACCHI
HEY, LIA.
WHAT ...?

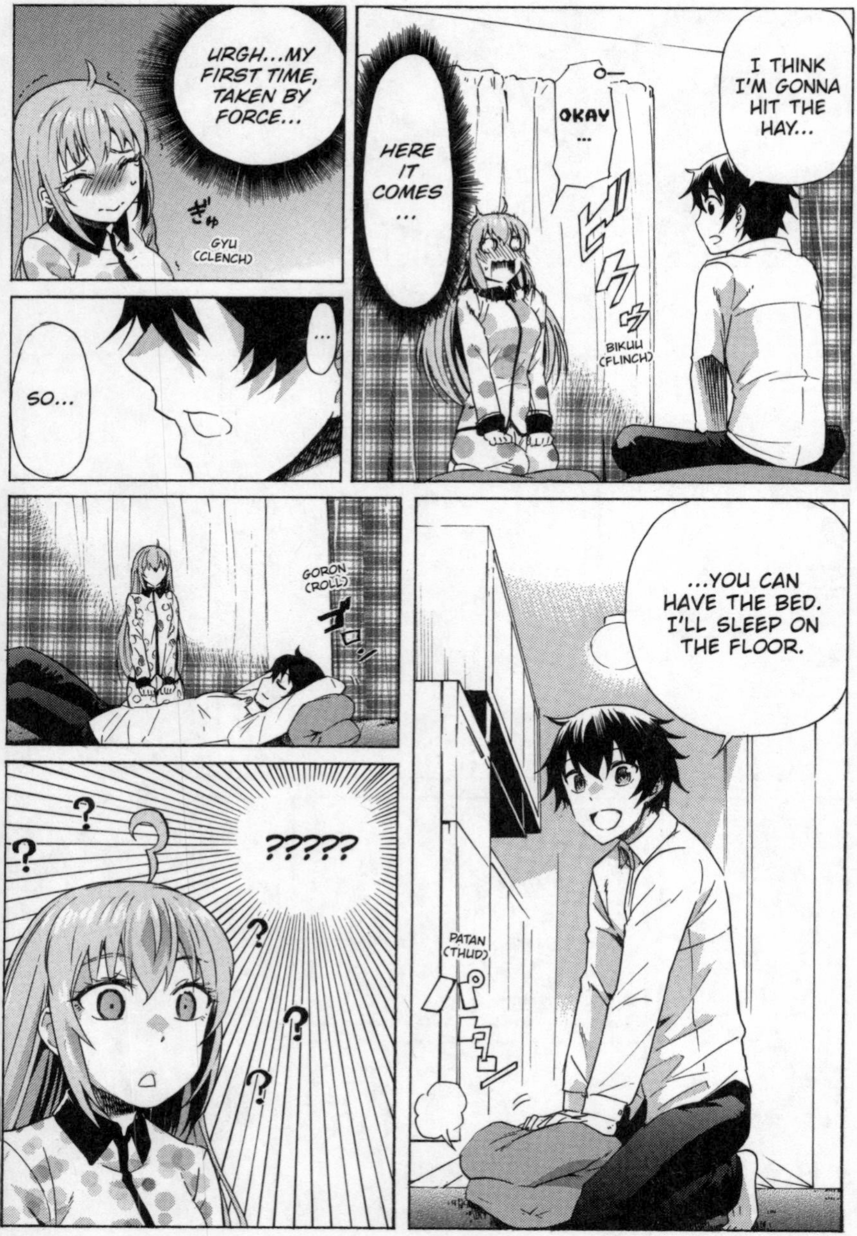
I THINK I'M GONNA HIT THE HAY...
OKAY...
HERE IT COMES...
BIKUU (FLINCH)
URGH...MY FIRST TIME, TAKEN BY FORCE...
ぎゅ
GYU (CLENCH)
...
SO...
...YOU CAN HAVE THE BED. I'LL SLEEP ON THE FLOOR.
PATAN (THUD)
GORON (ROLL)
?????

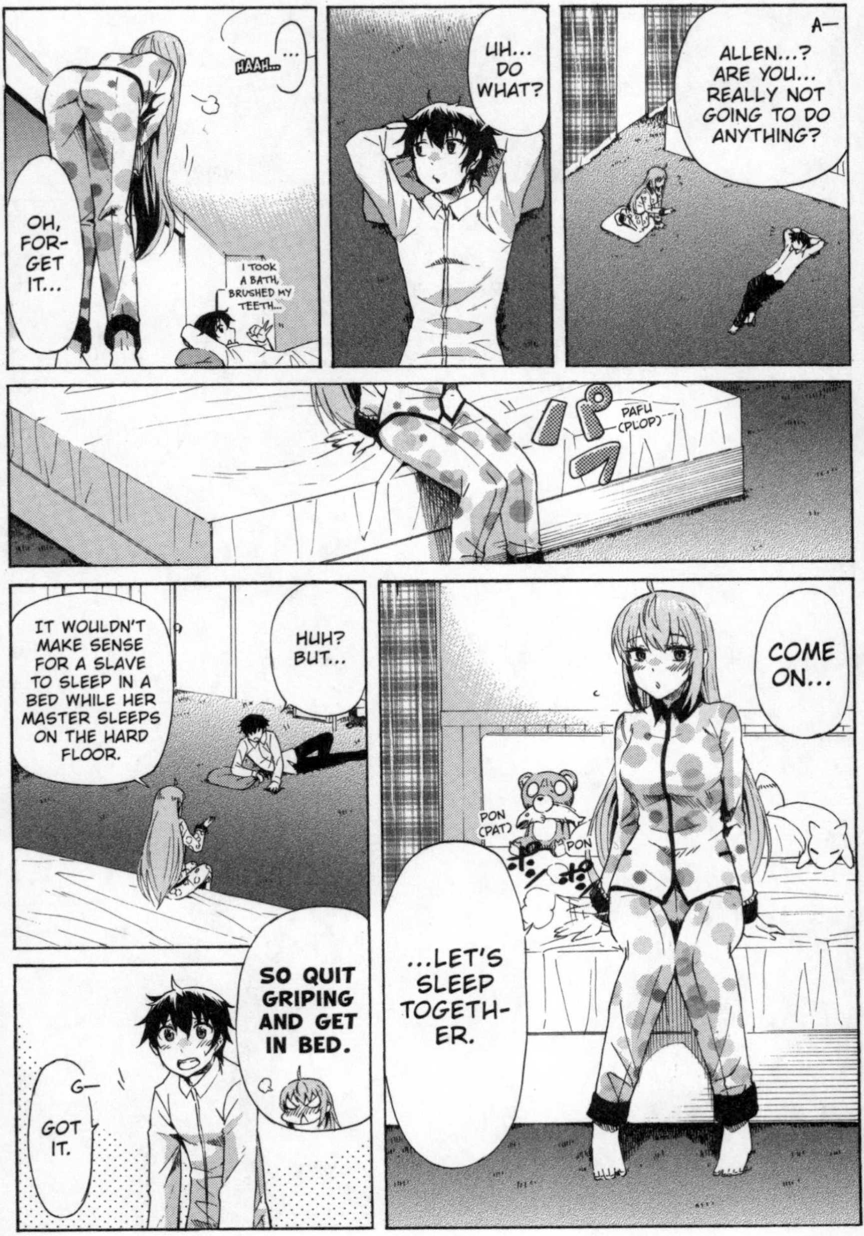
A—
ALLEN...? ARE YOU... REALLY NOT GOING TO DO ANYTHING?
UH... DO WHAT?
...
HAAH...
OH, FOR-GET IT...
I TOOK A BATH, BRUSHED MY TEETH...
PAFU (PLOP)
COME ON...
PON (PAT)
PON
...LET'S SLEEP TOGETH-ER.
HUH? BUT...
IT WOULDN'T MAKE SENSE FOR A SLAVE TO SLEEP IN A BED WHILE HER MASTER SLEEPS ON THE HARD FLOOR.
SO QUIT GRIPING AND GET IN BED.
G—
GOT IT.

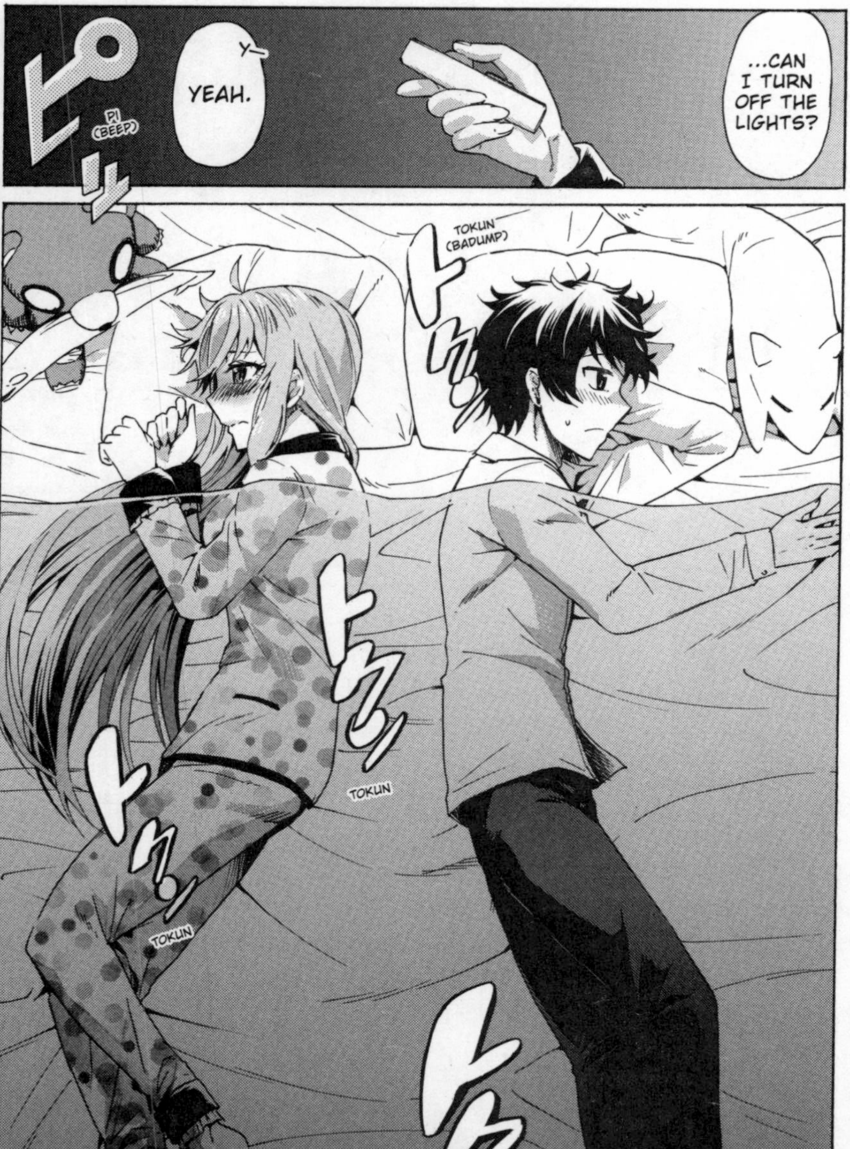
...CAN I TURN OFF THE LIGHTS?
Y— YEAH.
PI (BEEP)
TOKUN (BADUMP)
TOKUN
TOKUN
TOKUN

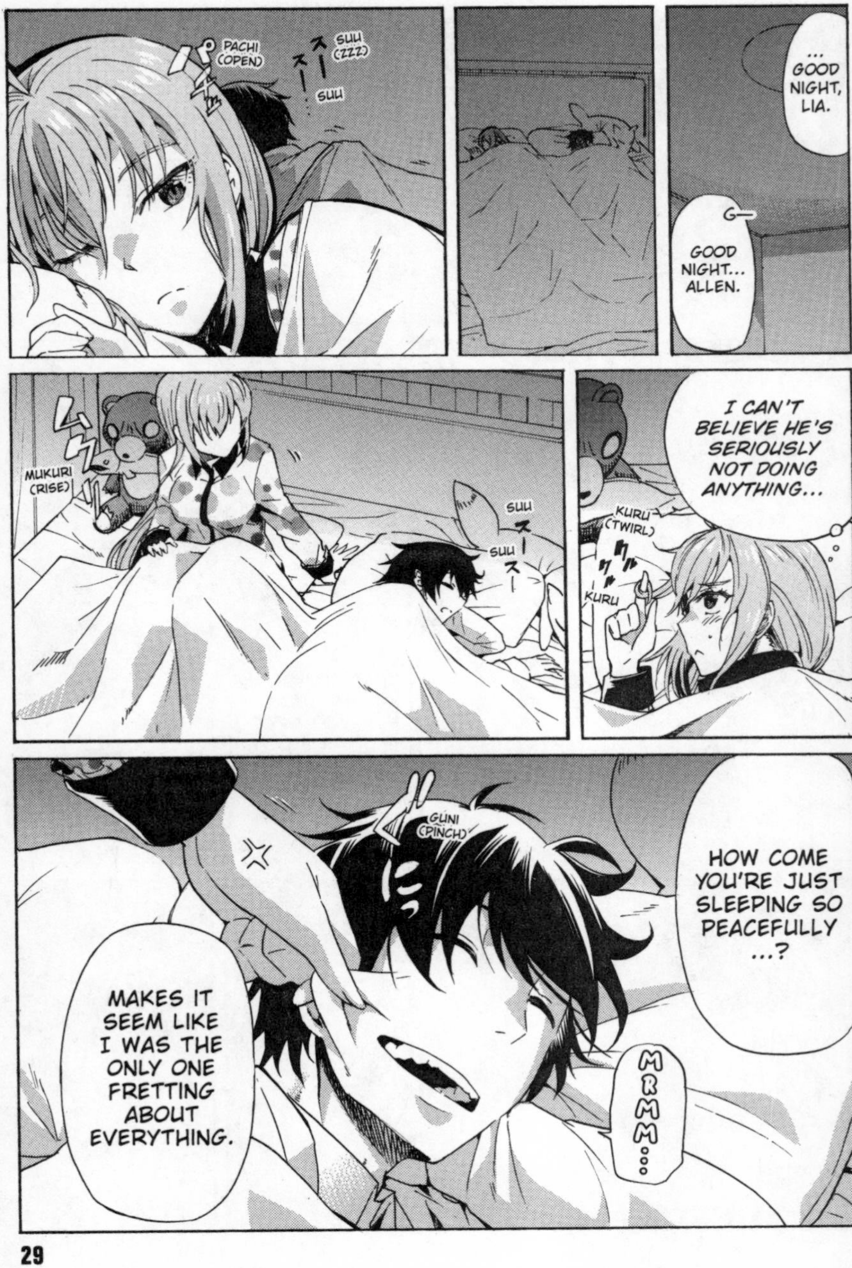
...GOOD NIGHT, LIA.
G— GOOD NIGHT... ALLEN.
SUU (ZZZ)
PACHI (OPEN)
SUU
I CAN'T BELIEVE HE'S SERIOUSLY NOT DOING ANYTHING...
KURU (TWIRL)
KURU
SUU
SUU
MUKURI (RISE)
HOW COME YOU'RE JUST SLEEPING SO PEACEFULLY ...?
GUNI (PINCH)
MRMM...
MAKES IT SEEM LIKE I WAS THE ONLY ONE FRETTING ABOUT EVERYTHING.

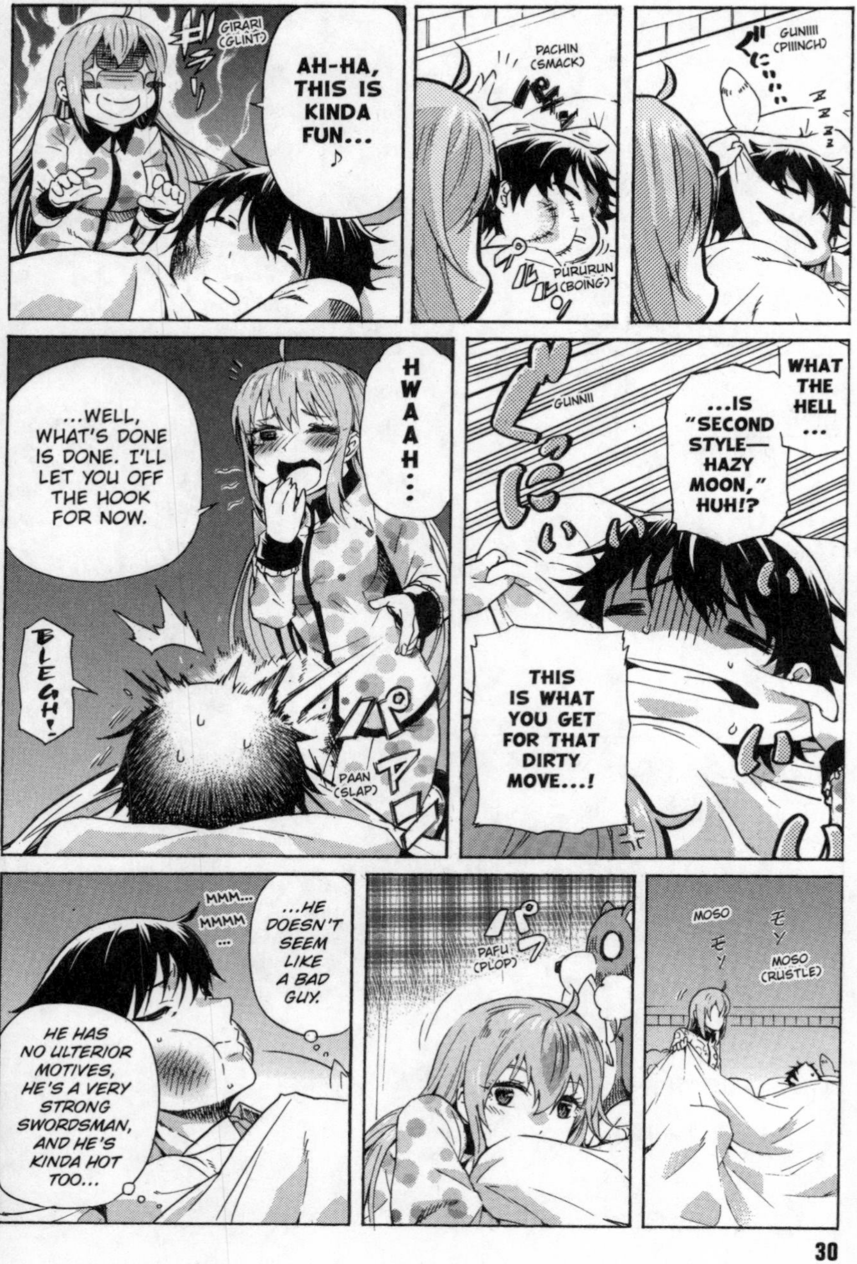
GUNIIII (PIIIINCH)
PACHIN (SMACK)
PURURUN (BOING)
GIRARI (GLINT)
AH-HA, THIS IS KINDA FUN... ♪
WHAT THE HELL ...
...IS "SECOND STYLE—HAZY MOON," HUH!?
GUNIII
THIS IS WHAT YOU GET FOR THAT DIRTY MOVE...!
HWAAH...
...WELL, WHAT'S DONE IS DONE. I'LL LET YOU OFF THE HOOK FOR NOW.
BLEGH!
PAAN (SLAP)
MOSO
MOSO (RUSTLE)
PAFU (PLOP)
MMM... MMMM ...
...HE DOESN'T SEEM LIKE A BAD GUY.
HE HAS NO ULTERIOR MOTIVES, HE'S A VERY STRONG SWORDSMAN, AND HE'S KINDA HOT TOO...

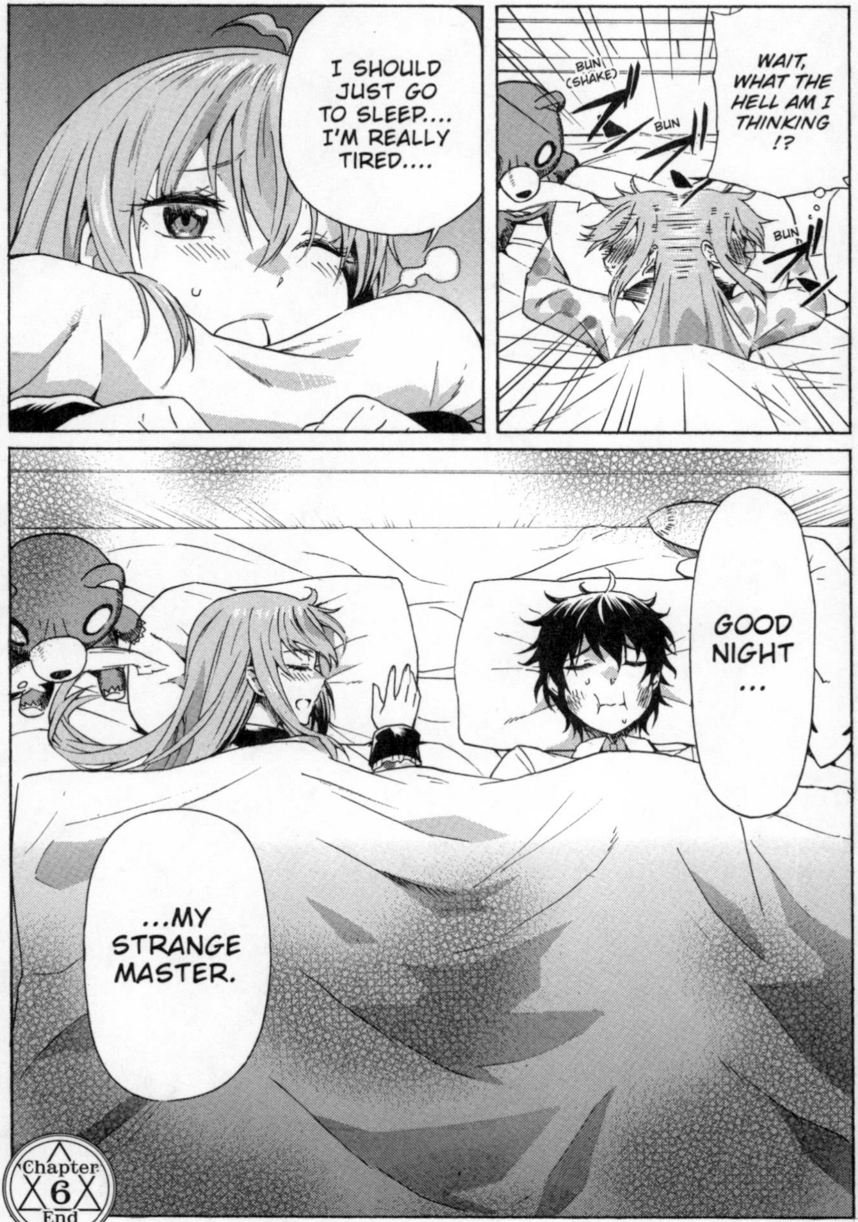
WAIT, WHAT THE HELL AM I THINKING !?
BUN (SHAKE)
BUN
BUN
I SHOULD JUST GO TO SLEEP.... I'M REALLY TIRED....
GOOD NIGHT ...
...MY STRANGE MASTER.
Chapter 6 End

I KEPT PRESSING THE 100-MILLION-YEAR BUTTON AND CAME OUT ON TOP

~THE UNBEATABLE REJECT SWORDSMAN~

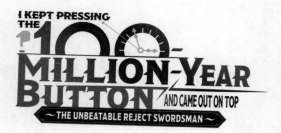

Chapter 7

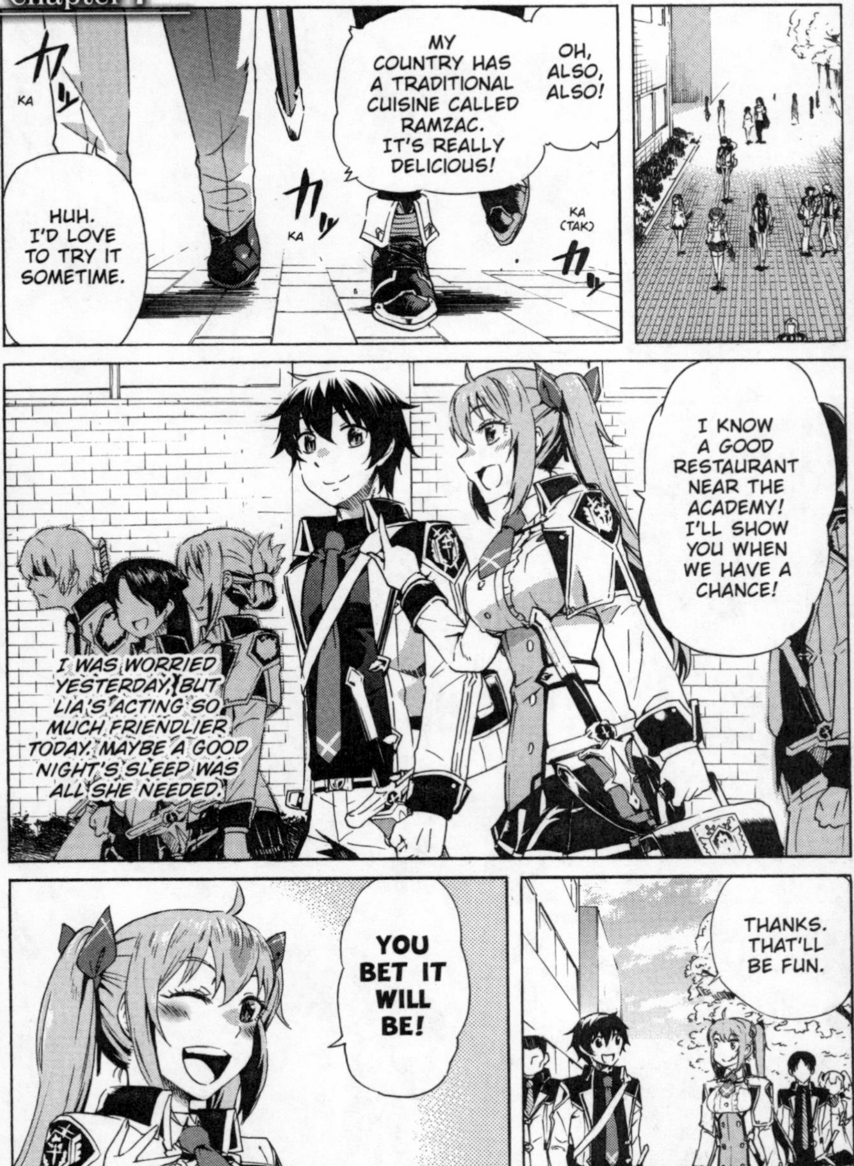
OH, ALSO, ALSO!
MY COUNTRY HAS A TRADITIONAL CUISINE CALLED RAMZAC. IT'S REALLY DELICIOUS!
KA (TAK)
KA
KA
HUH. I'D LOVE TO TRY IT SOMETIME.
I KNOW A GOOD RESTAURANT NEAR THE ACADEMY! I'LL SHOW YOU WHEN WE HAVE A CHANCE!
I WAS WORRIED YESTERDAY, BUT LIA'S ACTING SO MUCH FRIENDLIER TODAY. MAYBE A GOOD NIGHT'S SLEEP WAS ALL SHE NEEDED.
THANKS. THAT'LL BE FUN.
YOU BET IT WILL BE!

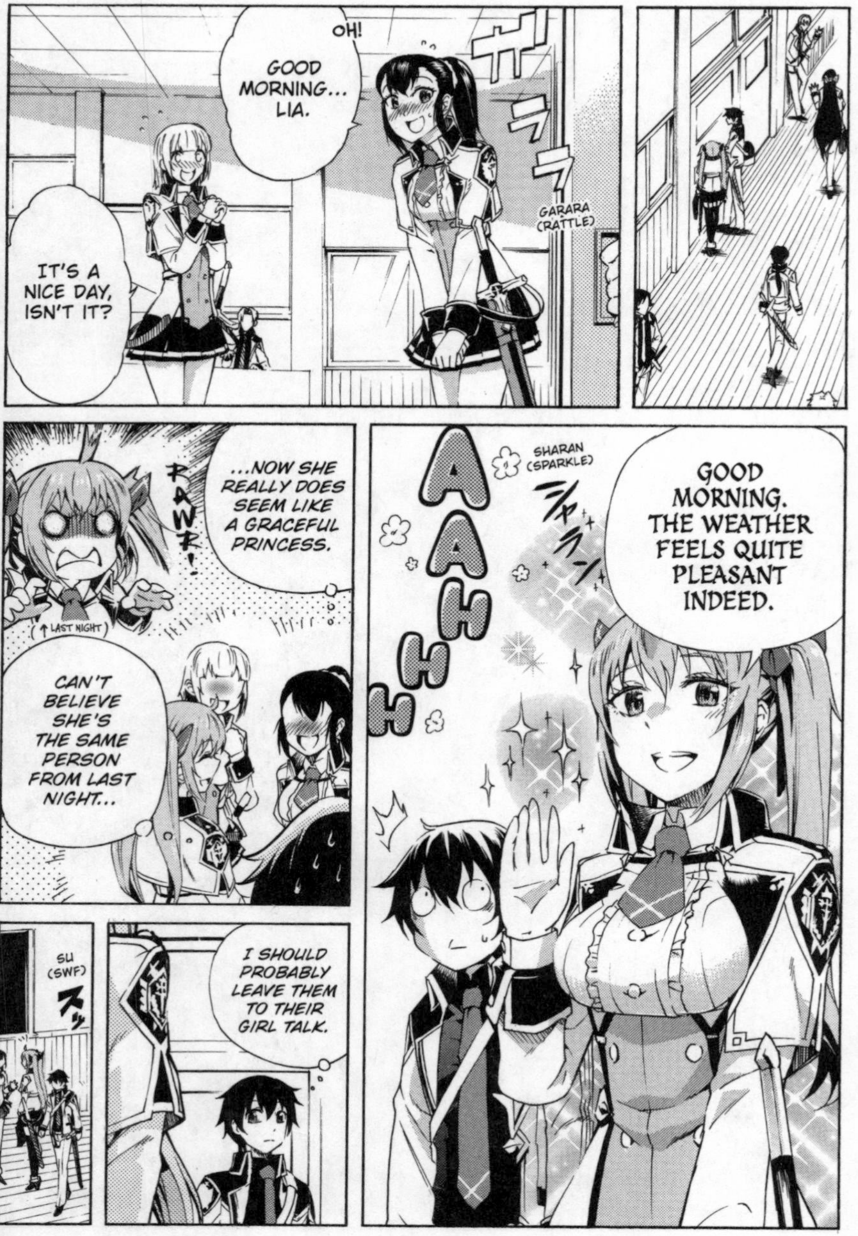
GARARA (RATTLE)
OH!
GOOD MORNING... LIA.
IT'S A NICE DAY, ISN'T IT?
SHARAN (SPARKLE)
GOOD MORNING. THE WEATHER FEELS QUITE PLEASANT INDEED.
AAAHHHH
RAWR!
...NOW SHE REALLY DOES SEEM LIKE A GRACEFUL PRINCESS.
(↑ LAST NIGHT)
CAN'T BELIEVE SHE'S THE SAME PERSON FROM LAST NIGHT...
I SHOULD PROBABLY LEAVE THEM TO THEIR GIRL TALK.
SU (SWF)

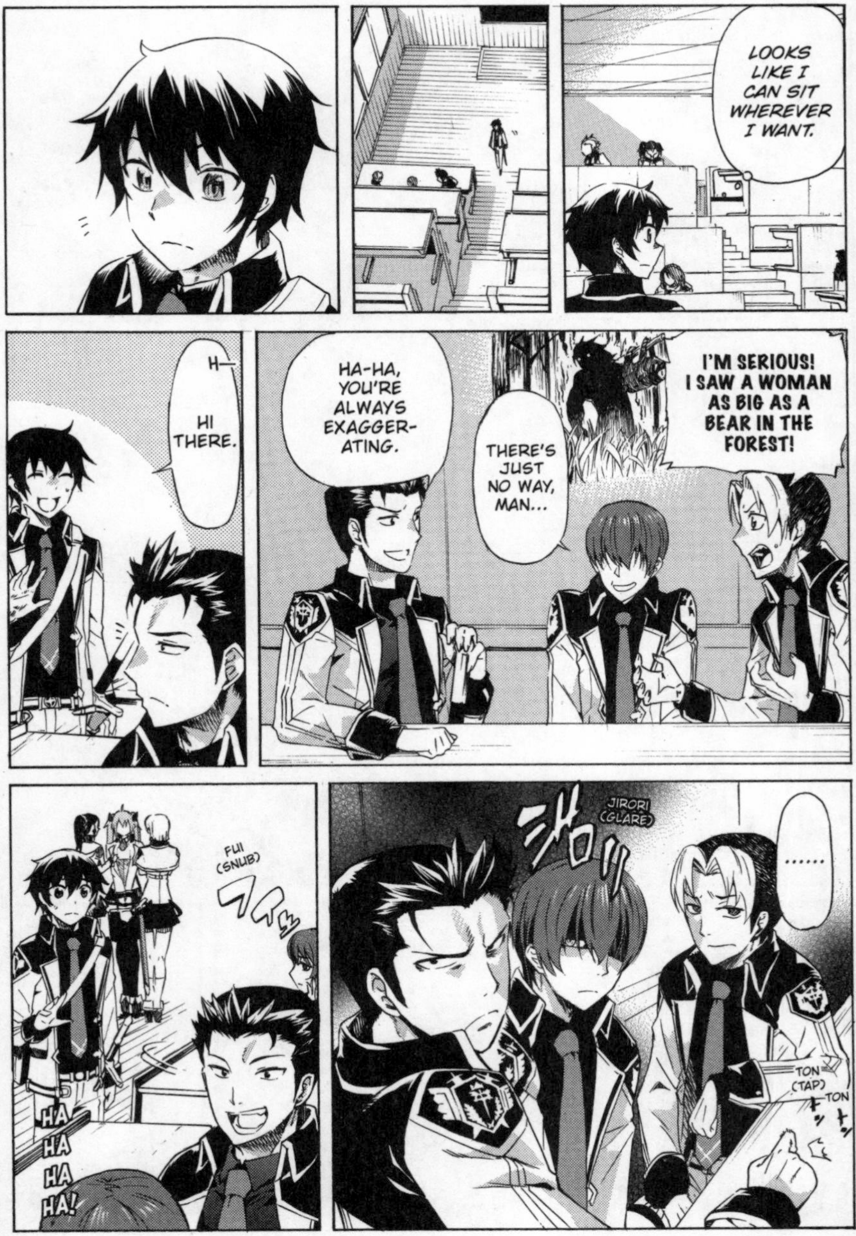

LOOKS LIKE I CAN SIT WHEREVER I WANT.
I'M SERIOUS! I SAW A WOMAN AS BIG AS A BEAR IN THE FOREST!
THERE'S JUST NO WAY, MAN...
HA-HA, YOU'RE ALWAYS EXAGGER-ATING.
H—
HI THERE.
......
JIRORI (GLARE)
TON (TAP)
TON
FUI (SNUB)
HA HA HA HA!

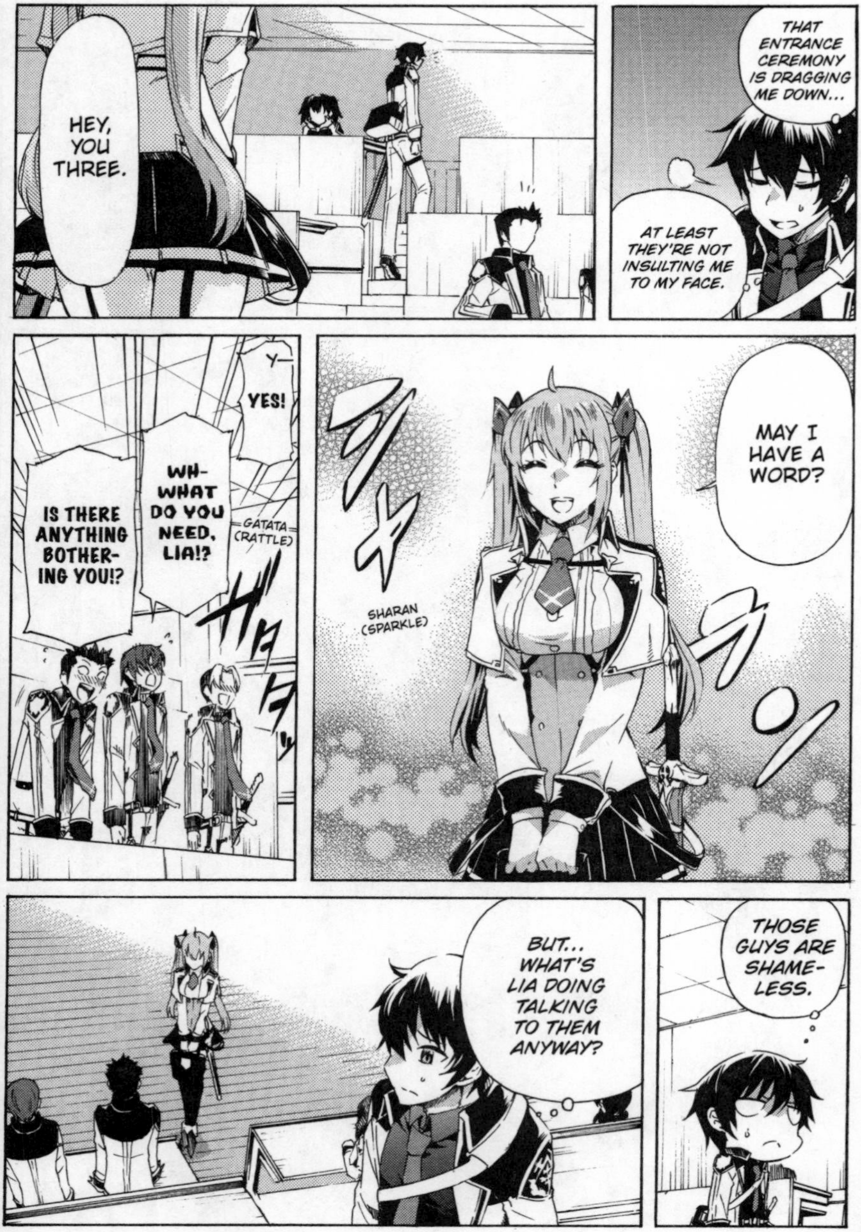
THAT ENTRANCE CEREMONY IS DRAGGING ME DOWN...
AT LEAST THEY'RE NOT INSULTING ME TO MY FACE.
HEY, YOU THREE.
MAY I HAVE A WORD?
SHARAN (SPARKLE)
Y— YES!
WH-WHAT DO YOU NEED, LIA!?
GATATA (RATTLE)
IS THERE ANYTHING BOTHERING YOU!?
THOSE GUYS ARE SHAMELESS.
BUT... WHAT'S LIA DOING TALKING TO THEM ANYWAY?

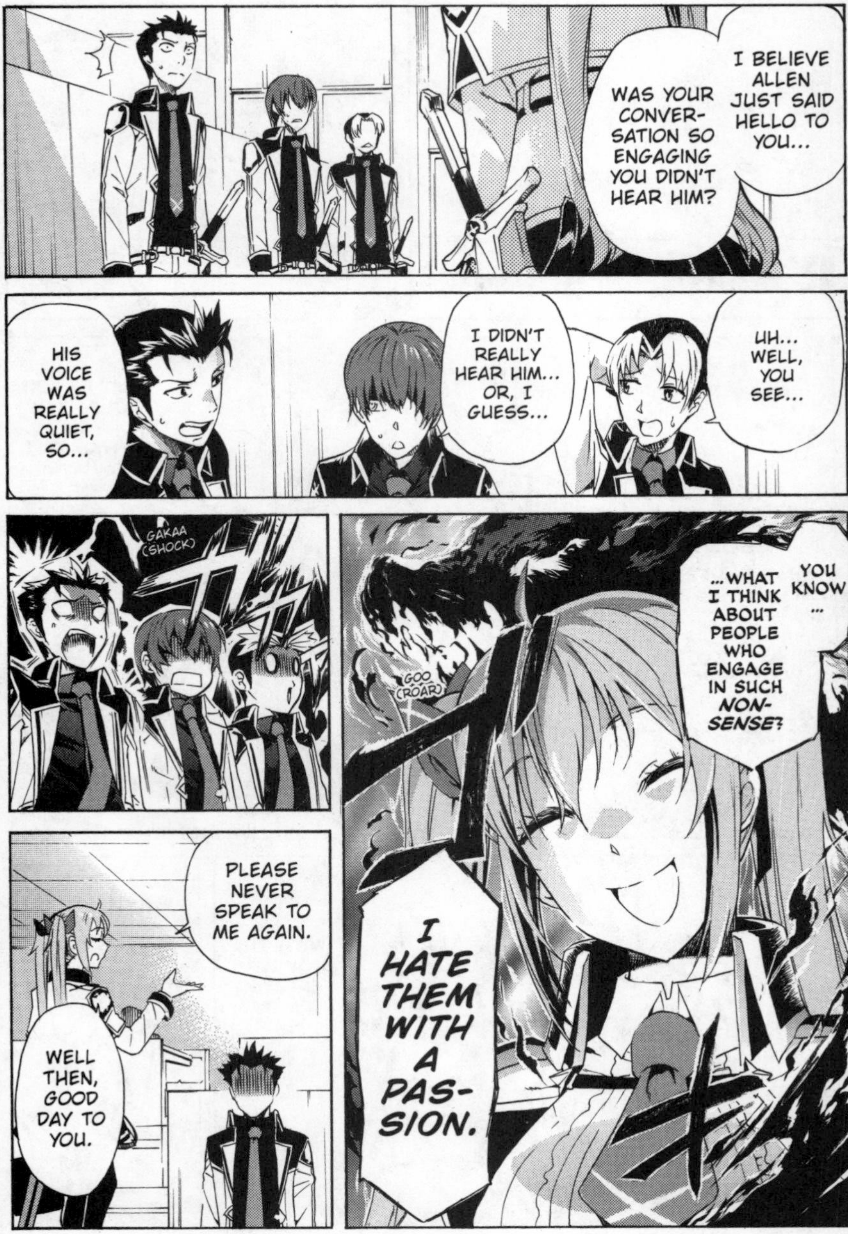
I BELIEVE ALLEN JUST SAID HELLO TO YOU...
WAS YOUR CONVER-SATION SO ENGAGING YOU DIDN'T HEAR HIM?
UH... WELL, YOU SEE...
I DIDN'T REALLY HEAR HIM... OR, I GUESS...
HIS VOICE WAS REALLY QUIET, SO...
YOU KNOW...
...WHAT I THINK ABOUT PEOPLE WHO ENGAGE IN SUCH NON-SENSE?
GOO (ROAR)
I HATE THEM WITH A PAS-SION.
GAKAA (SHOCK)
PLEASE NEVER SPEAK TO ME AGAIN.
WELL THEN, GOOD DAY TO YOU.

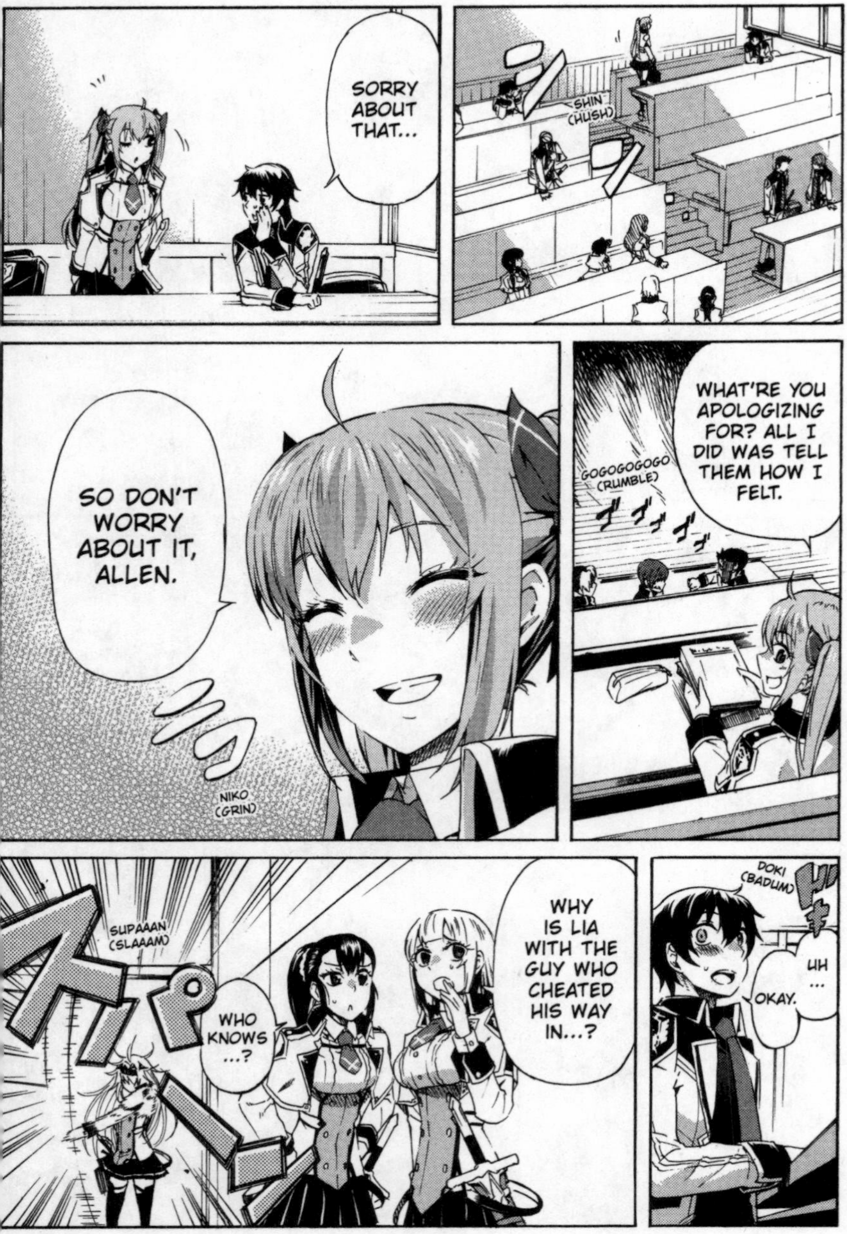
SHIN (HUSH)
SORRY ABOUT THAT...
WHAT'RE YOU APOLOGIZING FOR? ALL I DID WAS TELL THEM HOW I FELT.
GOGOGOGOGO (RUMBLE)
SO DON'T WORRY ABOUT IT, ALLEN.
NIKO (GRIN)
DOKI (BADUM)
UH ... OKAY.
WHY IS LIA WITH THE GUY WHO CHEATED HIS WAY IN...?
WHO KNOWS ...?
SUPAAAN (SLAAAM)

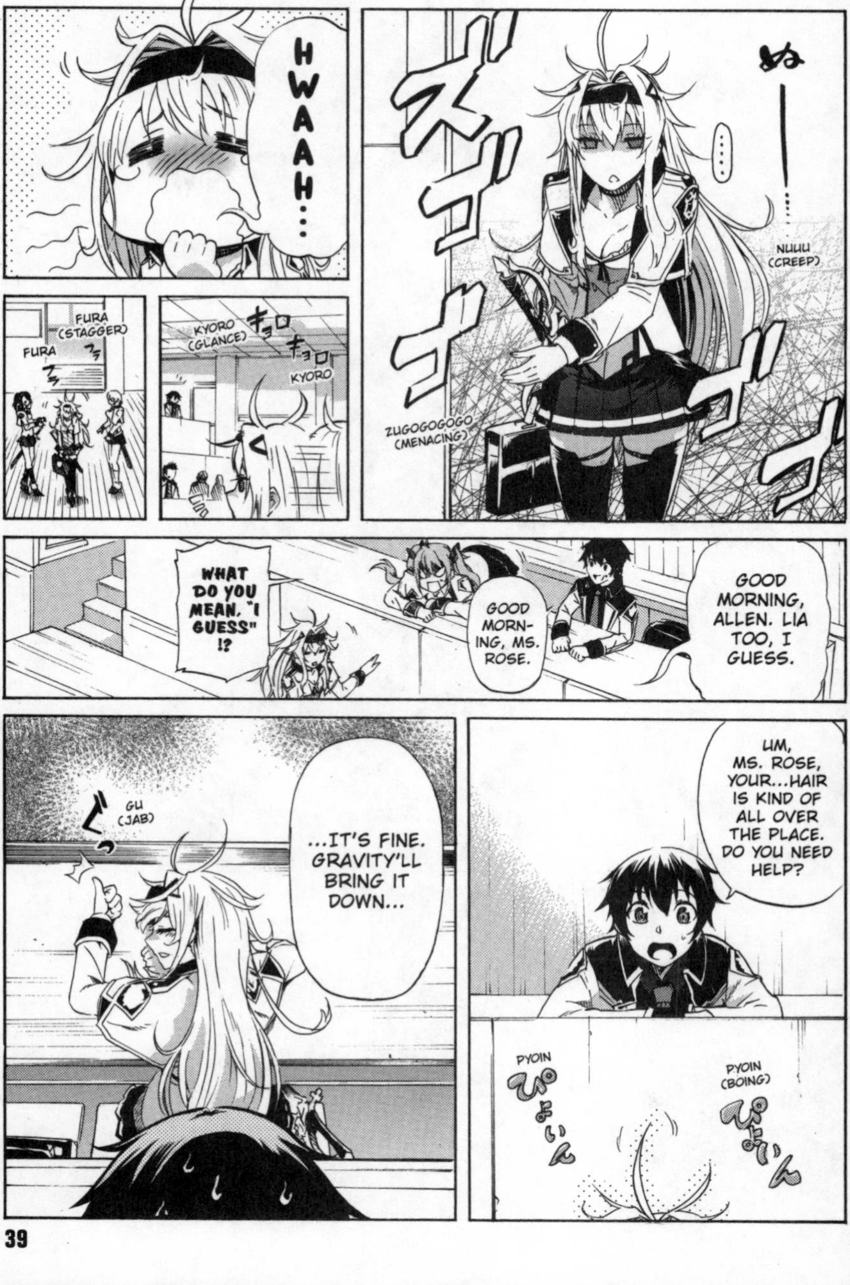
ぬー
...
NUUU (CREEP)
ズゴゴゴ
ZUGOGOGOGO (MENACING)
HWAAH...
キョロ キョロ
KYORO (GLANCE)
KYORO
FURA (STAGGER)
FURA
GOOD MORNING, ALLEN. LIA TOO, I GUESS.
GOOD MORNING, MS. ROSE.
WHAT DO YOU MEAN, "I GUESS" !?
UM, MS. ROSE, YOUR...HAIR IS KIND OF ALL OVER THE PLACE. DO YOU NEED HELP?
ぴょいん
PYOIN
ぴょいん
PYOIN (BOING)
...IT'S FINE. GRAVITY'LL BRING IT DOWN...
ぐっ
GU (JAB)

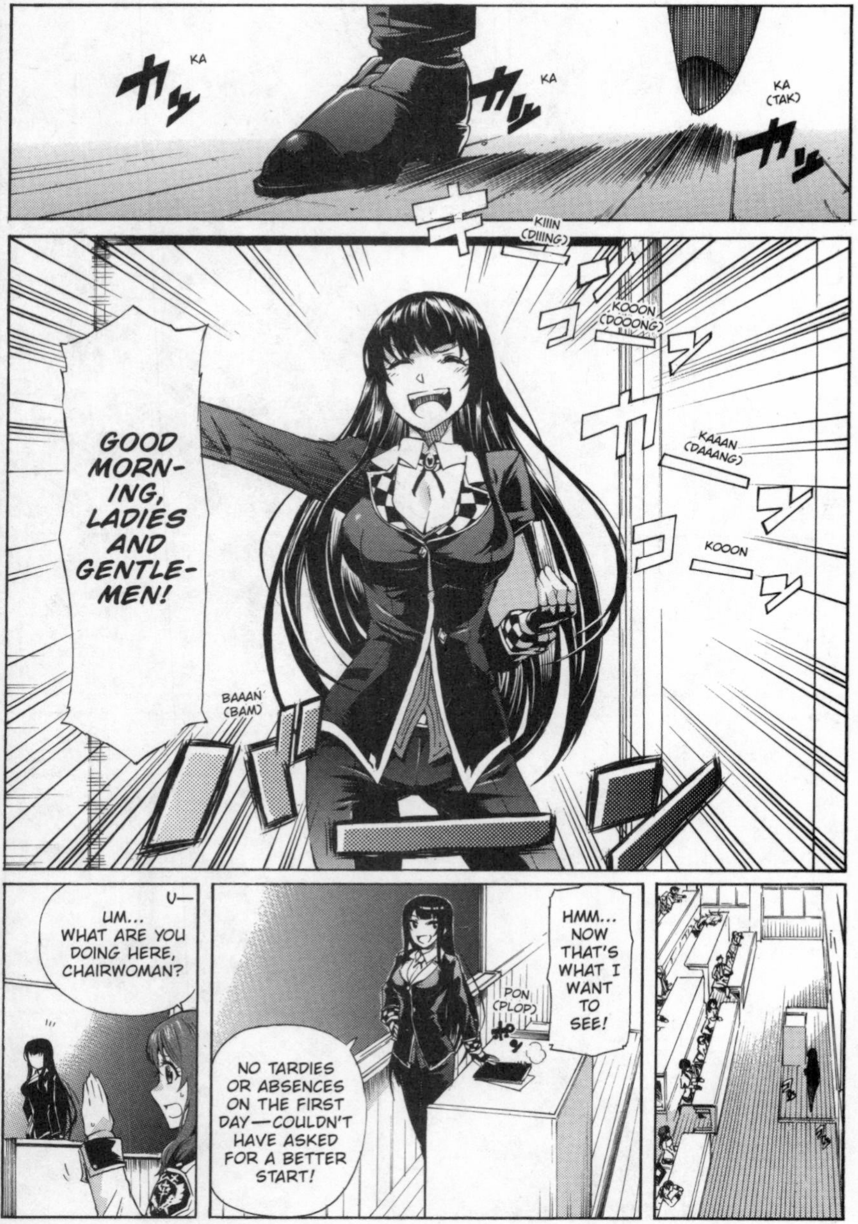

KA
(TAK)
KA
KA
KIIN
(DIIING)
KOOON
(DOOONG)
KAAAN
(DAAANG)
KOOON
GOOD MORNING, LADIES AND GENTLEMEN!
BAAAN
(BAM)
HMM... NOW THAT'S WHAT I WANT TO SEE!
PON
(PLOP)
NO TARDIES OR ABSENCES ON THE FIRST DAY—COULDN'T HAVE ASKED FOR A BETTER START!
U—
UM... WHAT ARE YOU DOING HERE, CHAIRWOMAN?

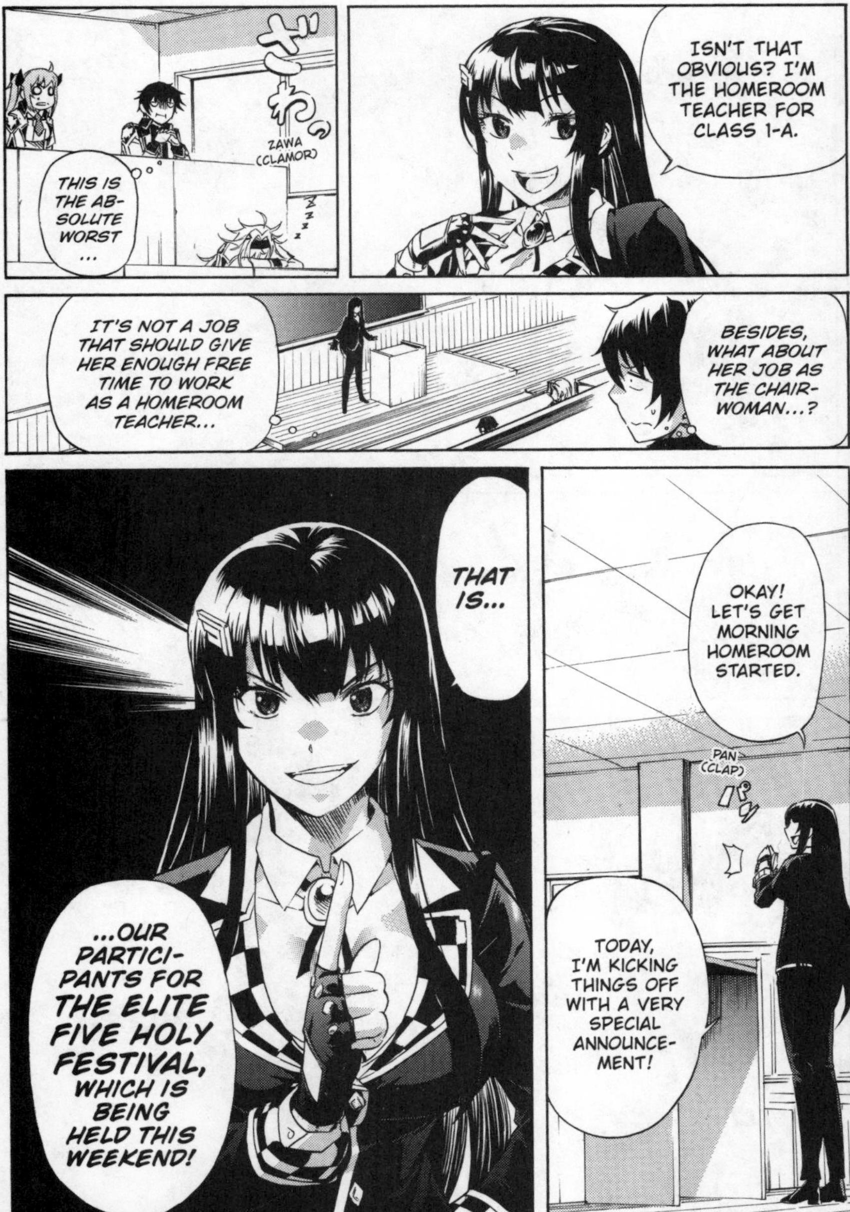

ISN'T THAT OBVIOUS? I'M THE HOMEROOM TEACHER FOR CLASS 1-A.
ZAWA (CLAMOR)
THIS IS THE AB-SOLUTE WORST ...
BESIDES, WHAT ABOUT HER JOB AS THE CHAIR-WOMAN...?
IT'S NOT A JOB THAT SHOULD GIVE HER ENOUGH FREE TIME TO WORK AS A HOMEROOM TEACHER...
OKAY! LET'S GET MORNING HOMEROOM STARTED.
PAN (CLAP)
TODAY, I'M KICKING THINGS OFF WITH A VERY SPECIAL ANNOUNCE-MENT!
THAT IS...
...OUR PARTICI-PANTS FOR THE ELITE FIVE HOLY FESTIVAL, WHICH IS BEING HELD THIS WEEKEND!

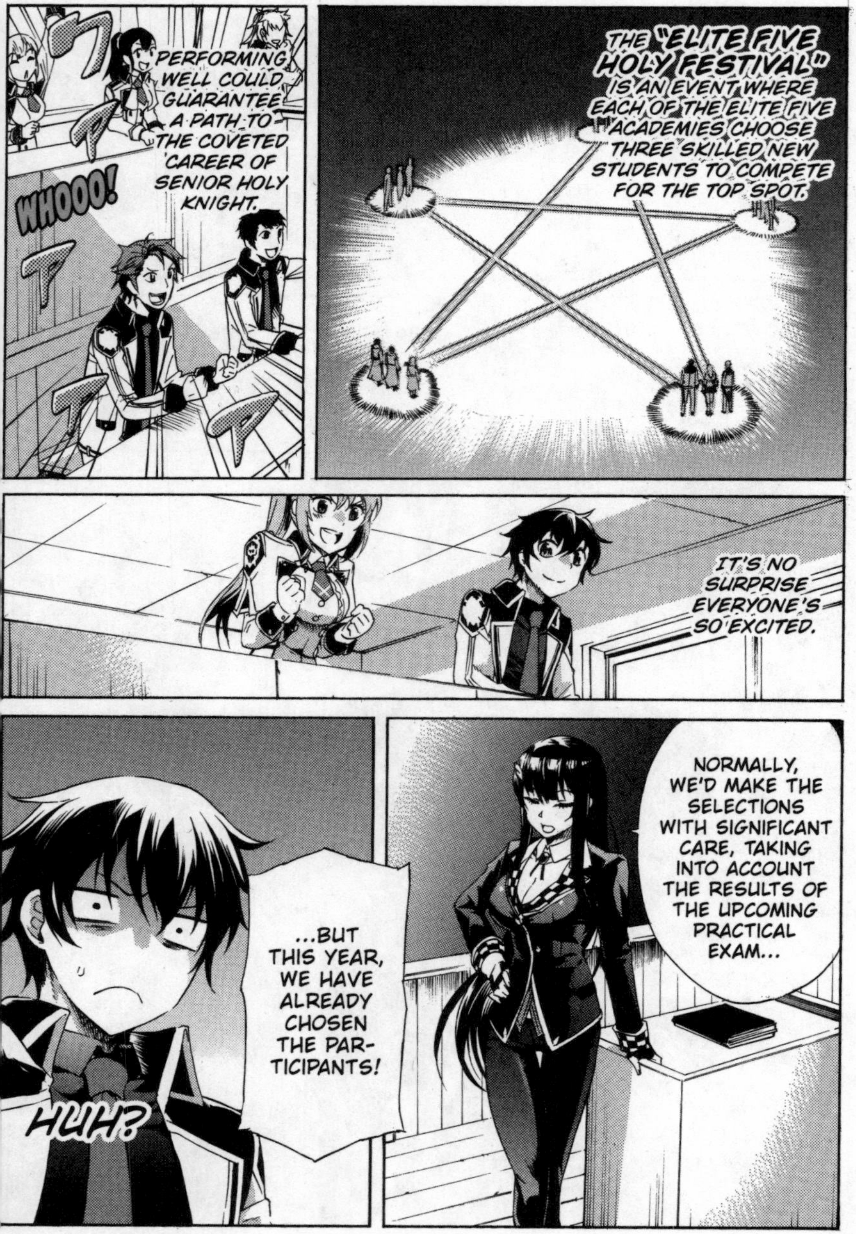
THE "ELITE FIVE HOLY FESTIVAL" IS AN EVENT WHERE EACH OF THE ELITE FIVE ACADEMIES CHOOSE THREE SKILLED NEW STUDENTS TO COMPETE FOR THE TOP SPOT.
PERFORMING WELL COULD GUARANTEE A PATH TO THE COVETED CAREER OF SENIOR HOLY KNIGHT.
WHOOO!
IT'S NO SURPRISE EVERYONE'S SO EXCITED.
NORMALLY, WE'D MAKE THE SELECTIONS WITH SIGNIFICANT CARE, TAKING INTO ACCOUNT THE RESULTS OF THE UPCOMING PRACTICAL EXAM...
...BUT THIS YEAR, WE HAVE ALREADY CHOSEN THE PAR-TICIPANTS!
HUH?

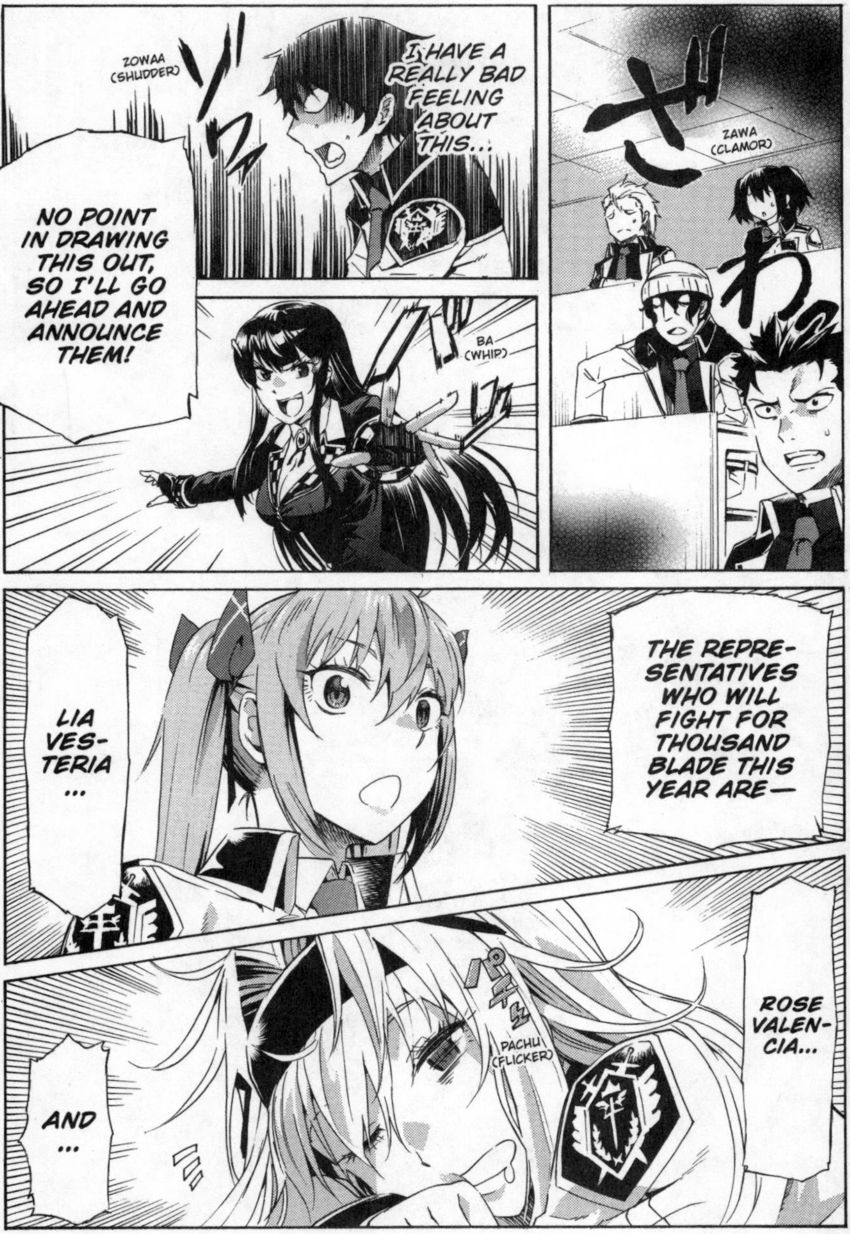
ZAWA (CLAMOR)
I HAVE A REALLY BAD FEELING ABOUT THIS...
ZOWAA (SHUDDER)
NO POINT IN DRAWING THIS OUT, SO I'LL GO AHEAD AND ANNOUNCE THEM!
BA (WHIP)
THE REPRE-SENTATIVES WHO WILL FIGHT FOR THOUSAND BLADE THIS YEAR ARE—
LIA VES-TERIA ...
ROSE VALEN-CIA...
PACHU (FLICKER)
AND ...

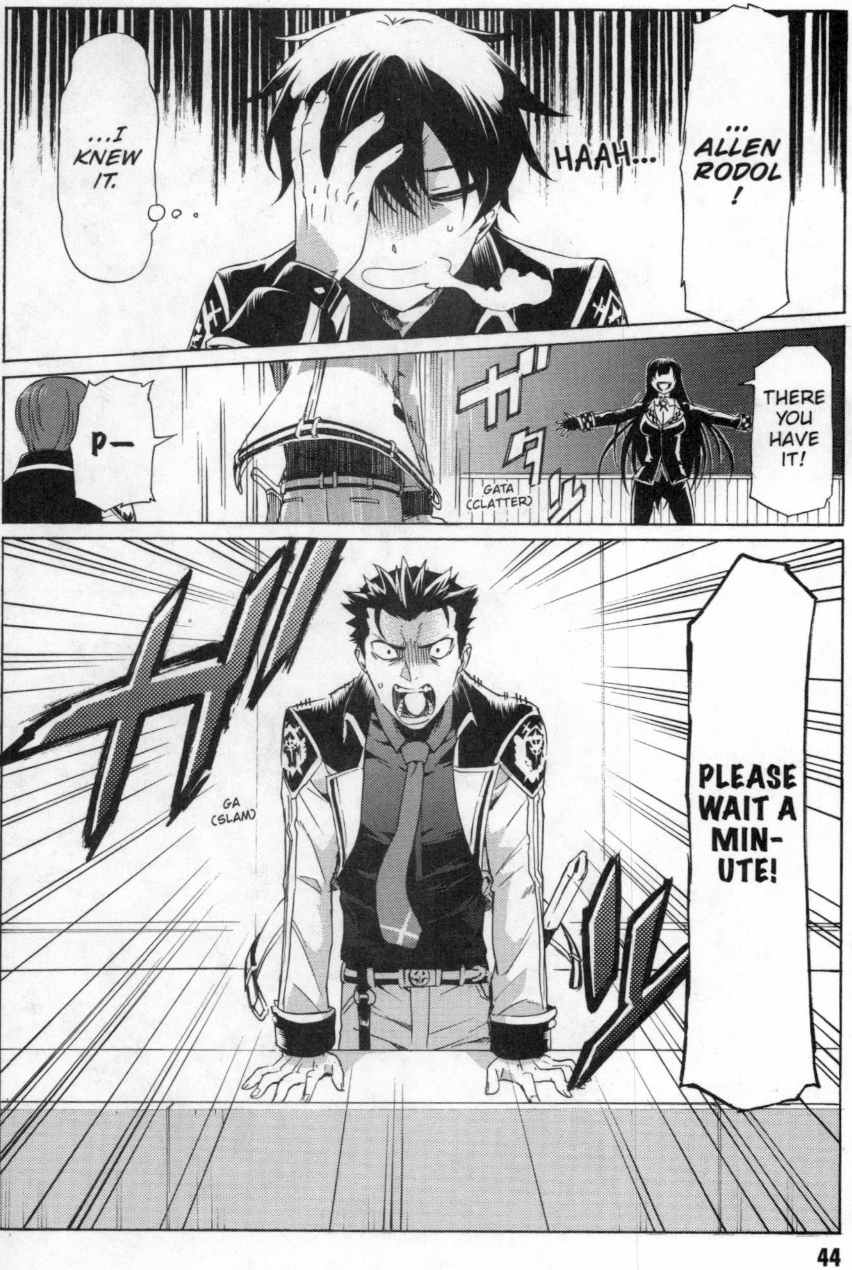
...ALLEN RODOL!
HAAH...
...I KNEW IT.
THERE YOU HAVE IT!
GATA (CLATTER)
P—
PLEASE WAIT A MIN-UTE!
GA (SLAM)

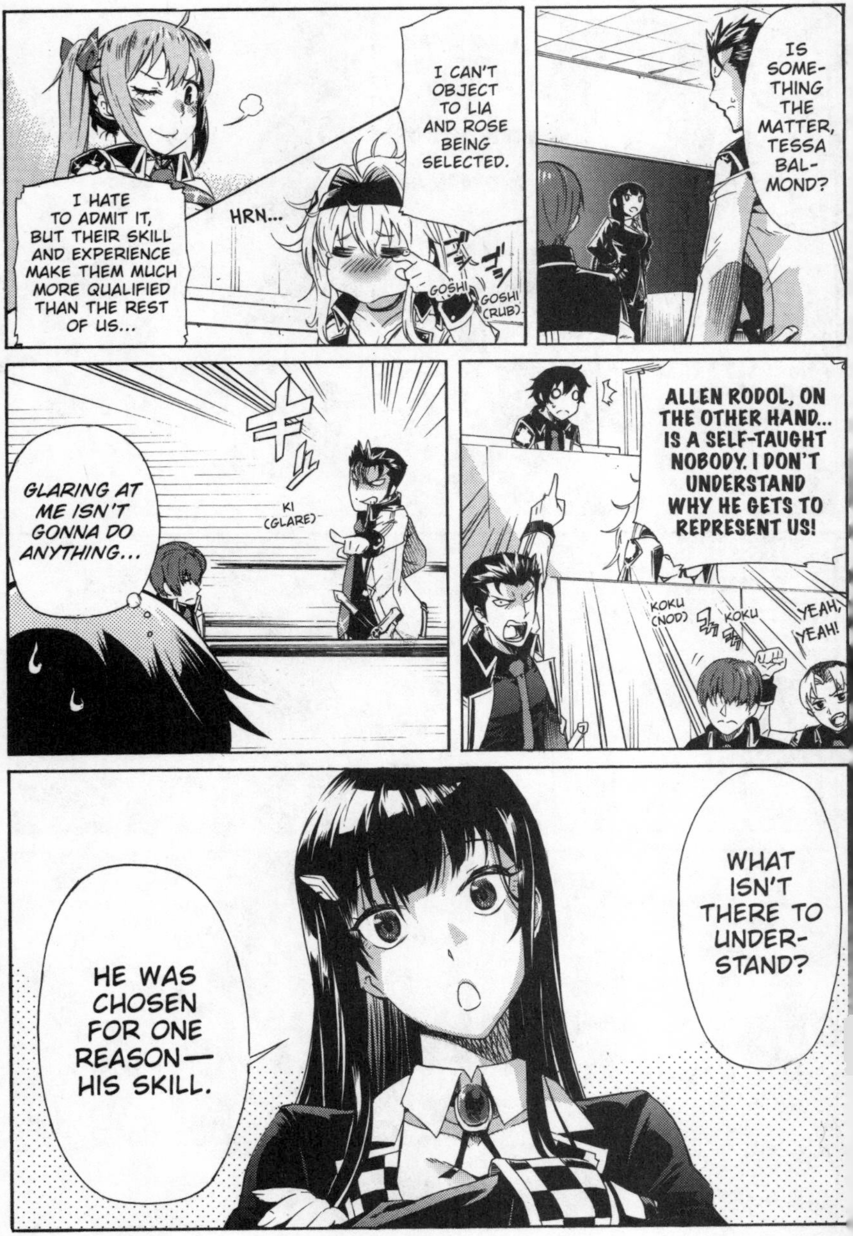
IS SOMETHING THE MATTER, TESSA BALMOND?
I CAN'T OBJECT TO LIA AND ROSE BEING SELECTED.
HRN...
GOSHI GOSHI (RUB)
I HATE TO ADMIT IT, BUT THEIR SKILL AND EXPERIENCE MAKE THEM MUCH MORE QUALIFIED THAN THE REST OF US...
ALLEN RODOL, ON THE OTHER HAND... IS A SELF-TAUGHT NOBODY. I DON'T UNDERSTAND WHY HE GETS TO REPRESENT US!
YEAH, YEAH!
KOKU (NOD) KOKU
KI (GLARE)
GLARING AT ME ISN'T GONNA DO ANYTHING...
WHAT ISN'T THERE TO UNDERSTAND?
HE WAS CHOSEN FOR ONE REASON—HIS SKILL.

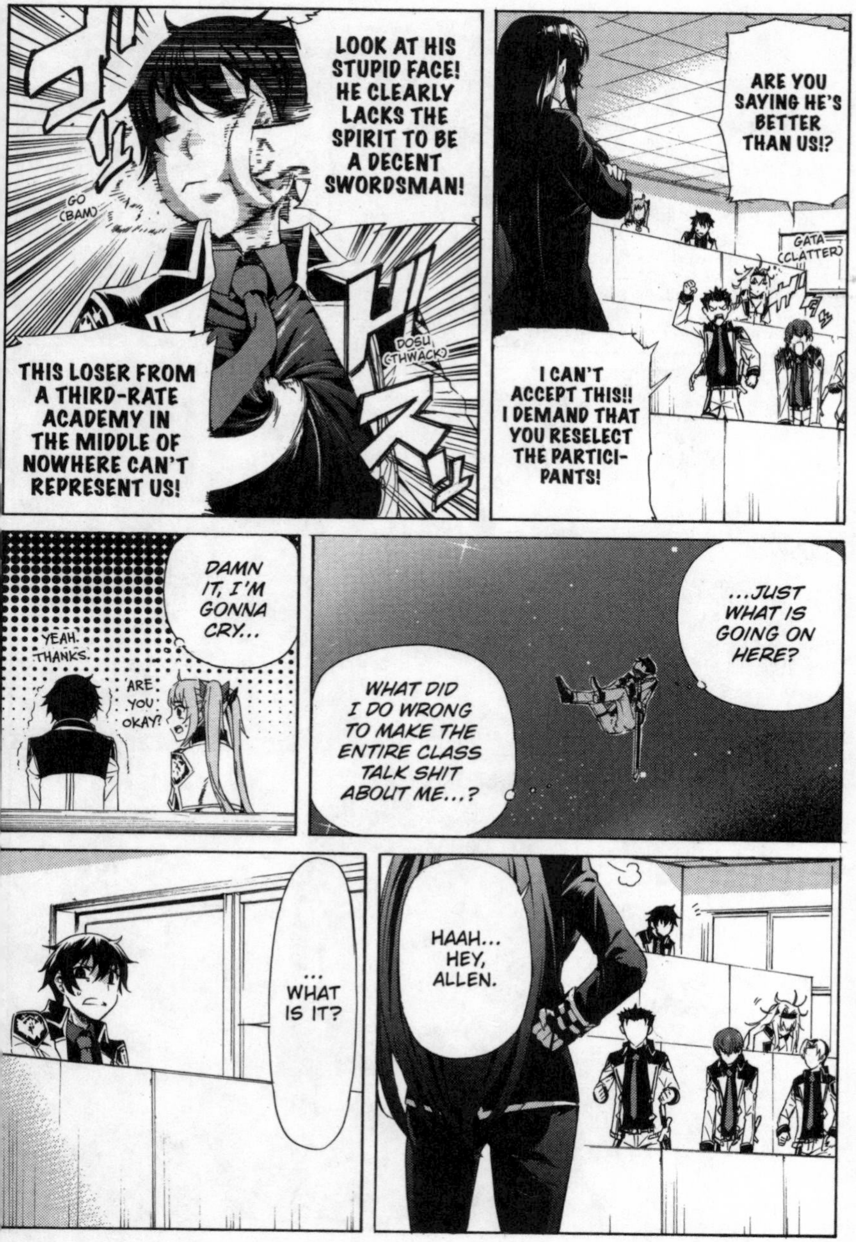
ARE YOU SAYING HE'S BETTER THAN US!?
GATA (CLATTER)
I CAN'T ACCEPT THIS!! I DEMAND THAT YOU RESELECT THE PARTICI-PANTS!
LOOK AT HIS STUPID FACE! HE CLEARLY LACKS THE SPIRIT TO BE A DECENT SWORDSMAN!
GO (BAM)
DOSU (THWACK)
THIS LOSER FROM A THIRD-RATE ACADEMY IN THE MIDDLE OF NOWHERE CAN'T REPRESENT US!
...JUST WHAT IS GOING ON HERE?
WHAT DID I DO WRONG TO MAKE THE ENTIRE CLASS TALK SHIT ABOUT ME...?
DAMN IT, I'M GONNA CRY...
ARE YOU OKAY?
YEAH. THANKS.
HAAH... HEY, ALLEN.
... WHAT IS IT?

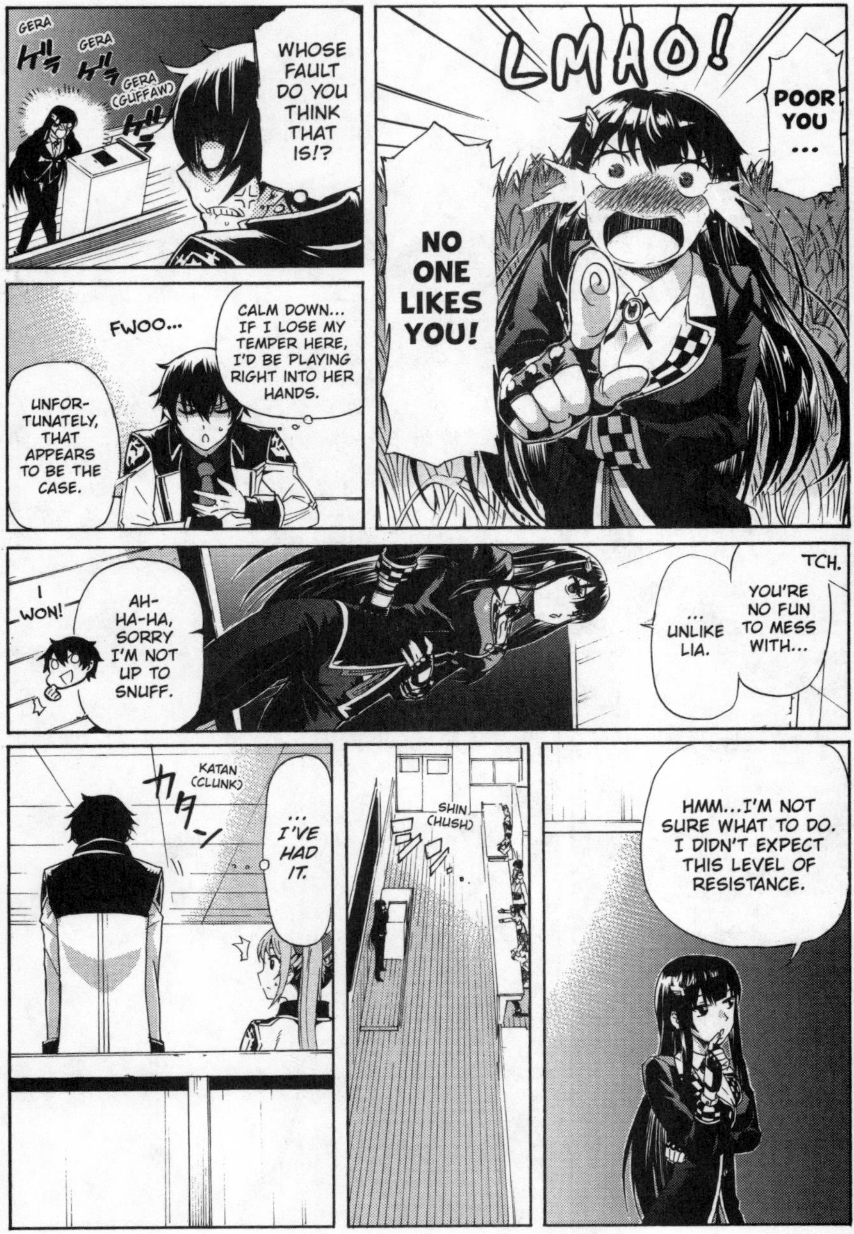
LMAO!
POOR YOU...
NO ONE LIKES YOU!
WHOSE FAULT DO YOU THINK THAT IS!?
GERA
GERA
GERA (GUFFAW)
CALM DOWN... IF I LOSE MY TEMPER HERE, I'D BE PLAYING RIGHT INTO HER HANDS.
FWOO...
UNFORTUNATELY, THAT APPEARS TO BE THE CASE.
TCH.
YOU'RE NO FUN TO MESS WITH...
...UNLIKE LIA.
AH-HA-HA, SORRY I'M NOT UP TO SNUFF.
I WON!
HMM...I'M NOT SURE WHAT TO DO. I DIDN'T EXPECT THIS LEVEL OF RESISTANCE.
SHIN (HUSH)
...I'VE HAD IT.
KATAN (CLUNK)

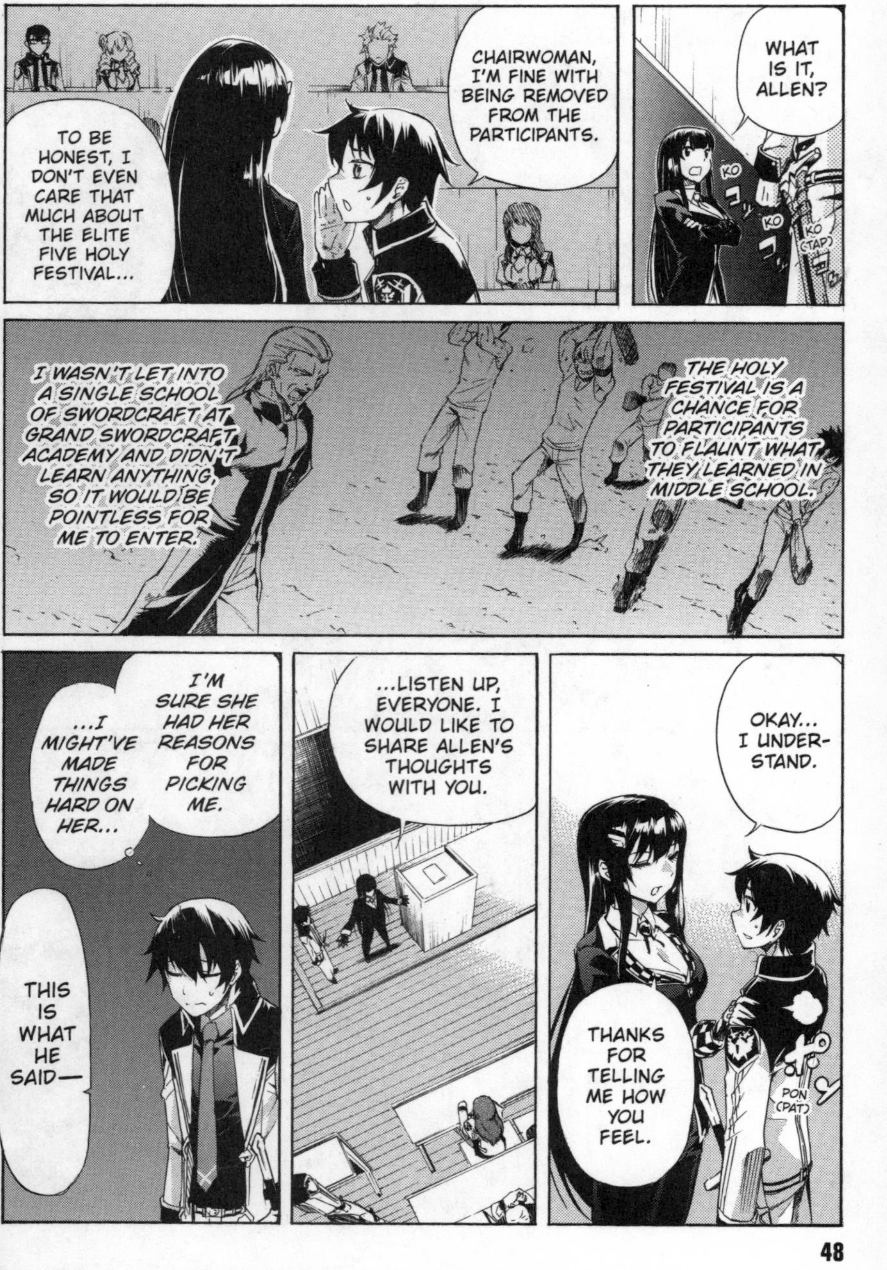
WHAT IS IT, ALLEN?
KO
KO
KO (TAP)
CHAIRWOMAN, I'M FINE WITH BEING REMOVED FROM THE PARTICIPANTS.
TO BE HONEST, I DON'T EVEN CARE THAT MUCH ABOUT THE ELITE FIVE HOLY FESTIVAL...
THE HOLY FESTIVAL IS A CHANCE FOR PARTICIPANTS TO FLAUNT WHAT THEY LEARNED IN MIDDLE SCHOOL.
I WASN'T LET INTO A SINGLE SCHOOL OF SWORDCRAFT AT GRAND SWORDCRAFT ACADEMY AND DIDN'T LEARN ANYTHING, SO IT WOULD BE POINTLESS FOR ME TO ENTER.
OKAY... I UNDER-STAND.
THANKS FOR TELLING ME HOW YOU FEEL.
PON (PAT)
...LISTEN UP, EVERYONE. I WOULD LIKE TO SHARE ALLEN'S THOUGHTS WITH YOU.
I'M SURE SHE HAD HER REASONS FOR PICKING ME.
...I MIGHT'VE MADE THINGS HARD ON HER...
THIS IS WHAT HE SAID—

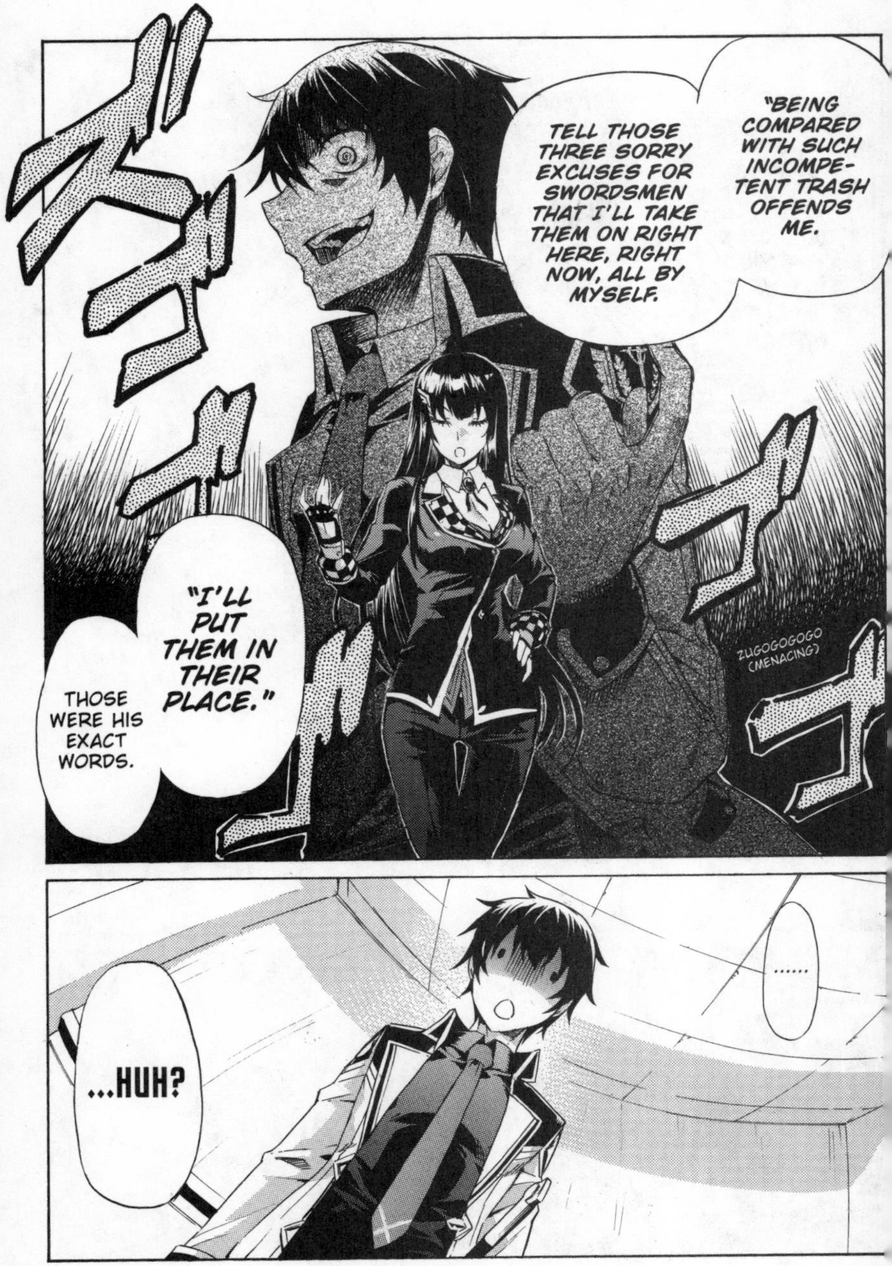
"BEING COMPARED WITH SUCH INCOMPETENT TRASH OFFENDS ME.
TELL THOSE THREE SORRY EXCUSES FOR SWORDSMEN THAT I'LL TAKE THEM ON RIGHT HERE, RIGHT NOW, ALL BY MYSELF.
ZUGOGOGOGO (MENACING)
"I'LL PUT THEM IN THEIR PLACE."
THOSE WERE HIS EXACT WORDS.
......
...HUH?

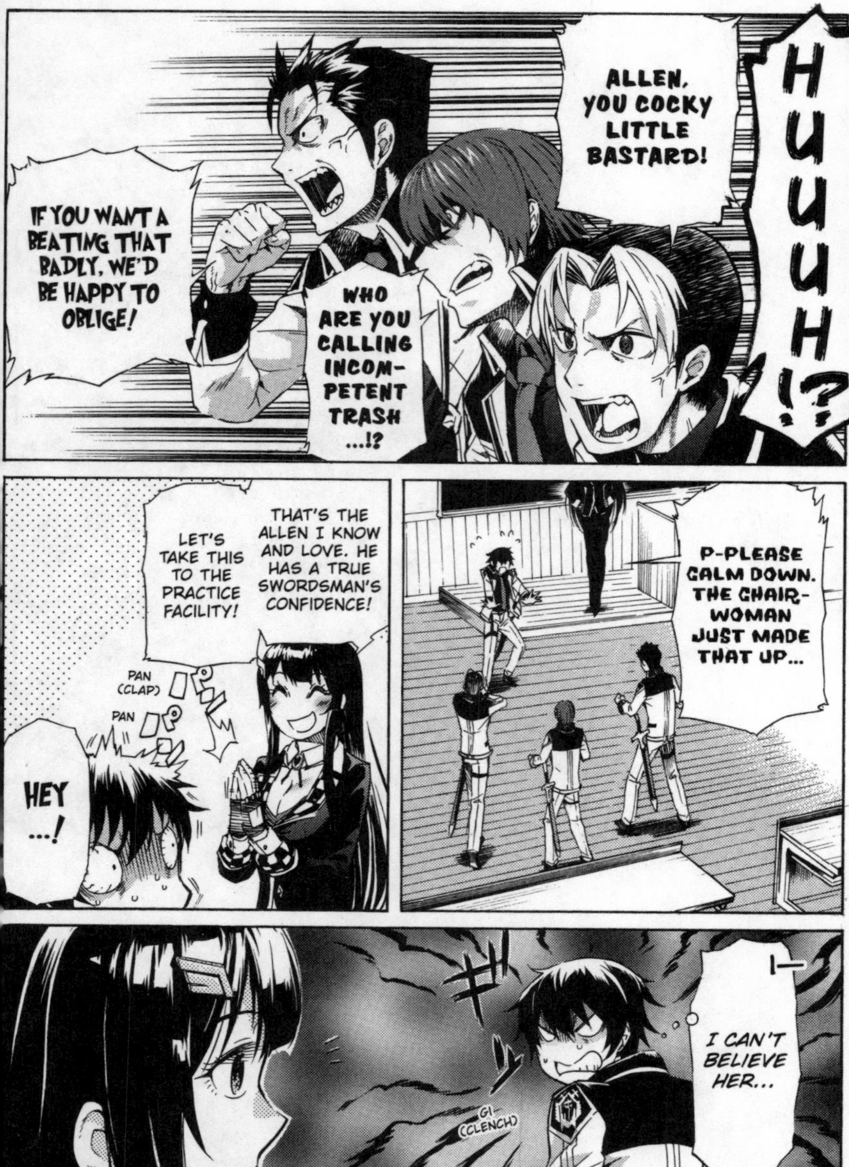
HUUUH!?
ALLEN, YOU COCKY LITTLE BASTARD!
WHO ARE YOU CALLING INCOMPETENT TRASH...!?
IF YOU WANT A BEATING THAT BADLY, WE'D BE HAPPY TO OBLIGE!
P-PLEASE CALM DOWN. THE CHAIRWOMAN JUST MADE THAT UP...
THAT'S THE ALLEN I KNOW AND LOVE. HE HAS A TRUE SWORDSMAN'S CONFIDENCE!
LET'S TAKE THIS TO THE PRACTICE FACILITY!
PAN (CLAP)
PAN
HEY...!
I–
I CAN'T BELIEVE HER...
GI (CLENCH)

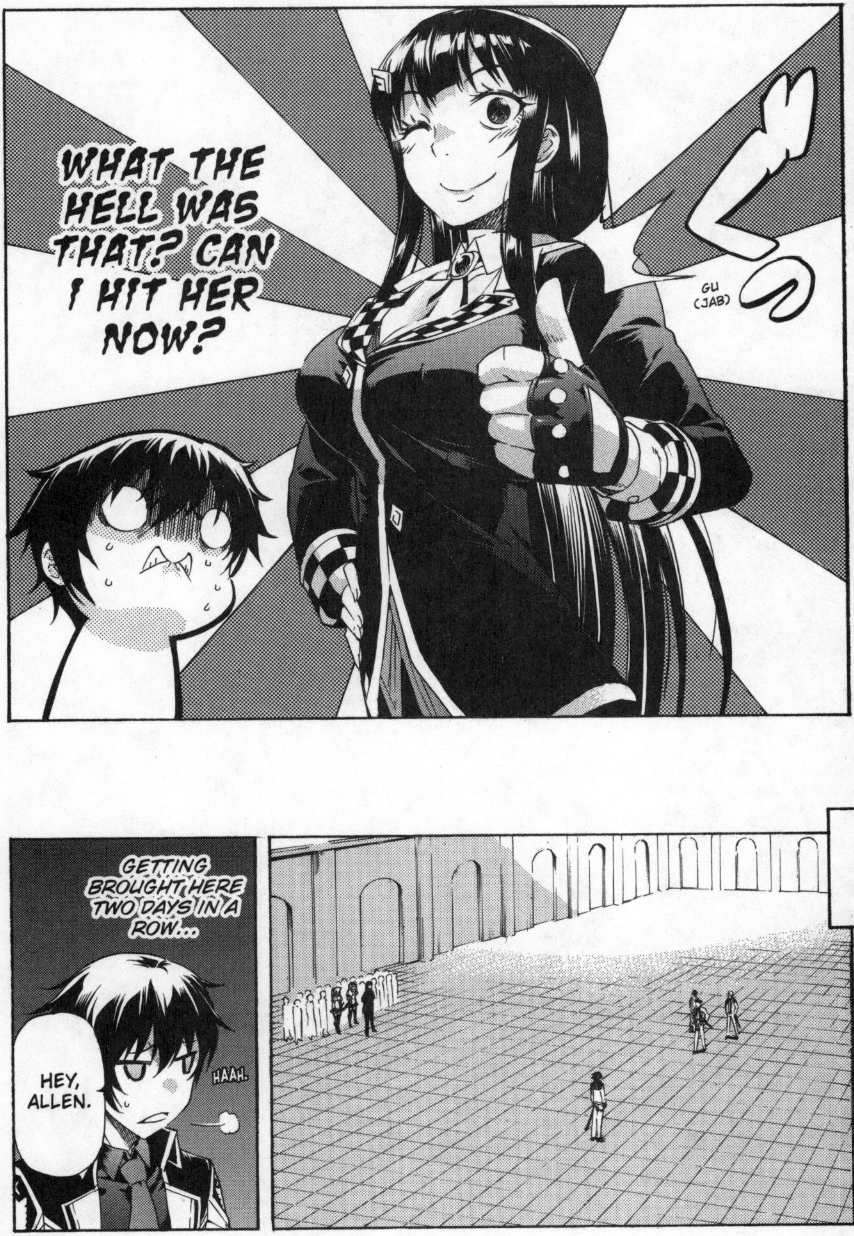
WHAT THE HELL WAS THAT? CAN I HIT HER NOW?
GU (JAB)
GETTING BROUGHT HERE TWO DAYS IN A ROW...
HAAH.
HEY, ALLEN.

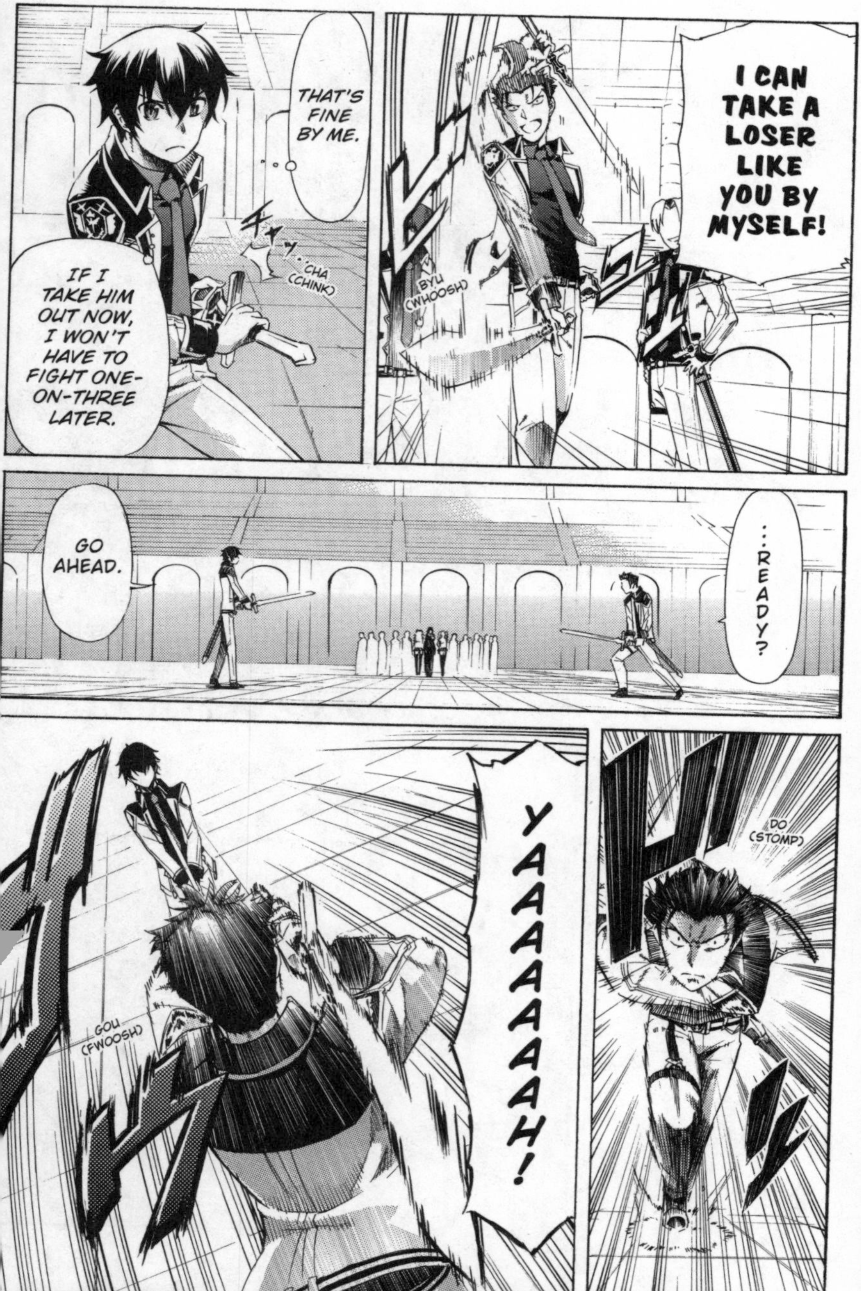
I CAN TAKE A LOSER LIKE YOU BY MYSELF!
BYU (WHOOSH)
THAT'S FINE BY ME.
IF I TAKE HIM OUT NOW, I WON'T HAVE TO FIGHT ONE-ON-THREE LATER.
CHA (CHINK)
...READY?
GO AHEAD.
DO (STOMP)
YAAAAAAAAAH!
GOU (FWOOSH)

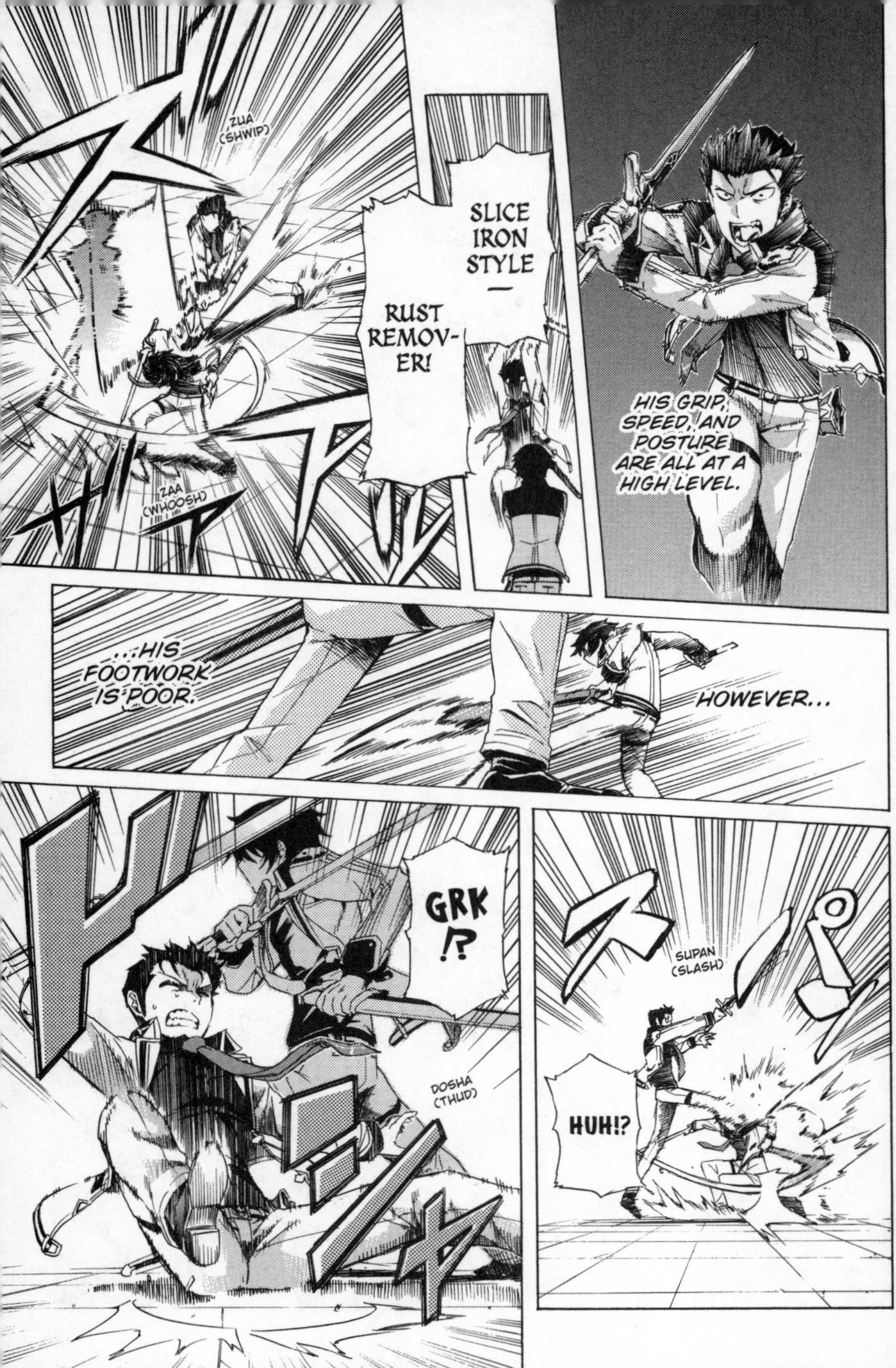
HIS GRIP, SPEED, AND POSTURE ARE ALL AT A HIGH LEVEL.
SLICE IRON STYLE — RUST REMOVER!
ZUA (SHWIP)
ZAA (WHOOSH)
HOWEVER...
...HIS FOOTWORK IS POOR.
SUPAN (SLASH)
HUH!?
GRK !?
DOSHA (THUD)

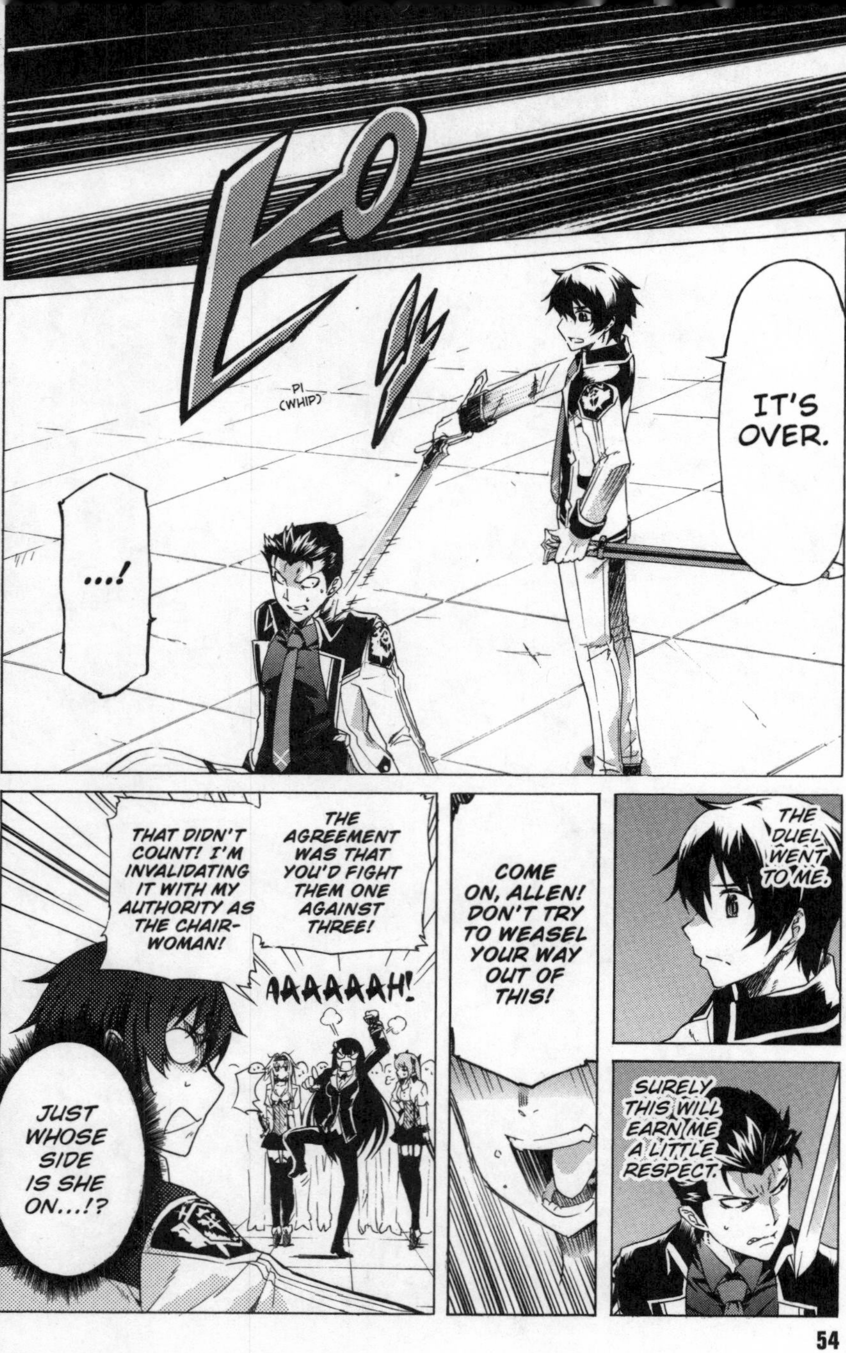
IT'S OVER.
PI
(WHIP)
...!
THE DUEL WENT TO ME.
SURELY THIS WILL EARN ME A LITTLE RESPECT.
COME ON, ALLEN! DON'T TRY TO WEASEL YOUR WAY OUT OF THIS!
THE AGREEMENT WAS THAT YOU'D FIGHT THEM ONE AGAINST THREE!
THAT DIDN'T COUNT! I'M INVALIDATING IT WITH MY AUTHORITY AS THE CHAIR-WOMAN!
AAAAAAH!
JUST WHOSE SIDE IS SHE ON...!?

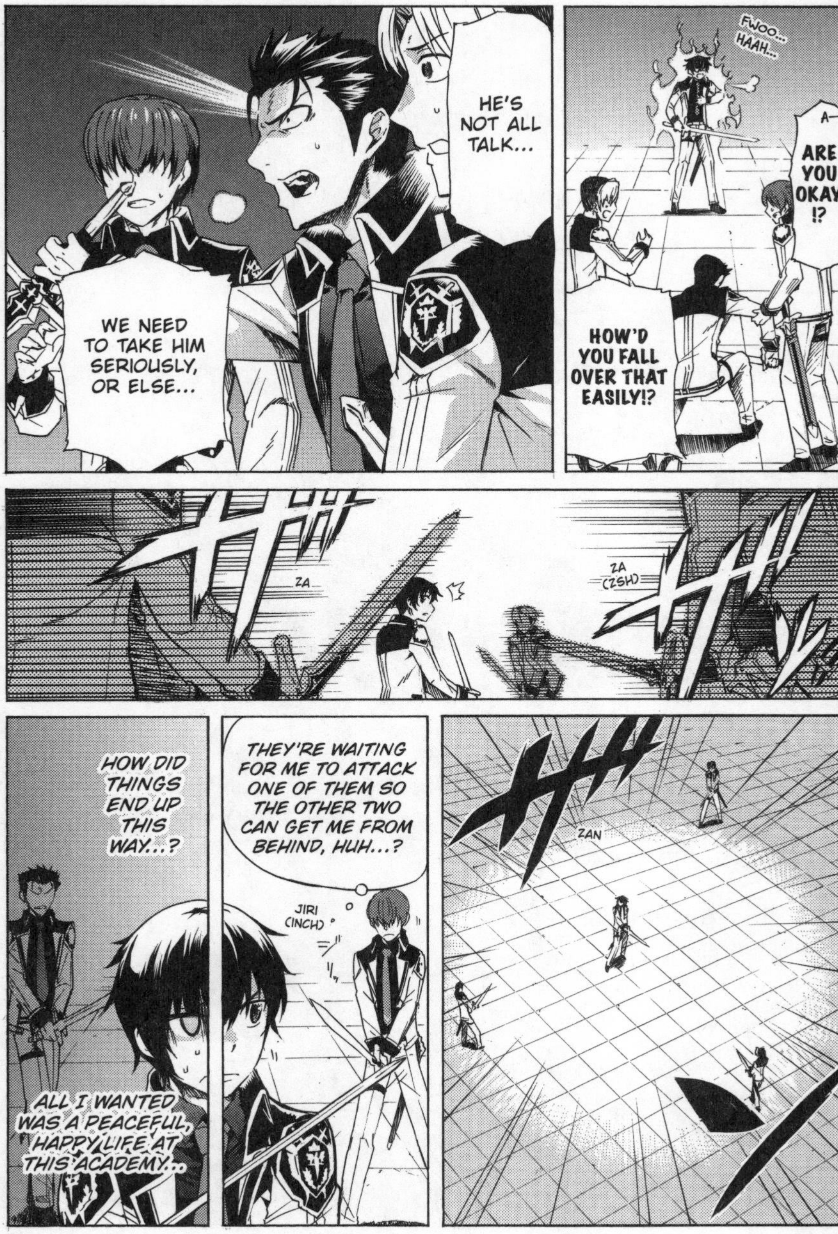
FWOO... HAAH...
A—
ARE YOU OKAY!?
HOW'D YOU FALL OVER THAT EASILY!?
HE'S NOT ALL TALK...
WE NEED TO TAKE HIM SERIOUSLY, OR ELSE...
ZA (ZSH)
ZA
ZAN
THEY'RE WAITING FOR ME TO ATTACK ONE OF THEM SO THE OTHER TWO CAN GET ME FROM BEHIND, HUH...?
JIRI (INCH)
HOW DID THINGS END UP THIS WAY...?
ALL I WANTED WAS A PEACEFUL, HAPPY LIFE AT THIS ACADEMY...

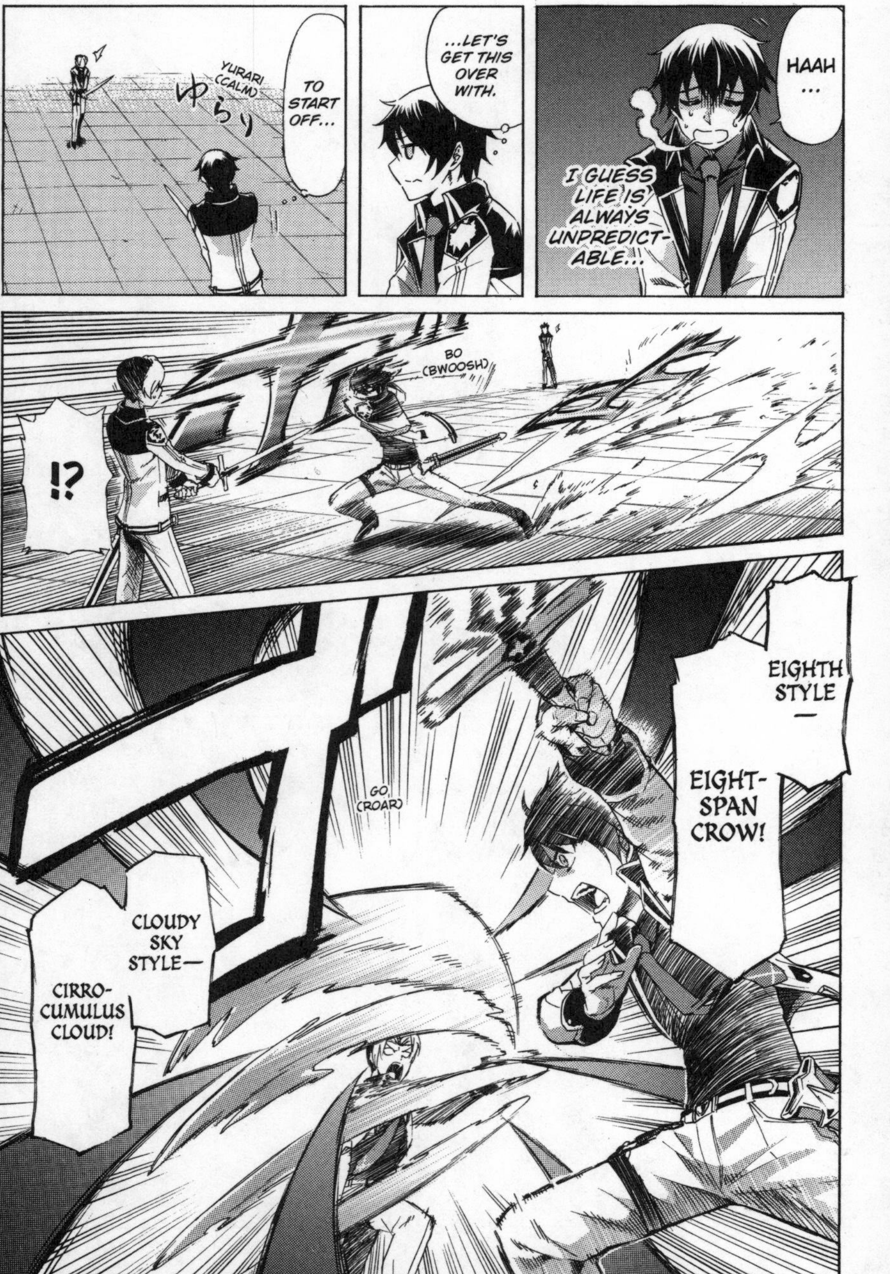
HAAH...
I GUESS LIFE IS ALWAYS UNPREDICT-ABLE...
...LET'S GET THIS OVER WITH.
TO START OFF...
YURARI (CALM)
ゆらり
BO (BWOOSH)
!?
EIGHTH STYLE—
EIGHT-SPAN CROW!
GO (ROAR)
CLOUDY SKY STYLE—
CIRRO-CUMULUS CLOUD!

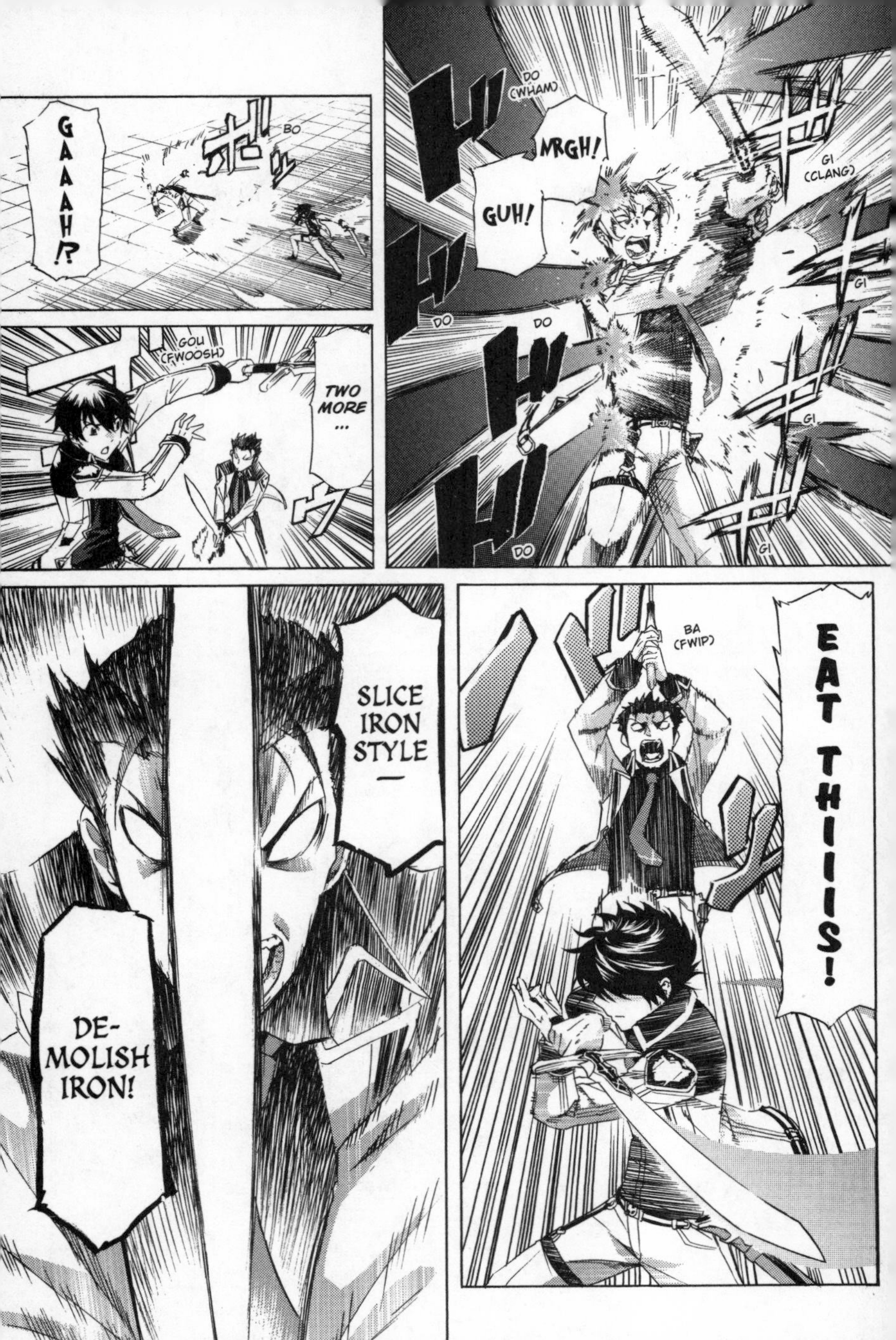
GI (CLANG)
DO (WHAM)
MRGH!
GUH!
GI
GI
DO
DO
GI
DO
BO
GAAAH!?
TWO MORE ...
GOU (FWOOSH)
EAT THIIIS!
BA (FWIP)
SLICE IRON STYLE —
DE-MOLISH IRON!

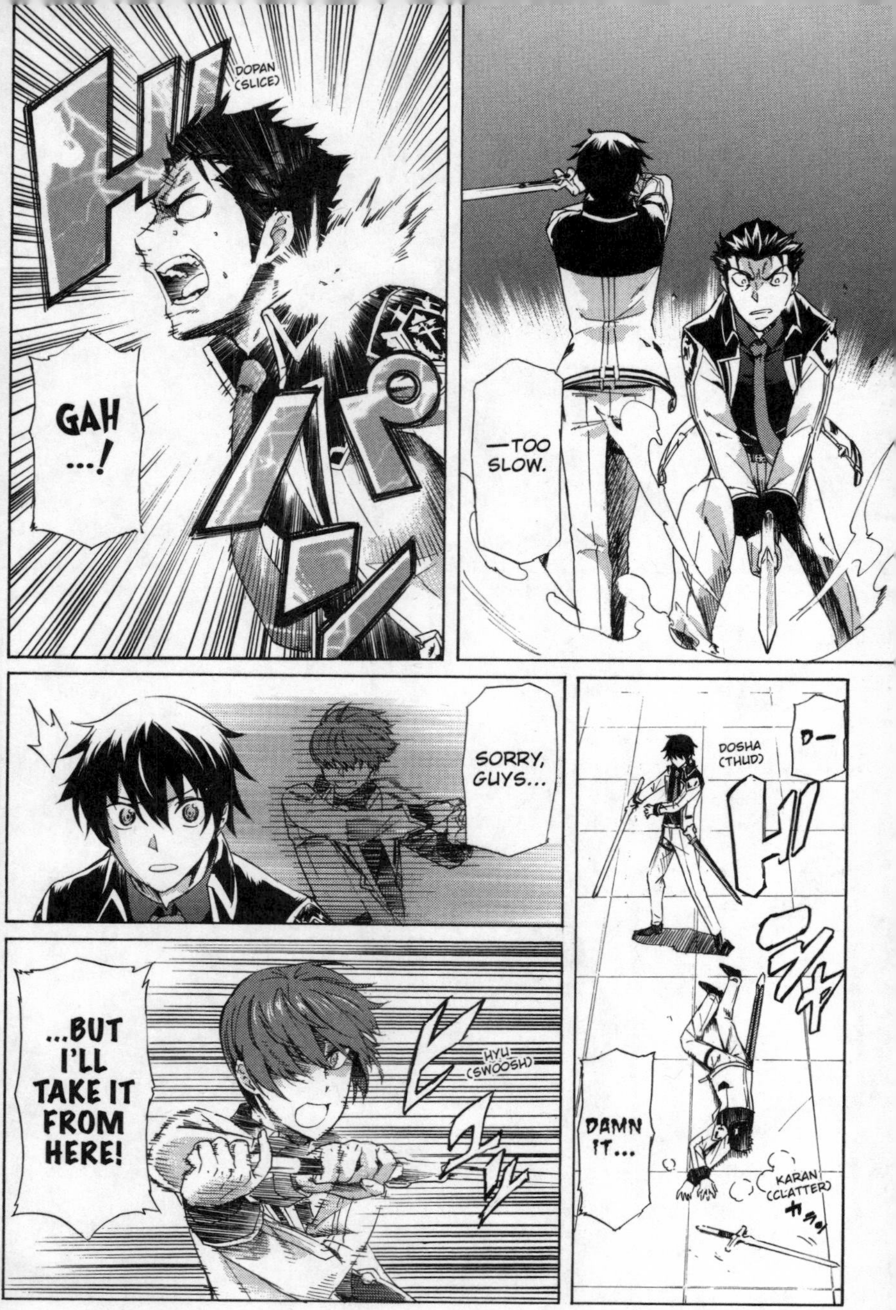
—TOO SLOW.
DOPAN (SLICE)
GAH ...!
D—
DOSHA (THUD)
DAMN IT...
KARAN (CLATTER)
SORRY, GUYS...
...BUT I'LL TAKE IT FROM HERE!
HYU (SWOOSH)

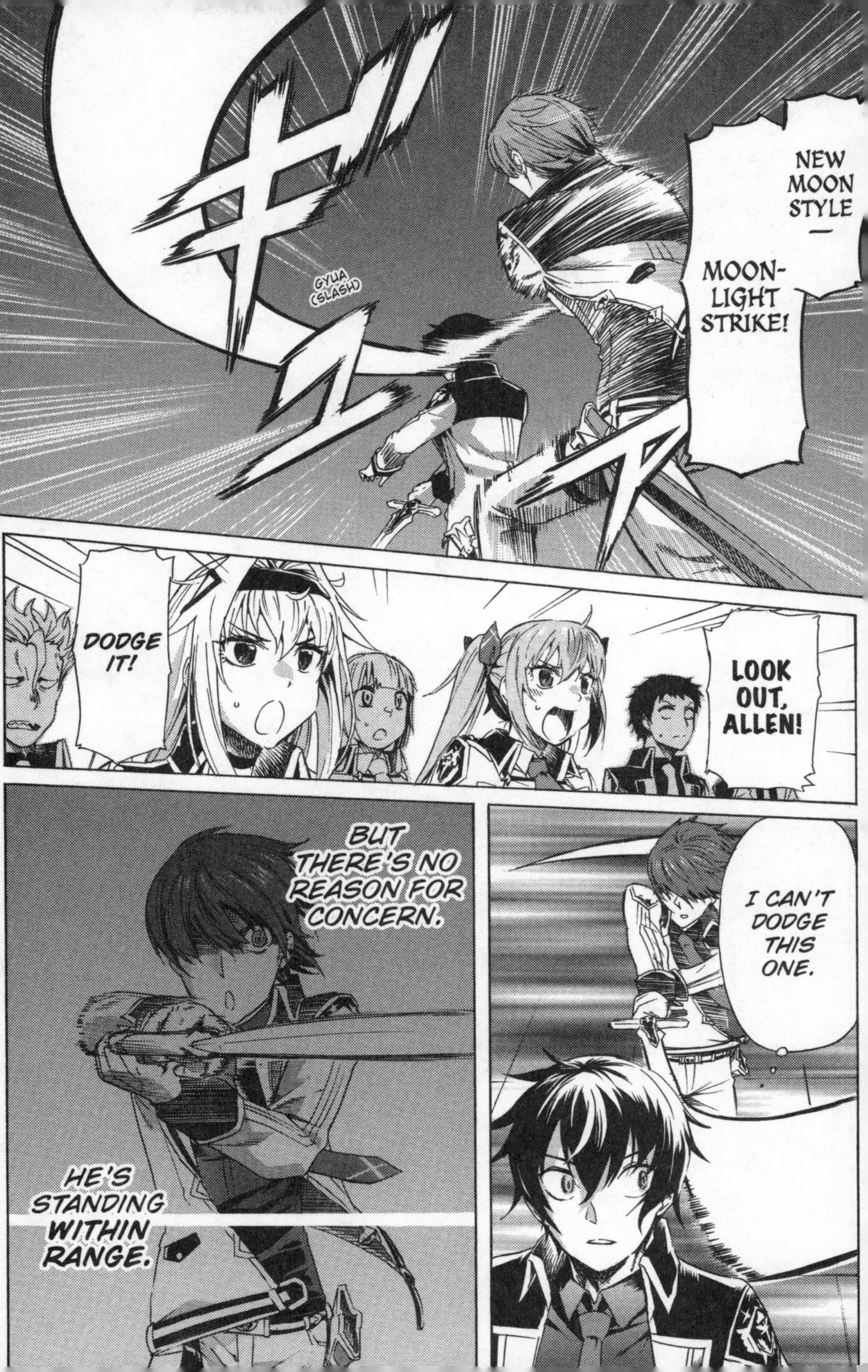
NEW MOON STYLE — MOONLIGHT STRIKE!
GYUA (SLASH)
LOOK OUT, ALLEN!
DODGE IT!
I CAN'T DODGE THIS ONE.
BUT THERE'S NO REASON FOR CONCERN.
HE'S STANDING WITHIN RANGE.

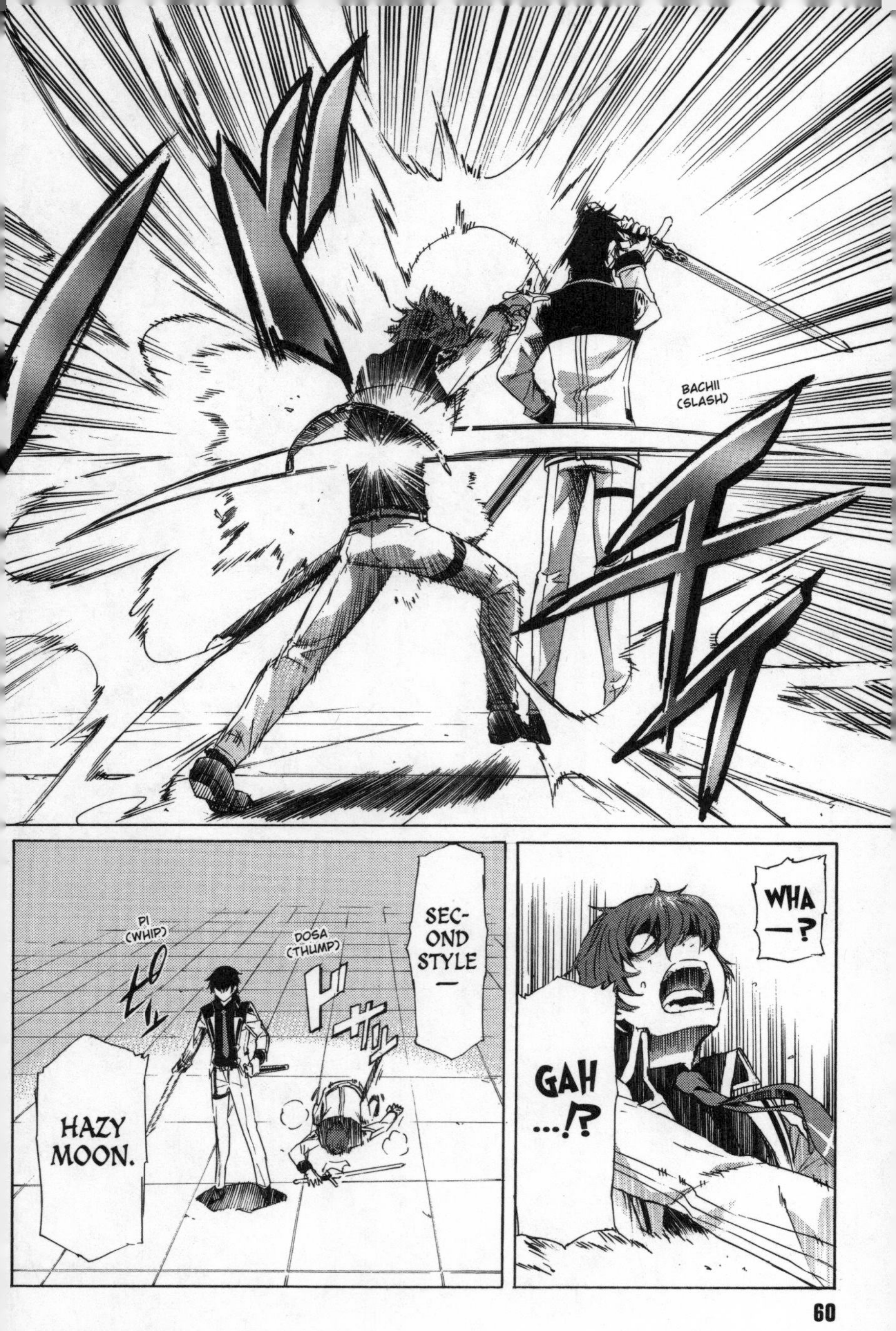
BACHII (SLASH)
WHA—?
GAH...!?
SEC-OND STYLE—
DOSA (THUMP)
PI (WHIP)
HAZY MOON.

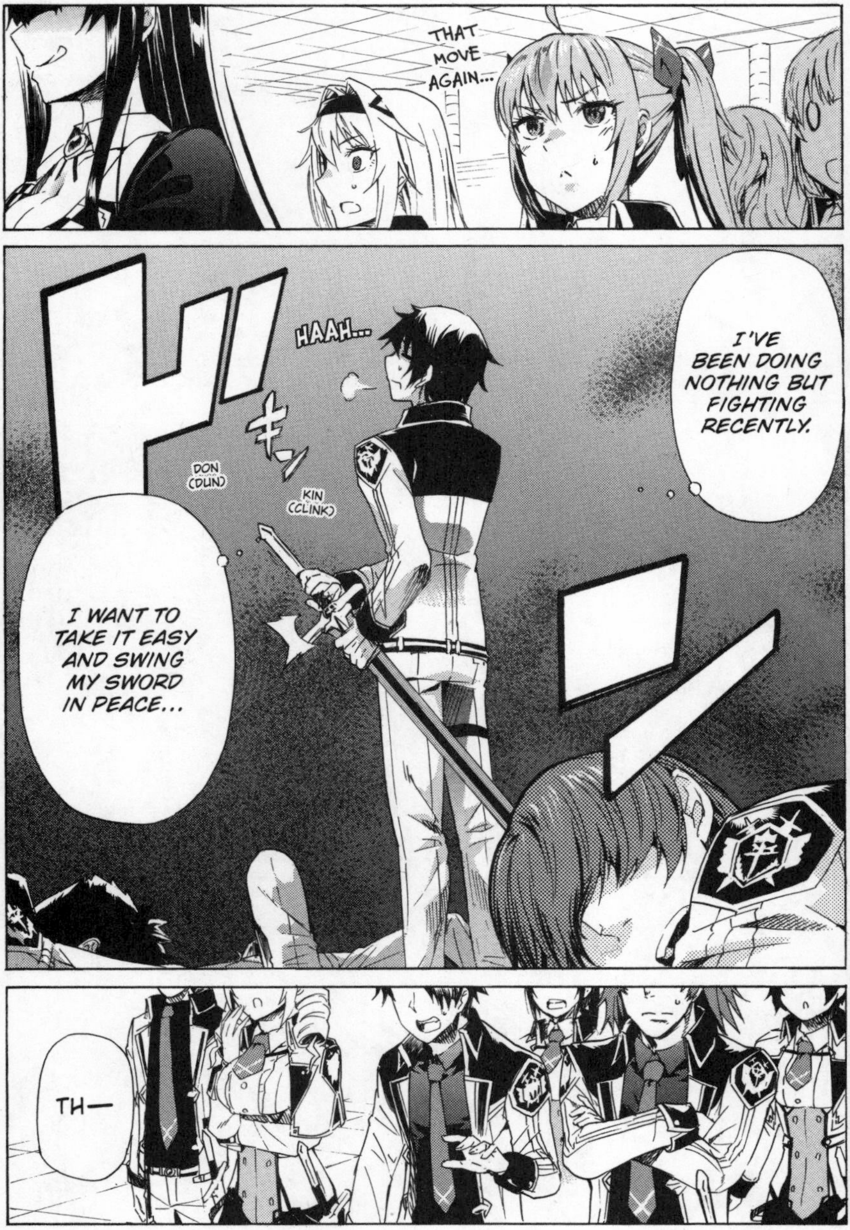
THAT MOVE AGAIN...
I'VE BEEN DOING NOTHING BUT FIGHTING RECENTLY.
HAAH...
KIN (CLINK)
DON (DUN)
I WANT TO TAKE IT EASY AND SWING MY SWORD IN PEACE...
TH—

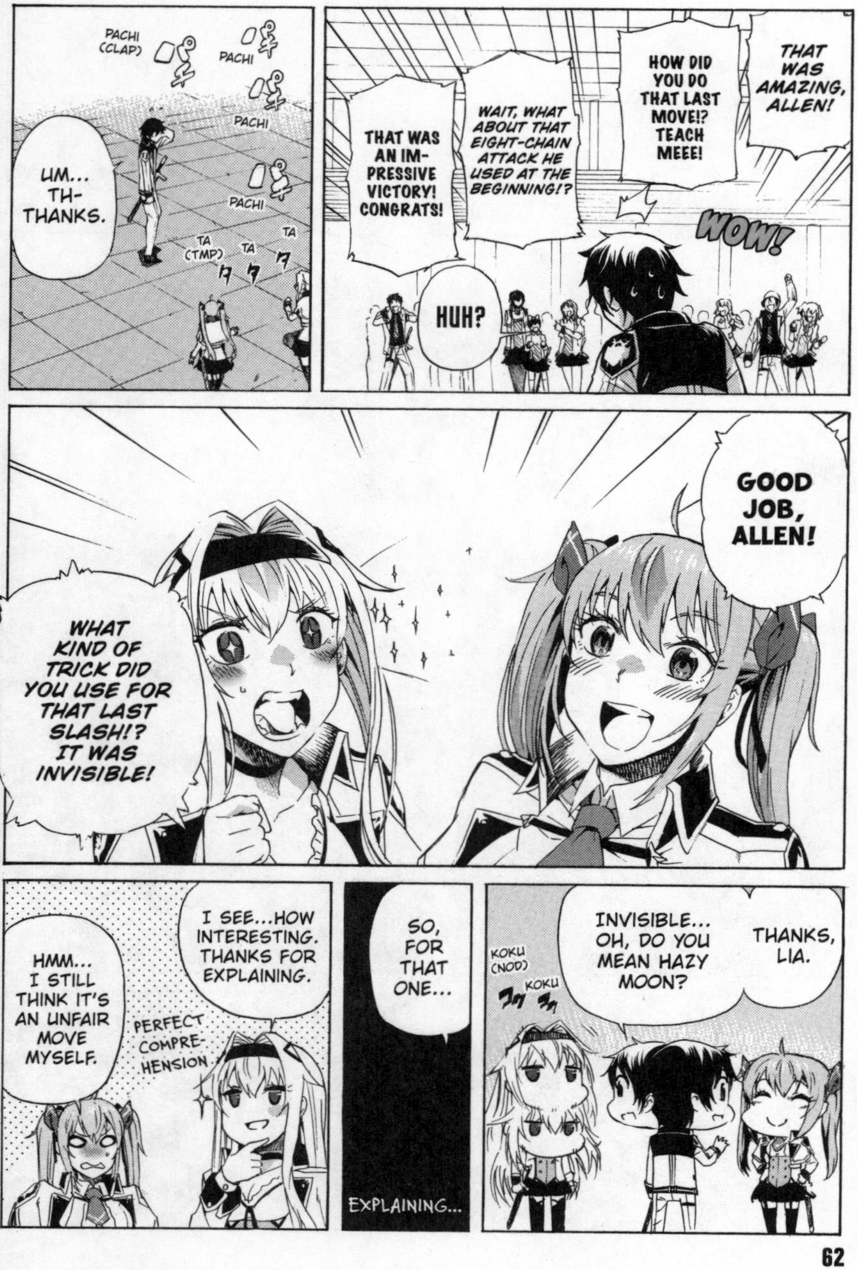
THAT WAS AMAZING, ALLEN!
HOW DID YOU DO THAT LAST MOVE!? TEACH MEEE!
WAIT, WHAT ABOUT THAT EIGHT-CHAIN ATTACK HE USED AT THE BEGINNING!?
THAT WAS AN IMPRESSIVE VICTORY! CONGRATS!
WOW!
HUH?
PACHI (CLAP)
PACHI
PACHI
PACHI
UM... TH-THANKS.
TA
TA
TA (TMP)
GOOD JOB, ALLEN!
WHAT KIND OF TRICK DID YOU USE FOR THAT LAST SLASH!? IT WAS INVISIBLE!
THANKS, LIA.
INVISIBLE... OH, DO YOU MEAN HAZY MOON?
KOKU (NOD)
KOKU
SO, FOR THAT ONE...
EXPLAINING...
I SEE...HOW INTERESTING. THANKS FOR EXPLAINING.
PERFECT COMPREHENSION
HMM... I STILL THINK IT'S AN UNFAIR MOVE MYSELF.

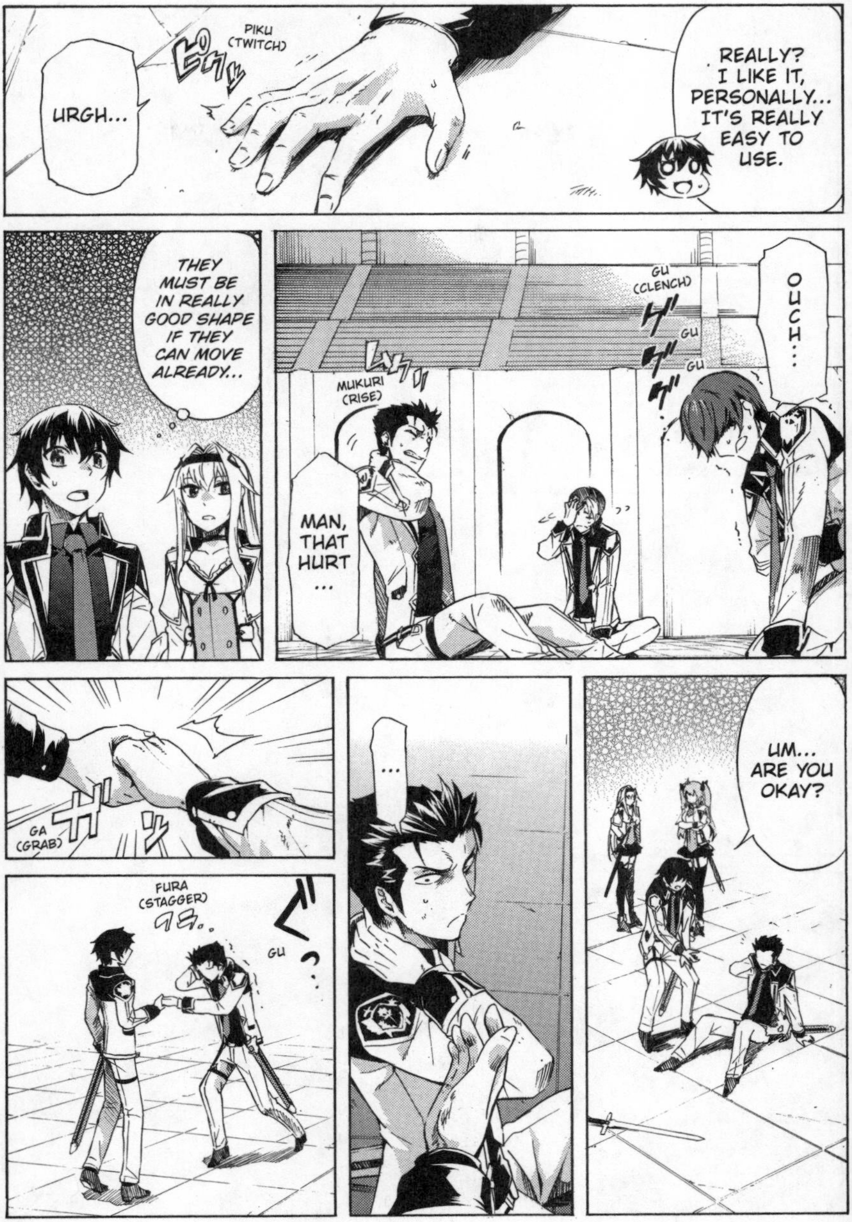
REALLY? I LIKE IT, PERSONALLY... IT'S REALLY EASY TO USE.
PIKU (TWITCH)
URGH...
OUCH...
GU (CLENCH)
GU
GU
MUKURI (RISE)
MAN, THAT HURT ...
THEY MUST BE IN REALLY GOOD SHAPE IF THEY CAN MOVE ALREADY...
UM... ARE YOU OKAY?
...
GA (GRAB)
FURA (STAGGER)
GU

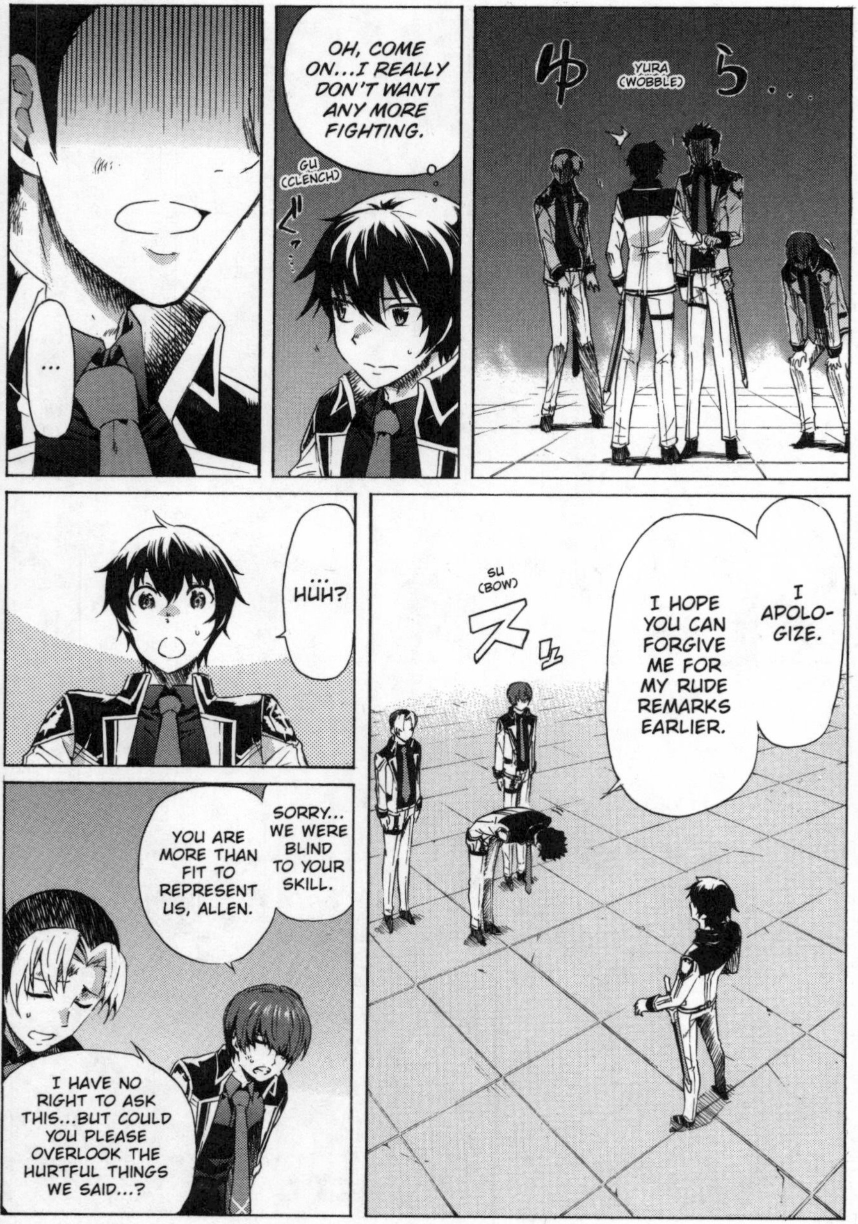

ゆら...
YURA (WOBBLE)
OH, COME ON...I REALLY DON'T WANT ANY MORE FIGHTING.
GU (CLENCH)
...
I APOLOGIZE.
I HOPE YOU CAN FORGIVE ME FOR MY RUDE REMARKS EARLIER.
SU (BOW)
...HUH?
SORRY... WE WERE BLIND TO YOUR SKILL.
YOU ARE MORE THAN FIT TO REPRESENT US, ALLEN.
I HAVE NO RIGHT TO ASK THIS...BUT COULD YOU PLEASE OVERLOOK THE HURTFUL THINGS WE SAID...?

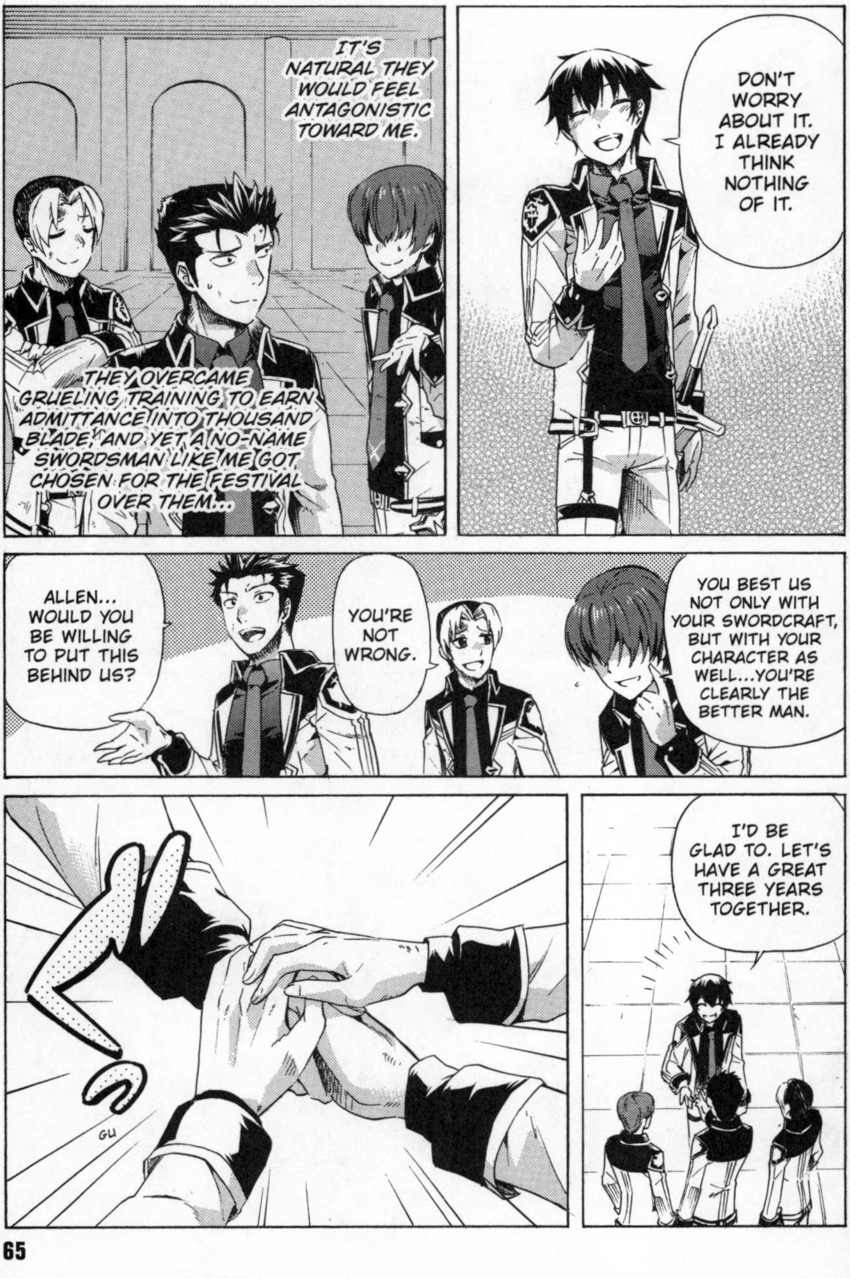
DON'T WORRY ABOUT IT. I ALREADY THINK NOTHING OF IT.
IT'S NATURAL THEY WOULD FEEL ANTAGONISTIC TOWARD ME.
THEY OVERCAME GRUELING TRAINING TO EARN ADMITTANCE INTO THOUSAND BLADE, AND YET A NO-NAME SWORDSMAN LIKE ME GOT CHOSEN FOR THE FESTIVAL OVER THEM...
YOU BEST US NOT ONLY WITH YOUR SWORDCRAFT, BUT WITH YOUR CHARACTER AS WELL...YOU'RE CLEARLY THE BETTER MAN.
YOU'RE NOT WRONG.
ALLEN... WOULD YOU BE WILLING TO PUT THIS BEHIND US?
I'D BE GLAD TO. LET'S HAVE A GREAT THREE YEARS TOGETHER.
GU

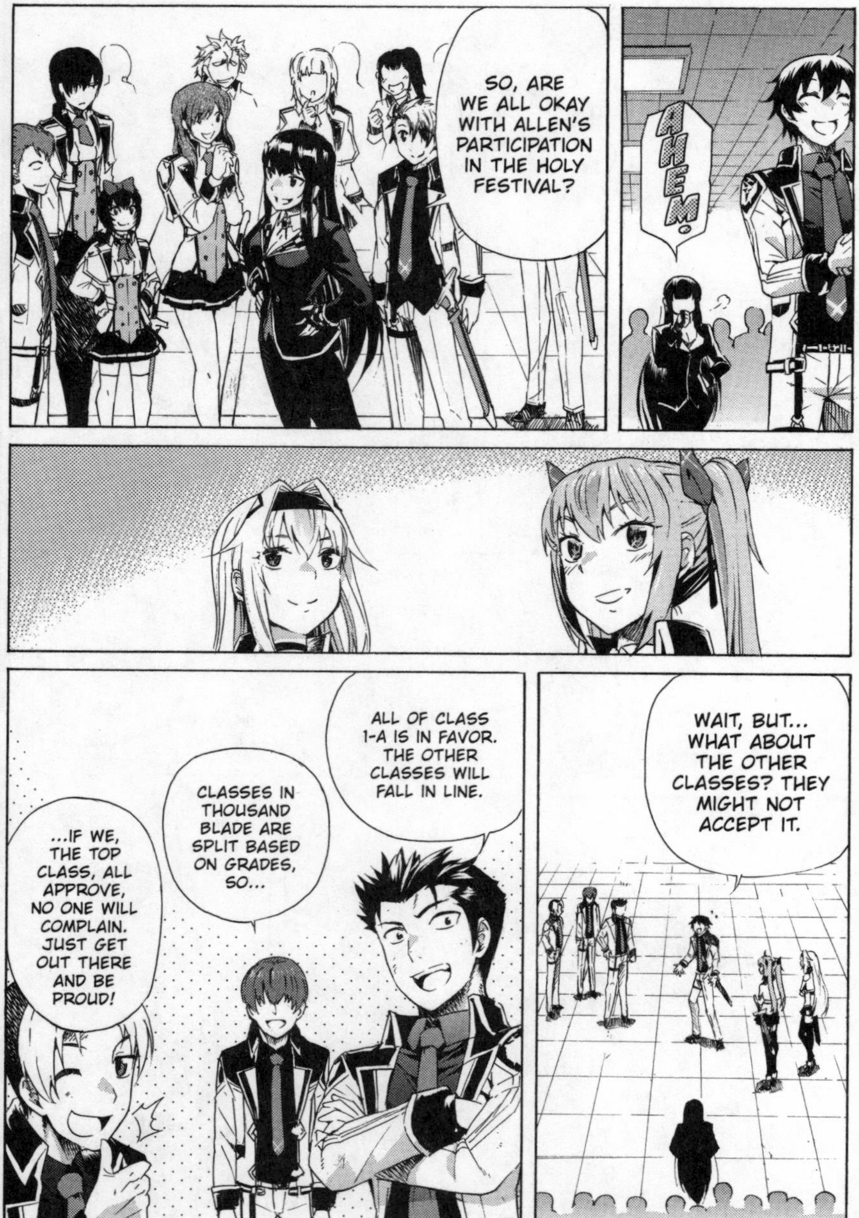
AHEM.
SO, ARE WE ALL OKAY WITH ALLEN'S PARTICIPATION IN THE HOLY FESTIVAL?
WAIT, BUT... WHAT ABOUT THE OTHER CLASSES? THEY MIGHT NOT ACCEPT IT.
ALL OF CLASS 1-A IS IN FAVOR. THE OTHER CLASSES WILL FALL IN LINE.
CLASSES IN THOUSAND BLADE ARE SPLIT BASED ON GRADES, SO...
...IF WE, THE TOP CLASS, ALL APPROVE, NO ONE WILL COMPLAIN. JUST GET OUT THERE AND BE PROUD!

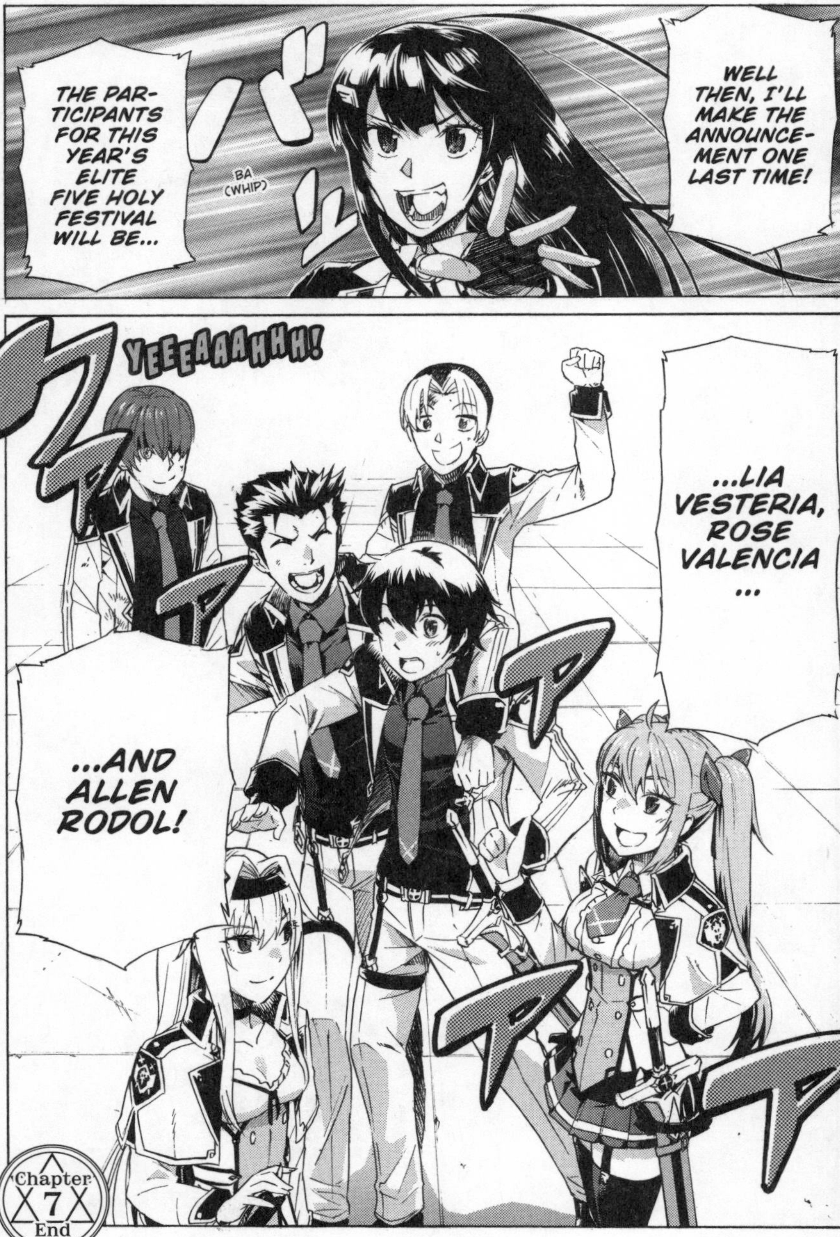
WELL THEN, I'LL MAKE THE ANNOUNCEMENT ONE LAST TIME!
BA (WHIP)
THE PARTICIPANTS FOR THIS YEAR'S ELITE FIVE HOLY FESTIVAL WILL BE...
YEEEAAAHHH!
...LIA VESTERIA, ROSE VALENCIA...
...AND ALLEN RODOL!
Chapter 7 End

I KEPT PRESSING THE 100-MILLION-YEAR BUTTON AND CAME OUT ON TOP

~THE UNBEATABLE REJECT SWORDSMAN~

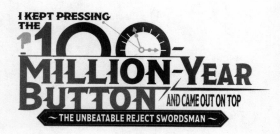

Chapter 8

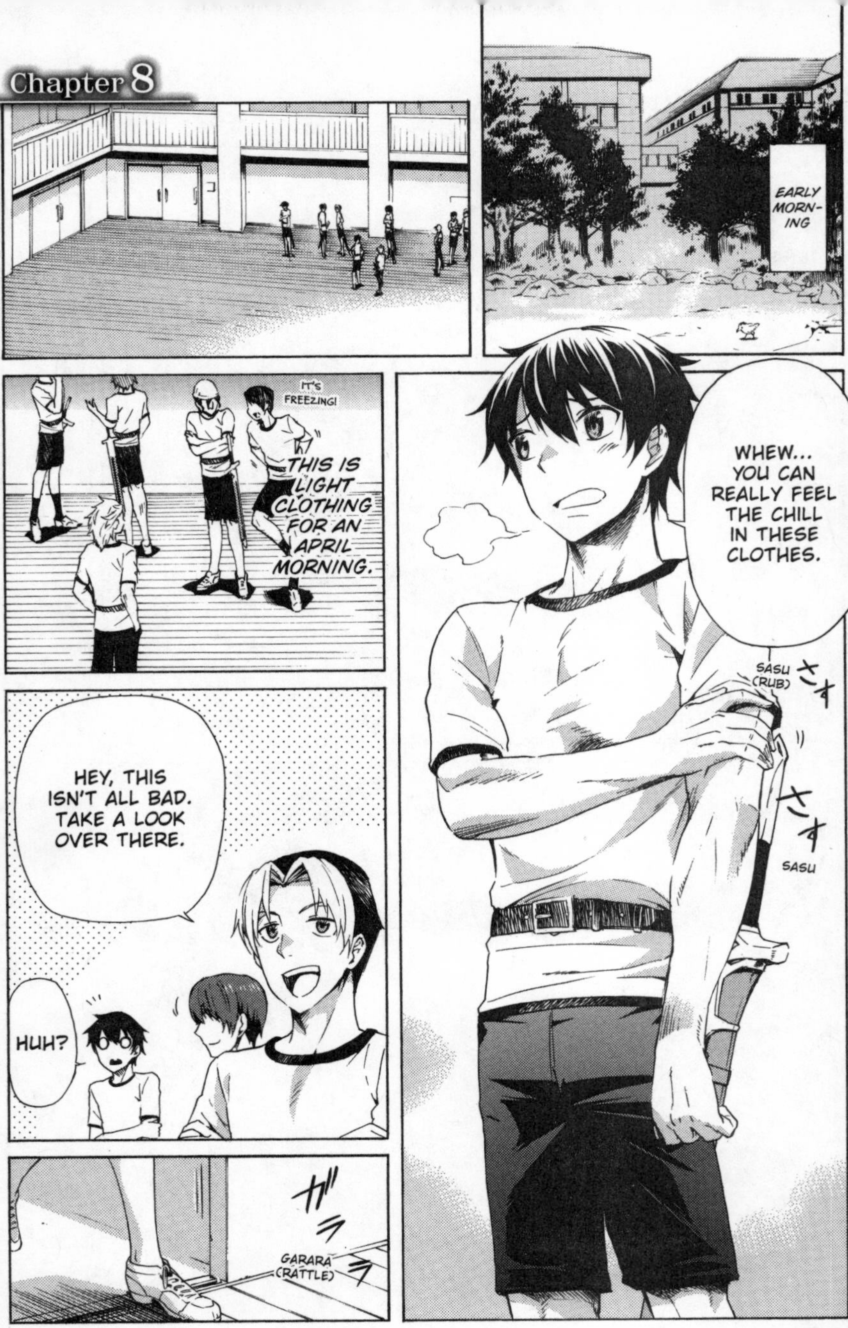
EARLY MORNING
WHEW... YOU CAN REALLY FEEL THE CHILL IN THESE CLOTHES.
SASU (RUB) さす
さす SASU
IT'S FREEZING!
THIS IS LIGHT CLOTHING FOR AN APRIL MORNING.
HEY, THIS ISN'T ALL BAD. TAKE A LOOK OVER THERE.
HUH?
ガラ ラ
GARARA (RATTLE)

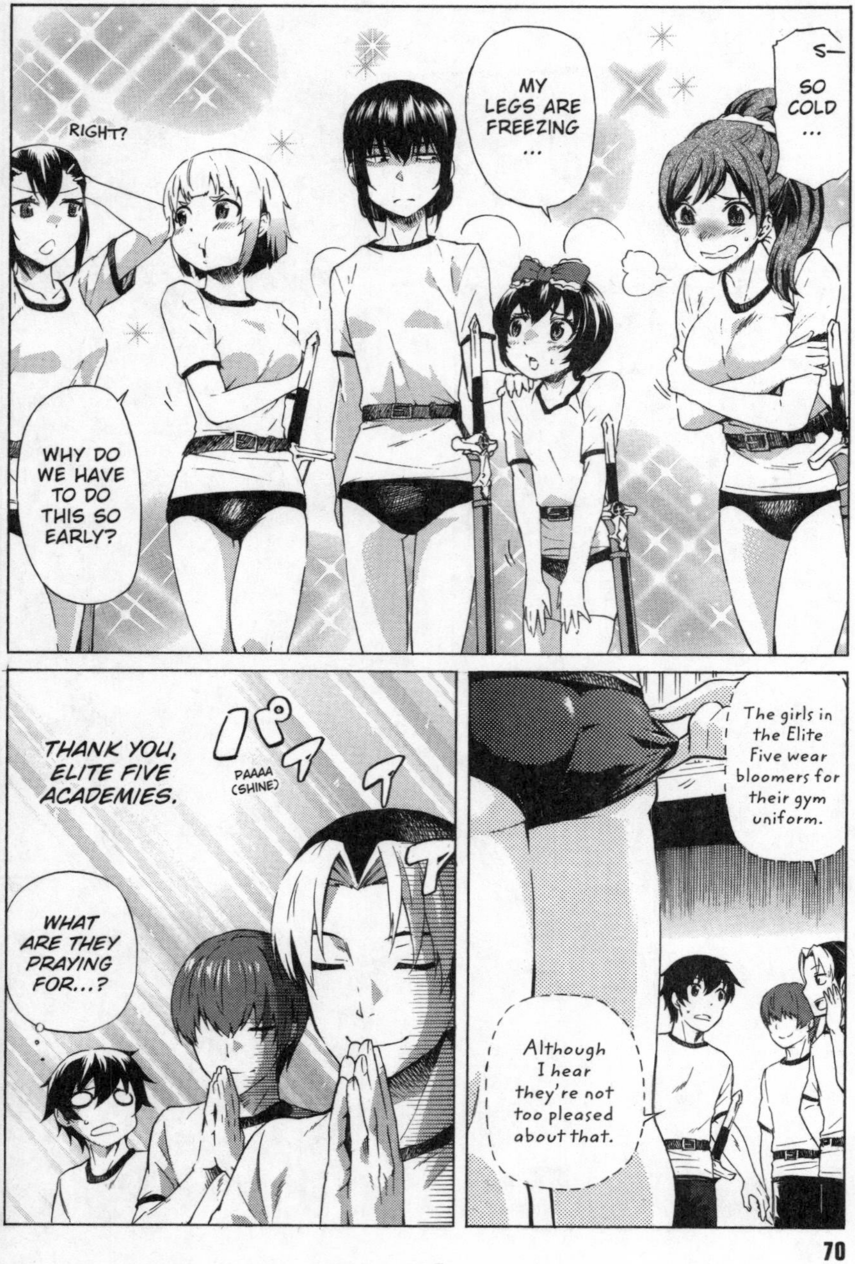
S— SO COLD ...
MY LEGS ARE FREEZING ...
RIGHT?
WHY DO WE HAVE TO DO THIS SO EARLY?
The girls in the Elite Five wear bloomers for their gym uniform.
Although I hear they're not too pleased about that.
PAAAA (SHINE)
THANK YOU, ELITE FIVE ACADEMIES.
WHAT ARE THEY PRAYING FOR...?

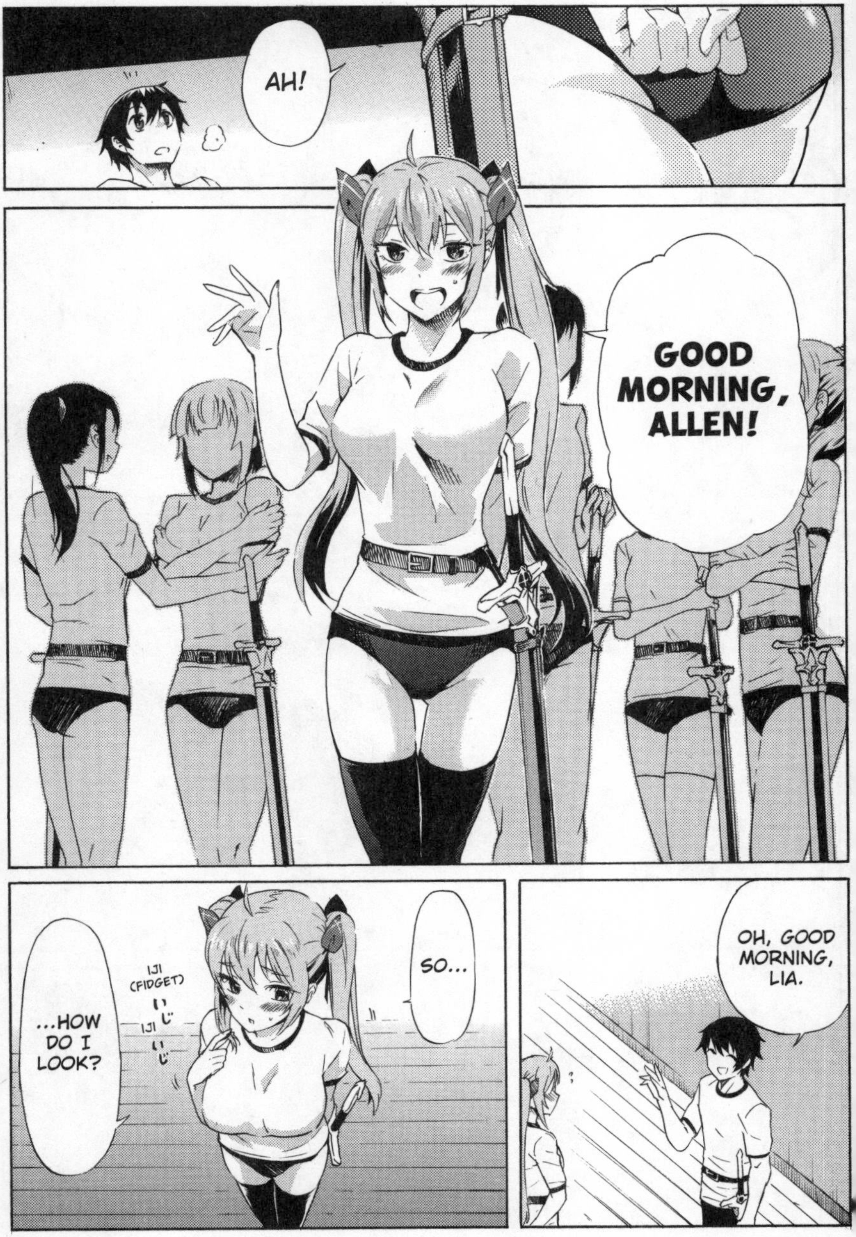

AH!
GOOD MORNING, ALLEN!
OH, GOOD MORNING, LIA.
SO...
IJI (FIDGET) いじ
IJI いじ
...HOW DO I LOOK?

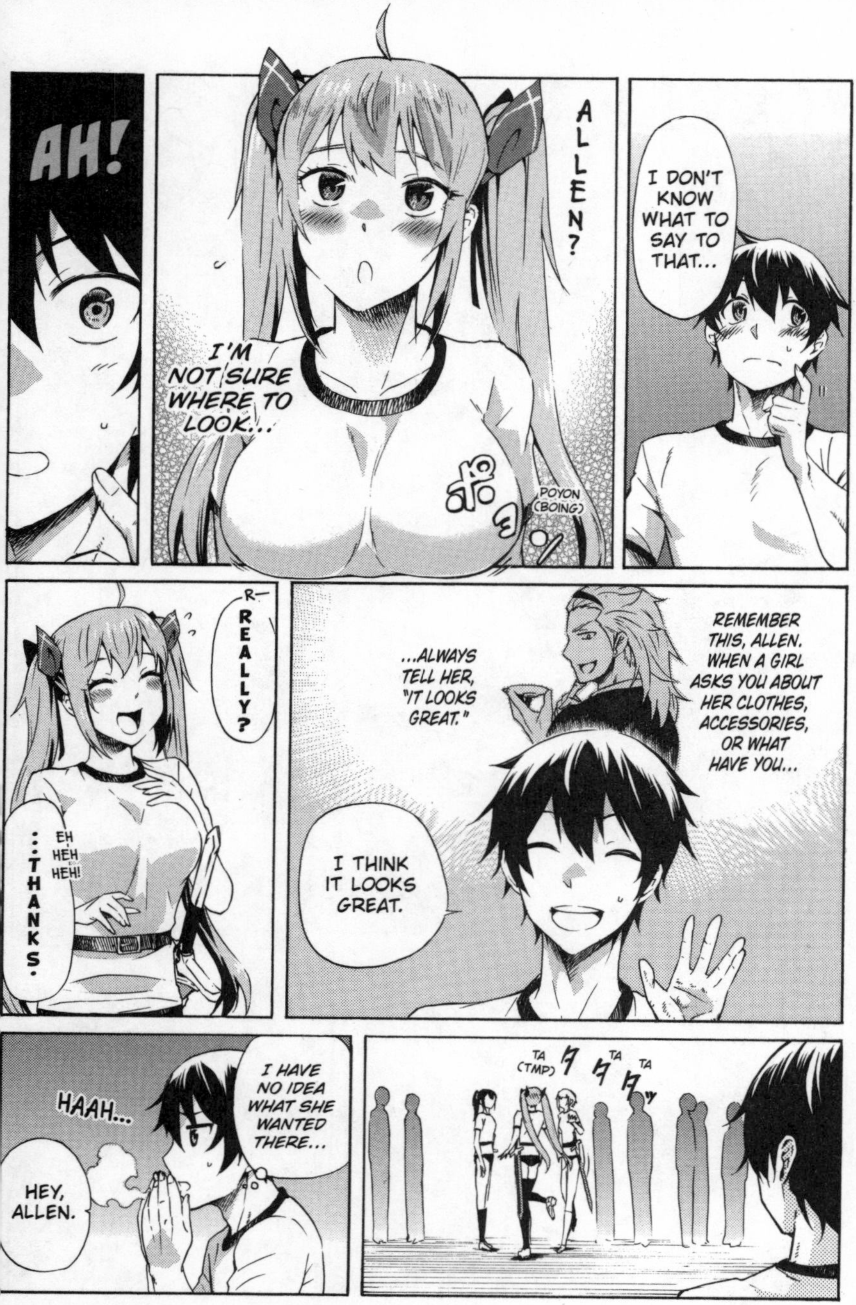
I DON'T KNOW WHAT TO SAY TO THAT...
ALLEN?
I'M NOT SURE WHERE TO LOOK...
POYON (BOING)
AH!
REMEMBER THIS, ALLEN. WHEN A GIRL ASKS YOU ABOUT HER CLOTHES, ACCESSORIES, OR WHAT HAVE YOU...
...ALWAYS TELL HER, "IT LOOKS GREAT."
I THINK IT LOOKS GREAT.
R-REALLY?
...THANKS.
EH HEH HEH!
TA (TMP) TA TA
I HAVE NO IDEA WHAT SHE WANTED THERE...
HAAH...
HEY, ALLEN.

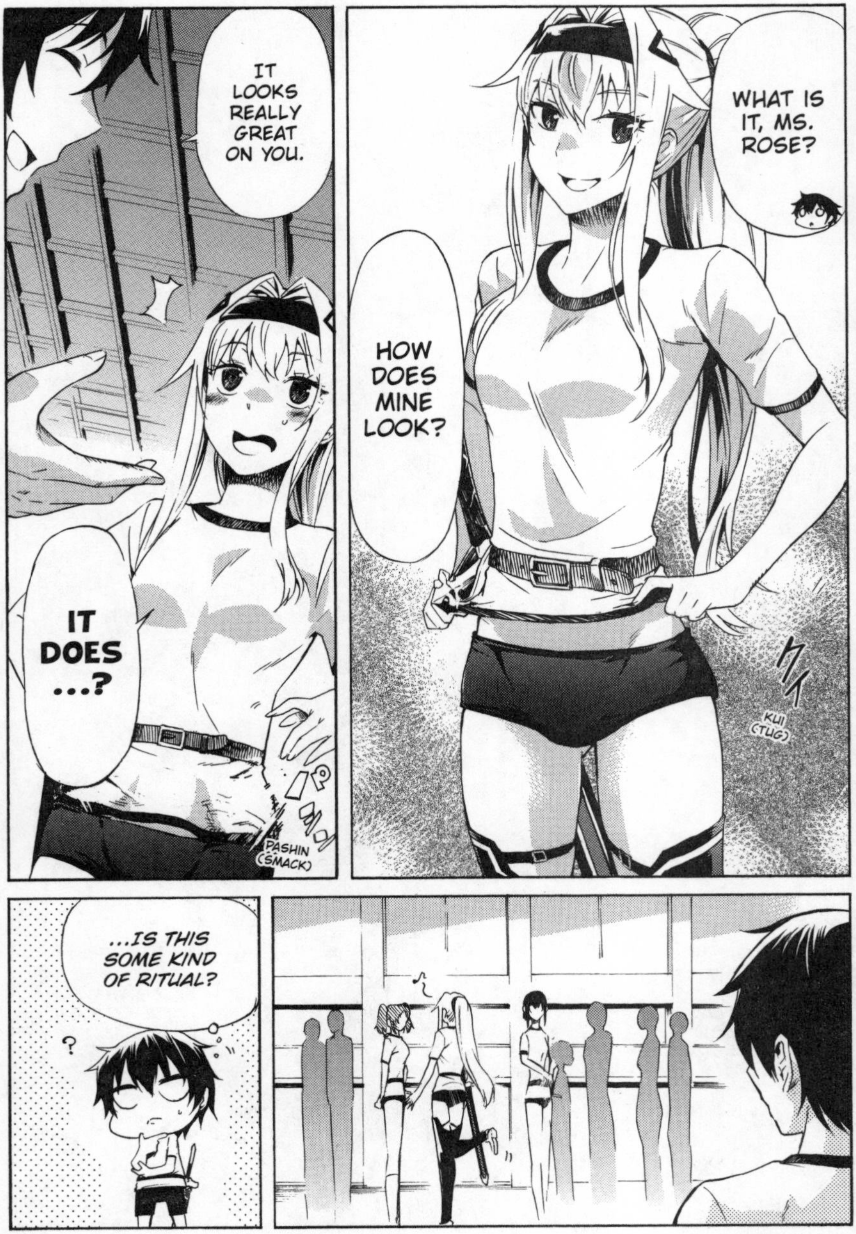
WHAT IS IT, MS. ROSE?
HOW DOES MINE LOOK?
KUI (TUG)
IT LOOKS REALLY GREAT ON YOU.
IT DOES ...?
PASHIN (SMACK)
...IS THIS SOME KIND OF RITUAL?

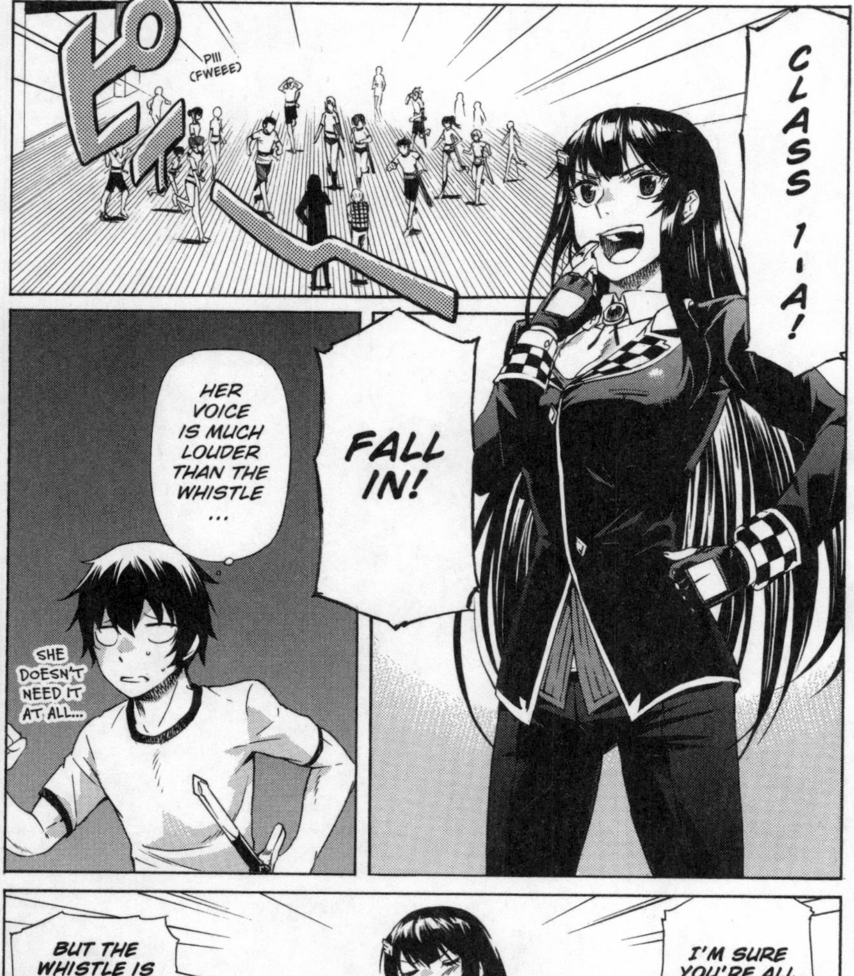
CLASS 1-A!
ピィー
PIII (FWEEE)
FALL IN!
HER VOICE IS MUCH LOUDER THAN THE WHISTLE ...
SHE DOESN'T NEED IT AT ALL...
I'M SURE YOU'RE ALL THINKING "DOES SHE REALLY NEED THAT WHISTLE?"
BUT THE WHISTLE IS ESSENTIAL! WE'VE GOTTA SET THE RIGHT MOOD IN HERE!

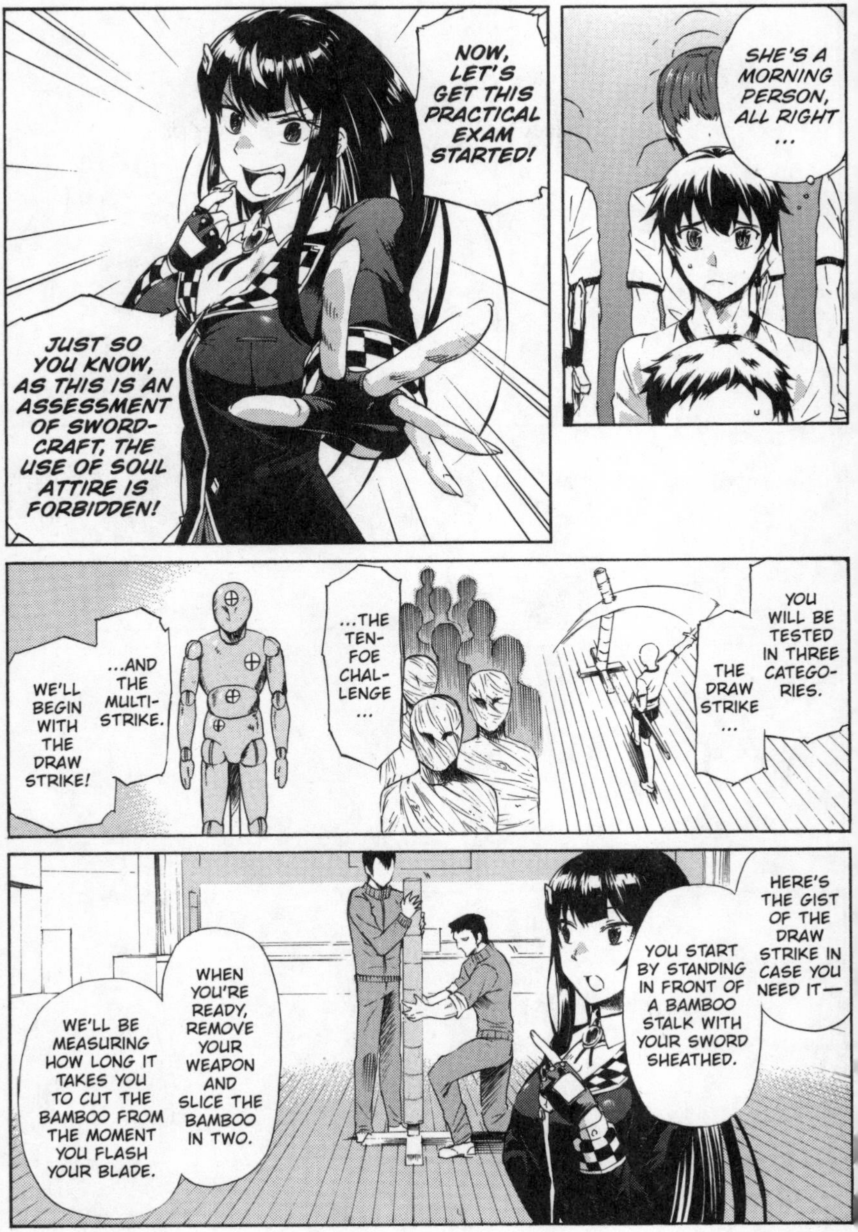
SHE'S A MORNING PERSON, ALL RIGHT ...
NOW, LET'S GET THIS PRACTICAL EXAM STARTED!
JUST SO YOU KNOW, AS THIS IS AN ASSESSMENT OF SWORD-CRAFT, THE USE OF SOUL ATTIRE IS FORBIDDEN!
YOU WILL BE TESTED IN THREE CATEGO-RIES.
THE DRAW STRIKE ...
...THE TEN-FOE CHAL-LENGE ...
...AND THE MULTI-STRIKE.
WE'LL BEGIN WITH THE DRAW STRIKE!
HERE'S THE GIST OF THE DRAW STRIKE IN CASE YOU NEED IT—
YOU START BY STANDING IN FRONT OF A BAMBOO STALK WITH YOUR SWORD SHEATHED.
WHEN YOU'RE READY, REMOVE YOUR WEAPON AND SLICE THE BAMBOO IN TWO.
WE'LL BE MEASURING HOW LONG IT TAKES YOU TO CUT THE BAMBOO FROM THE MOMENT YOU FLASH YOUR BLADE.

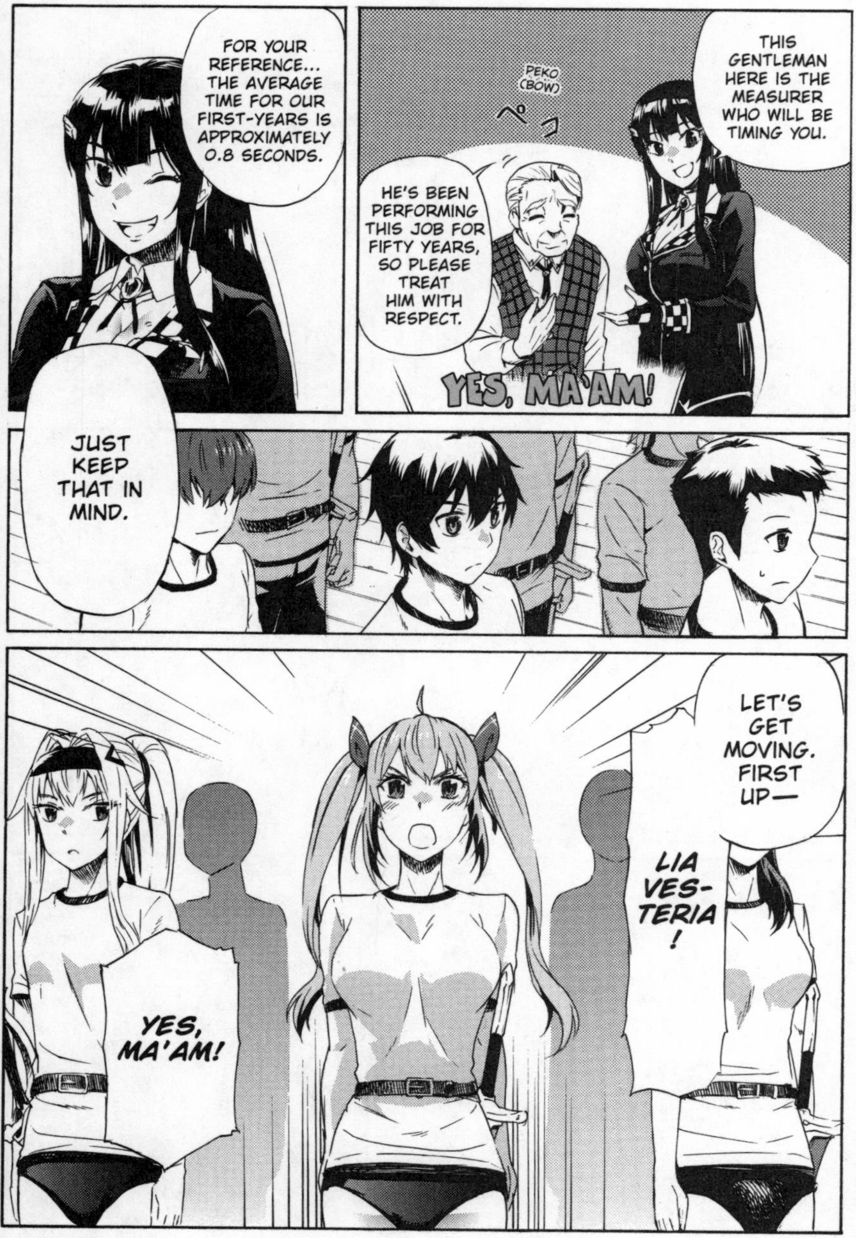
THIS GENTLEMAN HERE IS THE MEASURER WHO WILL BE TIMING YOU.
PEKO (BOW)
ペコ
HE'S BEEN PERFORMING THIS JOB FOR FIFTY YEARS, SO PLEASE TREAT HIM WITH RESPECT.
YES, MA'AM!
FOR YOUR REFERENCE... THE AVERAGE TIME FOR OUR FIRST-YEARS IS APPROXIMATELY 0.8 SECONDS.
JUST KEEP THAT IN MIND.
LET'S GET MOVING. FIRST UP—
LIA VESTERIA!
YES, MA'AM!

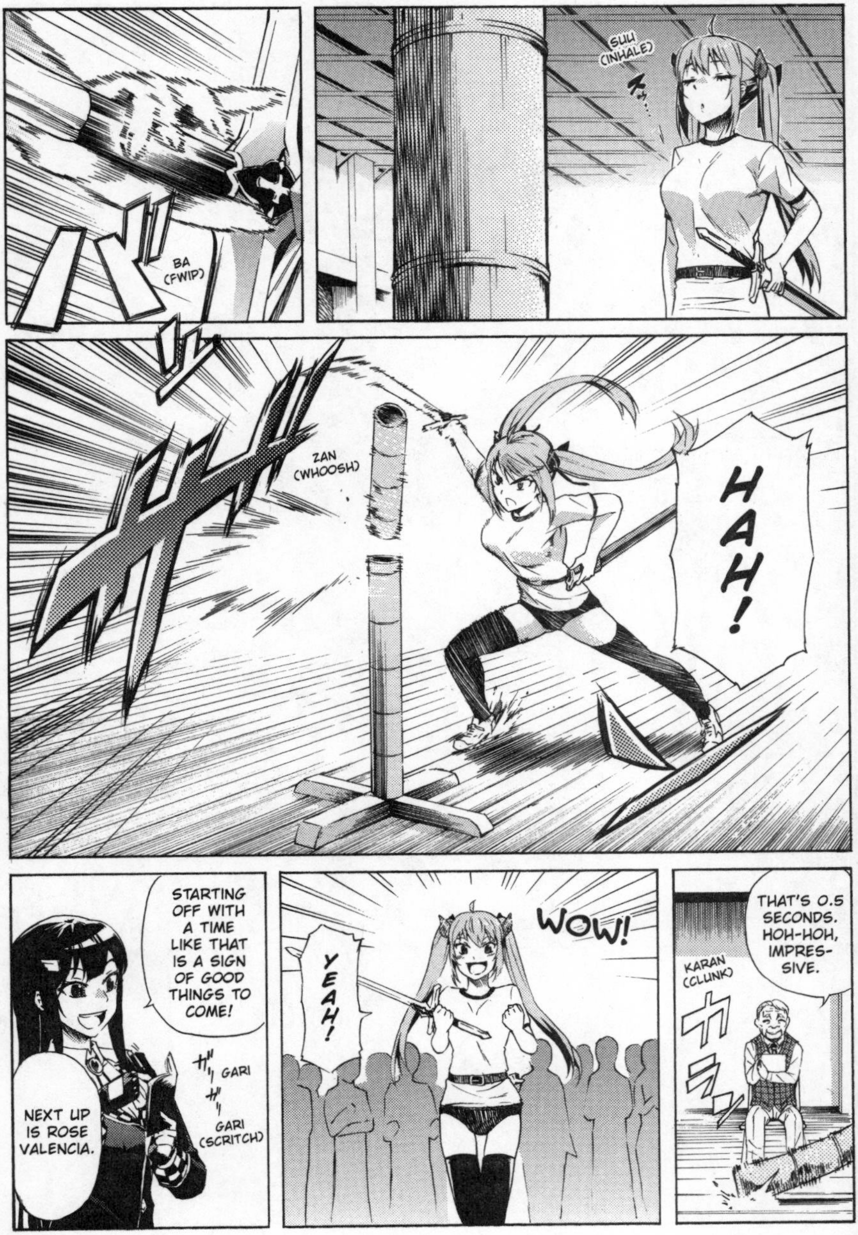
SUU (INHALE)
BA (FWIP)
ZAN (WHOOSH)
HAH!
THAT'S 0.5 SECONDS. HOH-HOH, IMPRES-SIVE.
KARAN (CLUNK)
WOW!
YEAH!
STARTING OFF WITH A TIME LIKE THAT IS A SIGN OF GOOD THINGS TO COME!
GARI
GARI (SCRITCH)
NEXT UP IS ROSE VALENCIA.

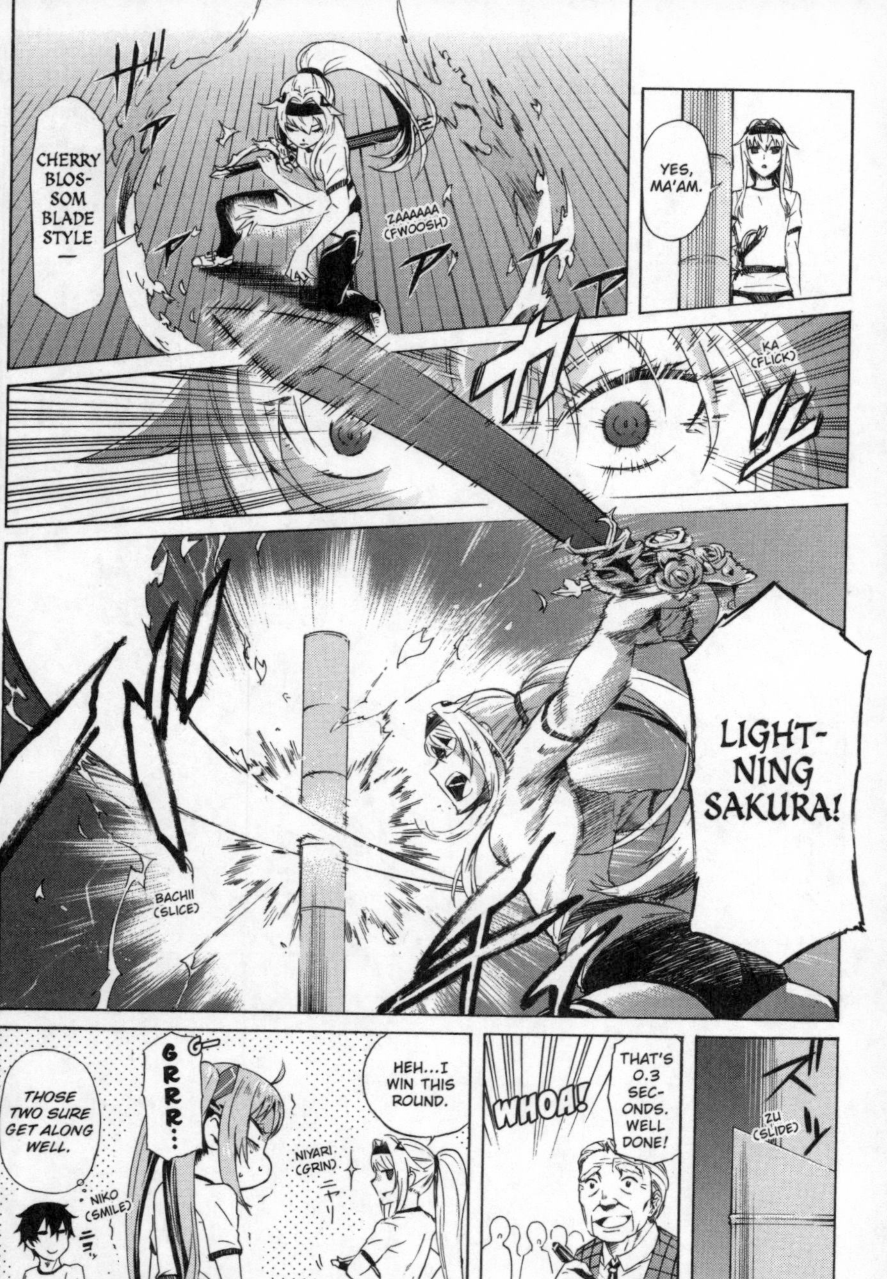
YES, MA'AM.
CHERRY BLOSSOM BLADE STYLE —
ZAAAAAA (FWOOSH)
KA (FLICK)
LIGHTNING SAKURA!
BACHII (SLICE)
ZU (SLIDE)
THAT'S 0.3 SECONDS. WELL DONE!
WHOA!
HEH...I WIN THIS ROUND.
NIYARI (GRIN)
GRRR...
THOSE TWO SURE GET ALONG WELL.
NIKO (SMILE)

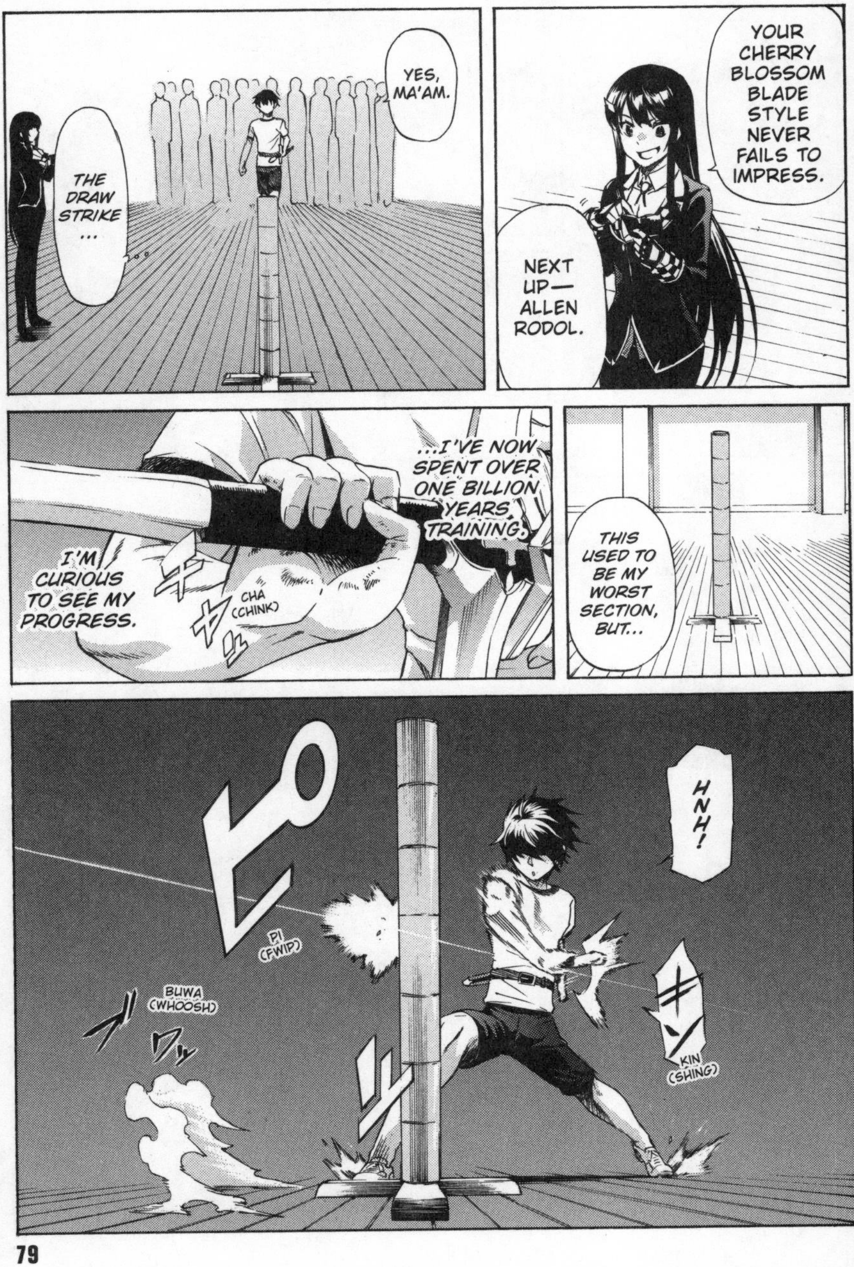
YOUR CHERRY BLOSSOM BLADE STYLE NEVER FAILS TO IMPRESS.
NEXT UP— ALLEN RODOL.
YES, MA'AM.
THE DRAW STRIKE ...
THIS USED TO BE MY WORST SECTION, BUT...
...I'VE NOW SPENT OVER ONE BILLION YEARS TRAINING.
CHA (CHINK)
I'M CURIOUS TO SEE MY PROGRESS.
HNH!
KIN (SHING)
PI (FWIP)
BUWA (WHOOSH)

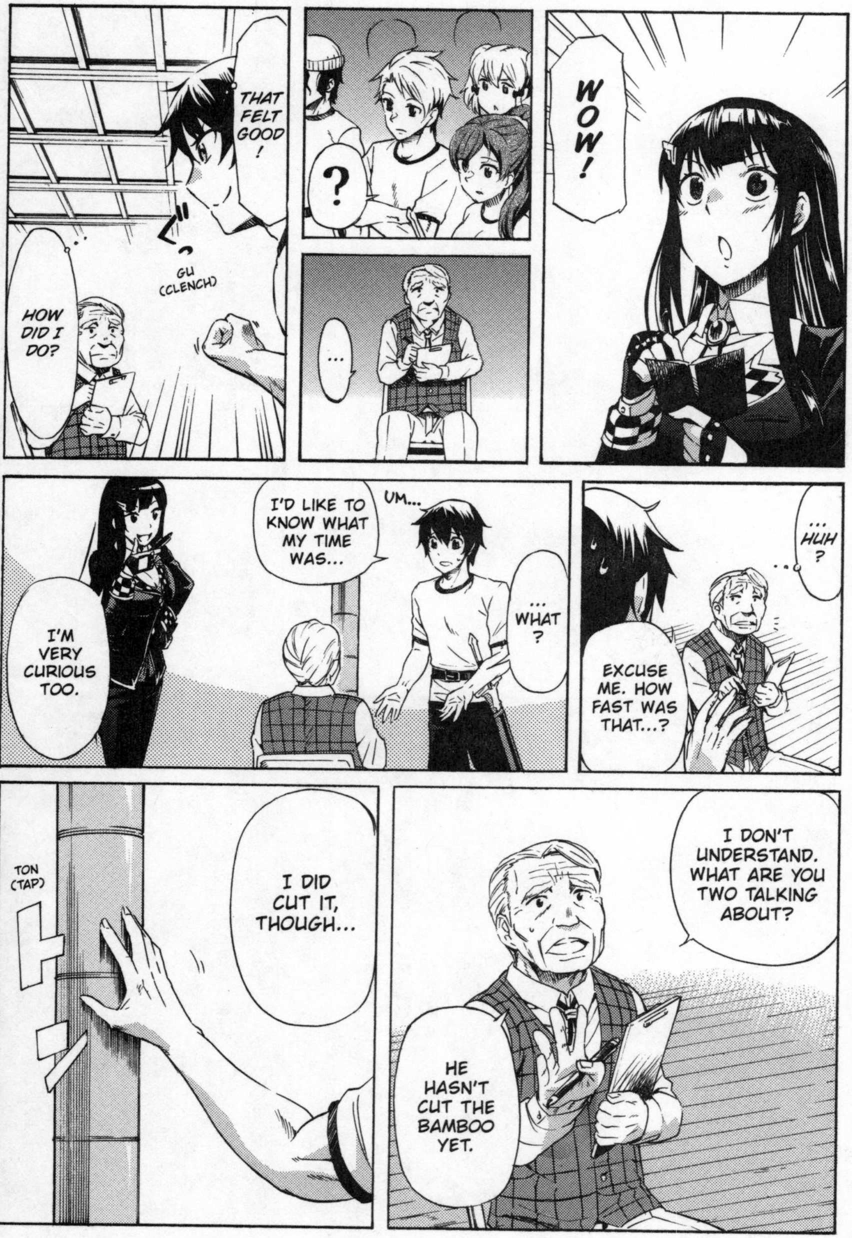
WOW!
?
...
THAT FELT GOOD!
GU (CLENCH)
...
HOW DID I DO?
... HUH?
..
EXCUSE ME. HOW FAST WAS THAT...?
UM...
I'D LIKE TO KNOW WHAT MY TIME WAS...
... WHAT?
I'M VERY CURIOUS TOO.
I DON'T UNDERSTAND. WHAT ARE YOU TWO TALKING ABOUT?
HE HASN'T CUT THE BAMBOO YET.
I DID CUT IT, THOUGH...
TON (TAP)

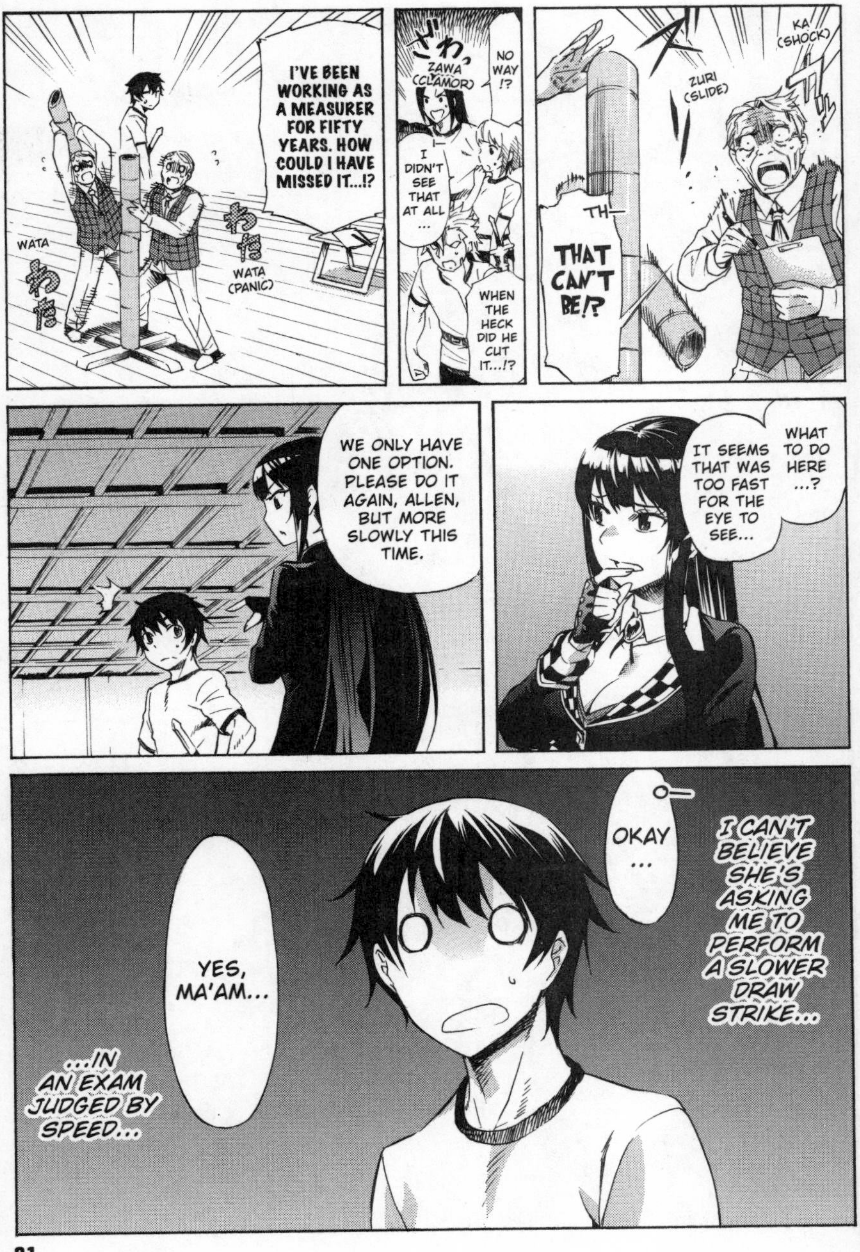
KA (SHOCK)
ZURI (SLIDE)
TH—
THAT CAN'T BE!?
ざわ
ZAWA (CLAMOR)
NO WAY !?
I DIDN'T SEE THAT AT ALL ...
WHEN THE HECK DID HE CUT IT...!?
I'VE BEEN WORKING AS A MEASURER FOR FIFTY YEARS. HOW COULD I HAVE MISSED IT...!?
わた
WATA (PANIC)
WATA
わた
WHAT TO DO HERE ...?
IT SEEMS THAT WAS TOO FAST FOR THE EYE TO SEE...
WE ONLY HAVE ONE OPTION. PLEASE DO IT AGAIN, ALLEN, BUT MORE SLOWLY THIS TIME.
I CAN'T BELIEVE SHE'S ASKING ME TO PERFORM A SLOWER DRAW STRIKE...
OKAY ...
YES, MA'AM...
...IN AN EXAM JUDGED BY SPEED...

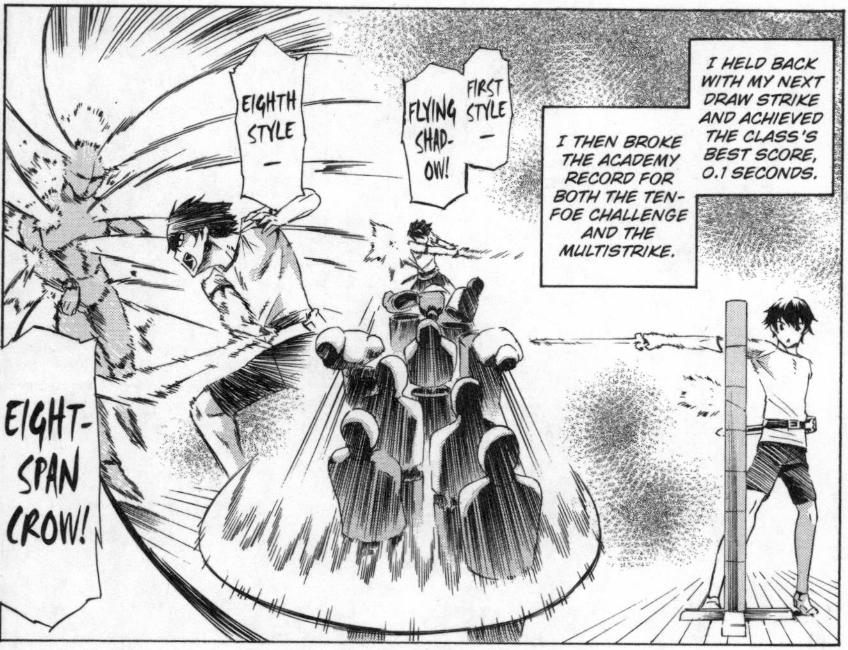
I HELD BACK WITH MY NEXT DRAW STRIKE AND ACHIEVED THE CLASS'S BEST SCORE, 0.1 SECONDS.
I THEN BROKE THE ACADEMY RECORD FOR BOTH THE TEN-FOE CHALLENGE AND THE MULTISTRIKE.
FIRST STYLE —
FLYING SHAD-OW!
EIGHTH STYLE —
EIGHT-SPAN CROW!

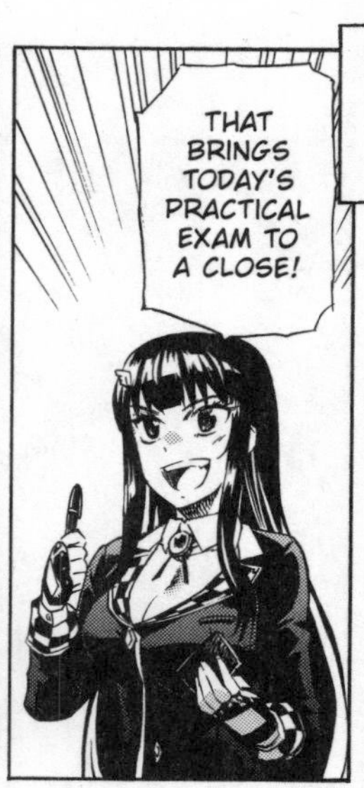
THAT BRINGS TODAY'S PRACTICAL EXAM TO A CLOSE!

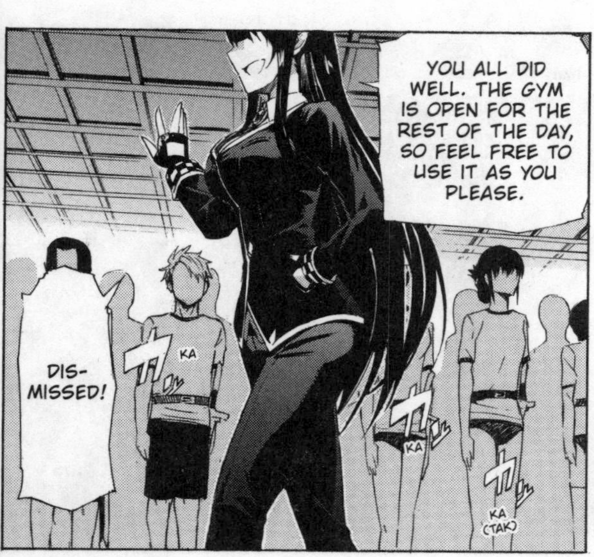
YOU ALL DID WELL. THE GYM IS OPEN FOR THE REST OF THE DAY, SO FEEL FREE TO USE IT AS YOU PLEASE.
KA
DIS-MISSED!
KA
KA (TAK)

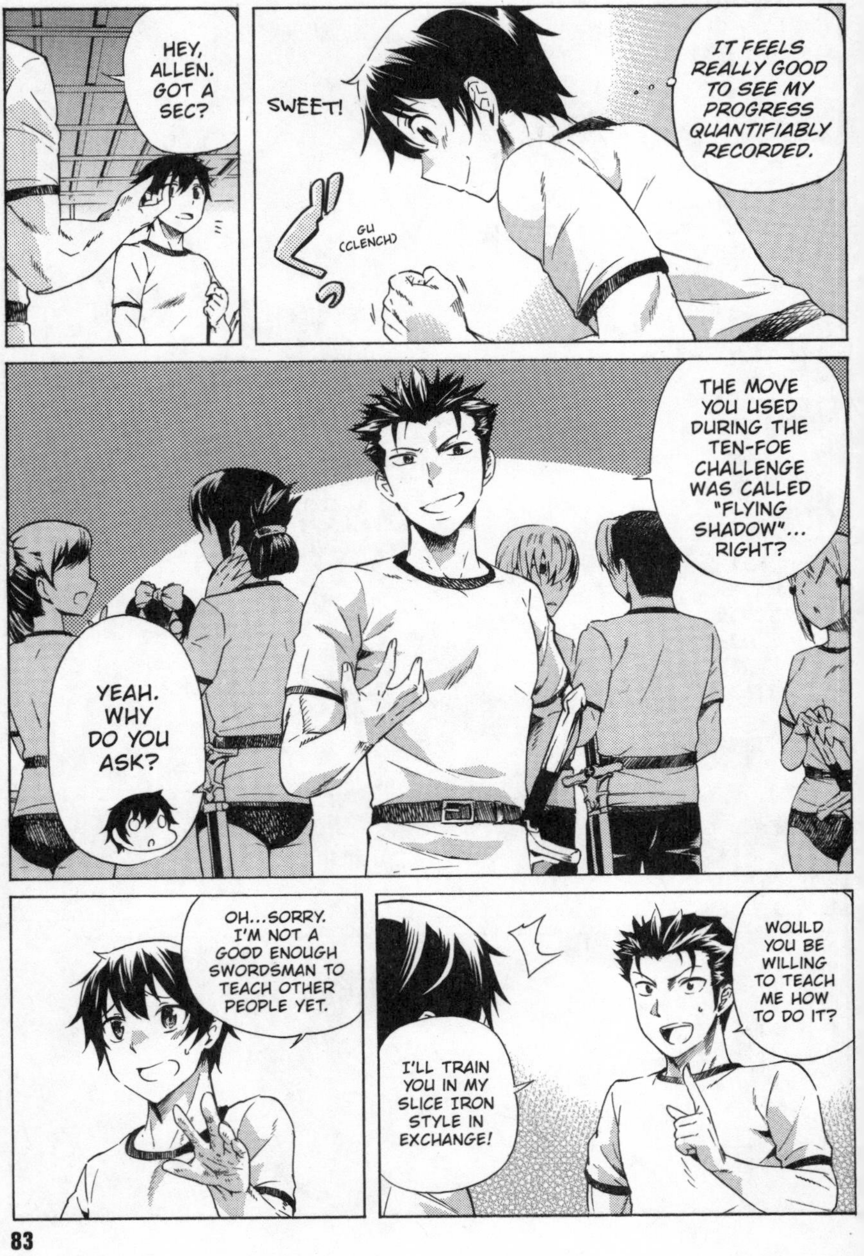
IT FEELS REALLY GOOD TO SEE MY PROGRESS QUANTIFIABLY RECORDED.
SWEET!
GU (CLENCH)
HEY, ALLEN. GOT A SEC?
THE MOVE YOU USED DURING THE TEN-FOE CHALLENGE WAS CALLED "FLYING SHADOW"... RIGHT?
YEAH. WHY DO YOU ASK?
WOULD YOU BE WILLING TO TEACH ME HOW TO DO IT?
I'LL TRAIN YOU IN MY SLICE IRON STYLE IN EXCHANGE!
OH...SORRY. I'M NOT A GOOD ENOUGH SWORDSMAN TO TEACH OTHER PEOPLE YET.

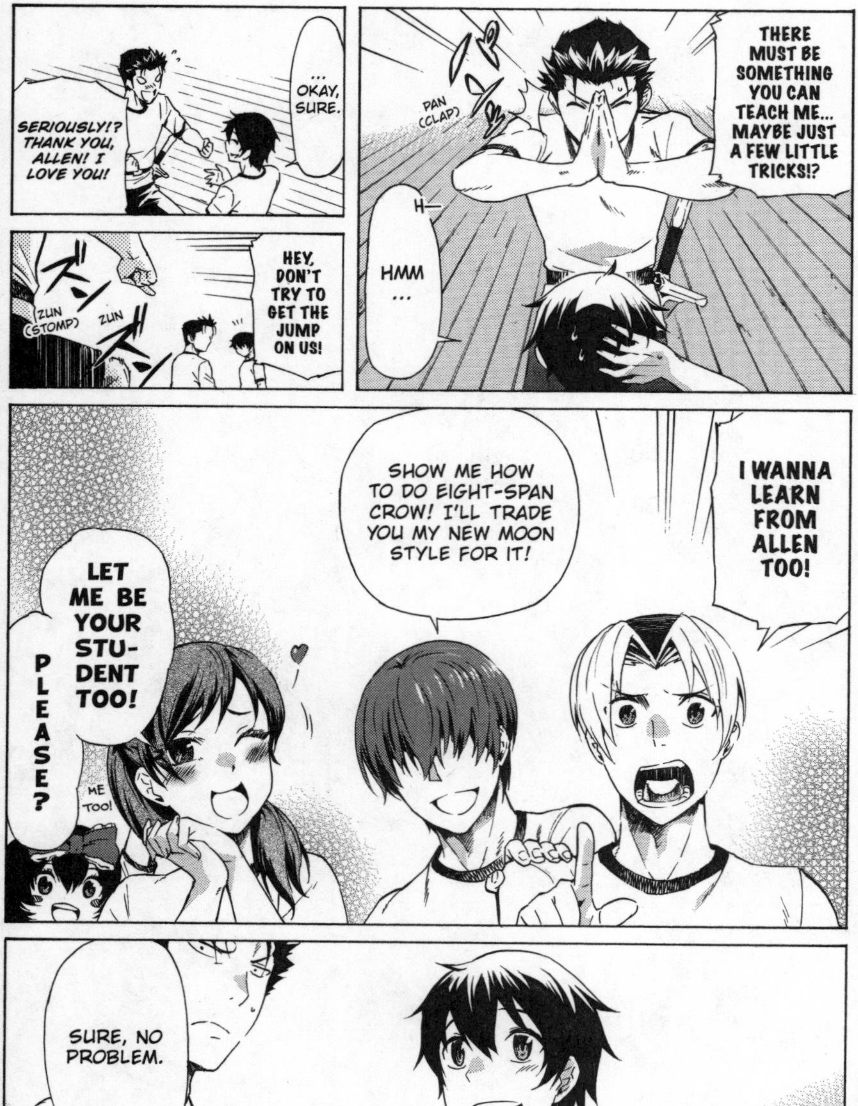
THERE MUST BE SOMETHING YOU CAN TEACH ME... MAYBE JUST A FEW LITTLE TRICKS!?
PAN (CLAP)
H— HMM...
...OKAY, SURE.
SERIOUSLY!? THANK YOU, ALLEN! I LOVE YOU!
HEY, DON'T TRY TO GET THE JUMP ON US!
ZUN (STOMP)
ZUN
I WANNA LEARN FROM ALLEN TOO!
SHOW ME HOW TO DO EIGHT-SPAN CROW! I'LL TRADE YOU MY NEW MOON STYLE FOR IT!
LET ME BE YOUR STU- DENT TOO!
PLEASE?
ME TOO!
SURE, NO PROBLEM.

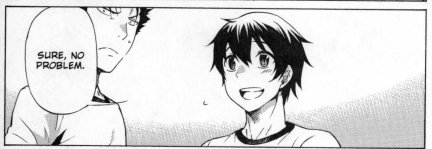

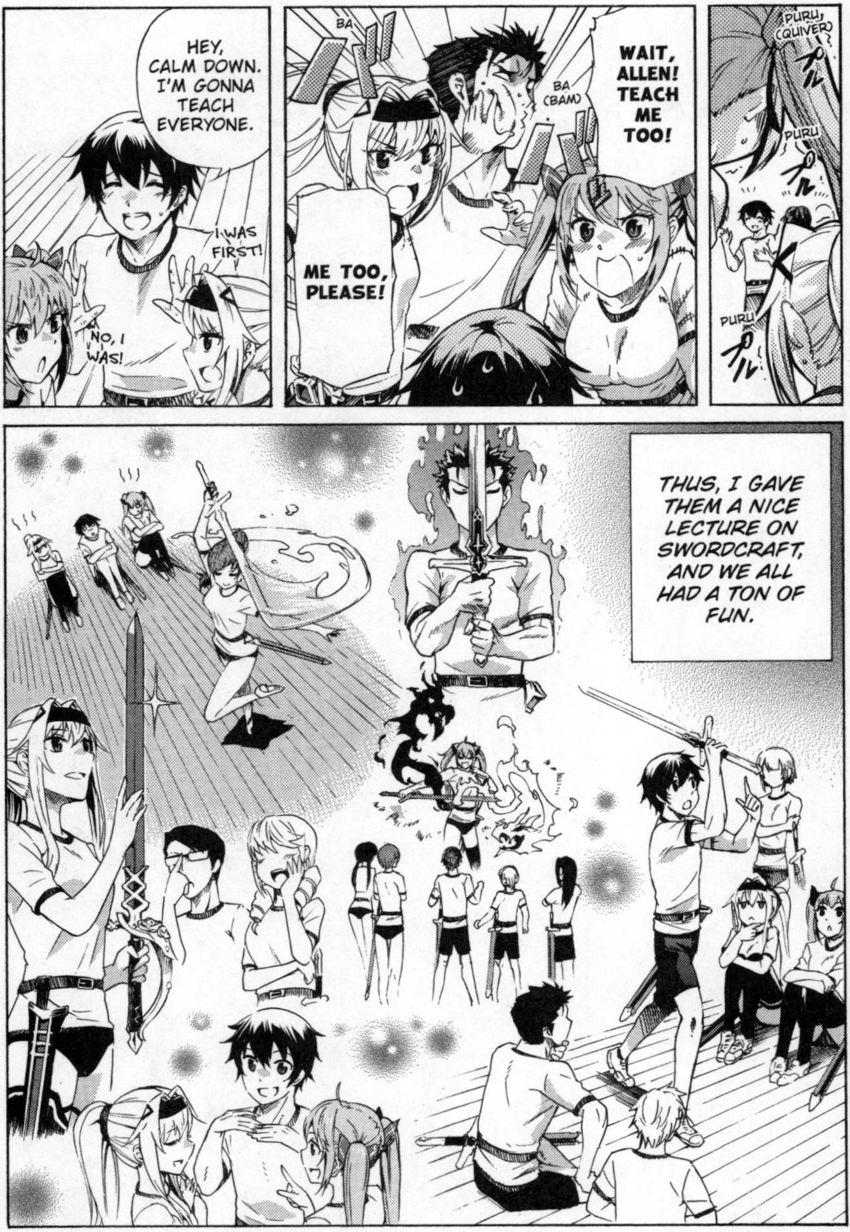
PURU (QUIVER)
PURU
PURU
WAIT, ALLEN! TEACH ME TOO!
BA (BAM)
BA
ME TOO, PLEASE!
HEY, CALM DOWN. I'M GONNA TEACH EVERYONE.
I WAS FIRST!
NO, I WAS!
THUS, I GAVE THEM A NICE LECTURE ON SWORDCRAFT, AND WE ALL HAD A TON OF FUN.

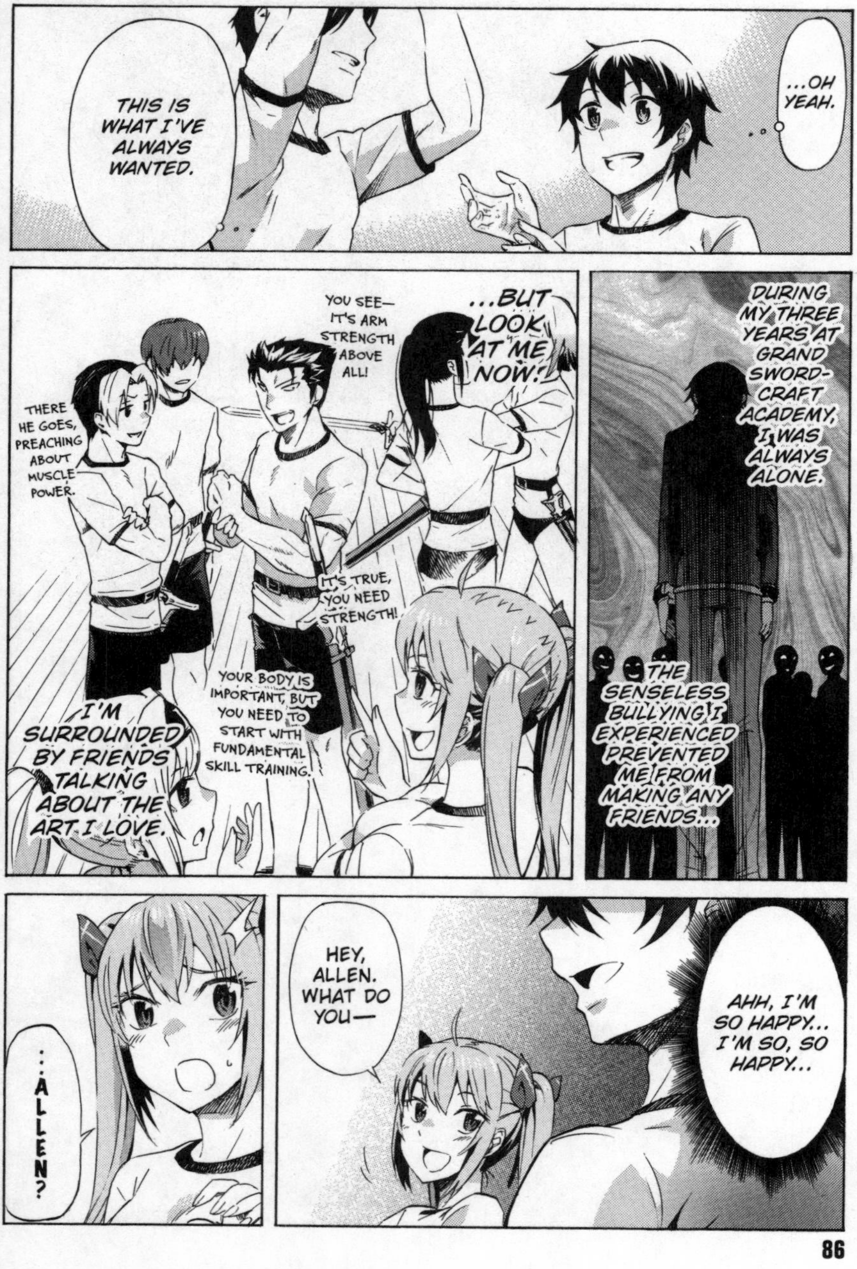
...OH YEAH.
THIS IS WHAT I'VE ALWAYS WANTED.
DURING MY THREE YEARS AT GRAND SWORD-CRAFT ACADEMY, I WAS ALWAYS ALONE.
THE SENSELESS BULLYING I EXPERIENCED PREVENTED ME FROM MAKING ANY FRIENDS...
...BUT LOOK AT ME NOW!
YOU SEE— IT'S ARM STRENGTH ABOVE ALL!
THERE HE GOES, PREACHING ABOUT MUSCLE POWER.
IT'S TRUE, YOU NEED STRENGTH!
YOUR BODY IS IMPORTANT, BUT YOU NEED TO START WITH FUNDAMENTAL SKILL TRAINING.
I'M SURROUNDED BY FRIENDS TALKING ABOUT THE ART I LOVE.
AHH, I'M SO HAPPY... I'M SO, SO HAPPY...
HEY, ALLEN. WHAT DO YOU—
...ALLEN?

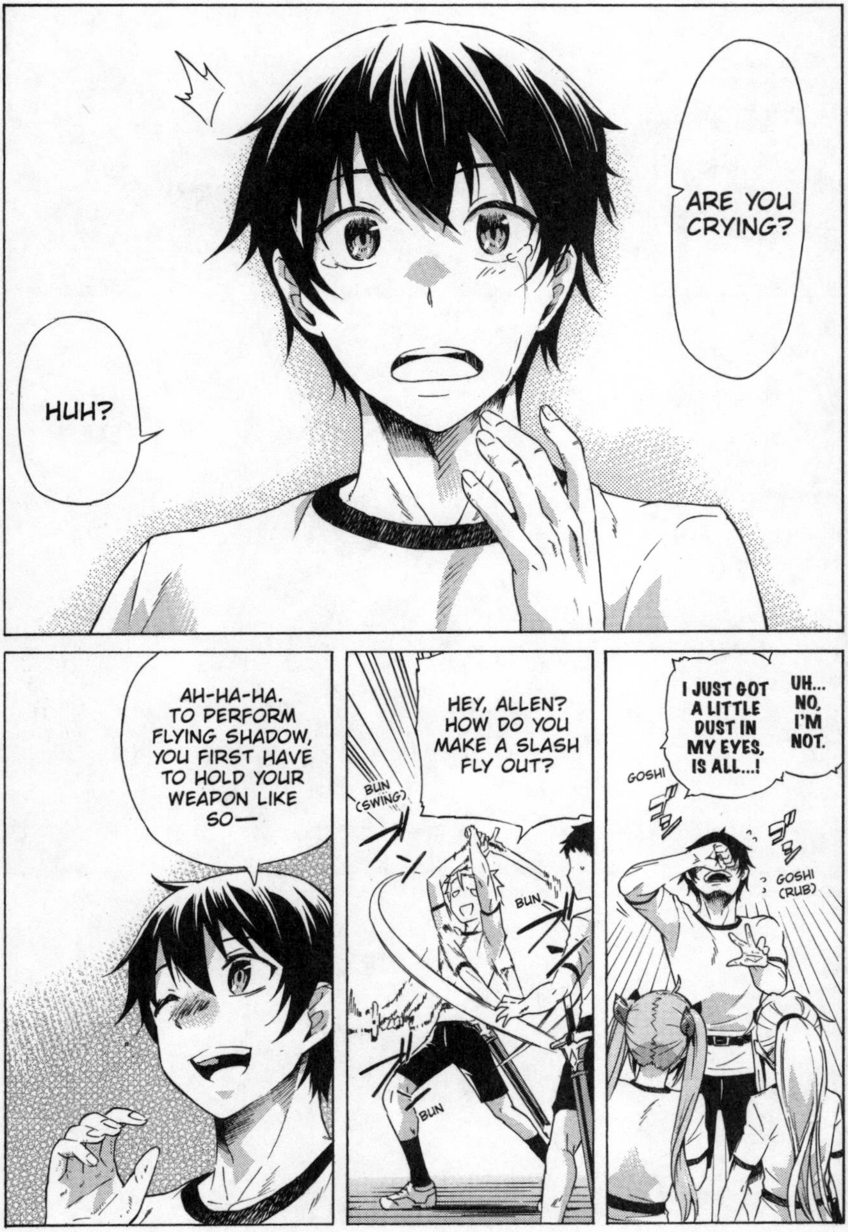
ARE YOU CRYING?
HUH?
UH... NO, I'M NOT.
I JUST GOT A LITTLE DUST IN MY EYES, IS ALL...!
GOSHI
GOSHI (RUB)
HEY, ALLEN? HOW DO YOU MAKE A SLASH FLY OUT?
BUN (SWING)
BUN
BUN
AH-HA-HA. TO PERFORM FLYING SHADOW, YOU FIRST HAVE TO HOLD YOUR WEAPON LIKE SO—

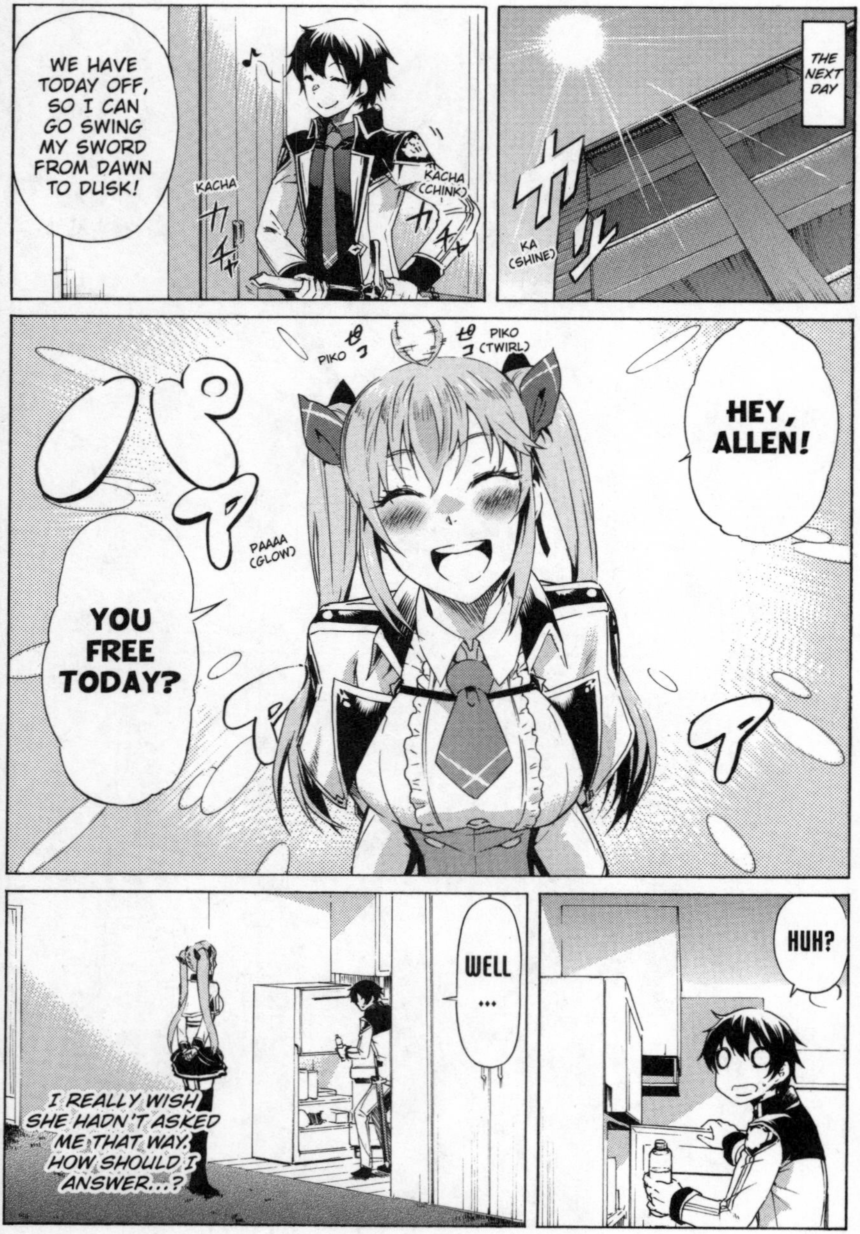
THE NEXT DAY
KA (SHINE)
WE HAVE TODAY OFF, SO I CAN GO SWING MY SWORD FROM DAWN TO DUSK!
KACHA (CHINK)
KACHA
HEY, ALLEN!
PIKO (TWIRL)
PIKO
PAAAA (GLOW)
YOU FREE TODAY?
HUH?
WELL...
I REALLY WISH SHE HADN'T ASKED ME THAT WAY. HOW SHOULD I ANSWER...?

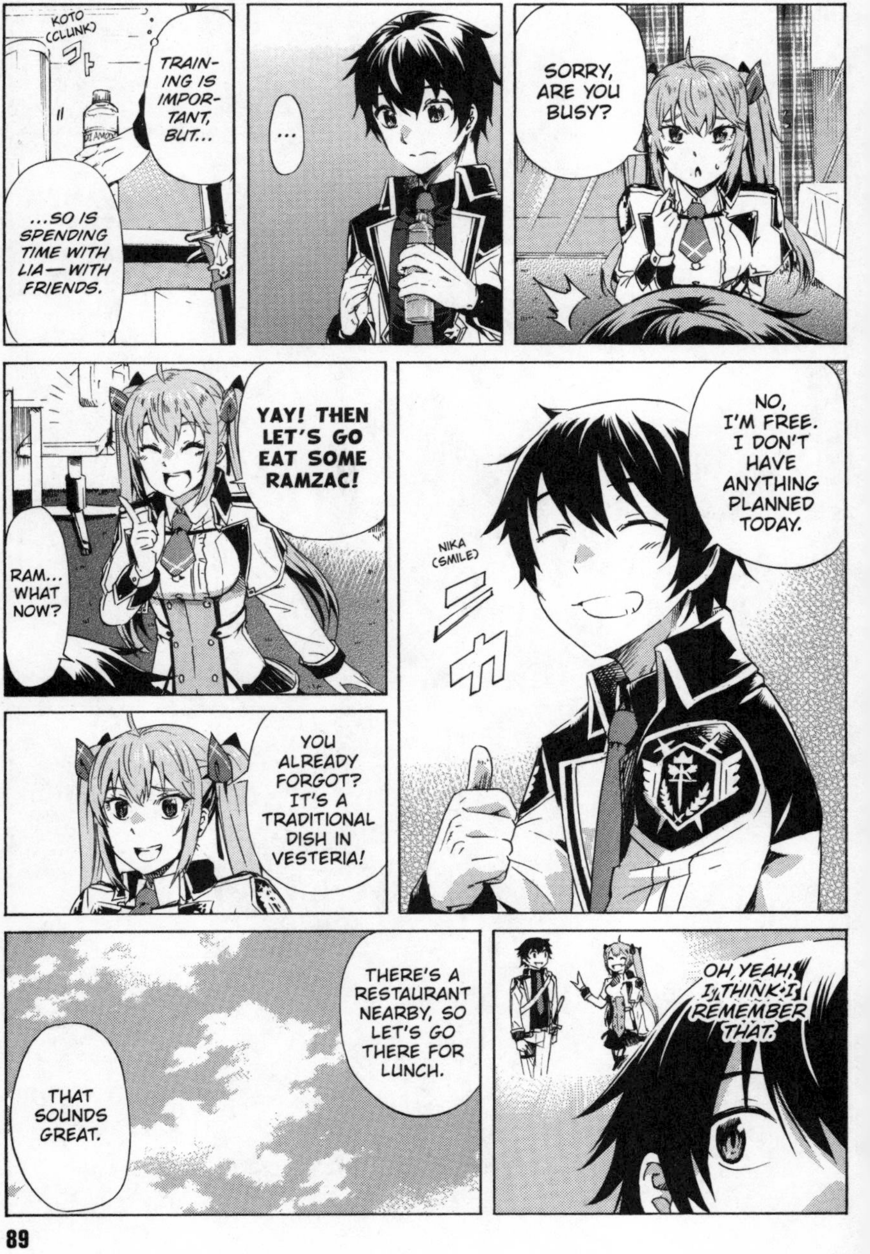
SORRY, ARE YOU BUSY?
...
KOTO (CLUNK)
TRAINING IS IMPORTANT, BUT...
...SO IS SPENDING TIME WITH LIA—WITH FRIENDS.
NO, I'M FREE. I DON'T HAVE ANYTHING PLANNED TODAY.
NIKA (SMILE)
YAY! THEN LET'S GO EAT SOME RAMZAC!
RAM... WHAT NOW?
YOU ALREADY FORGOT? IT'S A TRADITIONAL DISH IN VESTERIA!
OH, YEAH, I THINK I REMEMBER THAT.
THERE'S A RESTAURANT NEARBY, SO LET'S GO THERE FOR LUNCH.
THAT SOUNDS GREAT.

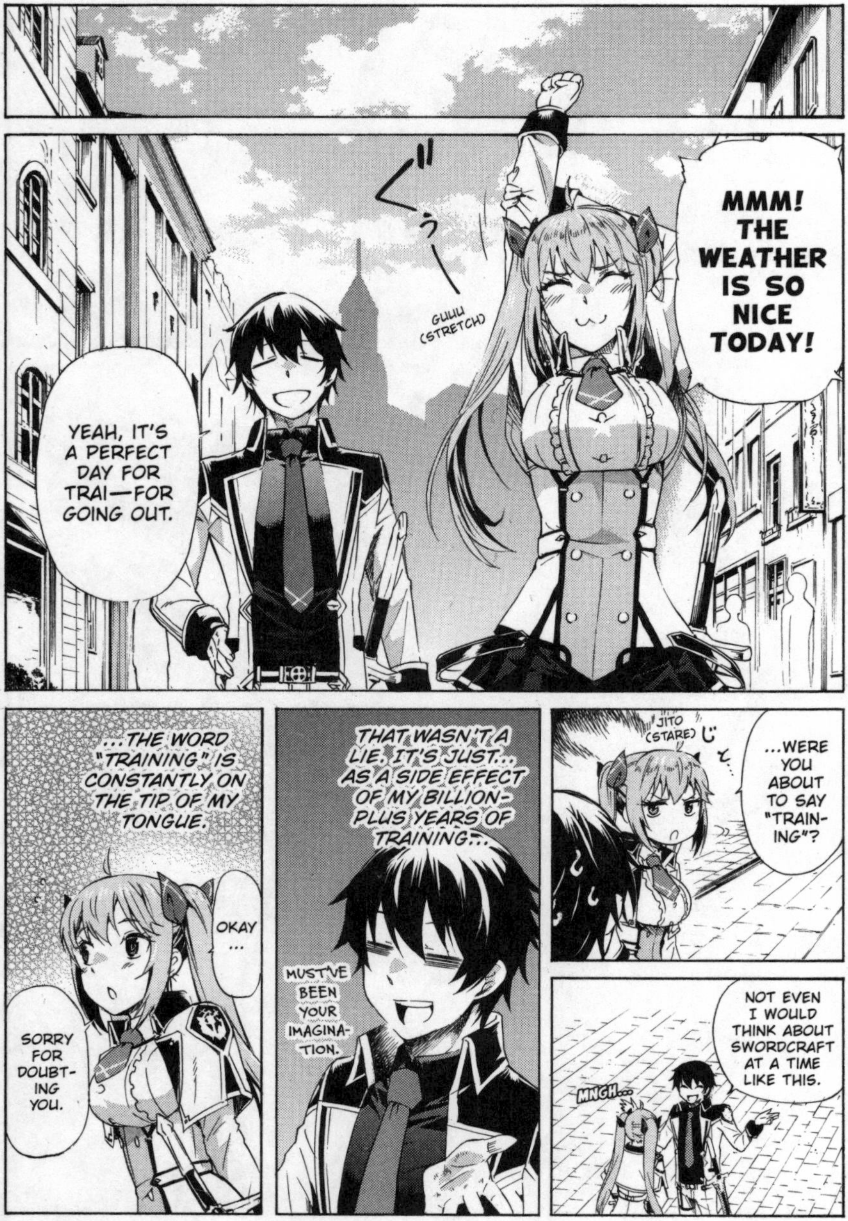
MMM! THE WEATHER IS SO NICE TODAY!
ぐぅー
GUUU (STRETCH)
YEAH, IT'S A PERFECT DAY FOR TRAI—FOR GOING OUT.
JITO (STARE) じと…
...WERE YOU ABOUT TO SAY "TRAIN-ING"?
NOT EVEN I WOULD THINK ABOUT SWORDCRAFT AT A TIME LIKE THIS.
MNGH...
THAT WASN'T A LIE. IT'S JUST... AS A SIDE EFFECT OF MY BILLION-PLUS YEARS OF TRAINING...
MUST'VE BEEN YOUR IMAGINA-TION.
...THE WORD "TRAINING" IS CONSTANTLY ON THE TIP OF MY TONGUE.
OKAY...
SORRY FOR DOUBT-ING YOU.

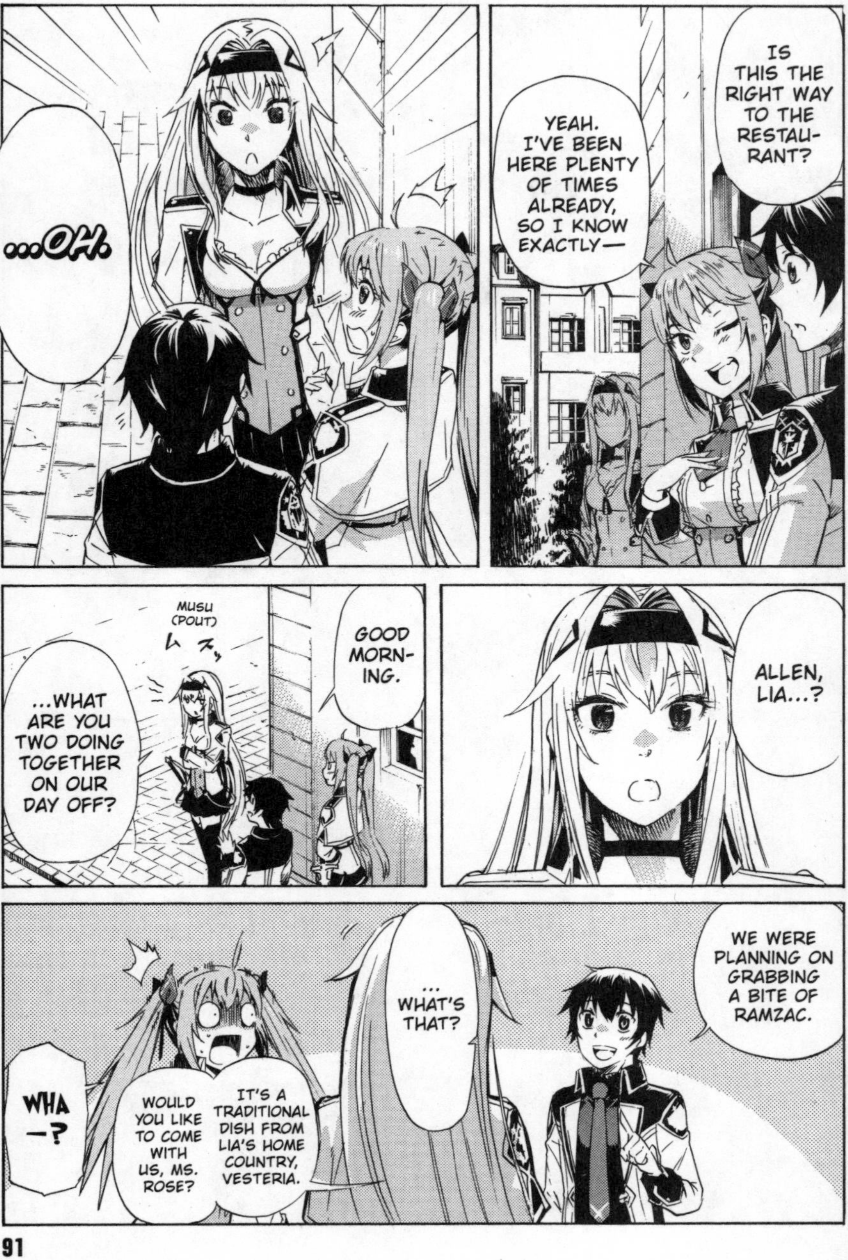
IS THIS THE RIGHT WAY TO THE RESTAU-RANT?
YEAH. I'VE BEEN HERE PLENTY OF TIMES ALREADY, SO I KNOW EXACTLY—
...OH.
ALLEN, LIA...?
GOOD MORN-ING.
MUSU (POUT)
ムスッ
...WHAT ARE YOU TWO DOING TOGETHER ON OUR DAY OFF?
WE WERE PLANNING ON GRABBING A BITE OF RAMZAC.
...WHAT'S THAT?
IT'S A TRADITIONAL DISH FROM LIA'S HOME COUNTRY, VESTERIA.
WOULD YOU LIKE TO COME WITH US, MS. ROSE?
WHA—?

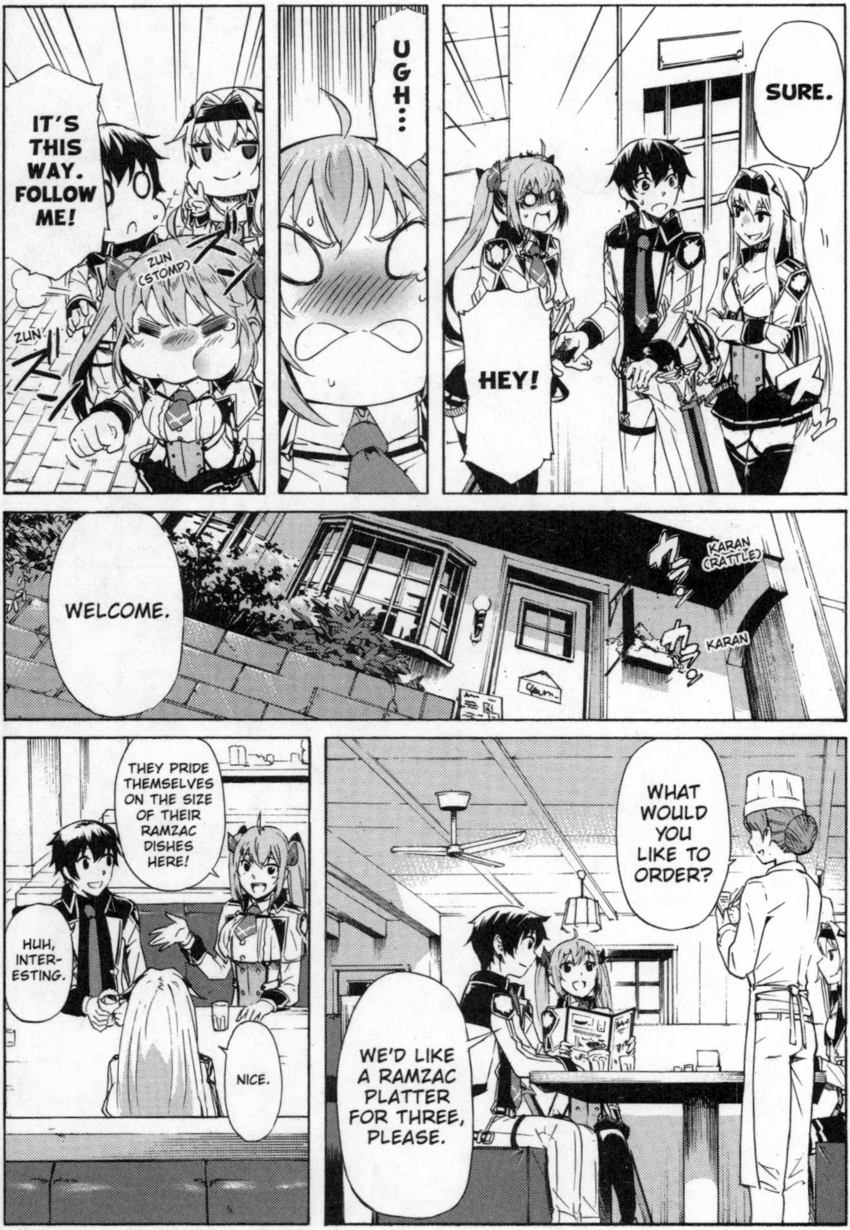
SURE.
HEY!
UGH...
IT'S THIS WAY. FOLLOW ME!
ZUN (STOMP)
ZUN
KARAN (RATTLE)
KARAN
WELCOME.
WHAT WOULD YOU LIKE TO ORDER?
WE'D LIKE A RAMZAC PLATTER FOR THREE, PLEASE.
THEY PRIDE THEMSELVES ON THE SIZE OF THEIR RAMZAC DISHES HERE!
HUH, INTERESTING.
NICE.

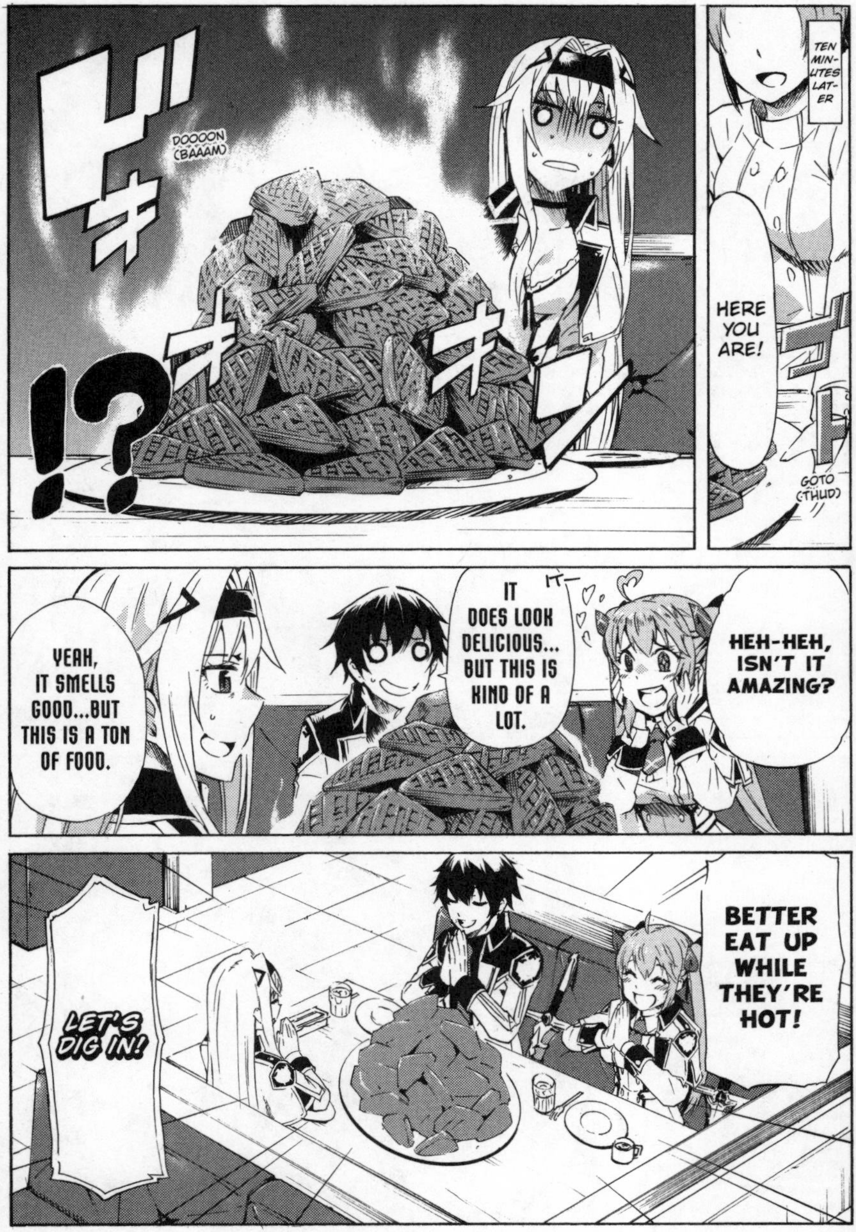
TEN MIN-UTES LAT-ER
HERE YOU ARE!
GOTO (THUD)
DOOOON (BAAAM)
!?
HEH-HEH, ISN'T IT AMAZING?
IT DOES LOOK DELICIOUS... BUT THIS IS KIND OF A LOT.
YEAH, IT SMELLS GOOD...BUT THIS IS A TON OF FOOD.
BETTER EAT UP WHILE THEY'RE HOT!
LET'S DIG IN!

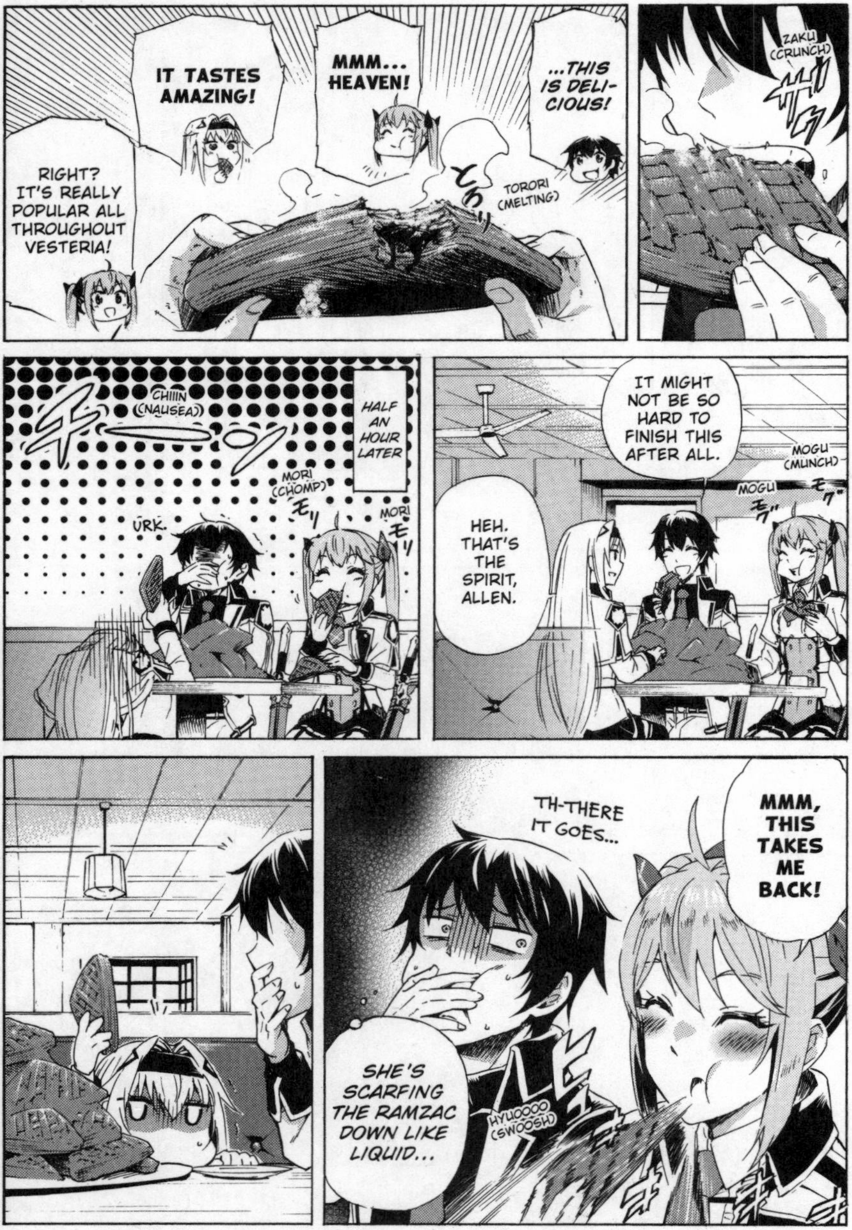
ZAKU (CRUNCH)
...THIS IS DELI-CIOUS!
TORORI (MELTING)
MMM... HEAVEN!
IT TASTES AMAZING!
RIGHT? IT'S REALLY POPULAR ALL THROUGHOUT VESTERIA!
IT MIGHT NOT BE SO HARD TO FINISH THIS AFTER ALL.
MOGU (MUNCH)
MOGU
HEH. THAT'S THE SPIRIT, ALLEN.
HALF AN HOUR LATER
MORI (CHOMP)
MORI
CHIIIN (NAUSEA)
URK.
MMM, THIS TAKES ME BACK!
TH-THERE IT GOES...
HYUOOOO (SWOOSH)
SHE'S SCARFING THE RAMZAC DOWN LIKE LIQUID...

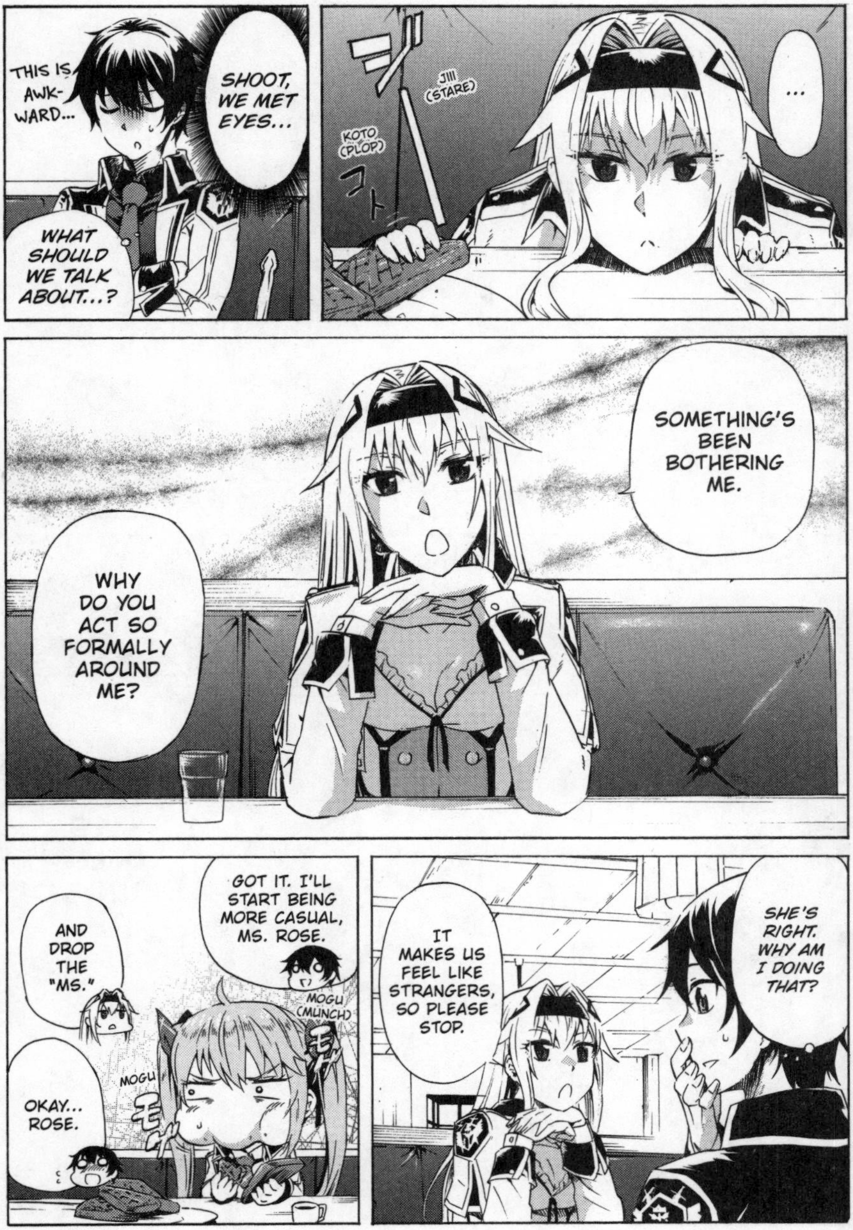
…
JIII (STARE)
KOTO (PLOP)
SHOOT, WE MET EYES…
THIS IS AWK-WARD…
WHAT SHOULD WE TALK ABOUT…?
SOMETHING'S BEEN BOTHERING ME.
WHY DO YOU ACT SO FORMALLY AROUND ME?
SHE'S RIGHT. WHY AM I DOING THAT?
IT MAKES US FEEL LIKE STRANGERS, SO PLEASE STOP.
GOT IT. I'LL START BEING MORE CASUAL, MS. ROSE.
AND DROP THE "MS."
MOGU (MUNCH)
MOGU
OKAY… ROSE.

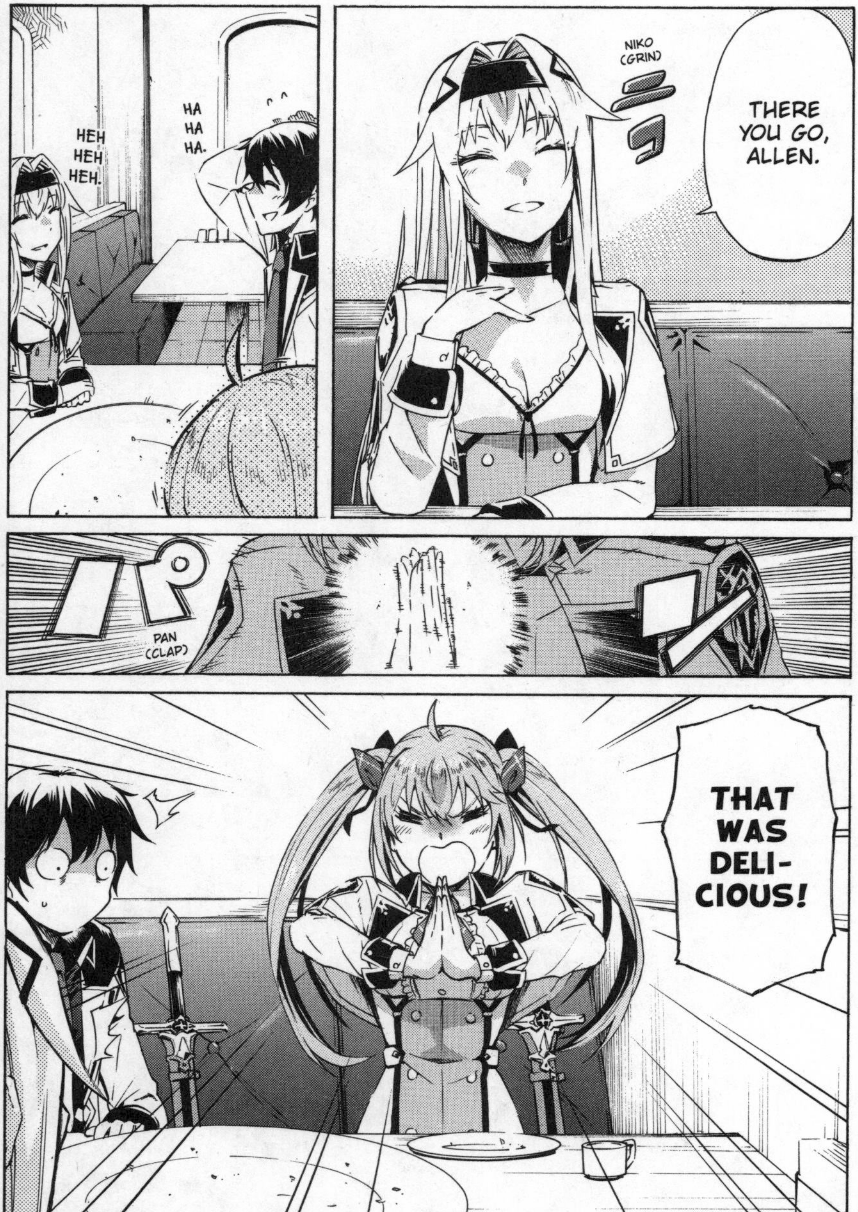
NIKO (GRIN)
THERE YOU GO, ALLEN.
HA HA HA.
HEH HEH HEH.
PAN (CLAP)
THAT WAS DELI- CIOUS!

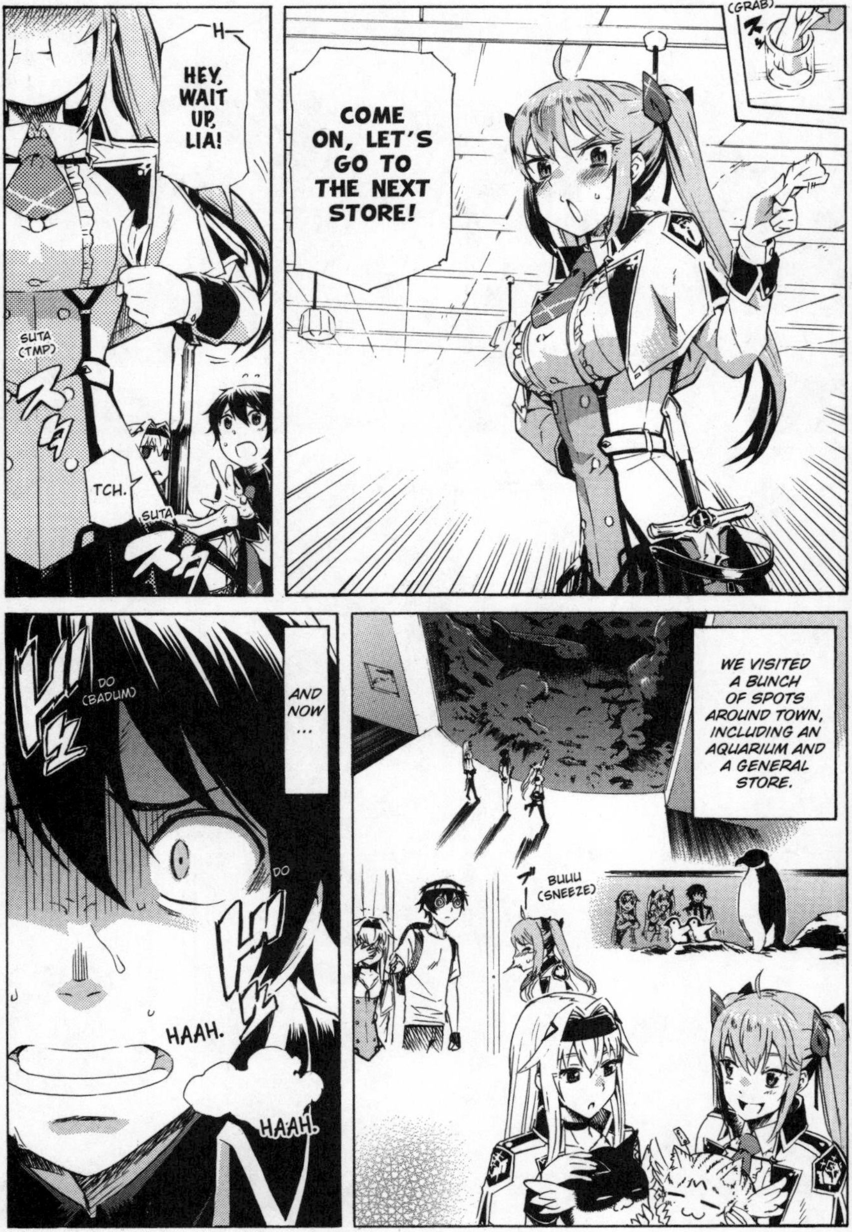
SU (GRAB)
COME ON, LET'S GO TO THE NEXT STORE!
H—
HEY, WAIT UP, LIA!
SUTA (TMP)
TCH.
SUTA
WE VISITED A BUNCH OF SPOTS AROUND TOWN, INCLUDING AN AQUARIUM AND A GENERAL STORE.
BUUU (SNEEZE)
AND NOW...
DO (BADUM)
DO
HAAH.
HAAH.

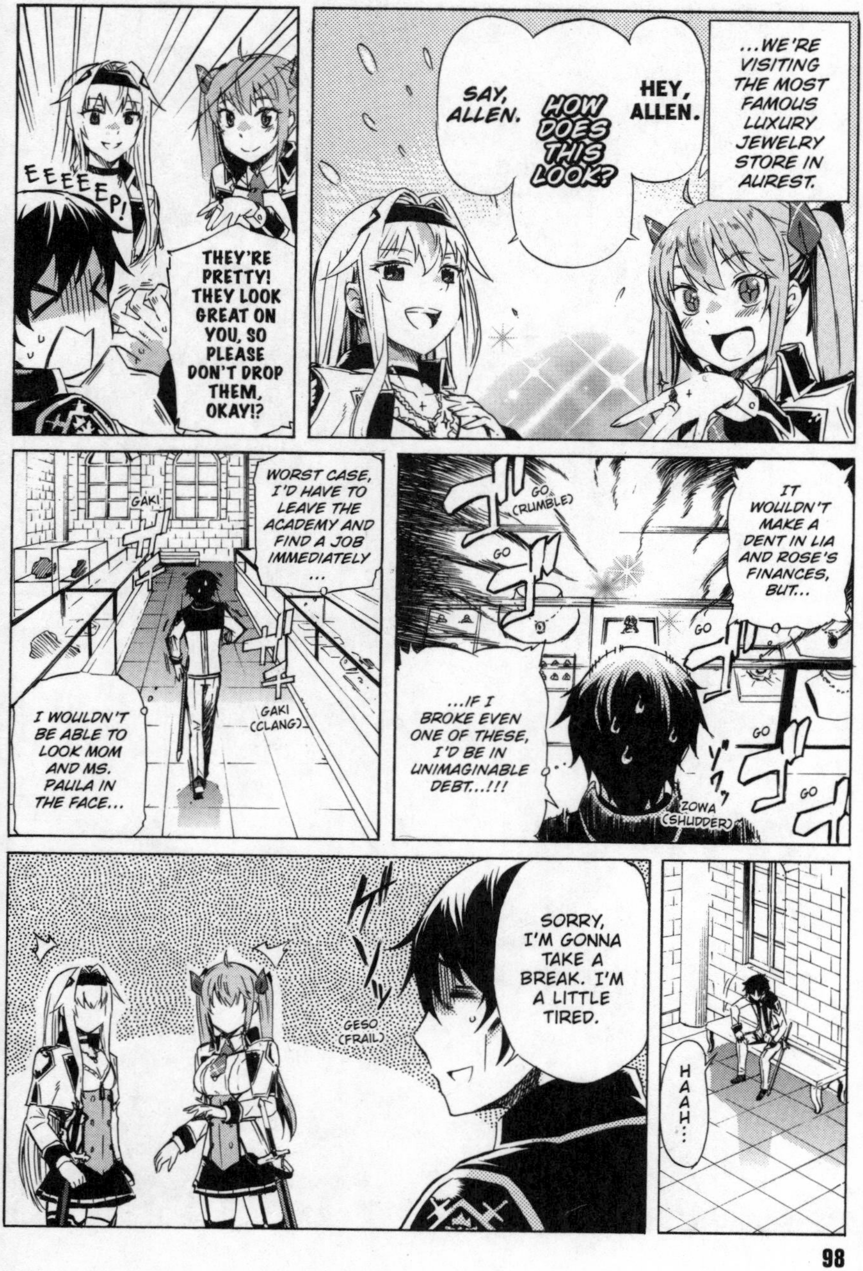
...WE'RE VISITING THE MOST FAMOUS LUXURY JEWELRY STORE IN AUREST.
HEY, ALLEN.
HOW DOES THIS LOOK?
SAY, ALLEN.
EEEEEP!
THEY'RE PRETTY! THEY LOOK GREAT ON YOU, SO PLEASE DON'T DROP THEM, OKAY!?
IT WOULDN'T MAKE A DENT IN LIA AND ROSE'S FINANCES, BUT...
GO (RUMBLE)
GO
GO
GO
GO
...IF I BROKE EVEN ONE OF THESE, I'D BE IN UNIMAGINABLE DEBT...!!!
ZOWA (SHUDDER)
WORST CASE, I'D HAVE TO LEAVE THE ACADEMY AND FIND A JOB IMMEDIATELY...
GAKI
GAKI (CLANG)
I WOULDN'T BE ABLE TO LOOK MOM AND MS. PAULA IN THE FACE...
HAAAH...
SORRY, I'M GONNA TAKE A BREAK. I'M A LITTLE TIRED.
GESO (FRAIL)

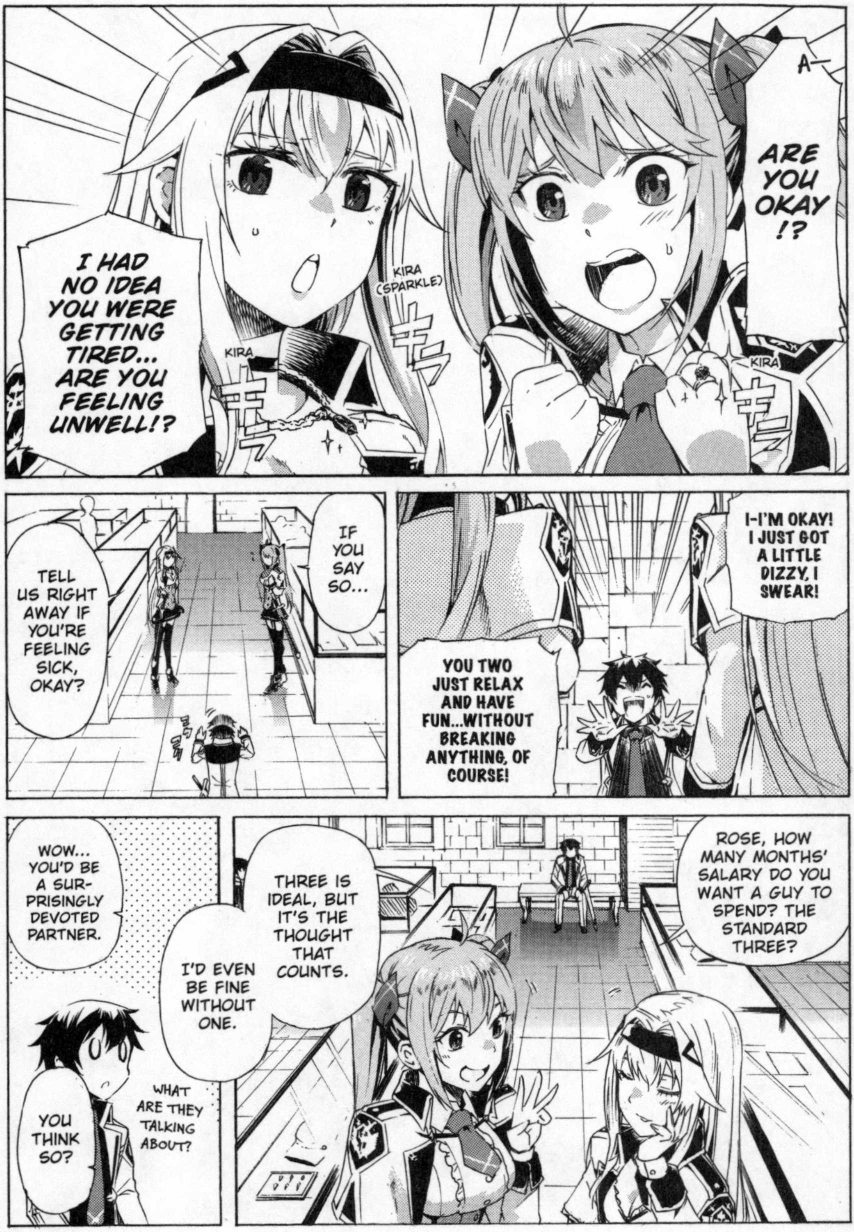
A—
ARE YOU OKAY!?
KIRA
KIRA (SPARKLE)
KIRA
I HAD NO IDEA YOU WERE GETTING TIRED... ARE YOU FEELING UNWELL!?
I-I'M OKAY! I JUST GOT A LITTLE DIZZY, I SWEAR!
YOU TWO JUST RELAX AND HAVE FUN...WITHOUT BREAKING ANYTHING, OF COURSE!
IF YOU SAY SO...
TELL US RIGHT AWAY IF YOU'RE FEELING SICK, OKAY?
ROSE, HOW MANY MONTHS' SALARY DO YOU WANT A GUY TO SPEND? THE STANDARD THREE?
THREE IS IDEAL, BUT IT'S THE THOUGHT THAT COUNTS.
I'D EVEN BE FINE WITHOUT ONE.
WOW... YOU'D BE A SUR-PRISINGLY DEVOTED PARTNER.
WHAT ARE THEY TALKING ABOUT?
YOU THINK SO?

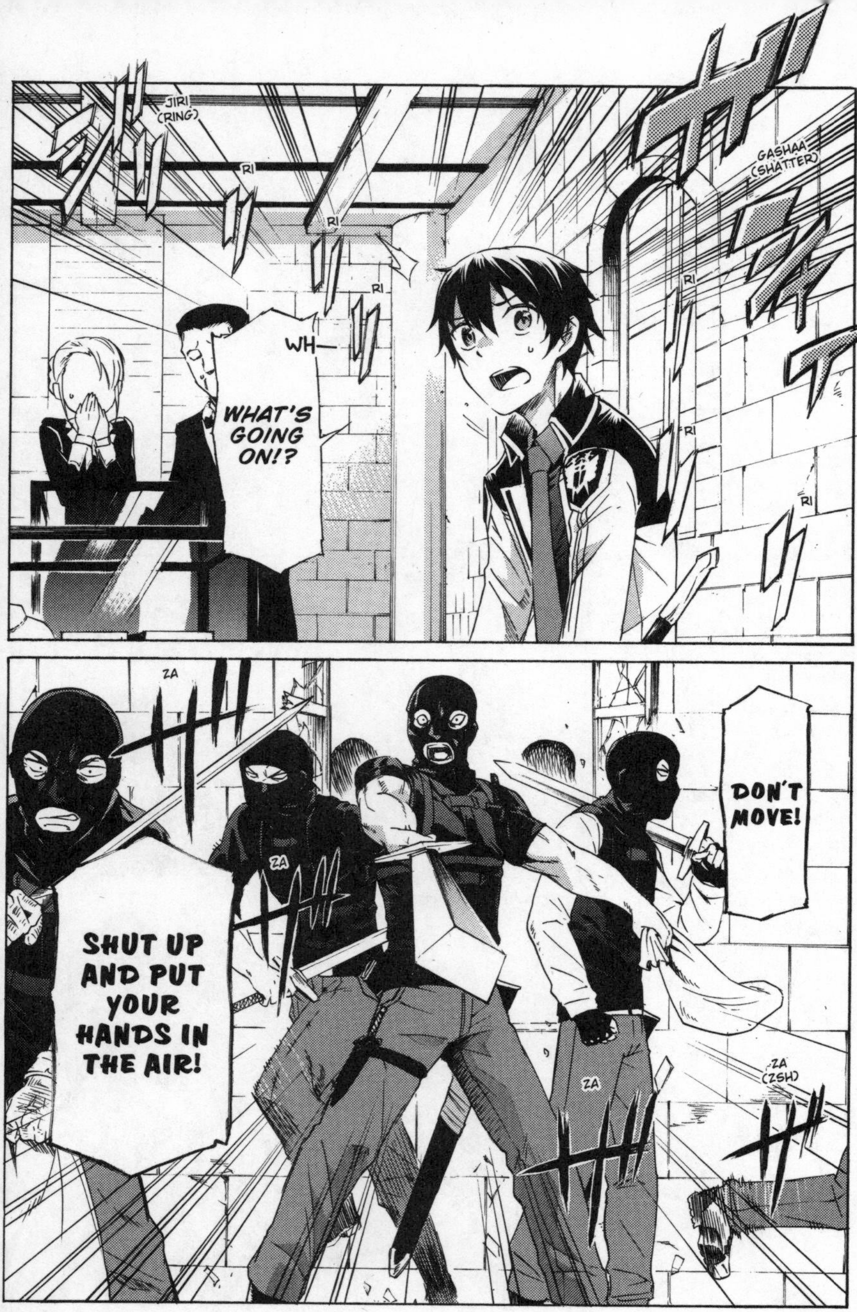
GASHAA (SHATTER)
RI
RI
RI
WH—
WHAT'S GOING ON!?
RI
RI
RI
JIRI (RING)
DON'T MOVE!
ZA (ZSH)
ZA
ZA
SHUT UP AND PUT YOUR HANDS IN THE AIR!
ZA

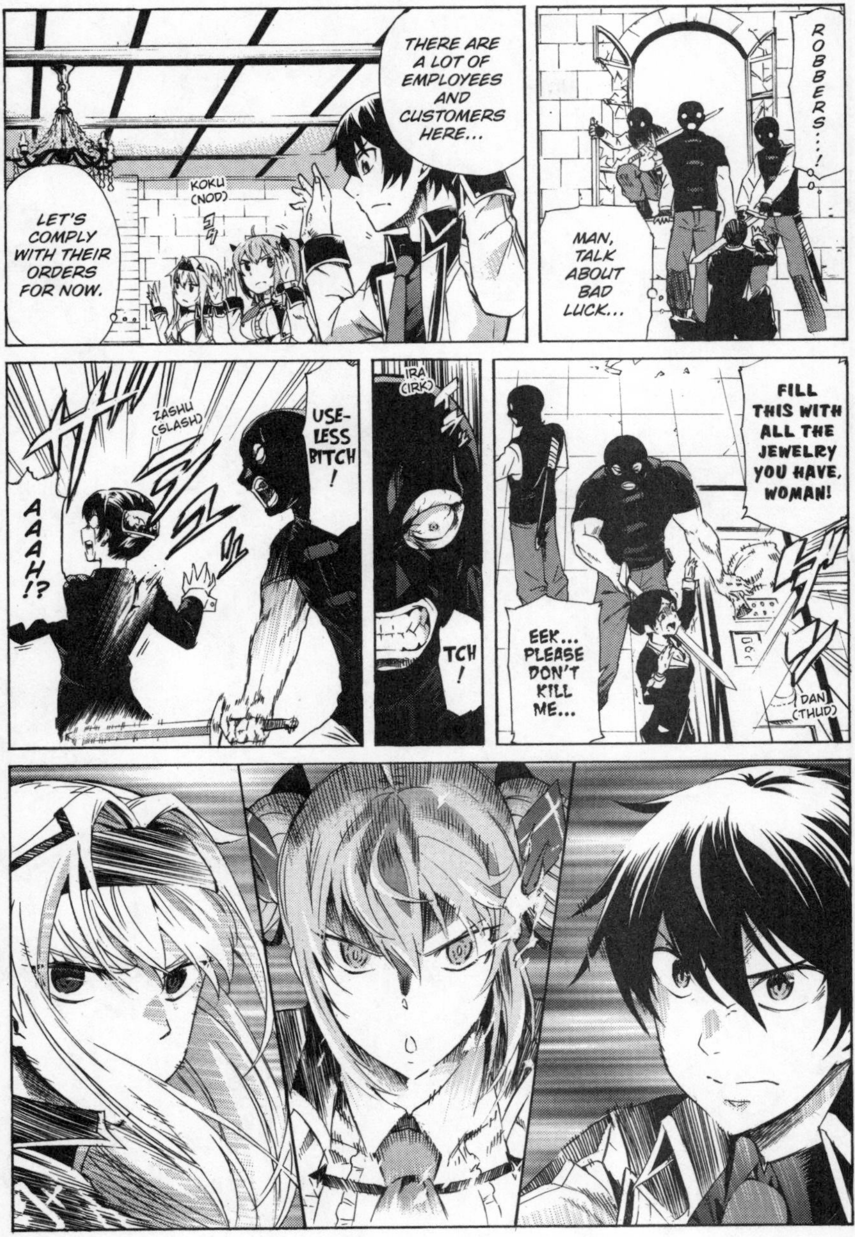
ROBBERS...!
MAN, TALK ABOUT BAD LUCK...
THERE ARE A LOT OF EMPLOYEES AND CUSTOMERS HERE...
KOKU (NOD)
LET'S COMPLY WITH THEIR ORDERS FOR NOW.
FILL THIS WITH ALL THE JEWELRY YOU HAVE, WOMAN!
EEK... PLEASE DON'T KILL ME...
DAN (THUD)
IRA (IRK)
TCH!
USE-LESS BITCH!
ZASHU (SLASH)
AAAAH!?

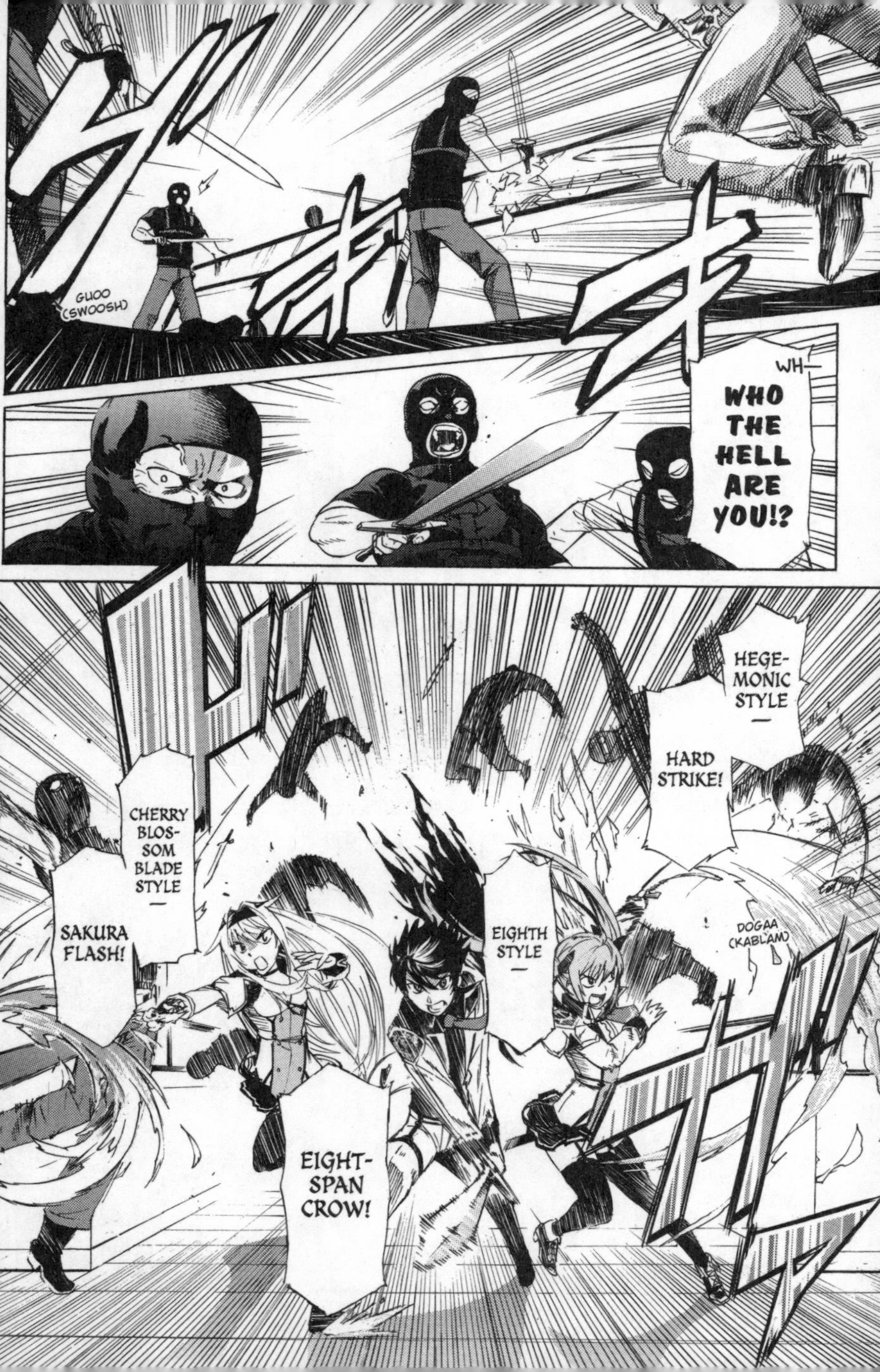
GUOO (SWOOSH)
WH—
WHO THE HELL ARE YOU!?
HEGE-MONIC STYLE —
HARD STRIKE!
DOGAA (KABLAM)
EIGHTH STYLE —
EIGHT-SPAN CROW!
CHERRY BLOS-SOM BLADE STYLE —
SAKURA FLASH!

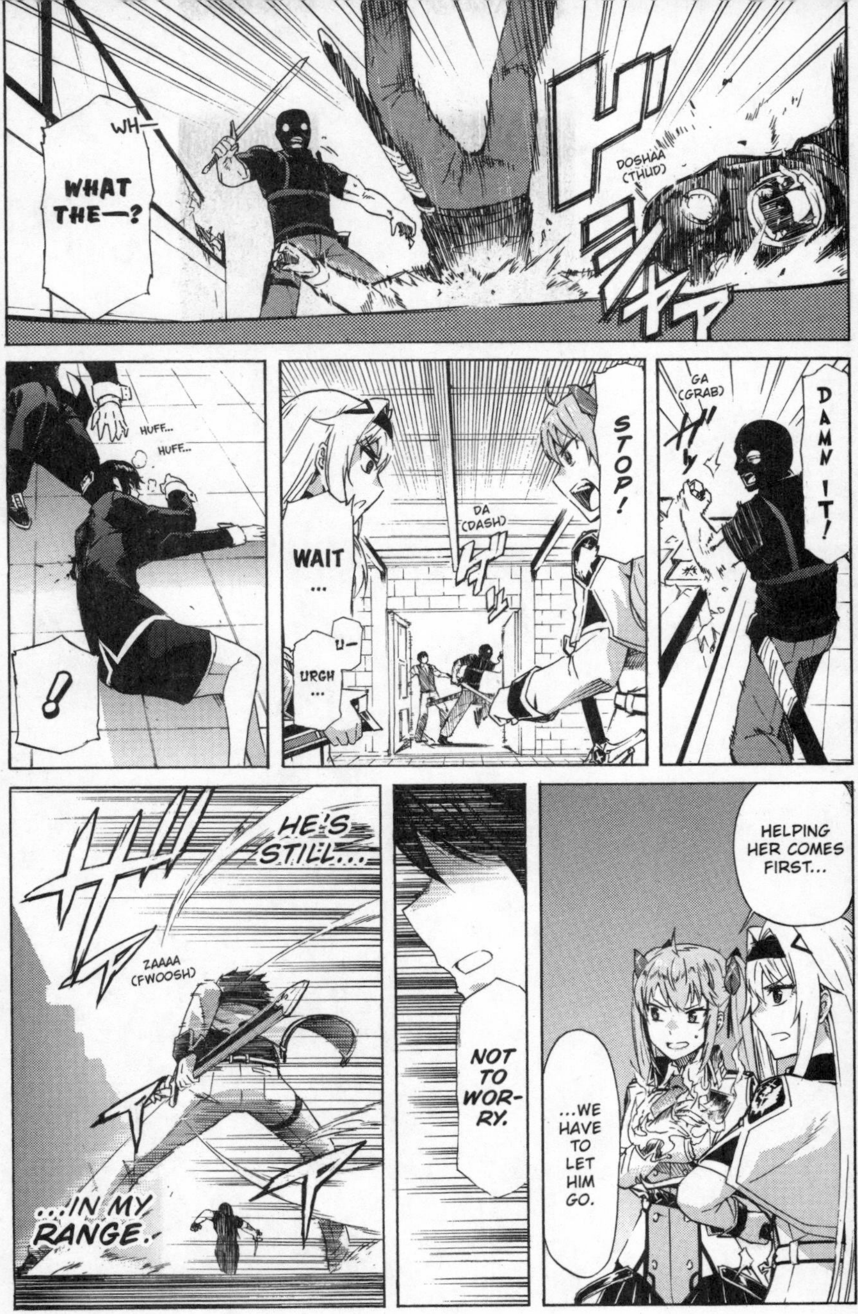
DOSHAA (THUD)
WH—
WHAT THE—?
DAMN IT!
GA (GRAB)
STOP!
DA (DASH)
WAIT...
U-URGH...
HUFF... HUFF...
!
HELPING HER COMES FIRST...
...WE HAVE TO LET HIM GO.
NOT TO WORRY.
HE'S STILL...
ZAAAA (FWOOSH)
...IN MY RANGE.

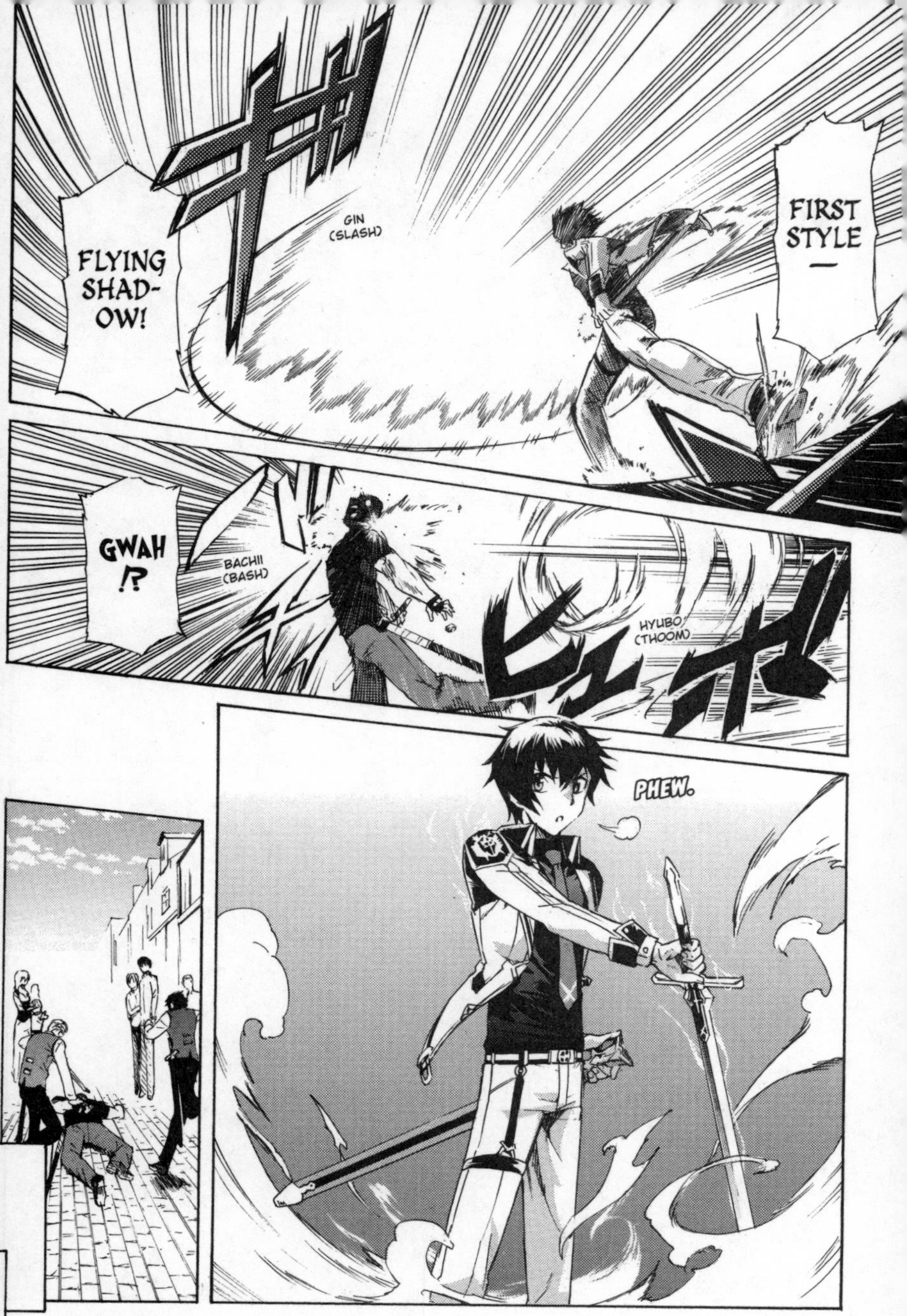
FIRST STYLE —
FLYING SHADOW!
GIN (SLASH)
HYUBO (THOOM)
BACHII (BASH)
GWAH !?
PHEW.

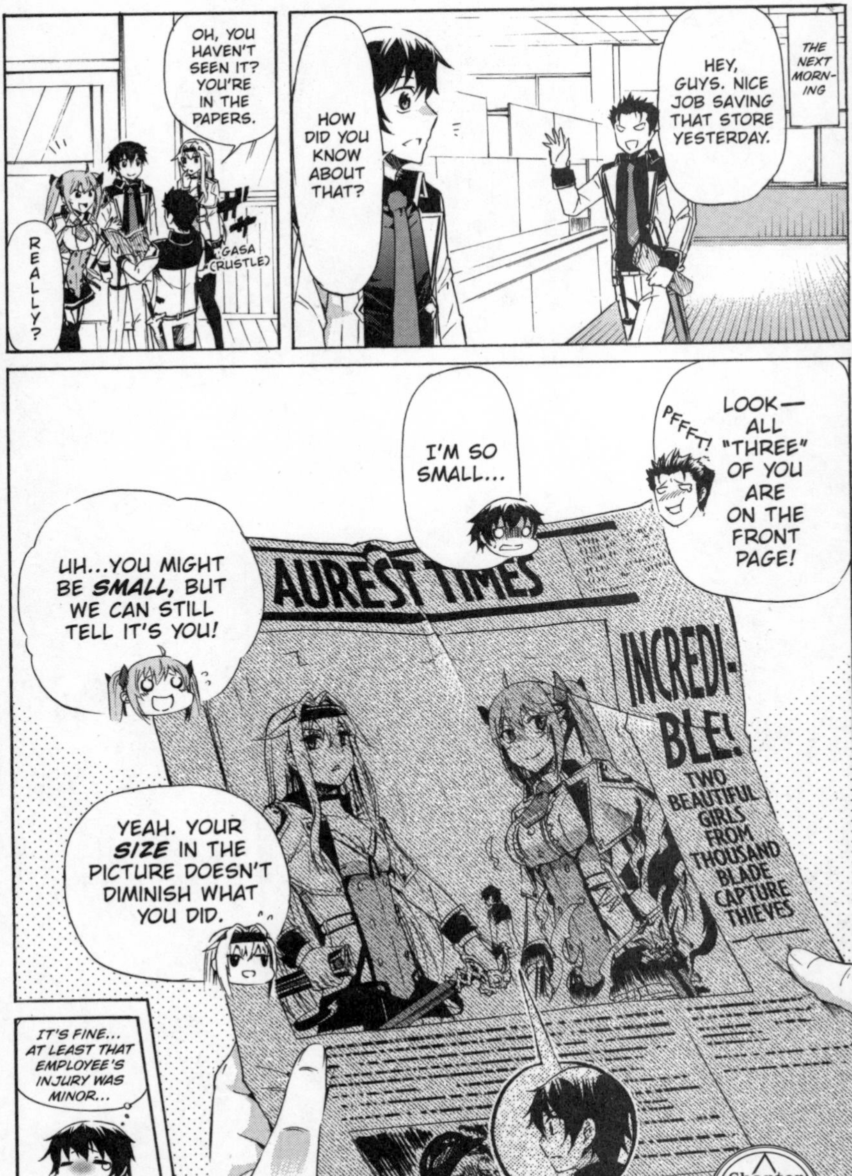
THE NEXT MORNING
HEY, GUYS. NICE JOB SAVING THAT STORE YESTERDAY.
HOW DID YOU KNOW ABOUT THAT?
OH, YOU HAVEN'T SEEN IT? YOU'RE IN THE PAPERS.
GASA (RUSTLE)
REALLY?
LOOK—ALL "THREE" OF YOU ARE ON THE FRONT PAGE!
PFFFT!
I'M SO SMALL...
AUREST TIMES
INCREDIBLE!
TWO BEAUTIFUL GIRLS FROM THOUSAND BLADE CAPTURE THIEVES
UH...YOU MIGHT BE SMALL, BUT WE CAN STILL TELL IT'S YOU!
YEAH. YOUR SIZE IN THE PICTURE DOESN'T DIMINISH WHAT YOU DID.
IT'S FINE... AT LEAST THAT EMPLOYEE'S INJURY WAS MINOR...
Chapter 8 End

I KEPT PRESSING THE 100-MILLION-YEAR BUTTON AND CAME OUT ON TOP

~THE UNBEATABLE REJECT SWORDSMAN~

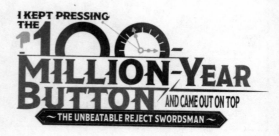

Chapter 9

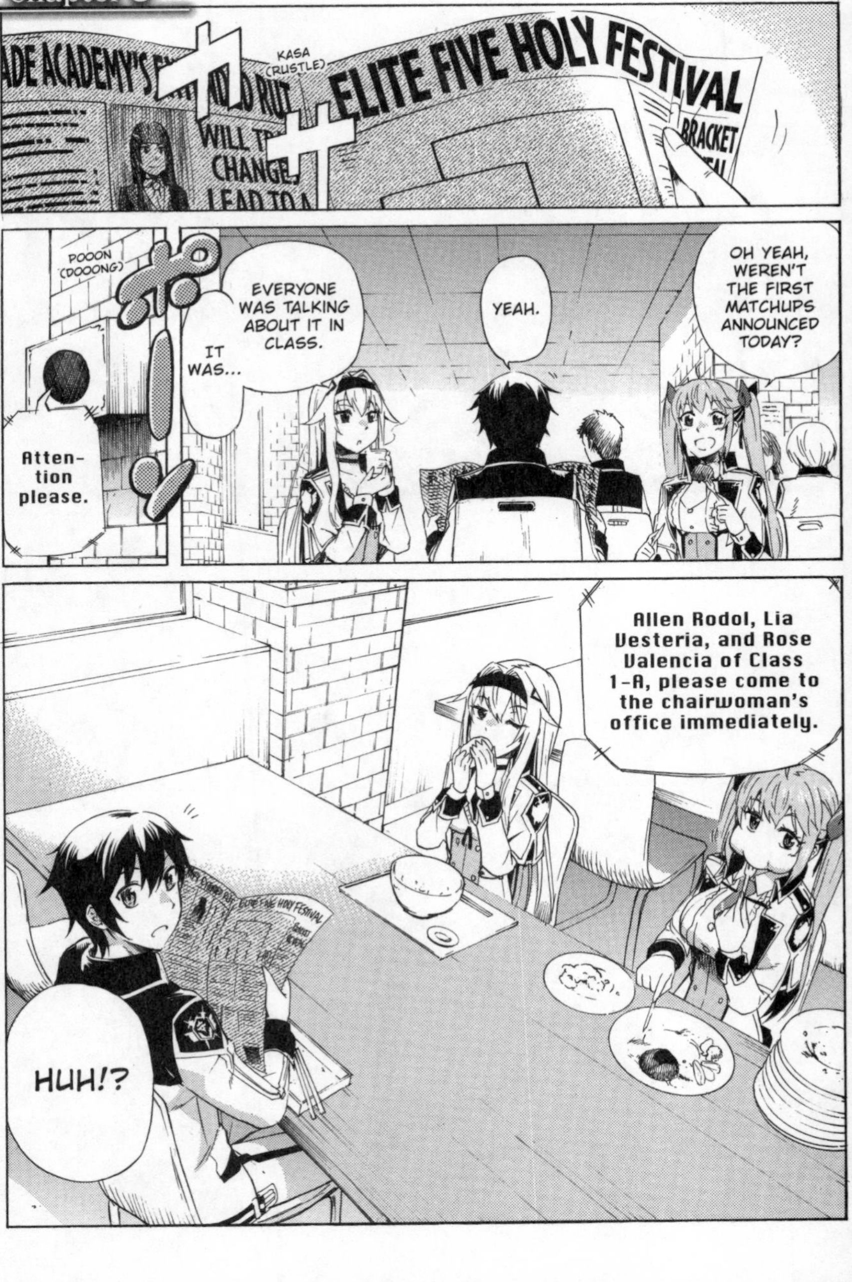
BRACKET
ELITE FIVE HOLY FESTIVAL
KASA (RUSTLE)
ADE ACADEMY'S
WILL TH
CHANGE,
OH YEAH, WEREN'T THE FIRST MATCHUPS ANNOUNCED TODAY?
YEAH.
EVERYONE WAS TALKING ABOUT IT IN CLASS.
IT WAS...
POOON (DOOONG)
Atten-tion please.
Allen Rodol, Lia Vesteria, and Rose Valencia of Class 1-A, please come to the chairwoman's office immediately.
HUH!?

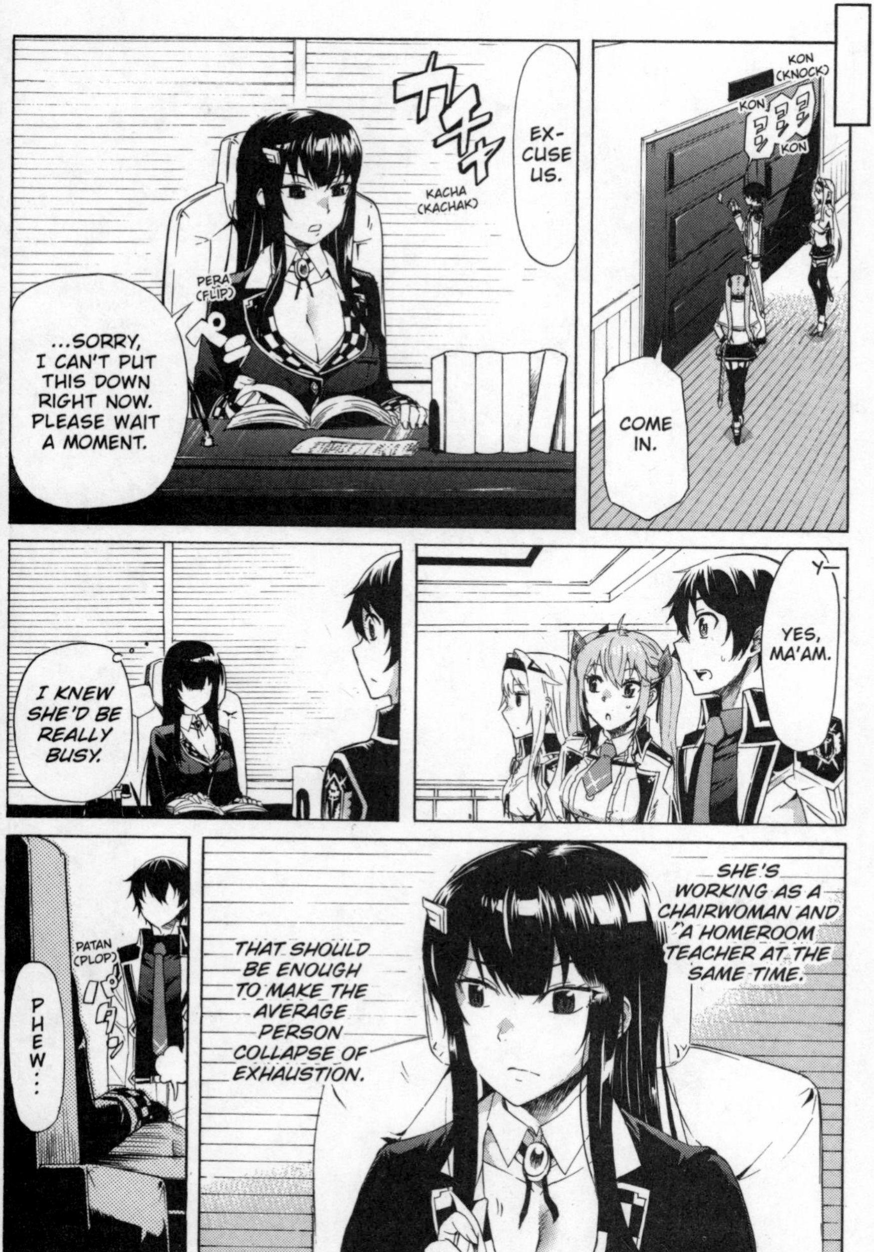
KON (KNOCK)
KON
KON
COME IN.
KACHA (KACHAK)
EX-CUSE US.
PERA (FLIP)
...SORRY, I CAN'T PUT THIS DOWN RIGHT NOW. PLEASE WAIT A MOMENT.
Y—
YES, MA'AM.
I KNEW SHE'D BE REALLY BUSY.
SHE'S WORKING AS A CHAIRWOMAN AND A HOMEROOM TEACHER AT THE SAME TIME.
THAT SHOULD BE ENOUGH TO MAKE THE AVERAGE PERSON COLLAPSE OF EXHAUSTION.
PATAN (PLOP)
PHEW...

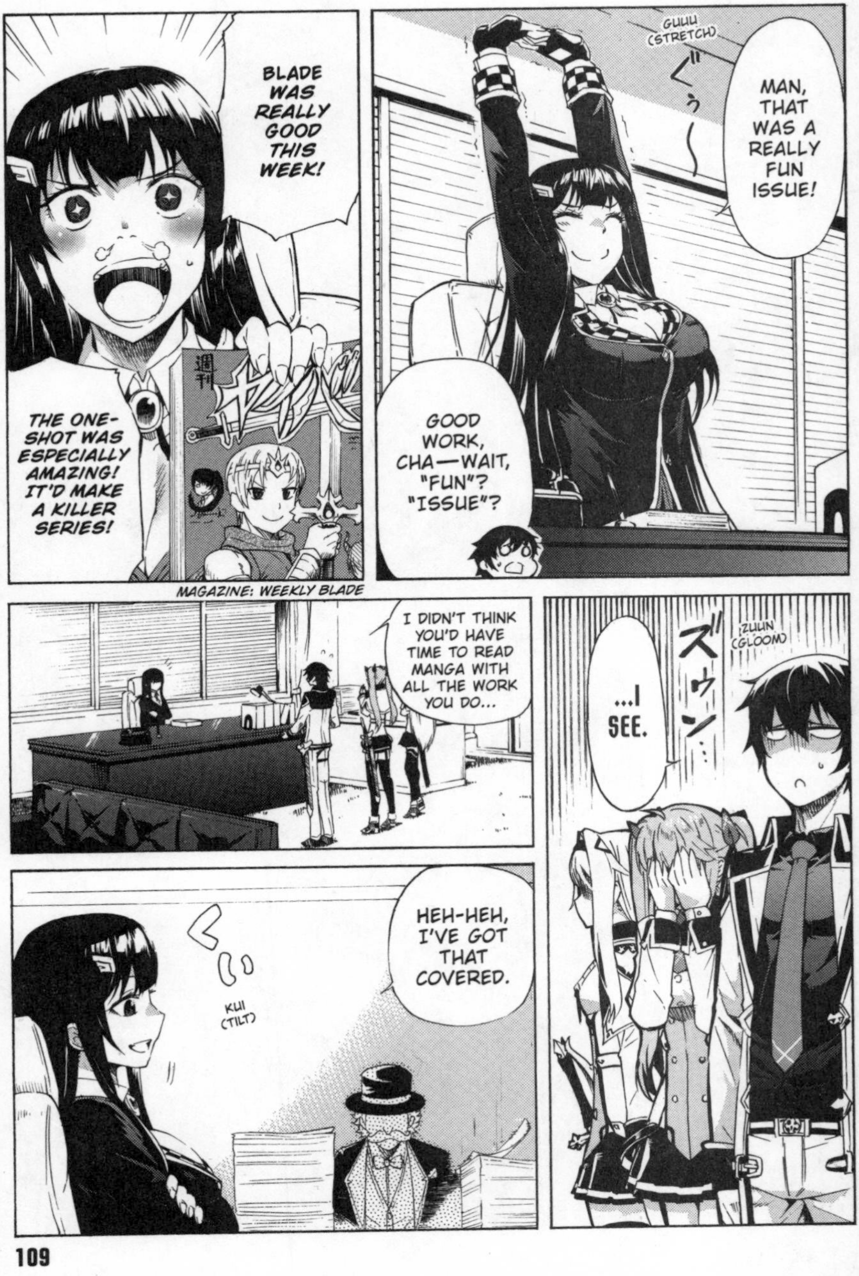
GUUU (STRETCH)
MAN, THAT WAS A REALLY FUN ISSUE!
GOOD WORK, CHA—WAIT, "FUN"? "ISSUE"?
BLADE WAS REALLY GOOD THIS WEEK!
THE ONE-SHOT WAS ESPECIALLY AMAZING! IT'D MAKE A KILLER SERIES!
MAGAZINE: WEEKLY BLADE
ZUUN (GLOOM)
...I SEE.
I DIDN'T THINK YOU'D HAVE TIME TO READ MANGA WITH ALL THE WORK YOU DO...
HEH-HEH, I'VE GOT THAT COVERED.
KUI (TILT)

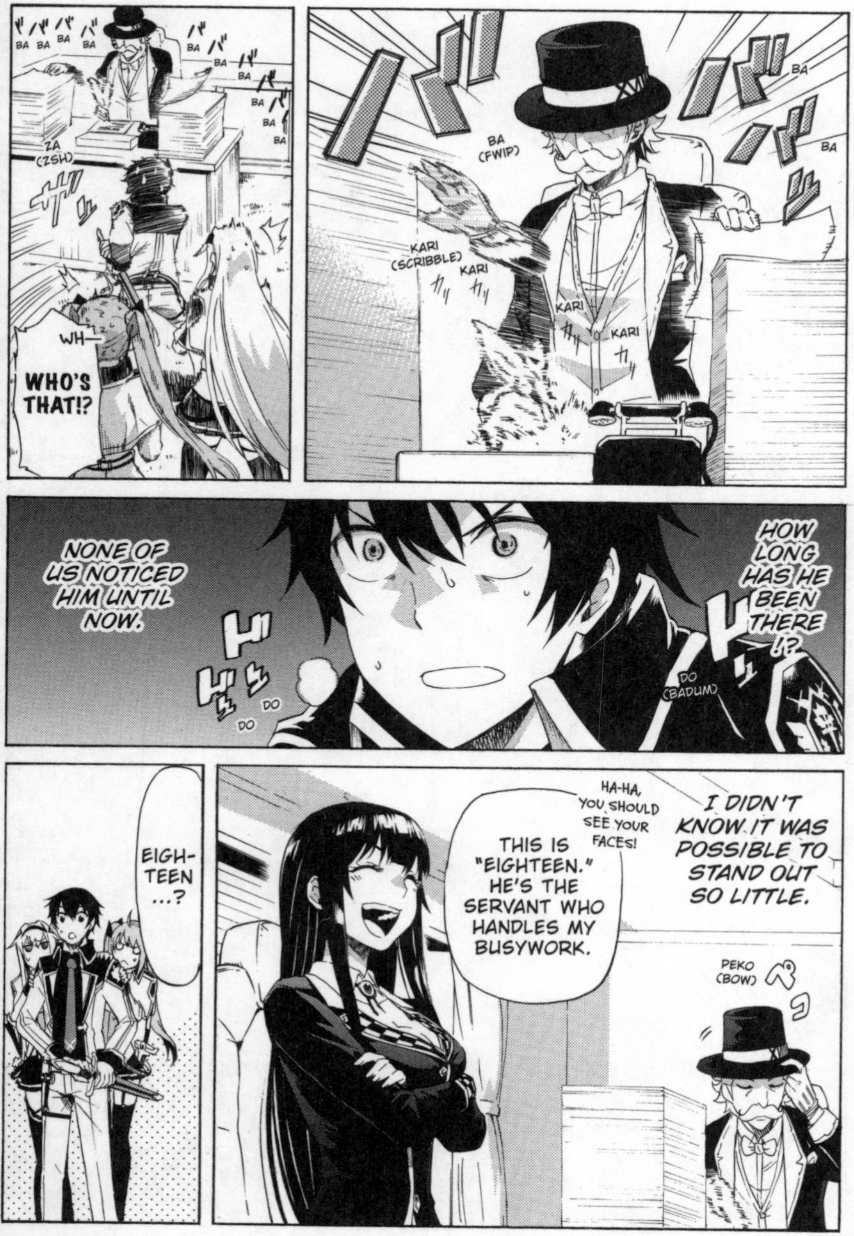
BA
BA
BA (FWIP)
KARI (SCRIBBLE) KARI
KARI
KARI
BA BA BA BA
BA BA BA BA BA
ZA (ZSH)
WH—
WHO'S THAT!?
HOW LONG HAS HE BEEN THERE!?
DO (BADUM)
NONE OF US NOTICED HIM UNTIL NOW.
DO
DO
I DIDN'T KNOW IT WAS POSSIBLE TO STAND OUT SO LITTLE.
HA-HA, YOU SHOULD SEE YOUR FACES!
THIS IS "EIGHTEEN." HE'S THE SERVANT WHO HANDLES MY BUSYWORK.
PEKO (BOW)
EIGH-TEEN ...?

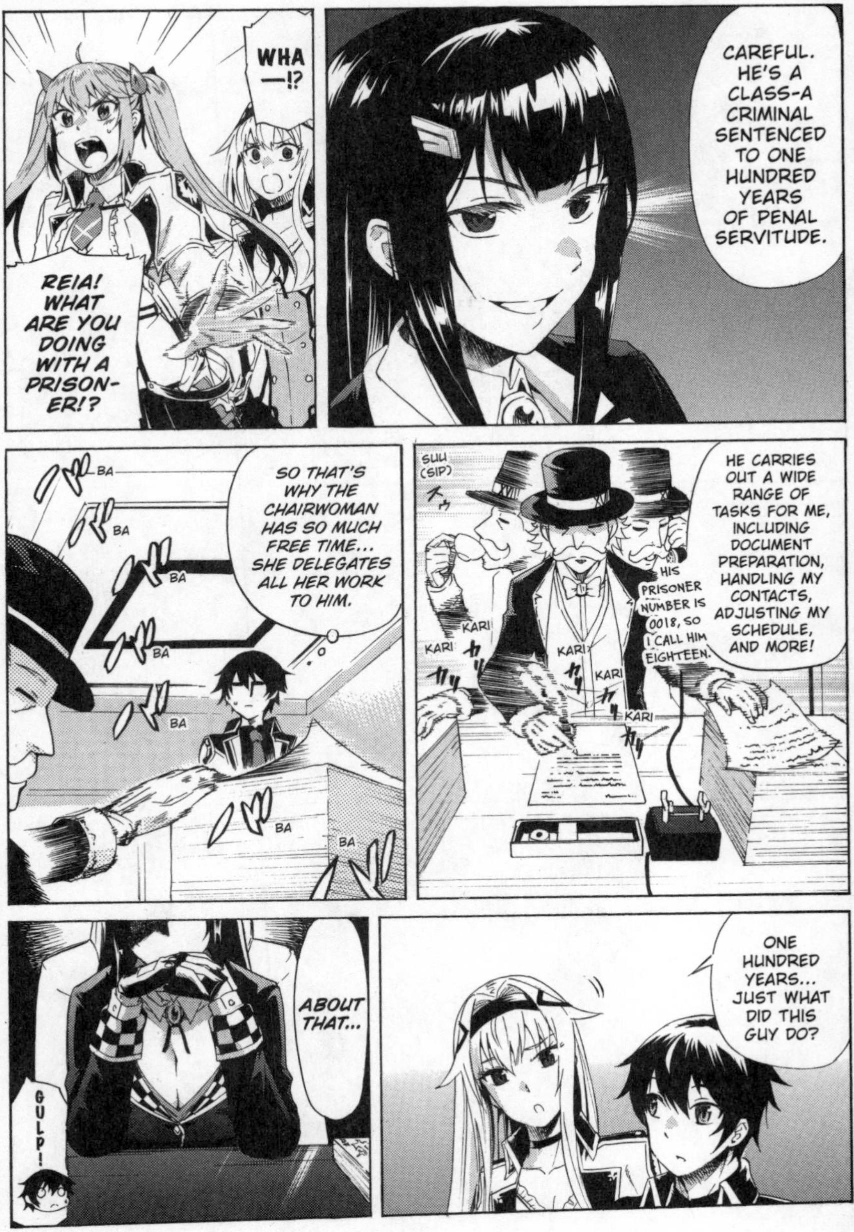
CAREFUL. HE'S A CLASS-A CRIMINAL SENTENCED TO ONE HUNDRED YEARS OF PENAL SERVITUDE.
WHA—!?
REIA! WHAT ARE YOU DOING WITH A PRISONER!?
HE CARRIES OUT A WIDE RANGE OF TASKS FOR ME, INCLUDING DOCUMENT PREPARATION, HANDLING MY CONTACTS, ADJUSTING MY SCHEDULE, AND MORE!
SUU (SIP)
HIS PRISONER NUMBER IS 0018, SO I CALL HIM EIGHTEEN.
KARI KARI KARI KARI KARI
SO THAT'S WHY THE CHAIRWOMAN HAS SO MUCH FREE TIME... SHE DELEGATES ALL HER WORK TO HIM.
BA BA BA BA BA BA BA
ONE HUNDRED YEARS... JUST WHAT DID THIS GUY DO?
ABOUT THAT...
GULP!

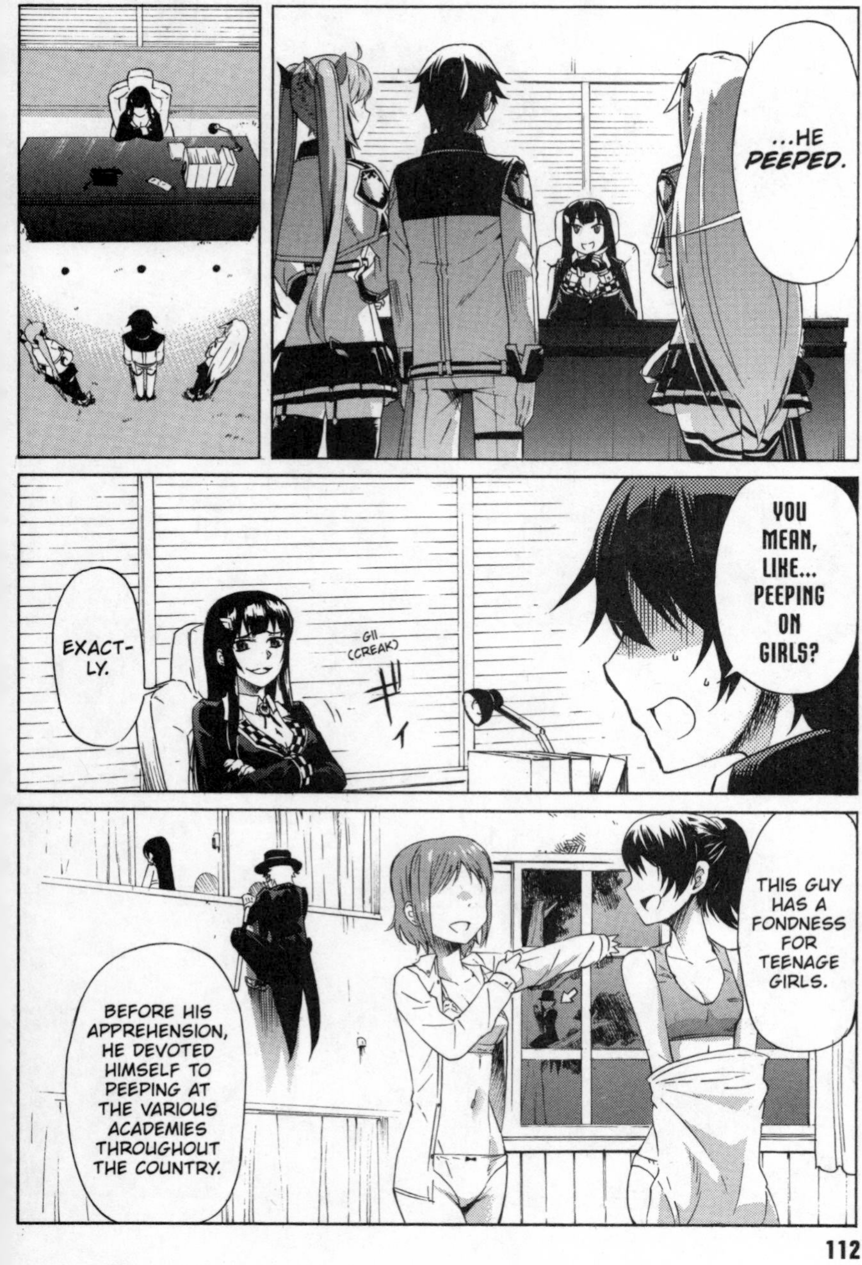
...HE PEEPED.
YOU MEAN, LIKE... PEEPING ON GIRLS?
GII (CREAK)
EXACT-LY.
THIS GUY HAS A FONDNESS FOR TEENAGE GIRLS.
BEFORE HIS APPREHENSION, HE DEVOTED HIMSELF TO PEEPING AT THE VARIOUS ACADEMIES THROUGHOUT THE COUNTRY.

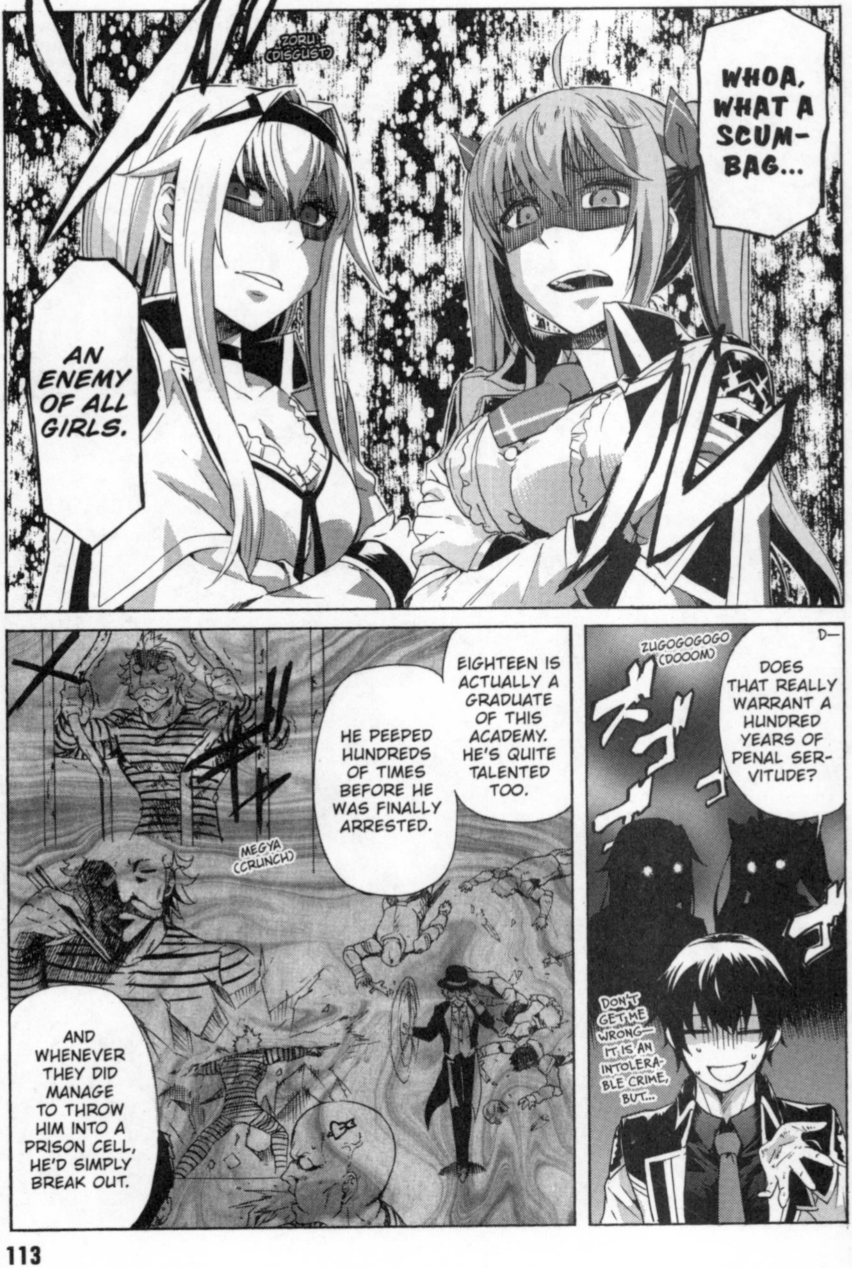
WHOA, WHAT A SCUM-BAG...
ZORU (DISGUST)
AN ENEMY OF ALL GIRLS.
D—
ZUGOGOGOGO (DOOOM)
DOES THAT REALLY WARRANT A HUNDRED YEARS OF PENAL SER-VITUDE?
DON'T GET ME WRONG—IT IS AN INTOLERA-BLE CRIME, BUT...
EIGHTEEN IS ACTUALLY A GRADUATE OF THIS ACADEMY. HE'S QUITE TALENTED TOO.
HE PEEPED HUNDREDS OF TIMES BEFORE HE WAS FINALLY ARRESTED.
MEGYA (CRUNCH)
AND WHENEVER THEY DID MANAGE TO THROW HIM INTO A PRISON CELL, HE'D SIMPLY BREAK OUT.

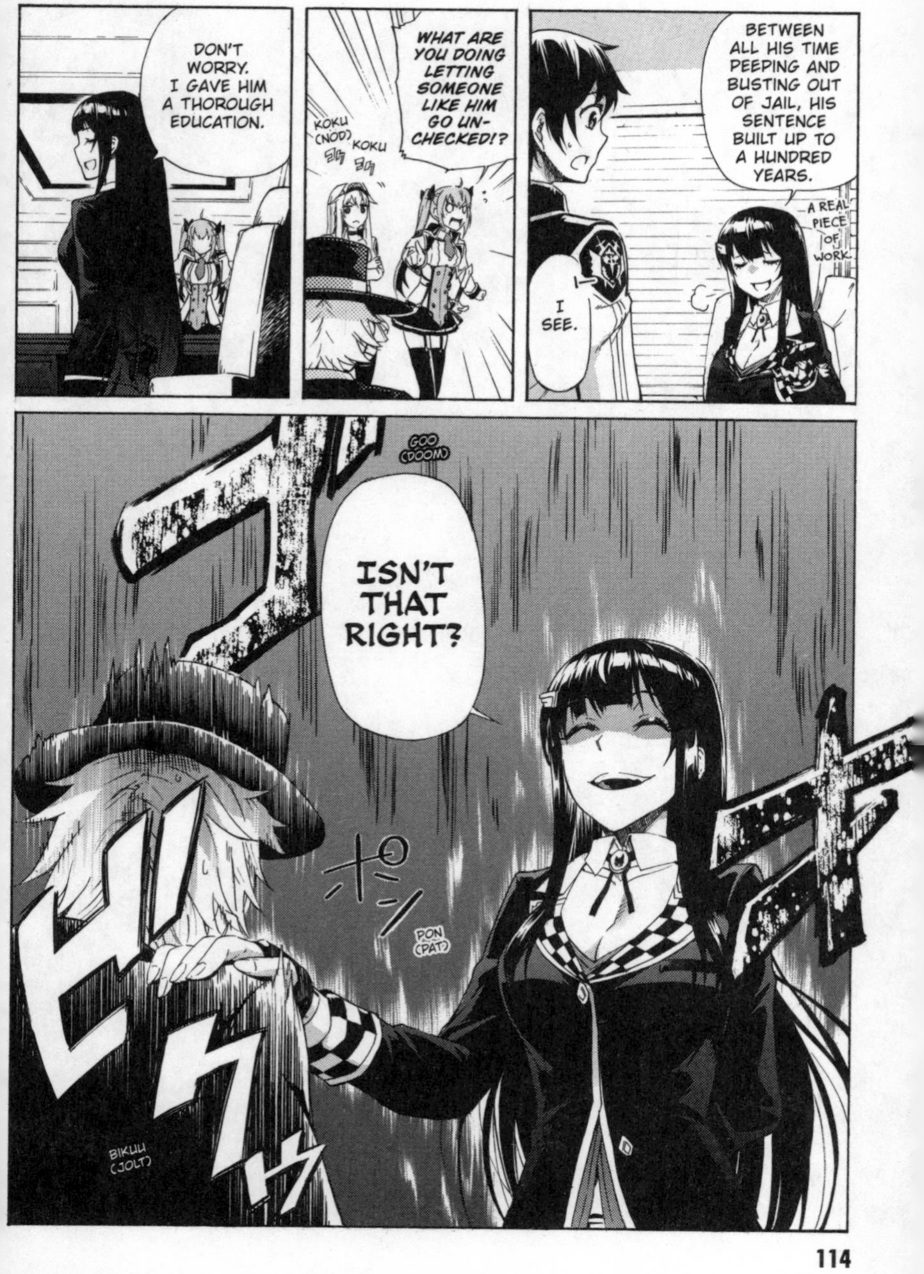
BETWEEN ALL HIS TIME PEEPING AND BUSTING OUT OF JAIL, HIS SENTENCE BUILT UP TO A HUNDRED YEARS.
A REAL PIECE OF WORK.
I SEE.
WHAT ARE YOU DOING LETTING SOMEONE LIKE HIM GO UN-CHECKED!?
KOKU (NOD) KOKU
DON'T WORRY. I GAVE HIM A THOROUGH EDUCATION.
GOO (DOOM)
ISN'T THAT RIGHT?
PON (PAT)
BIKUU (JOLT)

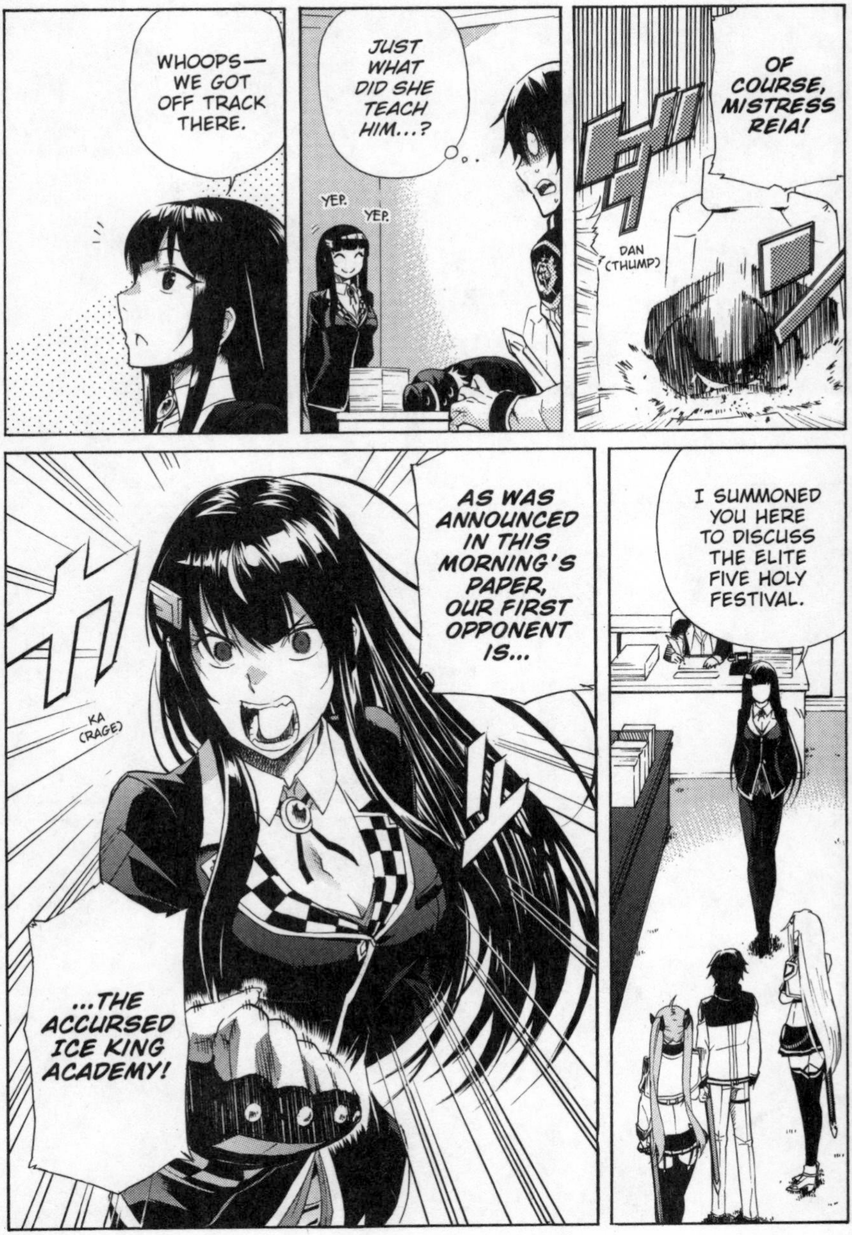
OF COURSE, MISTRESS REIA!
DAN (THUMP)
JUST WHAT DID SHE TEACH HIM...?
YEP.
YEP.
WHOOPS— WE GOT OFF TRACK THERE.
I SUMMONED YOU HERE TO DISCUSS THE ELITE FIVE HOLY FESTIVAL.
AS WAS ANNOUNCED IN THIS MORNING'S PAPER, OUR FIRST OPPONENT IS...
KA (RAGE)
...THE ACCURSED ICE KING ACADEMY!

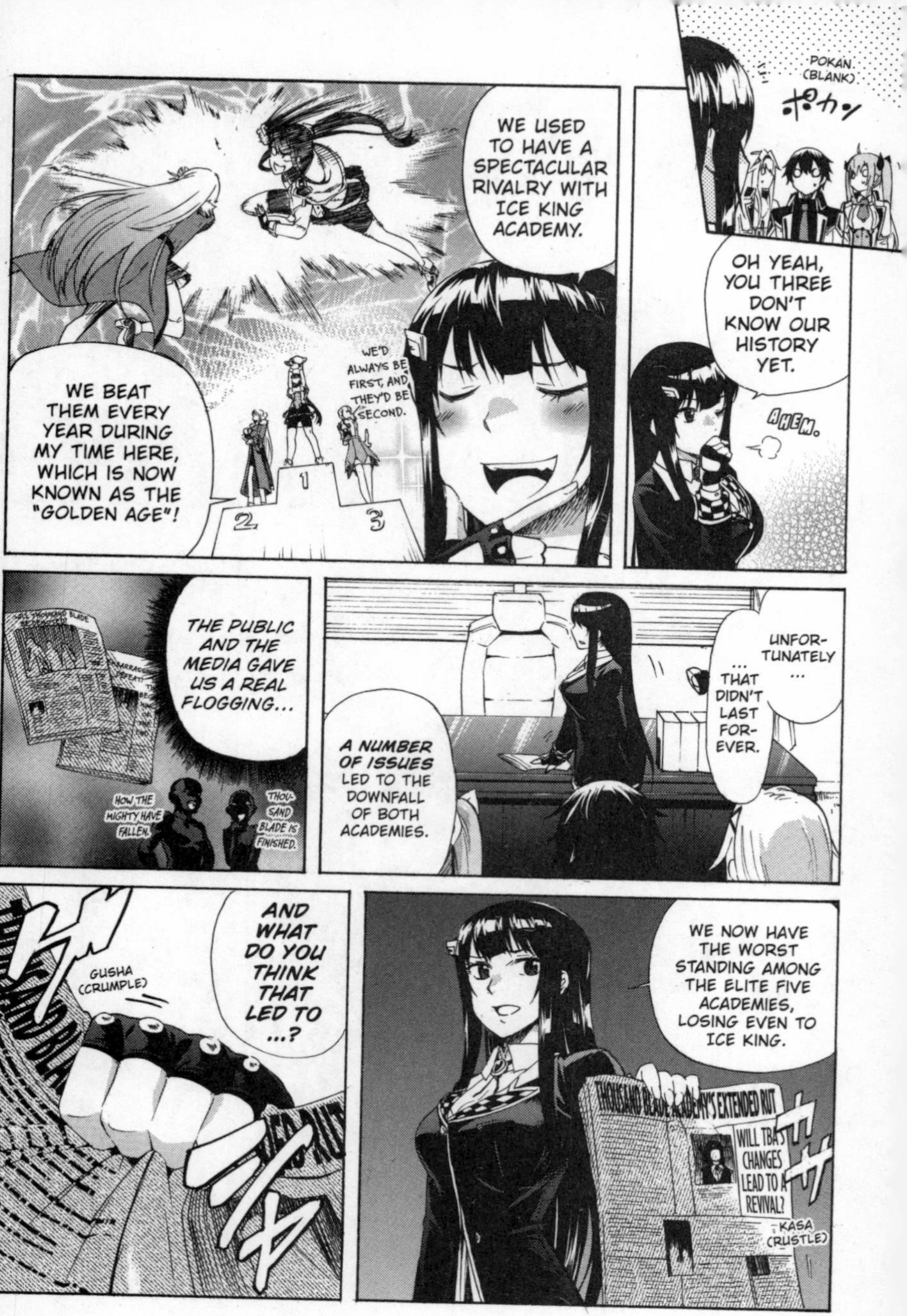
POKAN (BLANK)
OH YEAH, YOU THREE DON'T KNOW OUR HISTORY YET.
AHEM.
WE USED TO HAVE A SPECTACULAR RIVALRY WITH ICE KING ACADEMY.
WE'D ALWAYS BE FIRST, AND THEY'D BE SECOND.
1
2
3
WE BEAT THEM EVERY YEAR DURING MY TIME HERE, WHICH IS NOW KNOWN AS THE "GOLDEN AGE"!
UNFORTUNATELY ...
... THAT DIDN'T LAST FOREVER.
A NUMBER OF ISSUES LED TO THE DOWNFALL OF BOTH ACADEMIES.
THE PUBLIC AND THE MEDIA GAVE US A REAL FLOGGING...
THOUSAND BLADE IS FINISHED.
HOW THE MIGHTY HAVE FALLEN.
WE NOW HAVE THE WORST STANDING AMONG THE ELITE FIVE ACADEMIES, LOSING EVEN TO ICE KING.
THOUSAND BLADE ACADEMY'S EXTENDED RUT
WILL TBA'S CHANGES LEAD TO A REVIVAL?
KASA (RUSTLE)
AND WHAT DO YOU THINK THAT LED TO ...?
GUSHA (CRUMPLE)

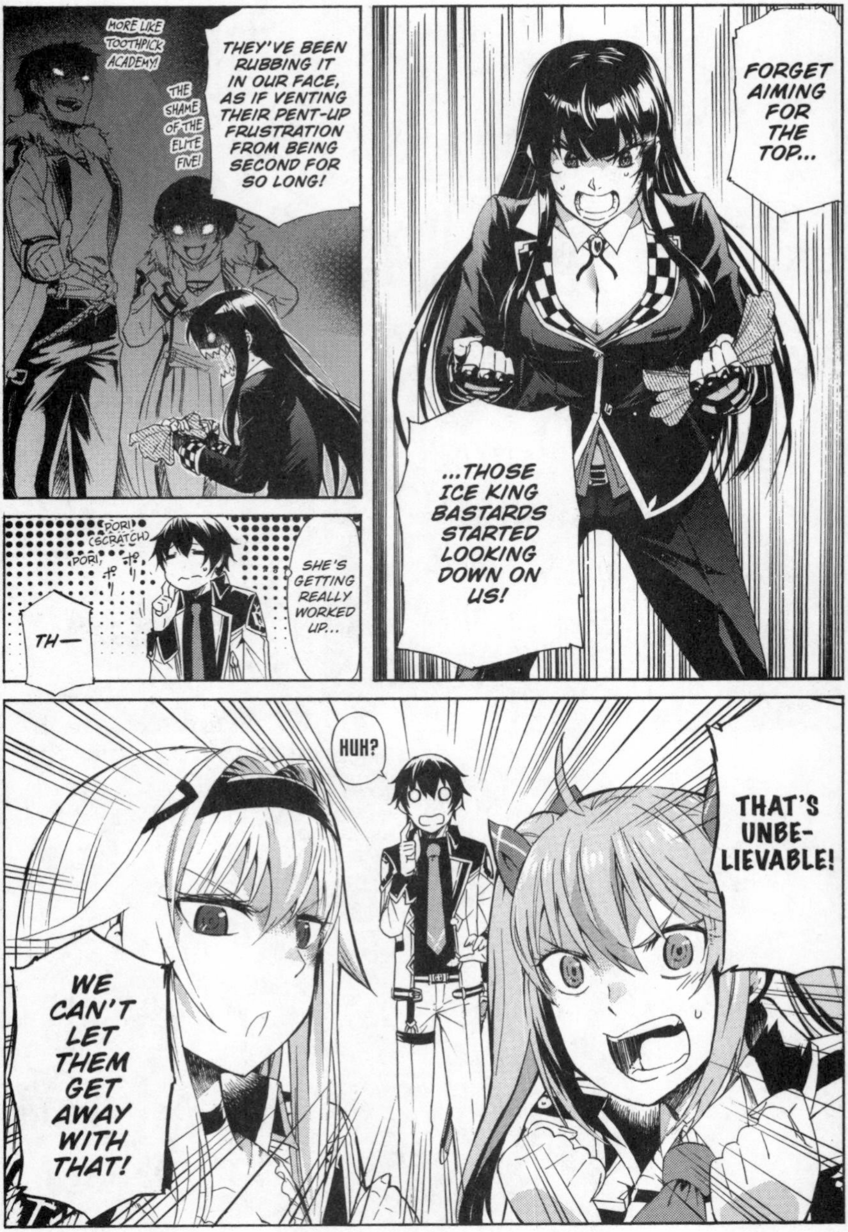
FORGET AIMING FOR THE TOP...
...THOSE ICE KING BASTARDS STARTED LOOKING DOWN ON US!
THEY'VE BEEN RUBBING IT IN OUR FACE, AS IF VENTING THEIR PENT-UP FRUSTRATION FROM BEING SECOND FOR SO LONG!
MORE LIKE TOOTHPICK ACADEMY!
THE SHAME OF THE ELITE FIVE!
SHE'S GETTING REALLY WORKED UP...
PORI (SCRATCH)
PORI
TH—
THAT'S UNBE-LIEVABLE!
HUH?
WE CAN'T LET THEM GET AWAY WITH THAT!

SO LAST NIGHT, I PULLED AN ALL-NIGHTER TO COME UP WITH OUR BEST POSSIBLE LINEUP!

NBA (WHOOSH)

MY POINT IS— WE CAN'T LOSE TO ICE KING ACADEMY, NO MATTER WHAT.

AHEM!

KASA (RUSTLE)

ELE___ H_Y FESTIVAL __TI_PANTS LIST

FIRST	ALLEN RODOL
SECOND	ROSE VALENCIA
CAPTAIN	LIA VESTERIA

DON (THUD)

TAKE A LOOK!

BAN (BAM)

MY ROLE AS THE FIRST WILL BE TO WEAR OUT OUR OPPONENTS, THEN ROSE AND LIA CAN FINISH THEM OFF.

IT'S A SOLID LINEUP.

...THIS IS ACTUALLY PRETTY REASONABLE FOR HER.

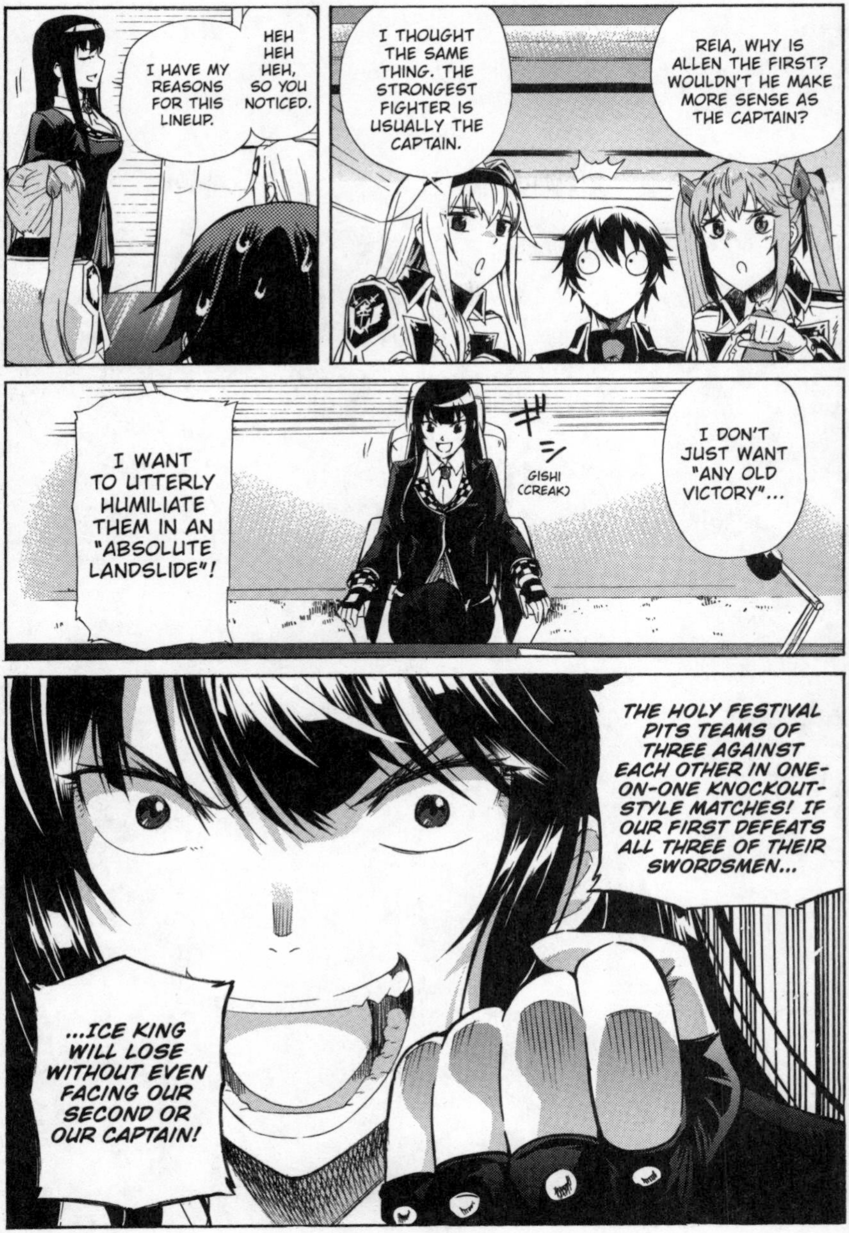
REIA, WHY IS ALLEN THE FIRST? WOULDN'T HE MAKE MORE SENSE AS THE CAPTAIN?
I THOUGHT THE SAME THING. THE STRONGEST FIGHTER IS USUALLY THE CAPTAIN.
HEH HEH HEH, SO YOU NOTICED.
I HAVE MY REASONS FOR THIS LINEUP.
I DON'T JUST WANT "ANY OLD VICTORY"...
GISHI (CREAK)
I WANT TO UTTERLY HUMILIATE THEM IN AN "ABSOLUTE LANDSLIDE"!
THE HOLY FESTIVAL PITS TEAMS OF THREE AGAINST EACH OTHER IN ONE-ON-ONE KNOCKOUT-STYLE MATCHES! IF OUR FIRST DEFEATS ALL THREE OF THEIR SWORDSMEN...
...ICE KING WILL LOSE WITHOUT EVEN FACING OUR SECOND OR OUR CAPTAIN!

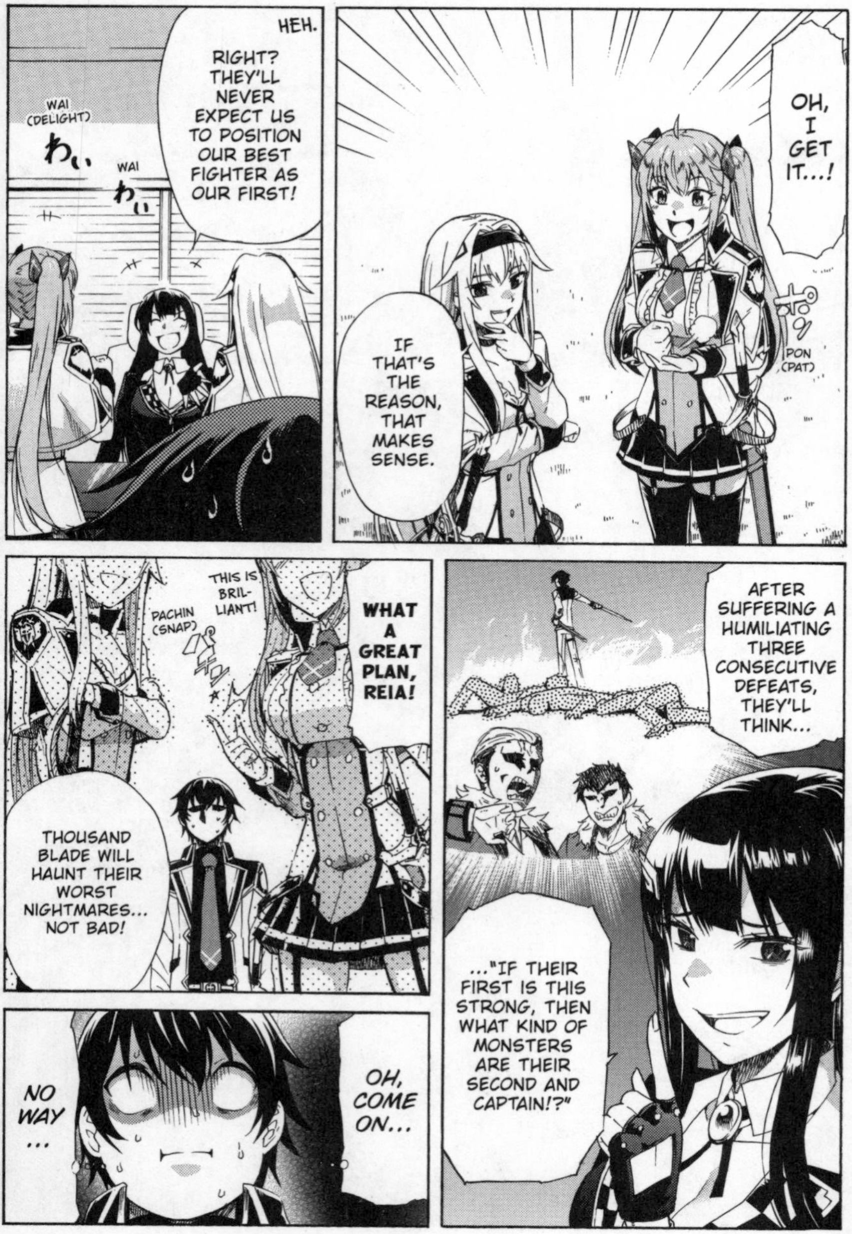

OH, I GET IT...!
PON (PAT)
IF THAT'S THE REASON, THAT MAKES SENSE.
HEH.
RIGHT? THEY'LL NEVER EXPECT US TO POSITION OUR BEST FIGHTER AS OUR FIRST!
WAI (DELIGHT)
わい
WAI
わい
AFTER SUFFERING A HUMILIATING THREE CONSECUTIVE DEFEATS, THEY'LL THINK...
..."IF THEIR FIRST IS THIS STRONG, THEN WHAT KIND OF MONSTERS ARE THEIR SECOND AND CAPTAIN!?"
WHAT A GREAT PLAN, REIA!
THIS IS BRIL-LIANT!
PACHIN (SNAP)
THOUSAND BLADE WILL HAUNT THEIR WORST NIGHTMARES... NOT BAD!
OH, COME ON...
NO WAY ...

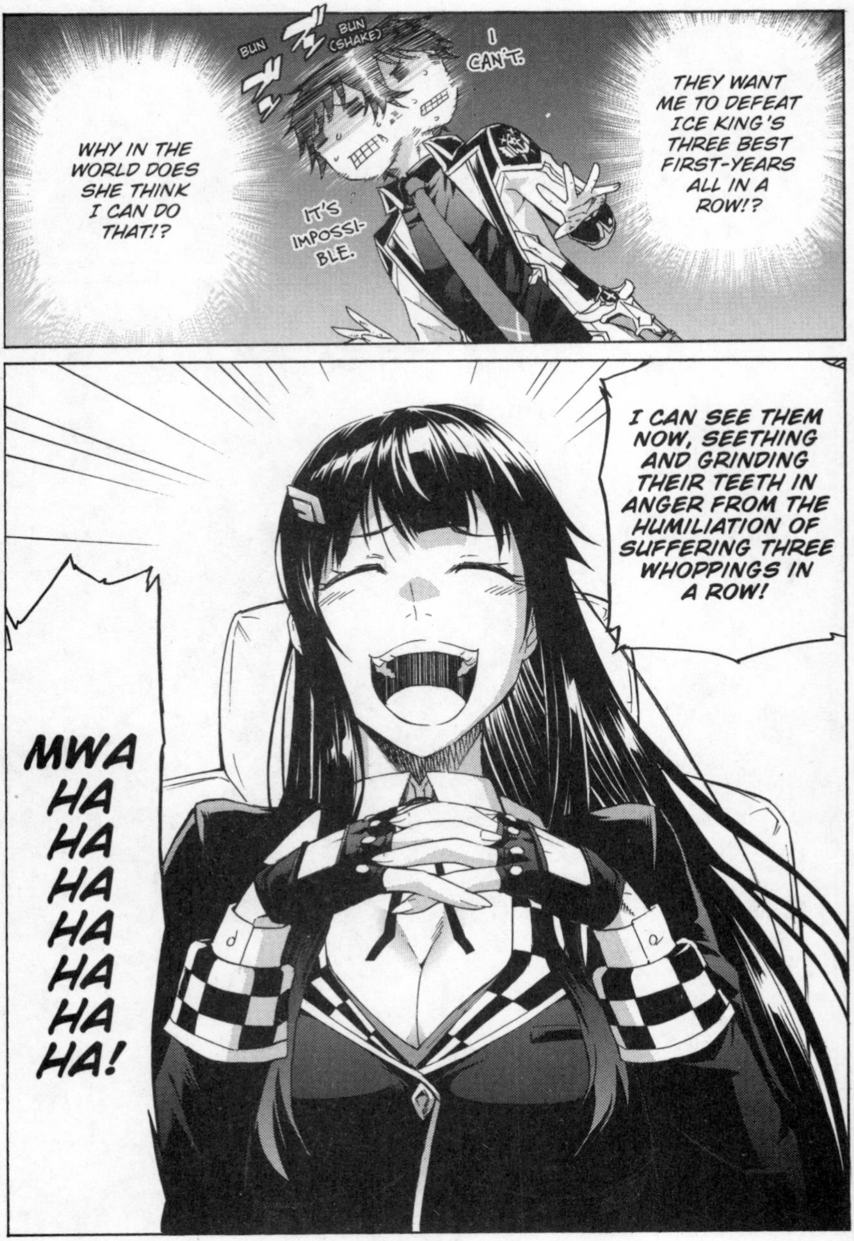
THEY WANT ME TO DEFEAT ICE KING'S THREE BEST FIRST-YEARS ALL IN A ROW!?
I CAN'T.
BUN (SHAKE)
BUN
IT'S IMPOSSI-BLE.
WHY IN THE WORLD DOES SHE THINK I CAN DO THAT!?
I CAN SEE THEM NOW, SEETHING AND GRINDING THEIR TEETH IN ANGER FROM THE HUMILIATION OF SUFFERING THREE WHOPPINGS IN A ROW!
MWA HA HA HA HA HA HA HA!

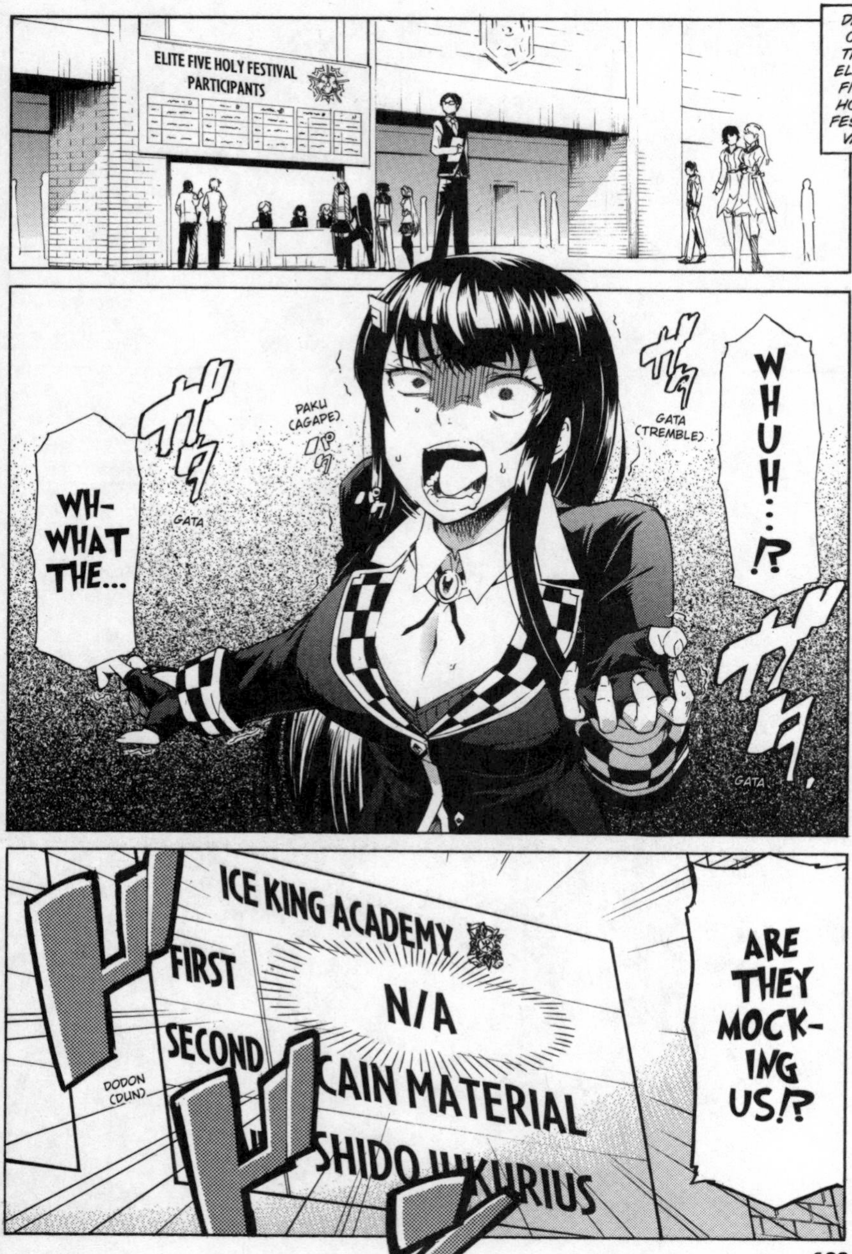
DAY OF THE ELITE FIVE HOLY FESTIVAL
ELITE FIVE HOLY FESTIVAL PARTICIPANTS
WHUH...!?
GATA (TREMBLE)
PAKU (AGAPE)
GATA
WH-WHAT THE...
GATA
ARE THEY MOCKING US!?
ICE KING ACADEMY
FIRST
N/A
SECOND
CAIN MATERIAL
DODON (DUN)

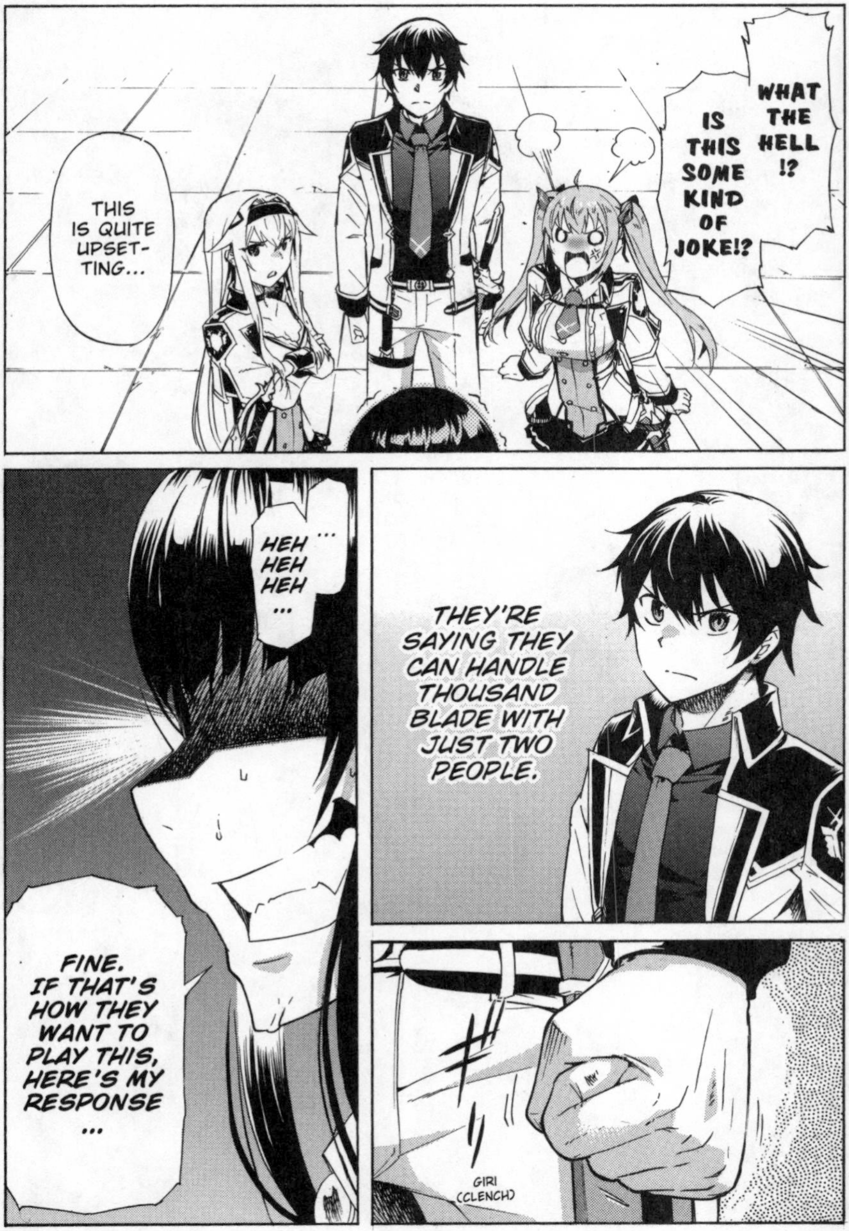
WHAT THE HELL!?
IS THIS SOME KIND OF JOKE!?
THIS IS QUITE UPSET-TING...
THEY'RE SAYING THEY CAN HANDLE THOUSAND BLADE WITH JUST TWO PEOPLE.
GIRI (CLENCH)
...HEH HEH HEH...
FINE. IF THAT'S HOW THEY WANT TO PLAY THIS, HERE'S MY RESPONSE...

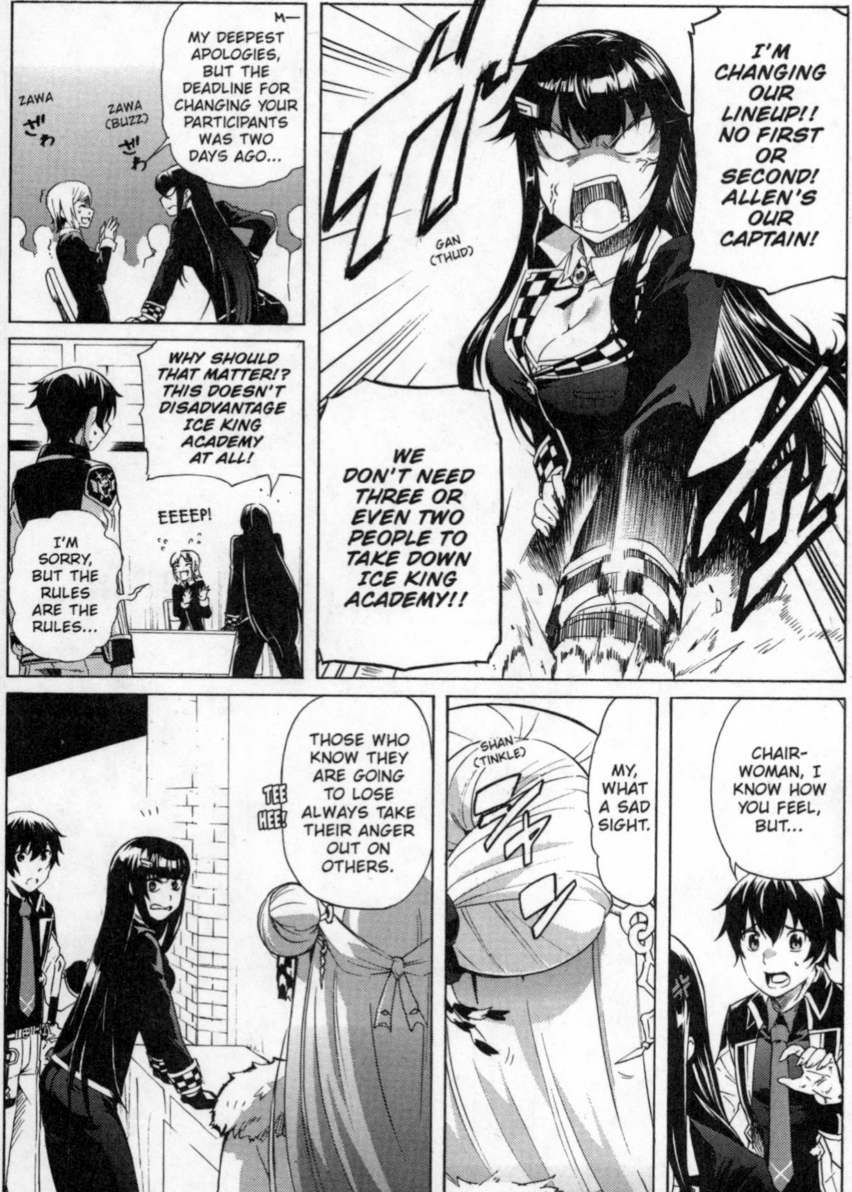
I'M CHANGING OUR LINEUP!! NO FIRST OR SECOND! ALLEN'S OUR CAPTAIN!
GAN (THUD)
WE DON'T NEED THREE OR EVEN TWO PEOPLE TO TAKE DOWN ICE KING ACADEMY!!
M—
MY DEEPEST APOLOGIES, BUT THE DEADLINE FOR CHANGING YOUR PARTICIPANTS WAS TWO DAYS AGO...
ZAWA (BUZZ)
ZAWA
WHY SHOULD THAT MATTER!? THIS DOESN'T DISADVANTAGE ICE KING ACADEMY AT ALL!
EEEEP!
I'M SORRY, BUT THE RULES ARE THE RULES...
CHAIR-WOMAN, I KNOW HOW YOU FEEL, BUT...
MY, WHAT A SAD SIGHT.
SHAN (TINKLE)
THOSE WHO KNOW THEY ARE GOING TO LOSE ALWAYS TAKE THEIR ANGER OUT ON OTHERS.
TEE HEE!

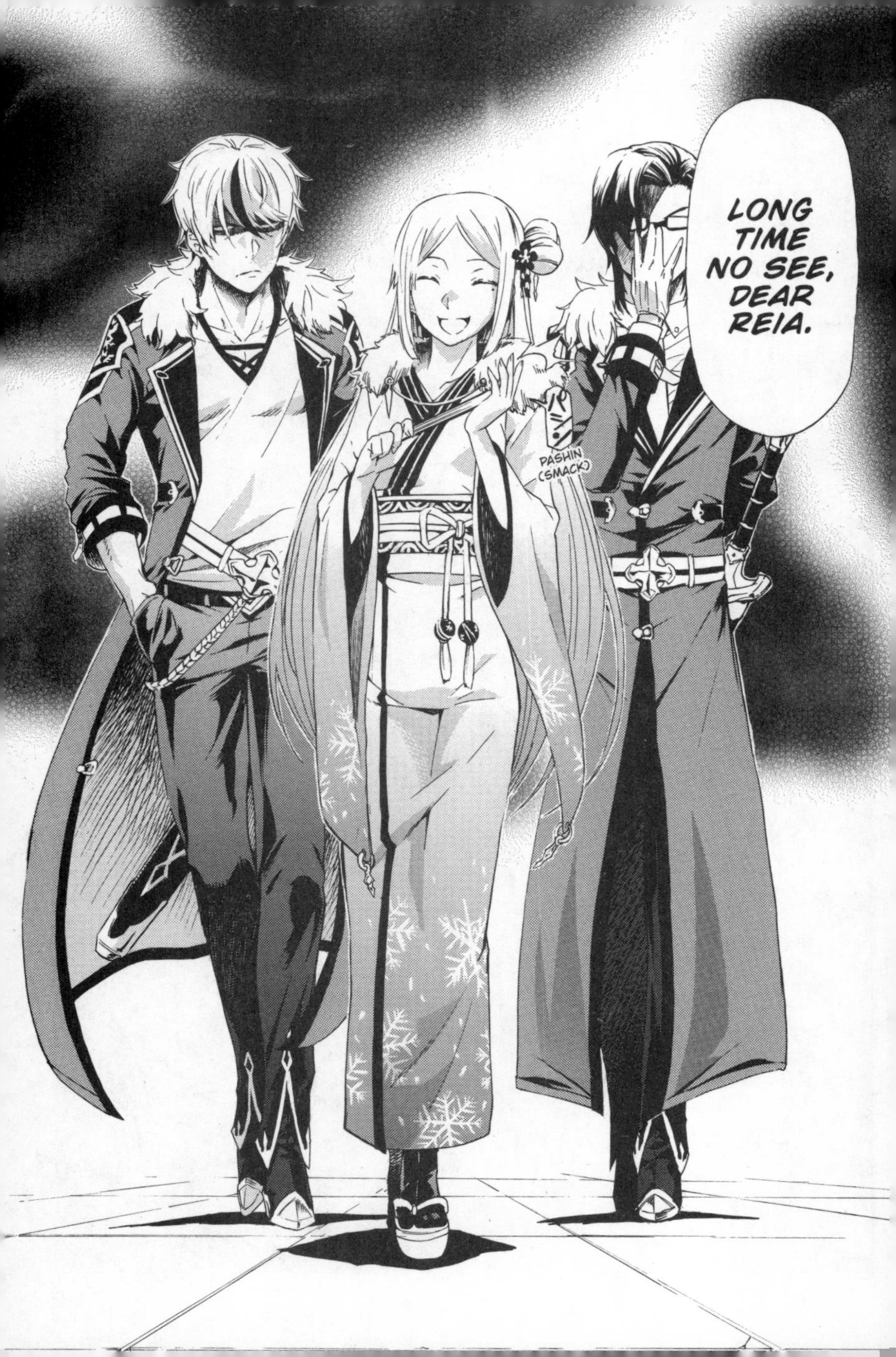
LONG TIME NO SEE, DEAR REIA.
パシン
PASHIN (SMACK)

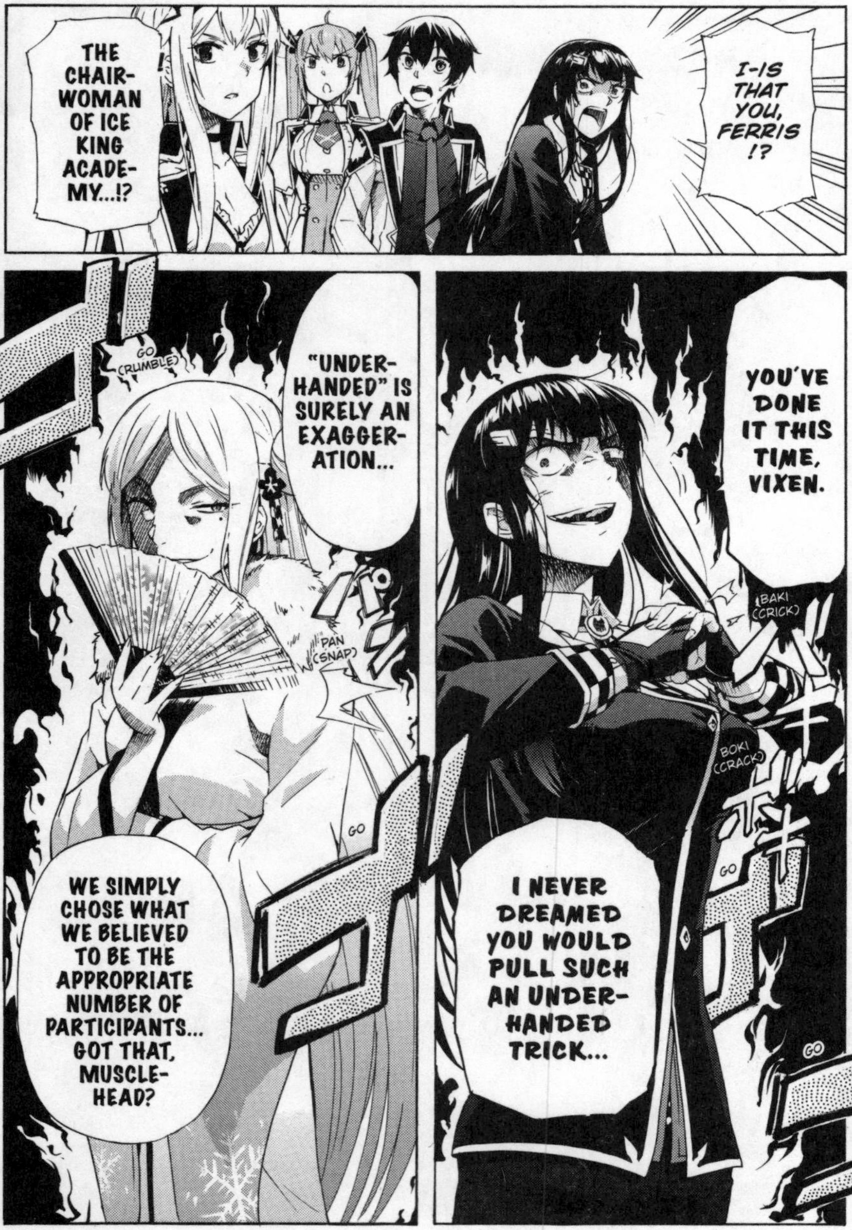
I-IS THAT YOU, FERRIS!?
THE CHAIRWOMAN OF ICE KING ACADEMY...!?
YOU'VE DONE IT THIS TIME, VIXEN.
BAKI (CRICK)
BOKI (CRACK)
I NEVER DREAMED YOU WOULD PULL SUCH AN UNDERHANDED TRICK...
GO
GO
GO (RUMBLE)
"UNDERHANDED" IS SURELY AN EXAGGERATION...
PAN (SNAP)
GO
WE SIMPLY CHOSE WHAT WE BELIEVED TO BE THE APPROPRIATE NUMBER OF PARTICIPANTS... GOT THAT, MUSCLEHEAD?

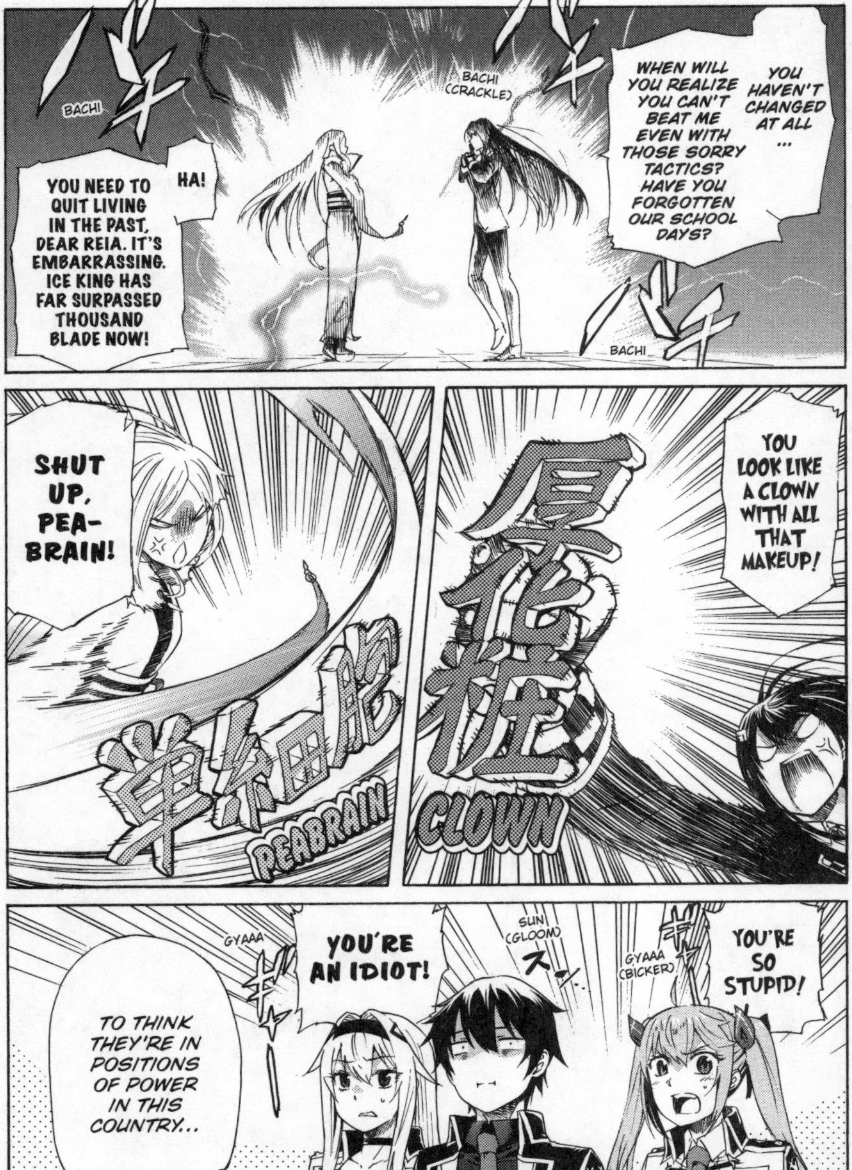

YOU HAVEN'T CHANGED AT ALL...
WHEN WILL YOU REALIZE YOU CAN'T BEAT ME EVEN WITH THOSE SORRY TACTICS? HAVE YOU FORGOTTEN OUR SCHOOL DAYS?
BACHI (CRACKLE)
BACHI
HA!
YOU NEED TO QUIT LIVING IN THE PAST, DEAR REIA. IT'S EMBARRASSING. ICE KING HAS FAR SURPASSED THOUSAND BLADE NOW!
BACHI
YOU LOOK LIKE A CLOWN WITH ALL THAT MAKEUP!
厚化粧
CLOWN
SHUT UP, PEA-BRAIN!
単細胞
PEABRAIN
YOU'RE SO STUPID!
GYAAA (BICKER)
SUN (GLOOM)
YOU'RE AN IDIOT!
GYAAA
TO THINK THEY'RE IN POSITIONS OF POWER IN THIS COUNTRY...

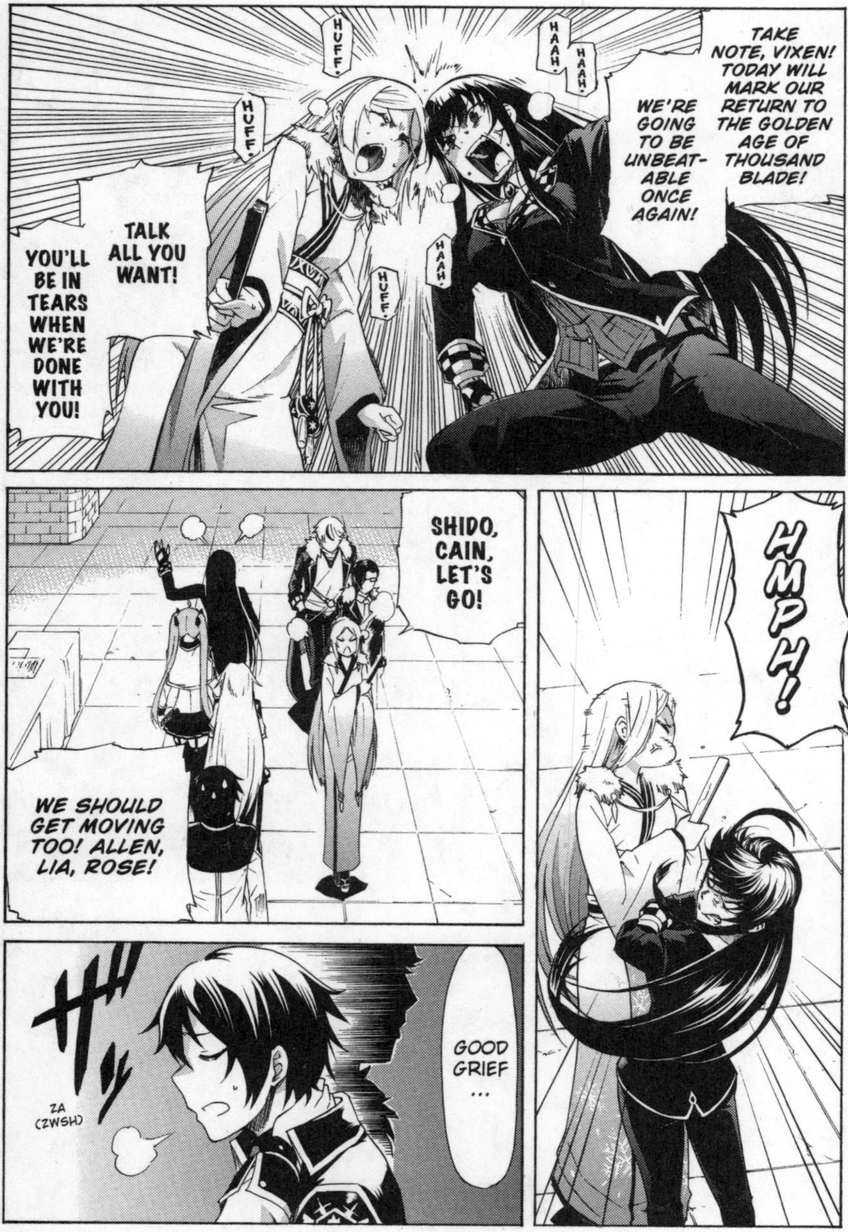
TAKE NOTE, VIXEN! TODAY WILL MARK OUR RETURN TO THE GOLDEN AGE OF THOUSAND BLADE!
WE'RE GOING TO BE UNBEAT-ABLE ONCE AGAIN!
HAAH. HAAH.
HUFF. HUFF.
HAAH.
HUFF.
TALK ALL YOU WANT!
YOU'LL BE IN TEARS WHEN WE'RE DONE WITH YOU!
HMPH!
SHIDO, CAIN, LET'S GO!
WE SHOULD GET MOVING TOO! ALLEN, LIA, ROSE!
GOOD GRIEF...
ZA (ZWSH)

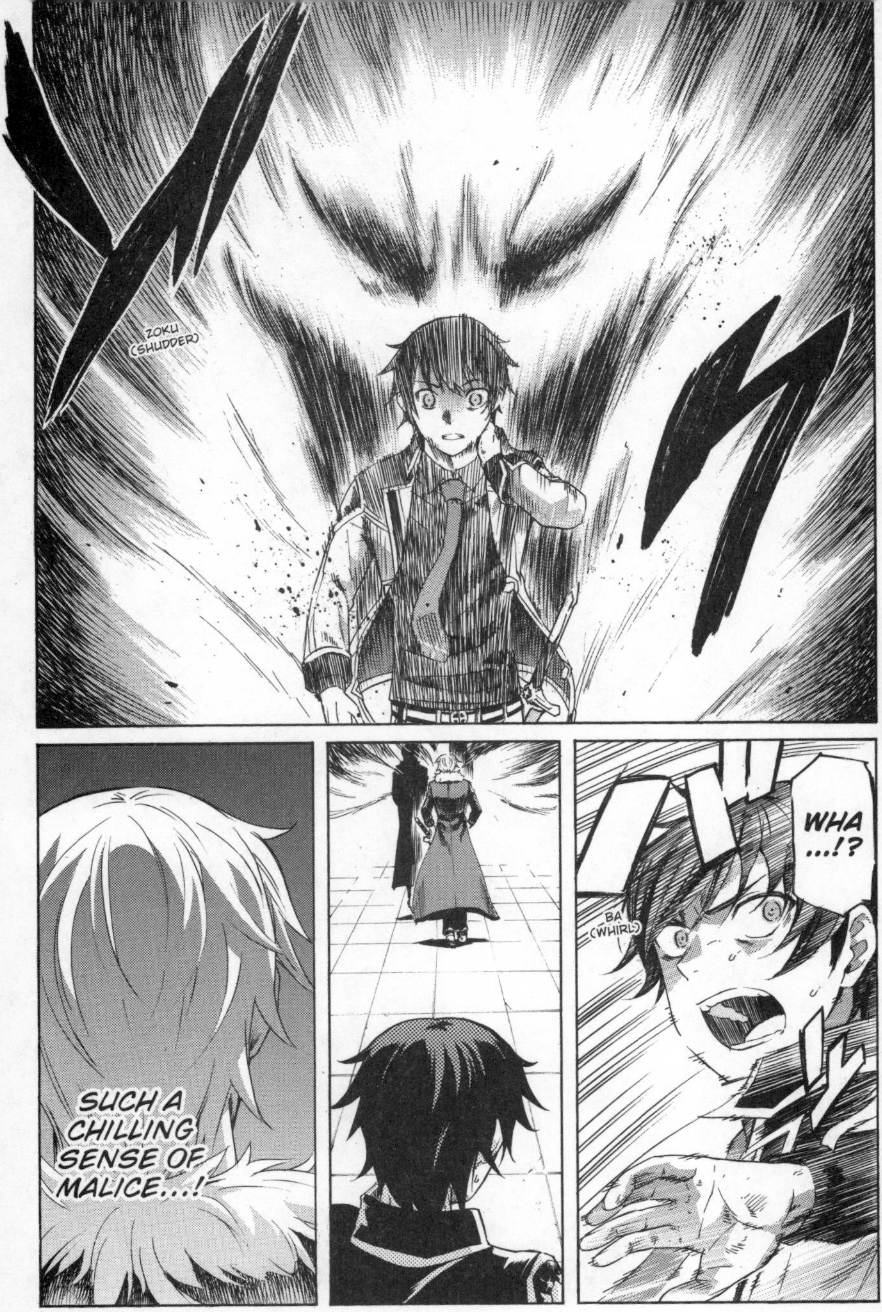
ZOKU (SHUDDER)
WHA ...!?
BA (WHIRL)
SUCH A CHILLING SENSE OF MALICE...!

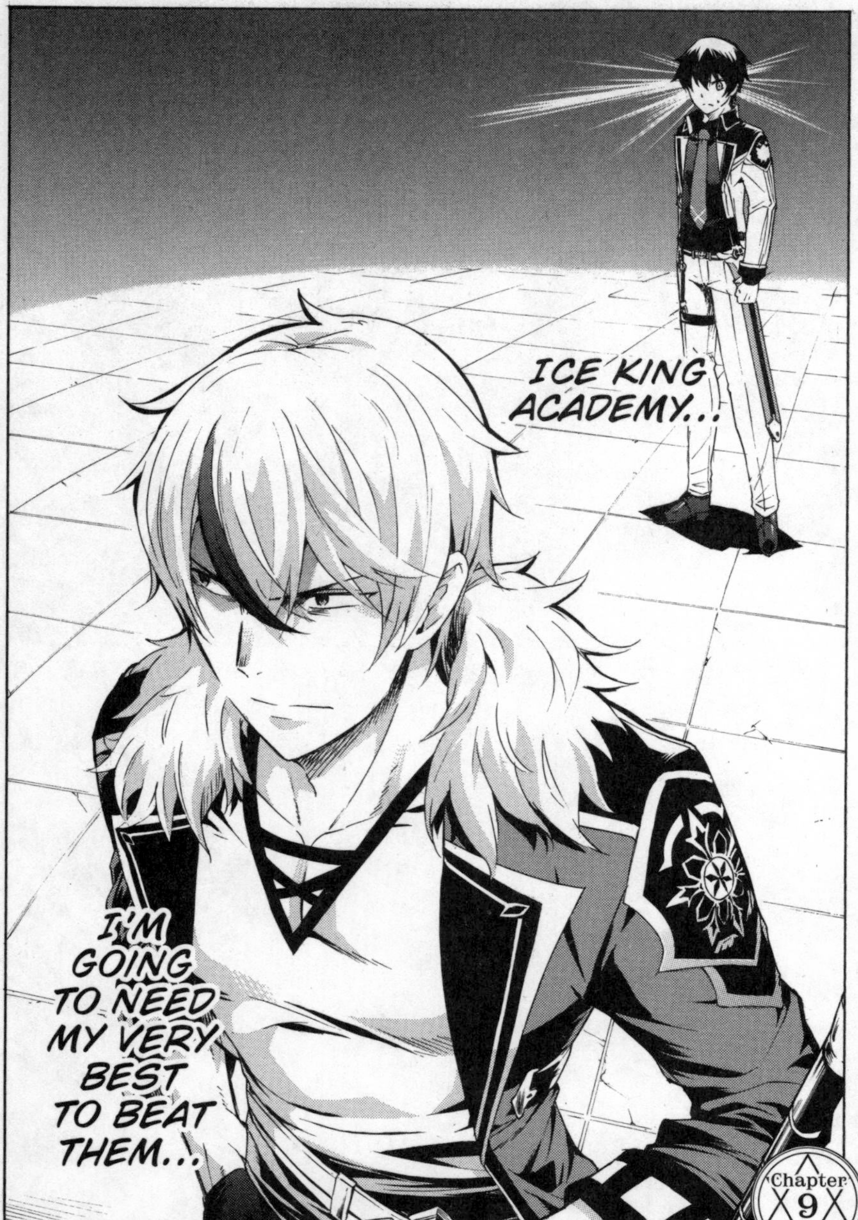
ICE KING ACADEMY...
I'M GOING TO NEED MY VERY BEST TO BEAT THEM...
Chapter 9 End

Chapter 10

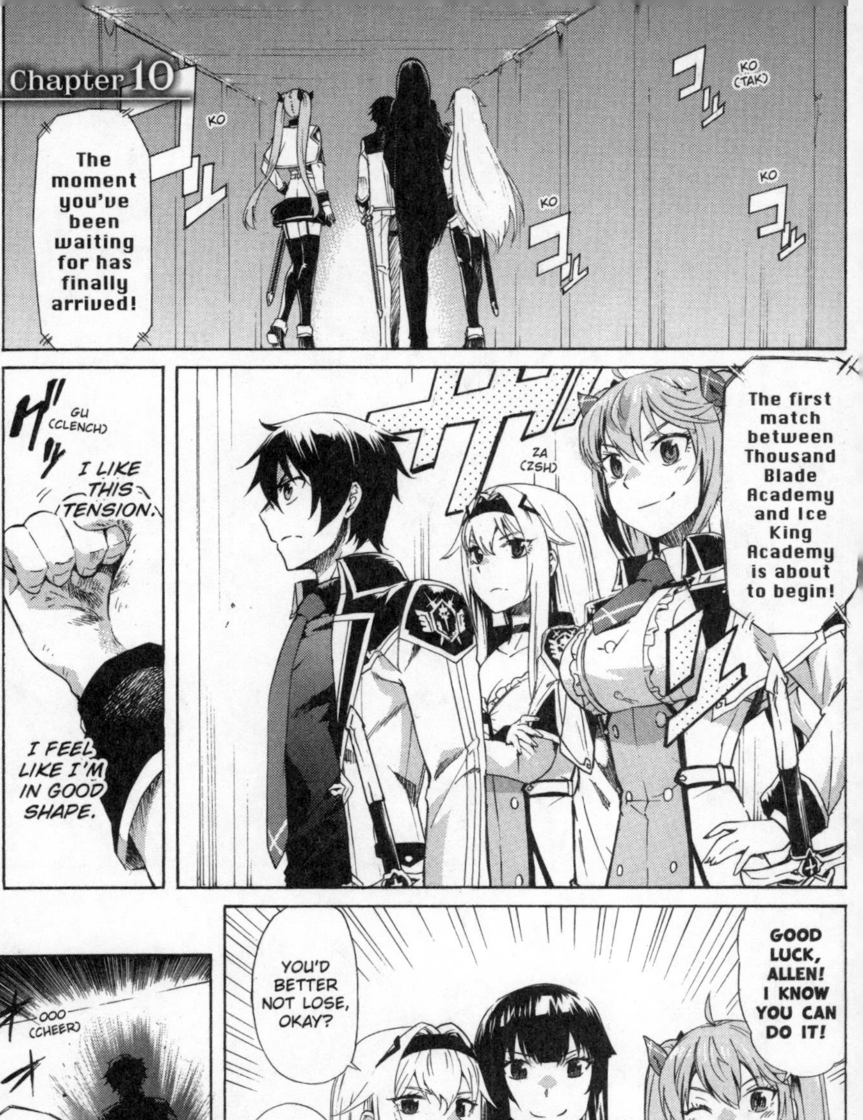
KO (TAK)
KO
KO
KO
The moment you've been waiting for has finally arrived!
The first match between Thousand Blade Academy and Ice King Academy is about to begin!
ZA (ZSH)
GU (CLENCH)
I LIKE THIS TENSION.
I FEEL LIKE I'M IN GOOD SHAPE.
GOOD LUCK, ALLEN! I KNOW YOU CAN DO IT!
YOU'D BETTER NOT LOSE, OKAY?
THANKS. I'LL GIVE IT MY BEST SHOT.
OOO (CHEER)
From the west gate...

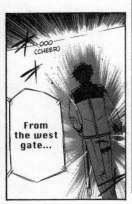

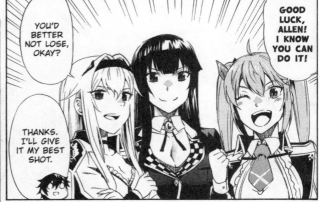

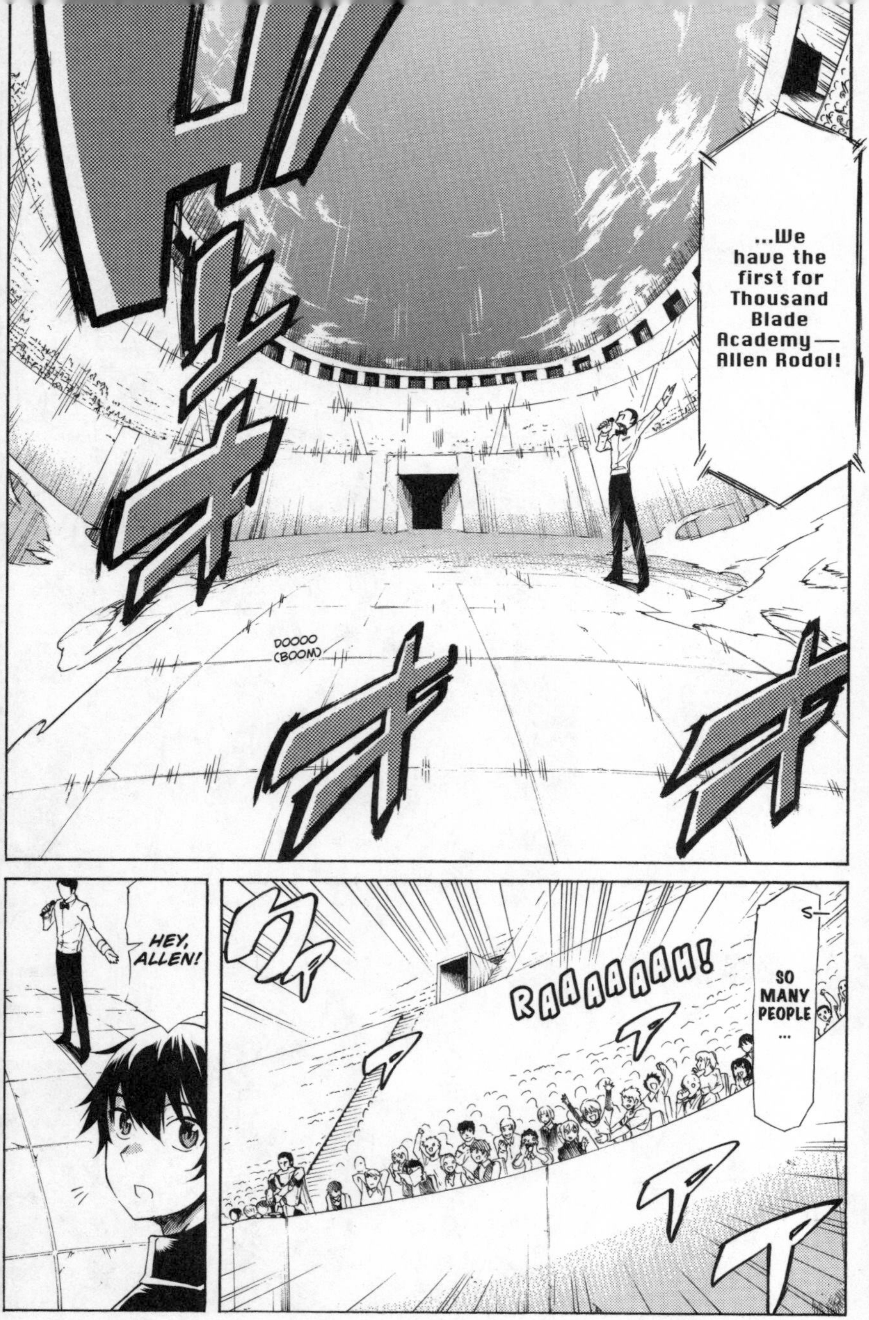

...We have the first for Thousand Blade Academy—Allen Rodol!
DOOOO (BOOM)
S—
SO MANY PEOPLE ...
RAAAAAAAH!
HEY, ALLEN!

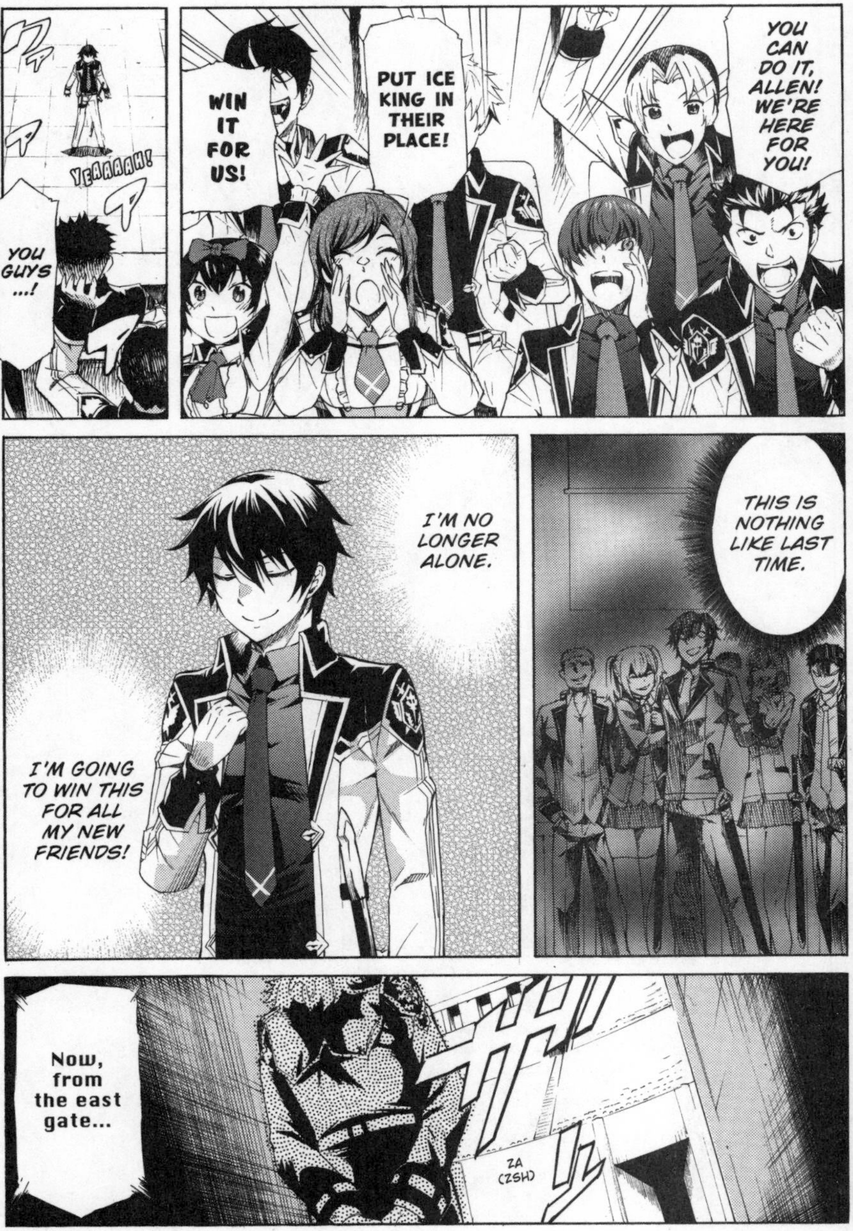
YOU CAN DO IT, ALLEN! WE'RE HERE FOR YOU!
PUT ICE KING IN THEIR PLACE!
WIN IT FOR US!
YEAAAAH!
YOU GUYS ...!
THIS IS NOTHING LIKE LAST TIME.
I'M NO LONGER ALONE.
I'M GOING TO WIN THIS FOR ALL MY NEW FRIENDS!
Now, from the east gate...
ZA (ZSH)

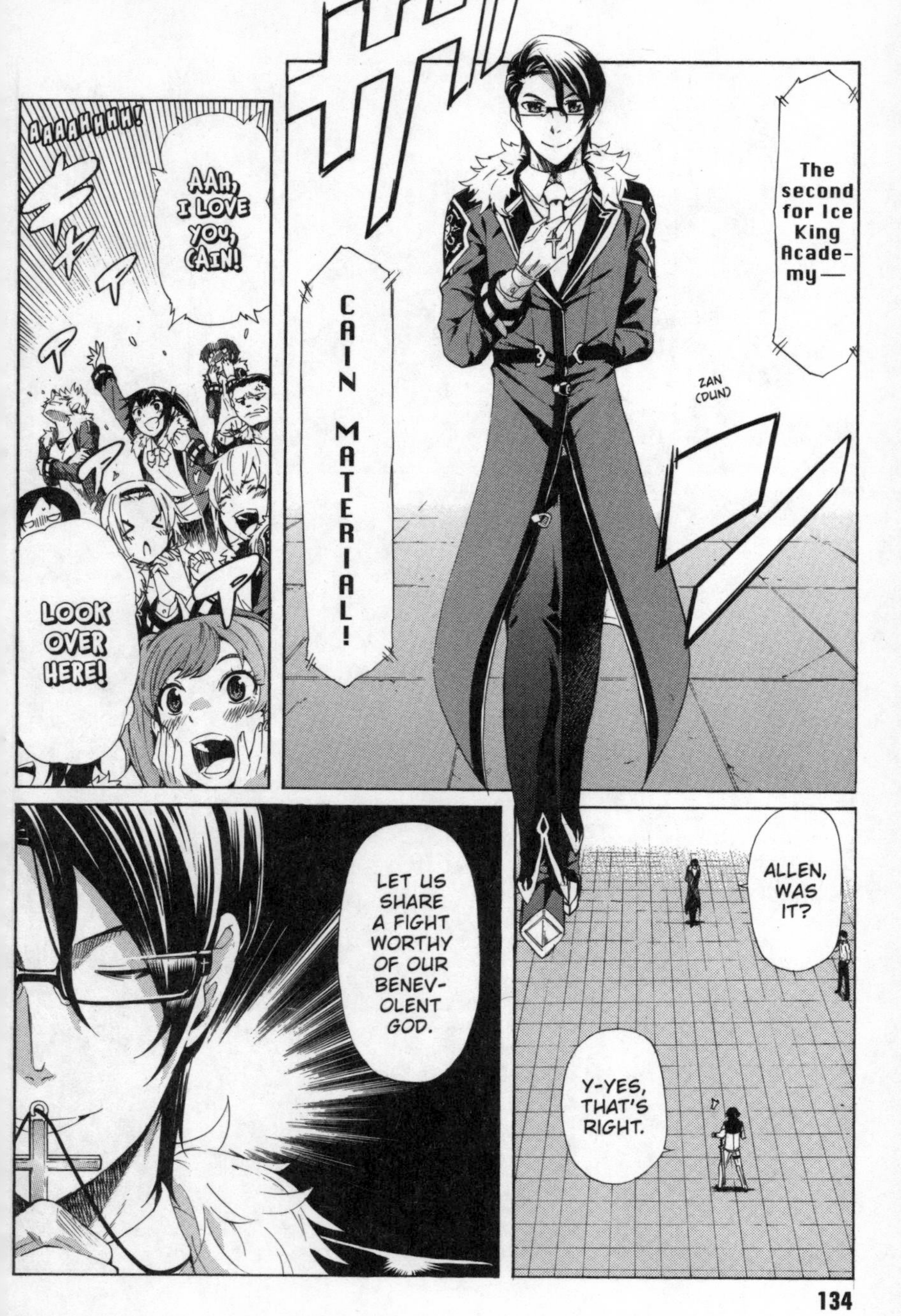
The second for Ice King Acade-my—
CAIN MATERIAL!
ZAN (DUN)
AAAAHHHH!
AAH, I LOVE YOU, CAIN!
LOOK OVER HERE!
ALLEN, WAS IT?
Y-YES, THAT'S RIGHT.
LET US SHARE A FIGHT WORTHY OF OUR BENEV-OLENT GOD.

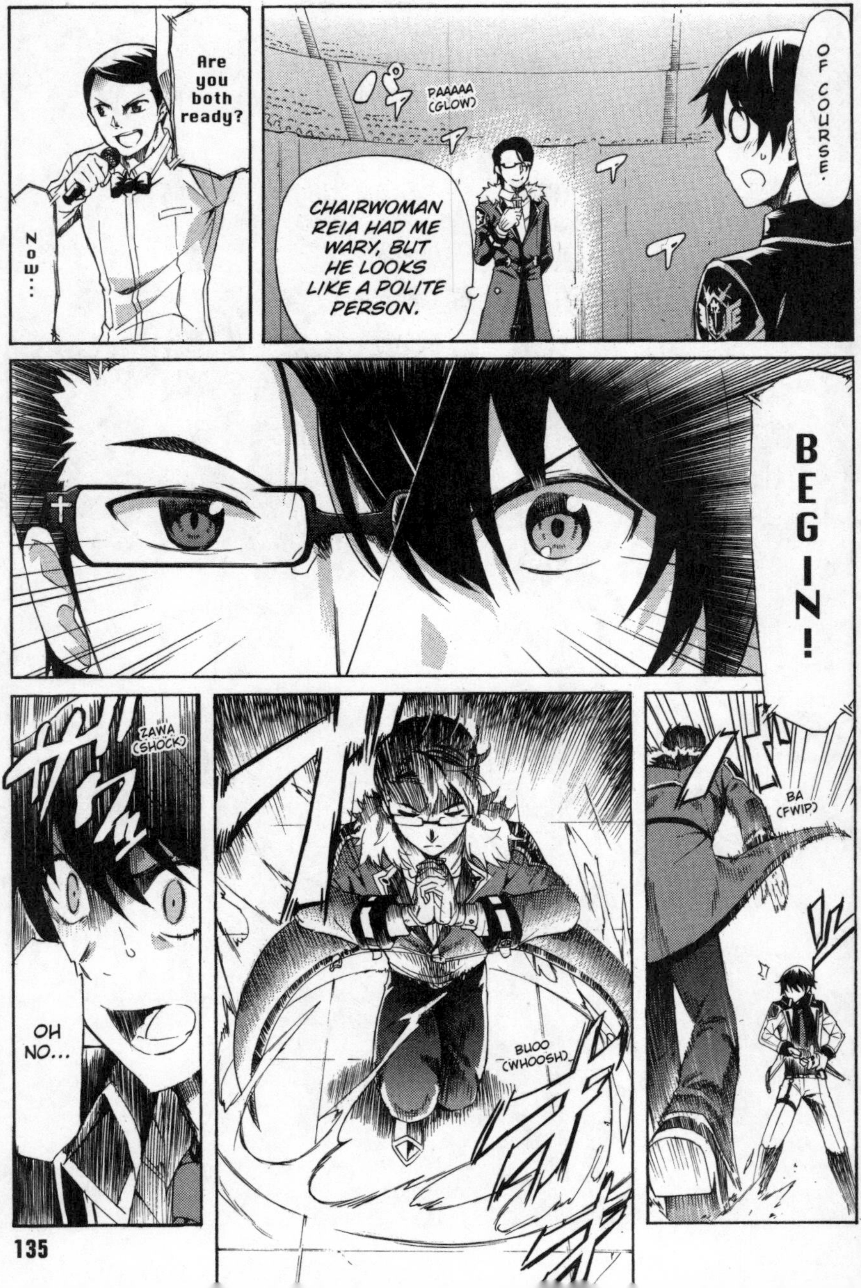
OF COURSE.
PAAAAA (GLOW)
CHAIRWOMAN REIA HAD ME WARY, BUT HE LOOKS LIKE A POLITE PERSON.
Are you both ready?
NOW...
BEGIN!
BA (FWIP)
BUOO (WHOOSH)
ZAWA (SHOCK)
OH NO...

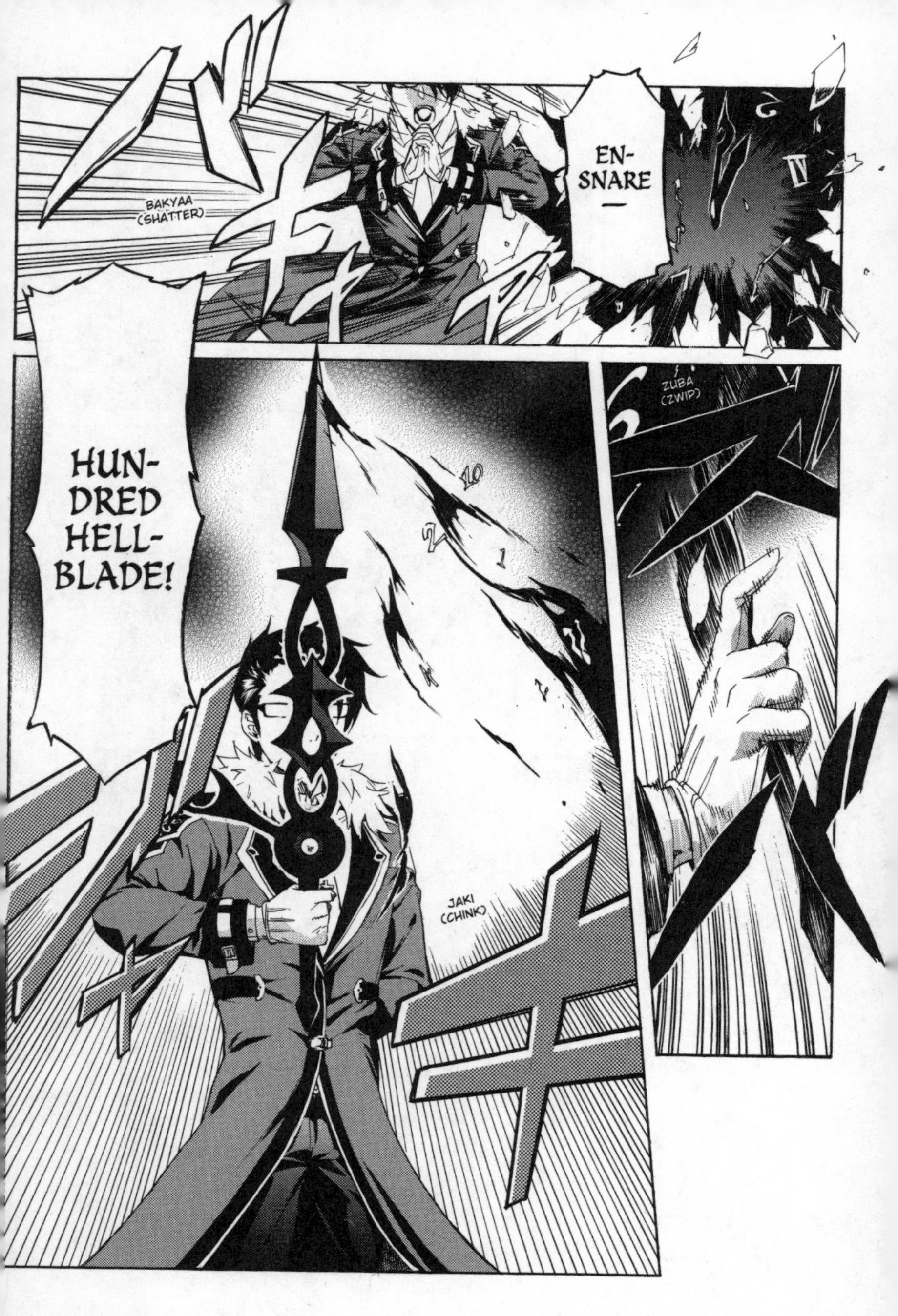
EN-
SNARE
—
BAKYAA
(SHATTER)
ZUBA
(ZWIP)
HUN-
DRED
HELL-
BLADE!
JAKI
(CHINK)

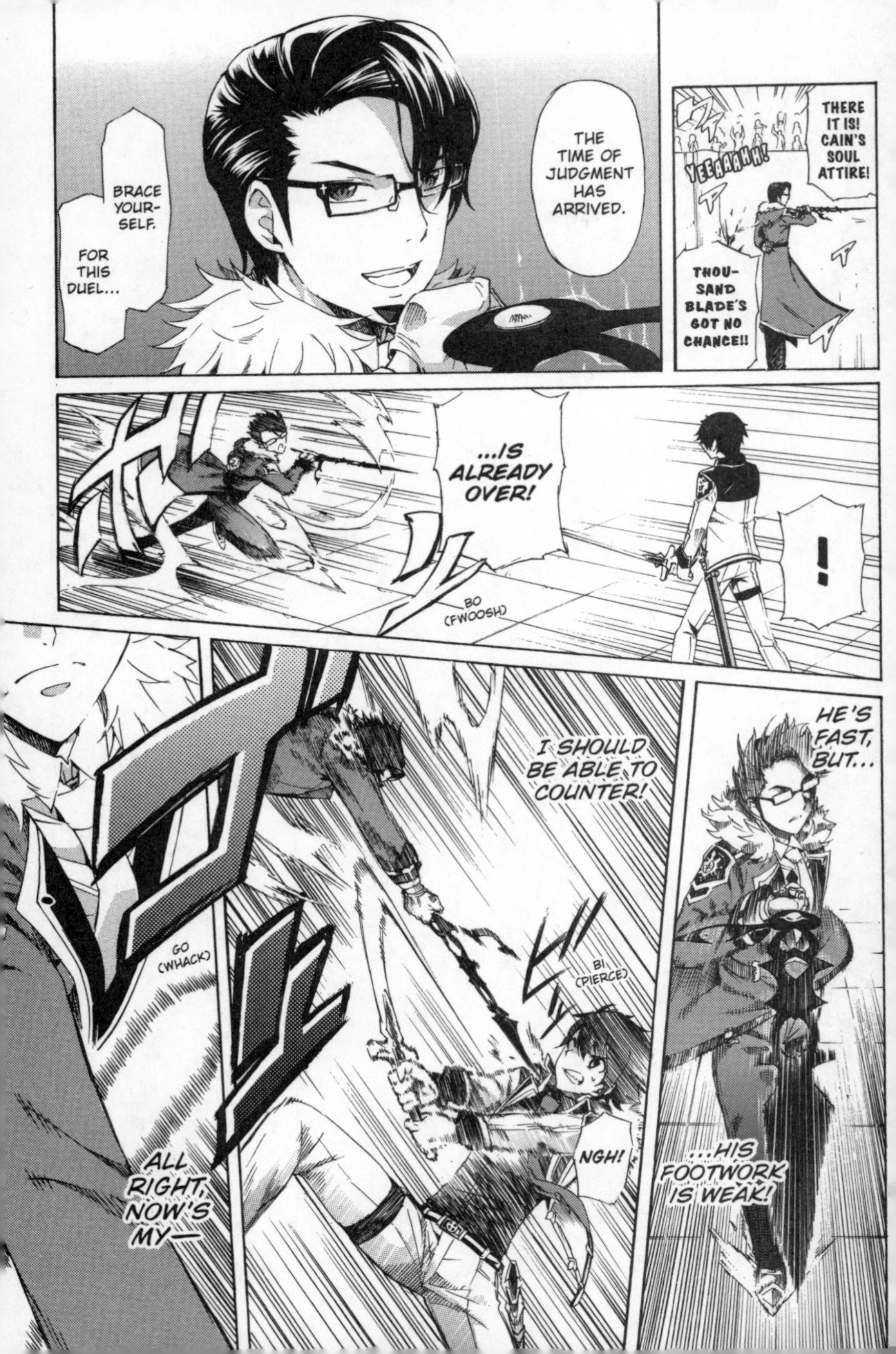
THERE IT IS! CAIN'S SOUL ATTIRE!
YEEAAAHH!
THOUSAND BLADE'S GOT NO CHANCE!!
THE TIME OF JUDGMENT HAS ARRIVED.
BRACE YOURSELF.
FOR THIS DUEL...
!
...IS ALREADY OVER!
BO (FWOOSH)
HE'S FAST, BUT...
...HIS FOOTWORK IS WEAK!
I SHOULD BE ABLE TO COUNTER!
BI (PIERCE)
NGH!
GO (WHACK)
ALL RIGHT, NOW'S MY—

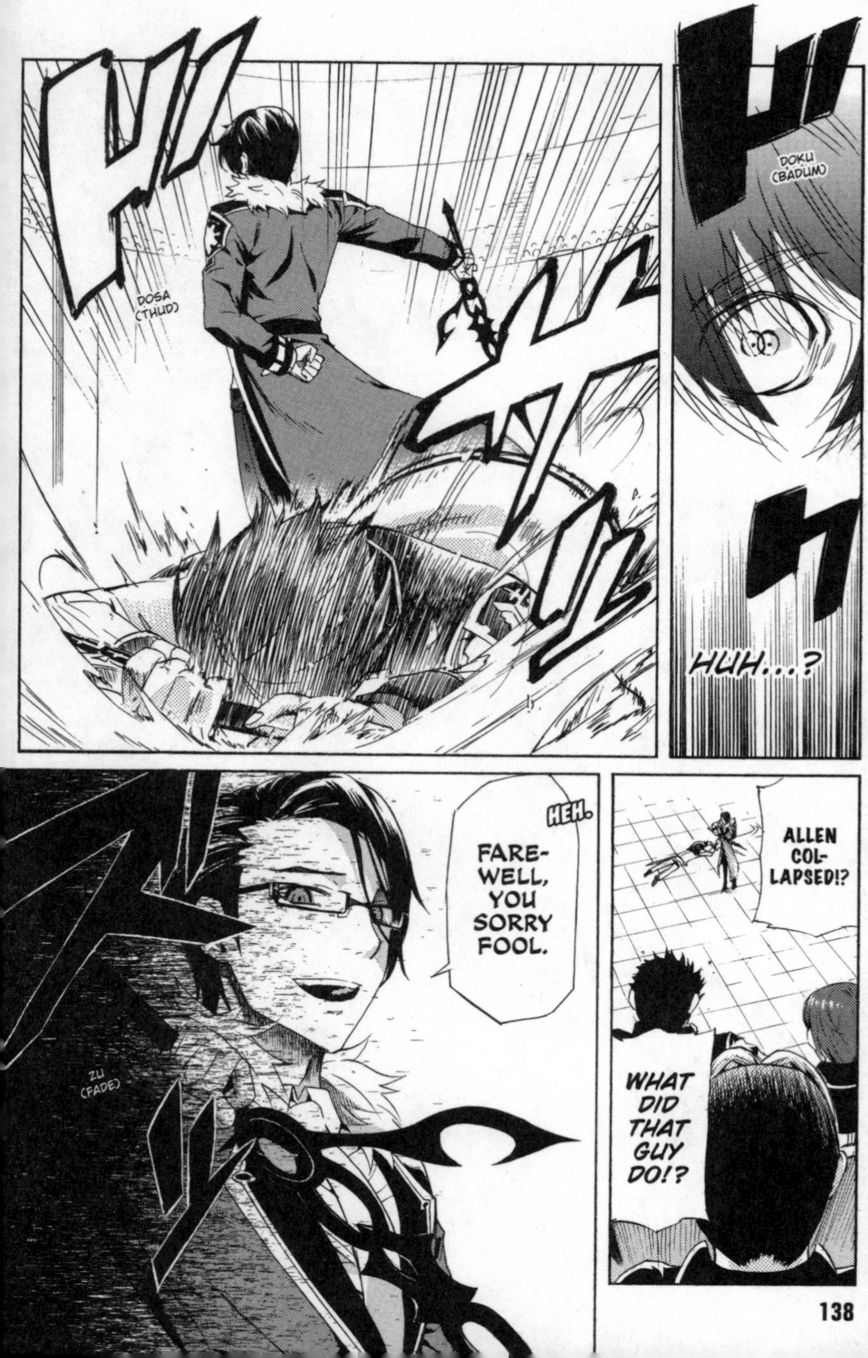
DOKU (BADUM)
HUH...?
DOSA (THUD)
ALLEN COL-LAPSED!?
WHAT DID THAT GUY DO!?
HEH.
FARE-WELL, YOU SORRY FOOL.
ZU (FADE)

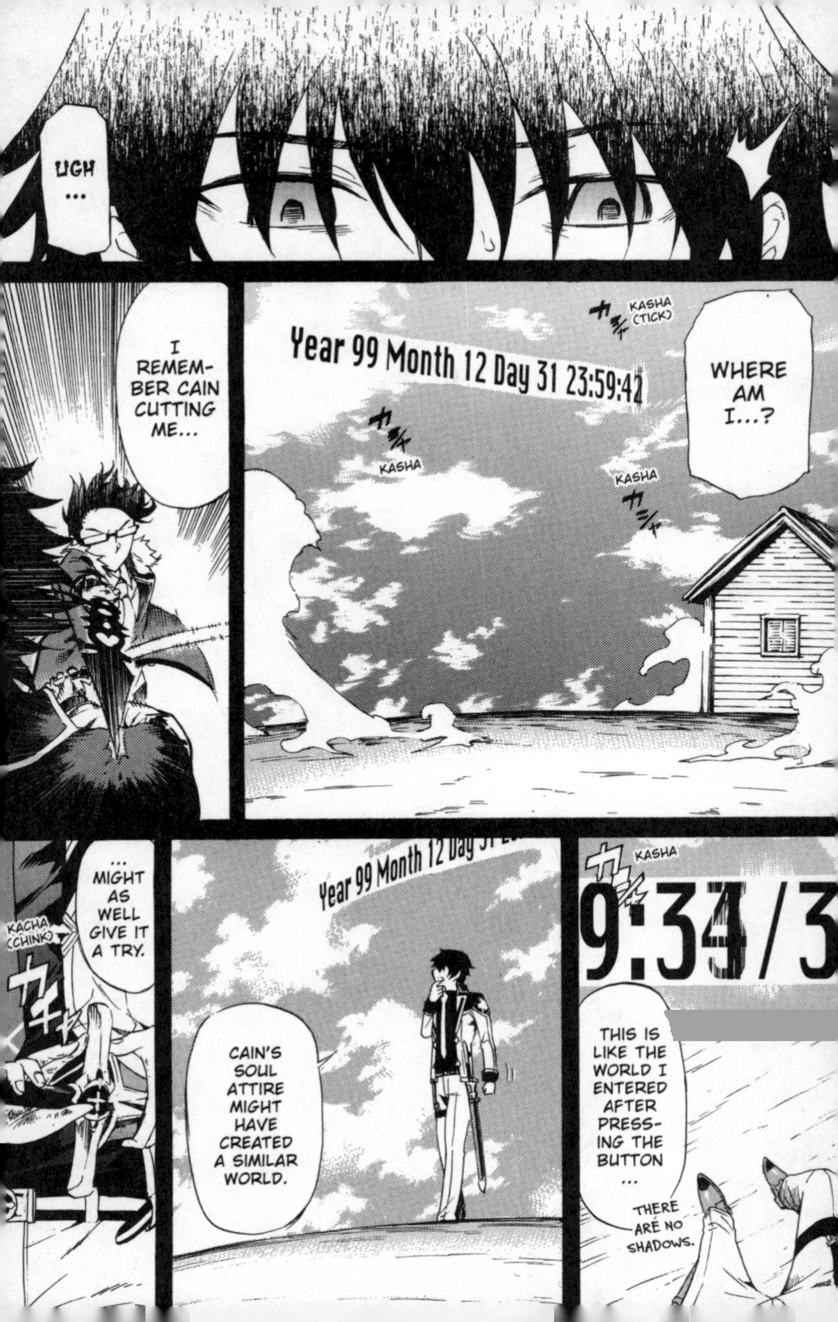
UGH ...
KASHA (TICK)
WHERE AM I...?
Year 99 Month 12 Day 31 23:59:42
KASHA
KASHA
I REMEMBER CAIN CUTTING ME...
KASHA
9:34/3
THIS IS LIKE THE WORLD I ENTERED AFTER PRESSING THE BUTTON ...
THERE ARE NO SHADOWS.
Year 99 Month 12 Day 31
CAIN'S SOUL ATTIRE MIGHT HAVE CREATED A SIMILAR WORLD.
... MIGHT AS WELL GIVE IT A TRY.
KACHA (CHINK)

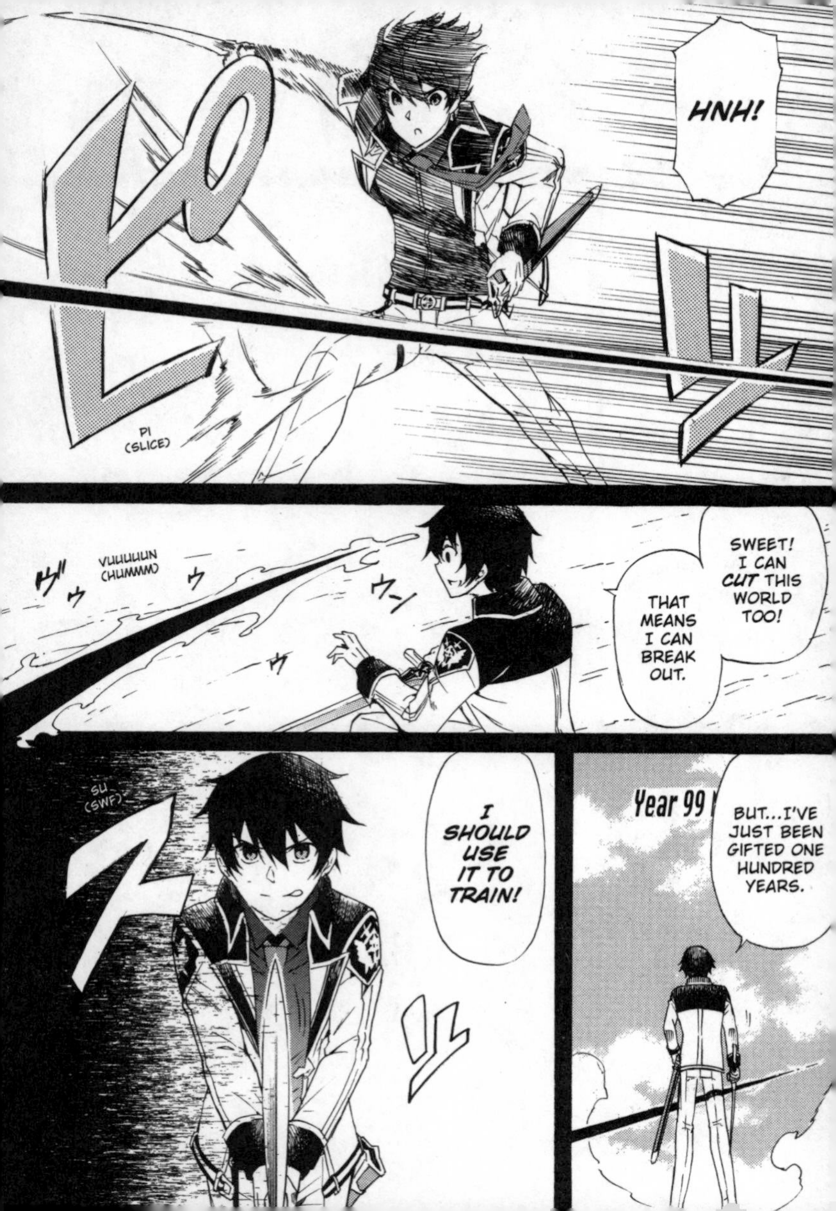
HNH!
PI
(SLICE)
SWEET! I CAN CUT THIS WORLD TOO!
THAT MEANS I CAN BREAK OUT.
VUUUUUN
(HUMMM)
Year 99
BUT...I'VE JUST BEEN GIFTED ONE HUNDRED YEARS.
I SHOULD USE IT TO TRAIN!
SU
(SWF)

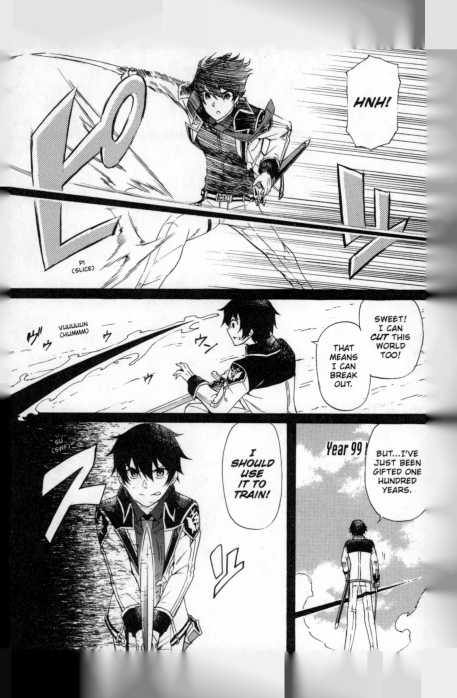

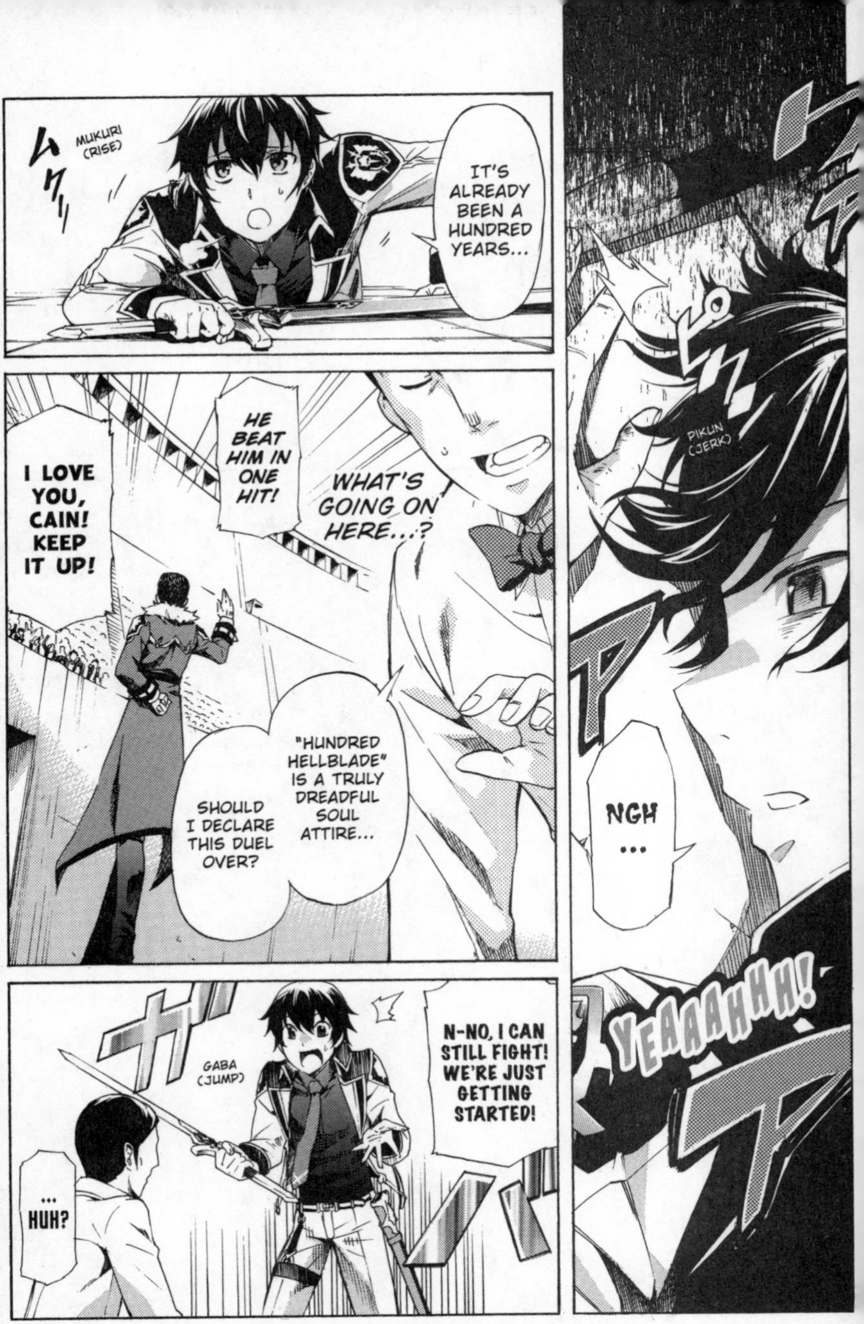
PIKUN (JERK)
NGH...
YEAAAHHH!
IT'S ALREADY BEEN A HUNDRED YEARS...
MUKURI (RISE)
WHAT'S GOING ON HERE...?
HE BEAT HIM IN ONE HIT!
I LOVE YOU, CAIN! KEEP IT UP!
"HUNDRED HELLBLADE" IS A TRULY DREADFUL SOUL ATTIRE...
SHOULD I DECLARE THIS DUEL OVER?
N-NO, I CAN STILL FIGHT! WE'RE JUST GETTING STARTED!
GABA (JUMP)
...HUH?

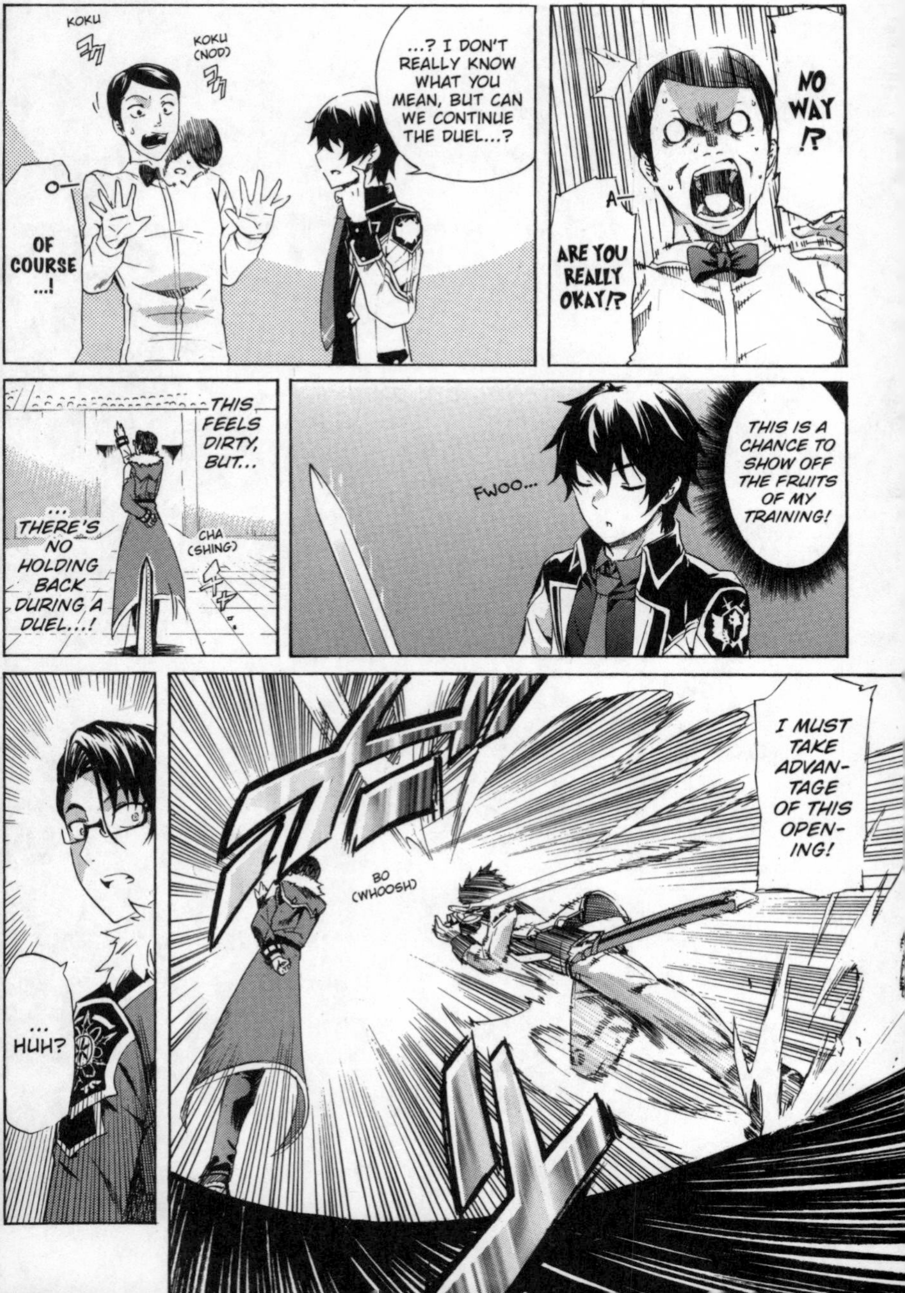
NO WAY!?
A—
ARE YOU REALLY OKAY!?
...? I DON'T REALLY KNOW WHAT YOU MEAN, BUT CAN WE CONTINUE THE DUEL...?
KOKU (NOD)
KOKU
O—
OF COURSE...!
THIS IS A CHANCE TO SHOW OFF THE FRUITS OF MY TRAINING!
FWOO...
THIS FEELS DIRTY, BUT...
...THERE'S NO HOLDING BACK DURING A DUEL...!
CHA (SHING)
I MUST TAKE ADVANTAGE OF THIS OPENING!
BO (WHOOSH)
...HUH?

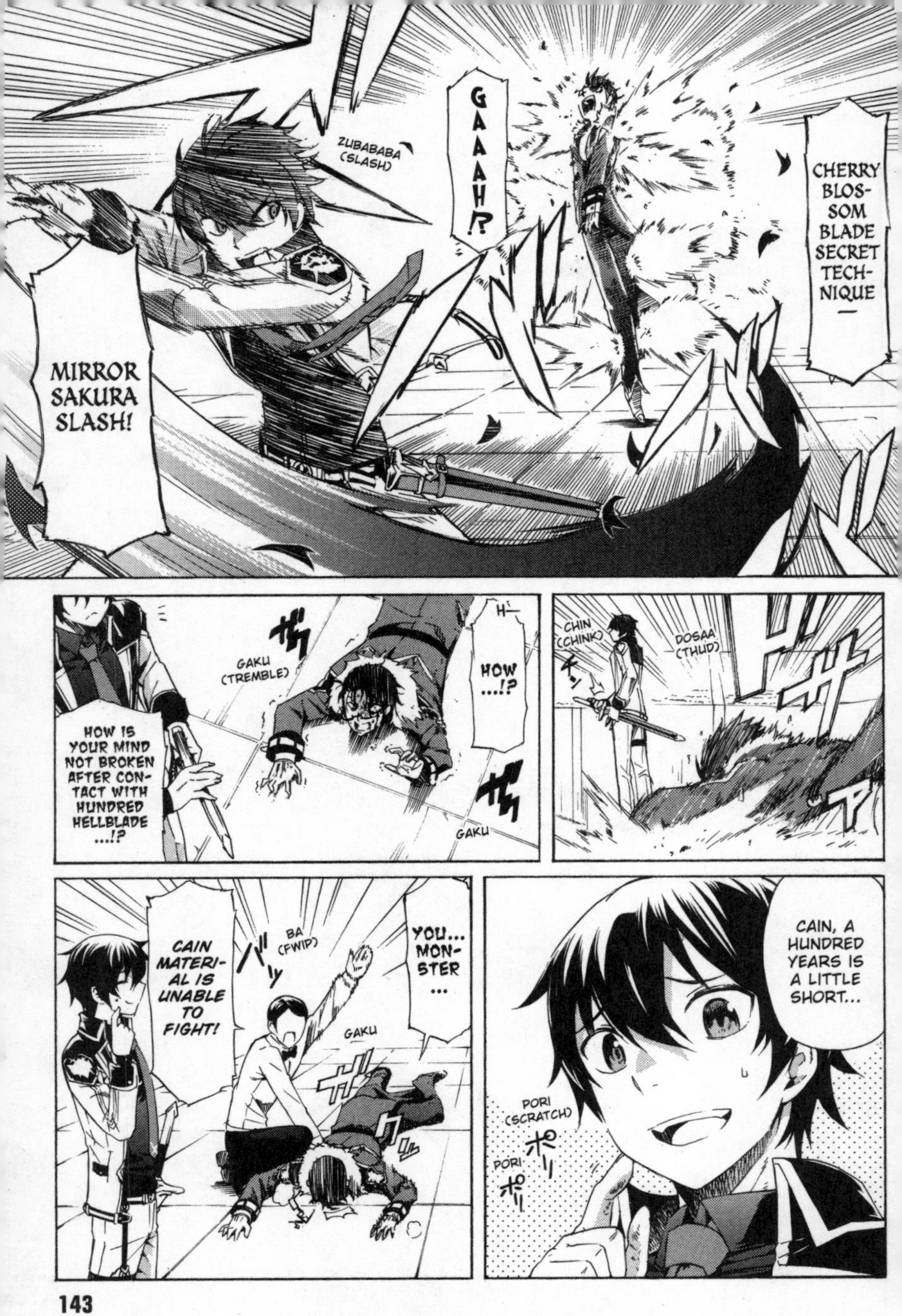
CHERRY BLOSSOM BLADE SECRET TECHNIQUE—
GAAAH!?
ZUBABABA (SLASH)
MIRROR SAKURA SLASH!
CHIN (CHINK)
DOSAA (THUD)
H—
HOW ...!?
GAKU (TREMBLE)
HOW IS YOUR MIND NOT BROKEN AFTER CONTACT WITH HUNDRED HELLBLADE ...!?
GAKU
CAIN, A HUNDRED YEARS IS A LITTLE SHORT...
PORI (SCRATCH)
PORI
YOU... MONSTER ...
BA (FWIP)
CAIN MATERIAL IS UNABLE TO FIGHT!
GAKU

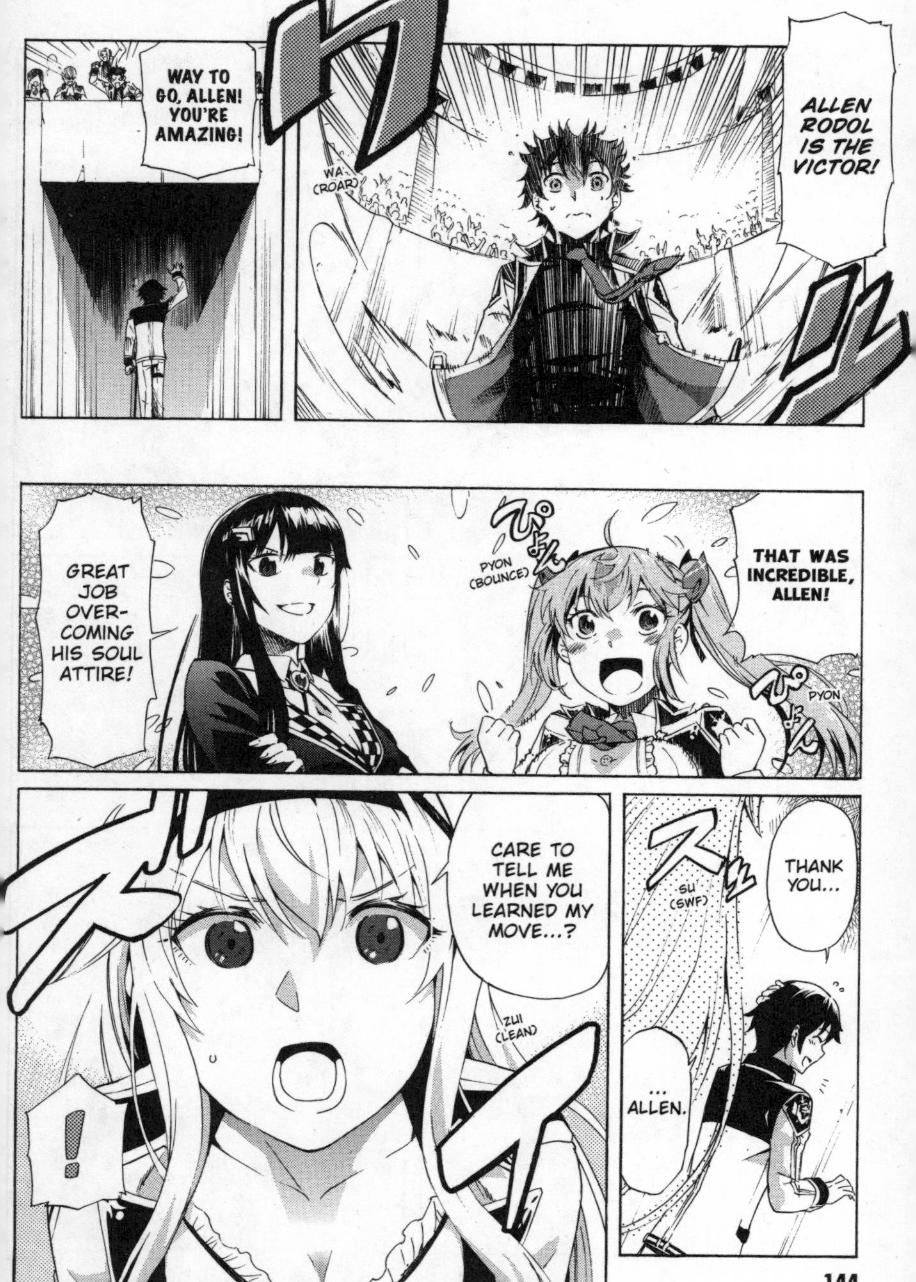
ALLEN RODOL IS THE VICTOR!
WA (ROAR)
WAY TO GO, ALLEN! YOU'RE AMAZING!
THAT WAS INCREDIBLE, ALLEN!
ぴょん
PYON
ぴょん
PYON (BOUNCE)
GREAT JOB OVERCOMING HIS SOUL ATTIRE!
THANK YOU...
SU (SWF)
... ALLEN.
CARE TO TELL ME WHEN YOU LEARNED MY MOVE...?
ZUI (LEAN)
!

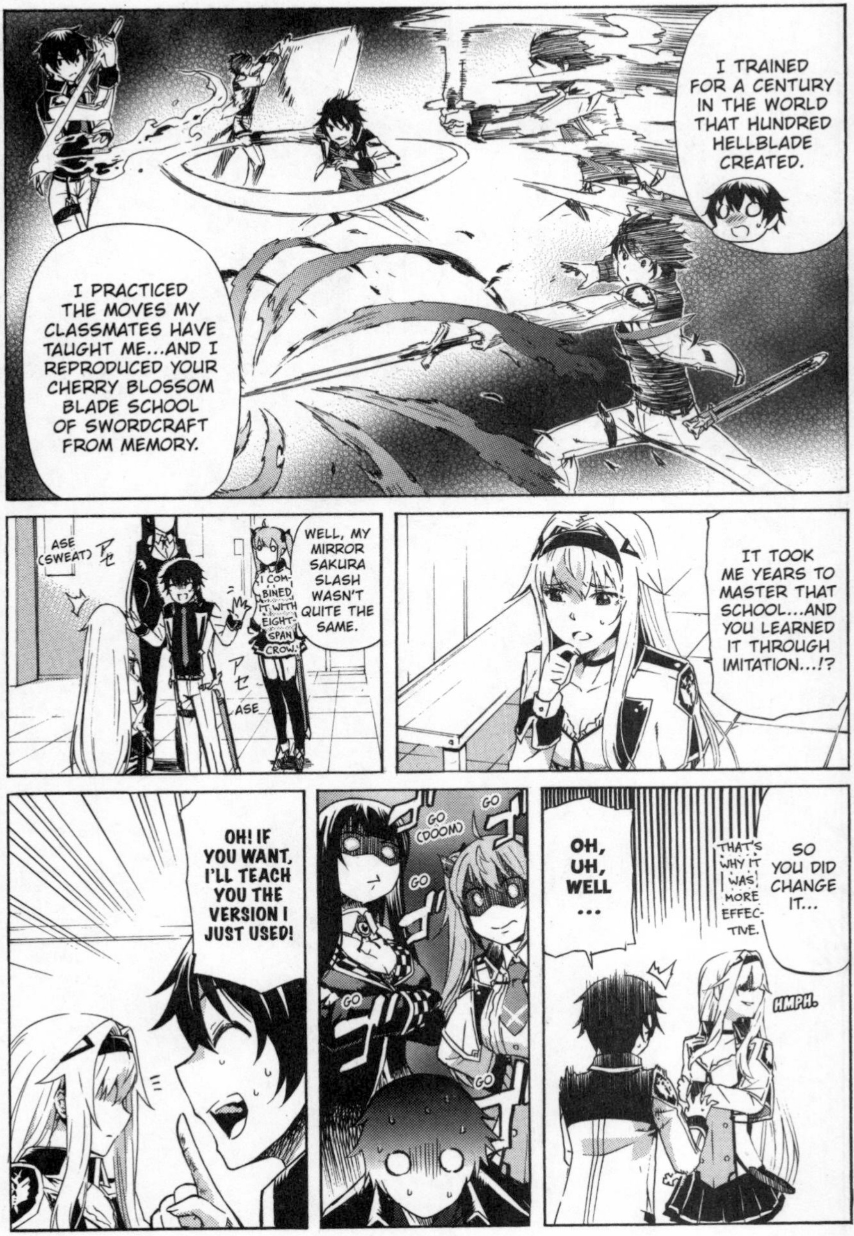
I TRAINED FOR A CENTURY IN THE WORLD THAT HUNDRED HELLBLADE CREATED.
I PRACTICED THE MOVES MY CLASSMATES HAVE TAUGHT ME...AND I REPRODUCED YOUR CHERRY BLOSSOM BLADE SCHOOL OF SWORDCRAFT FROM MEMORY.
IT TOOK ME YEARS TO MASTER THAT SCHOOL...AND YOU LEARNED IT THROUGH IMITATION...!?
WELL, MY MIRROR SAKURA SLASH WASN'T QUITE THE SAME.
I COMBINED IT WITH EIGHT-SPAN CROW.
ASE (SWEAT)
ASE
SO YOU DID CHANGE IT...
THAT'S WHY IT WAS MORE EFFECTIVE.
HMPH.
OH, UH, WELL...
GO
GO (DOOM)
GO
GO
GO
OH! IF YOU WANT, I'LL TEACH YOU THE VERSION I JUST USED!

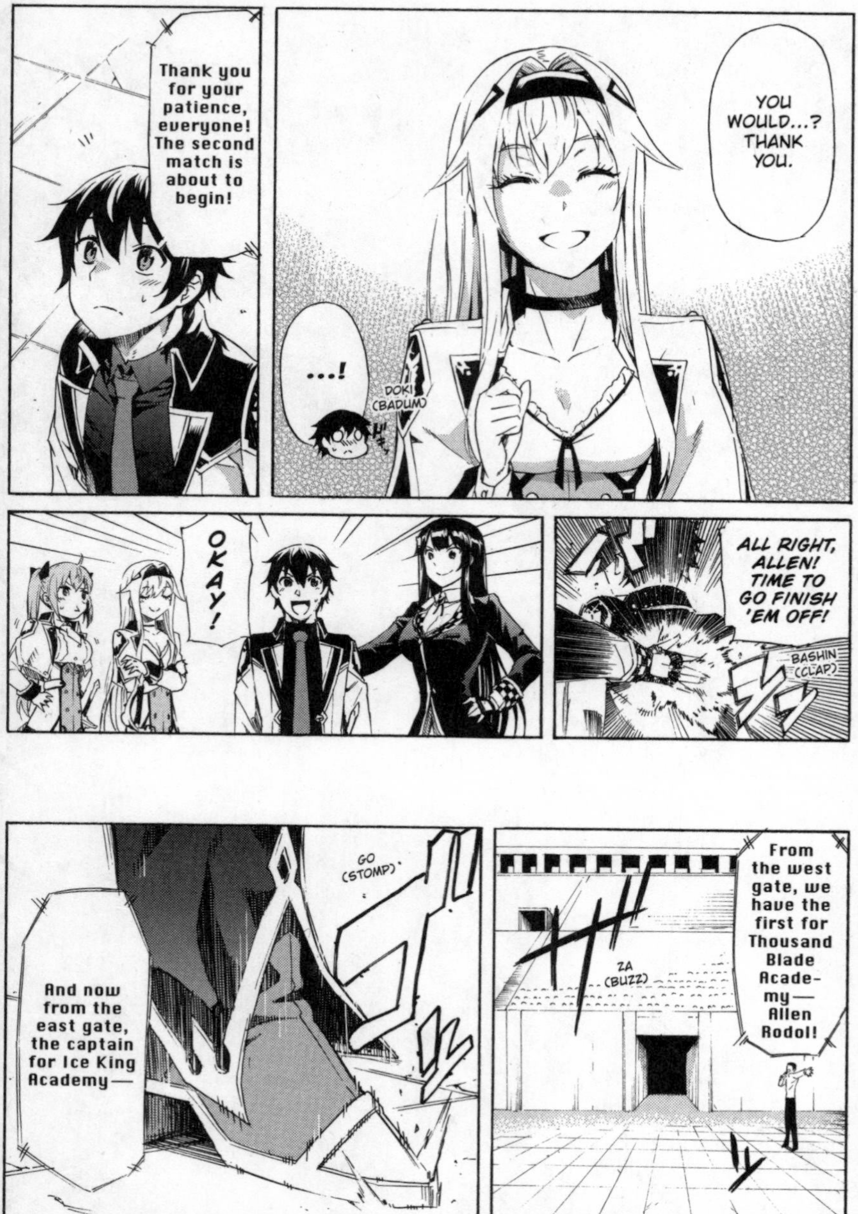
YOU WOULD...? THANK YOU.
...!
DOKI (BADUM)
Thank you for your patience, everyone! The second match is about to begin!
ALL RIGHT, ALLEN! TIME TO GO FINISH 'EM OFF!
BASHIN (CLAP)
OKAY!
From the west gate, we have the first for Thousand Blade Academy—Allen Rodol!
ZA (BUZZ)
GO (STOMP)
And now from the east gate, the captain for Ice King Academy—

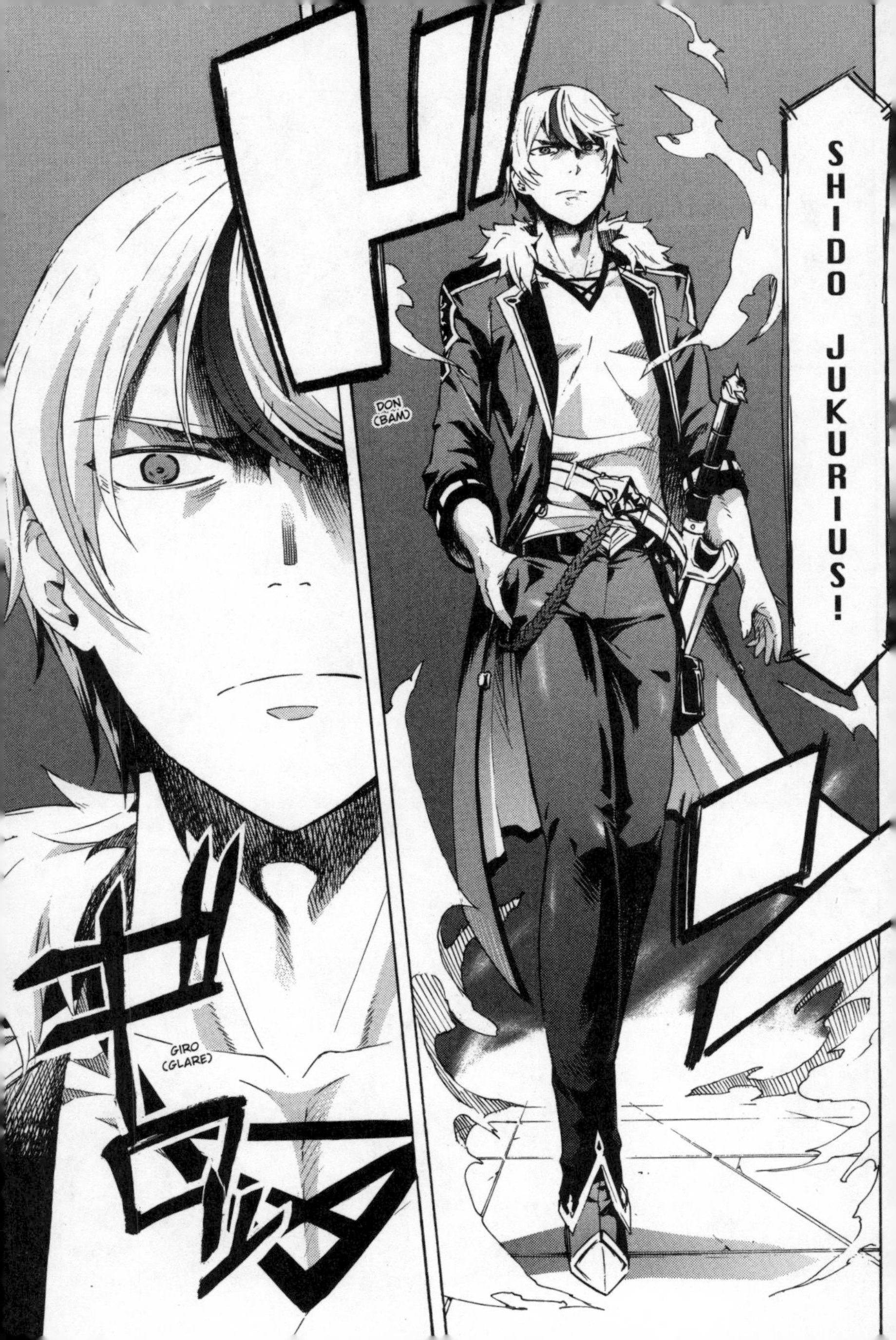
SHIDO JUKURIUS!
DON (BAM)
GIRO (GLARE)

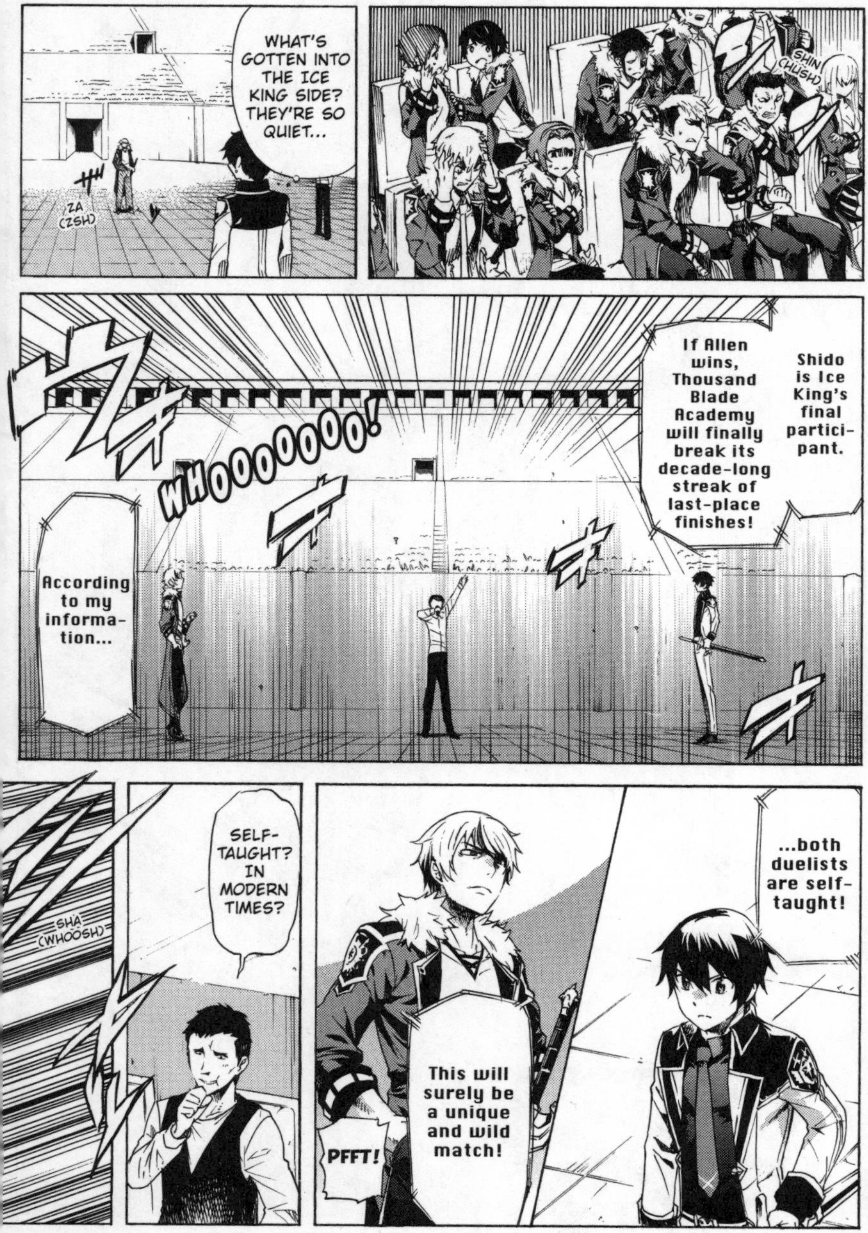
SHIN (HUSH)
WHAT'S GOTTEN INTO THE ICE KING SIDE? THEY'RE SO QUIET...
ZA (ZSH)
Shido is Ice King's final partici-pant.
If Allen wins, Thousand Blade Academy will finally break its decade-long streak of last-place finishes!
WHOOOOOOOO!
According to my informa-tion...
...both duelists are self-taught!
This will surely be a unique and wild match!
PFFT!
SELF-TAUGHT? IN MODERN TIMES?
SHA (WHOOSH)

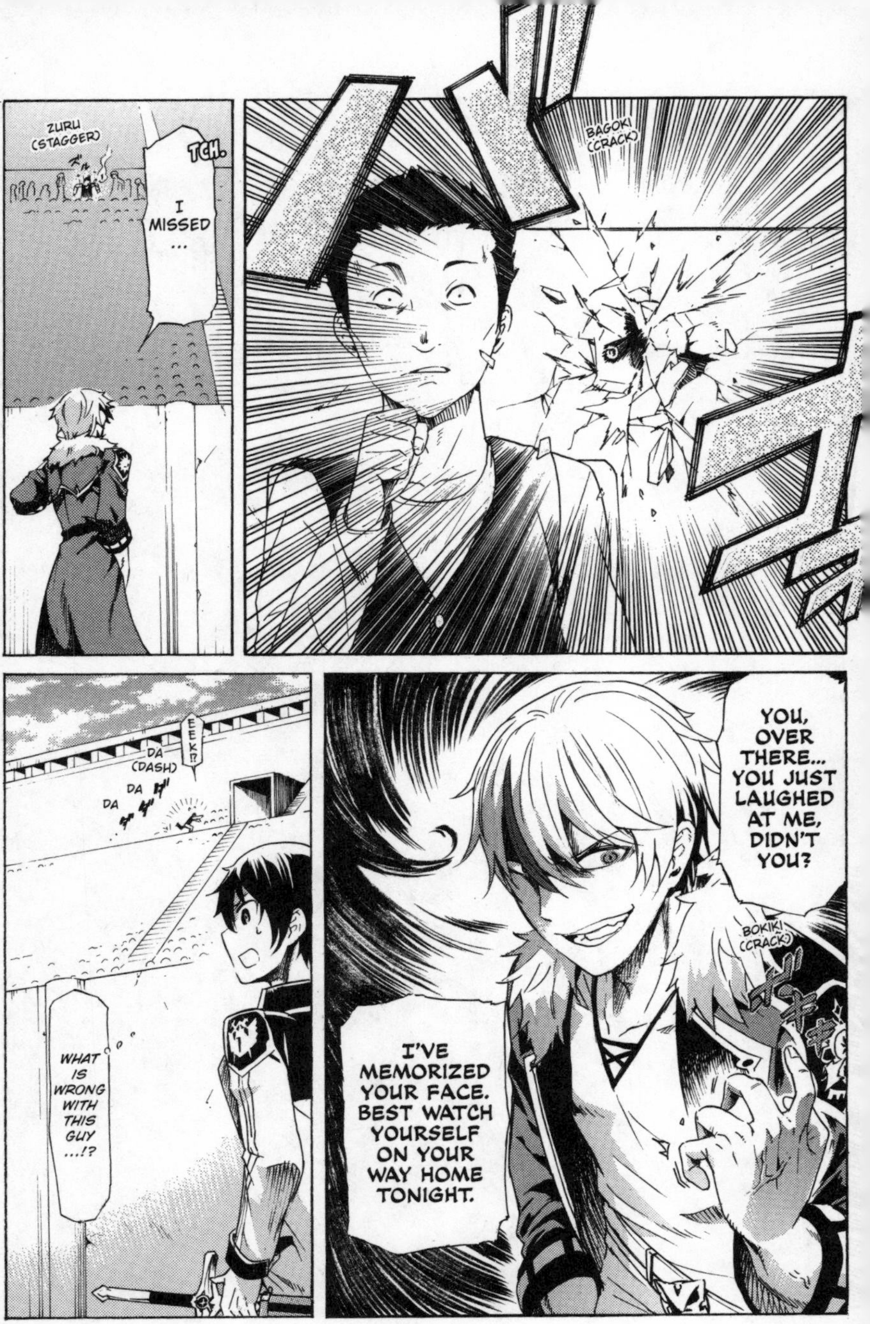

BAGOKI (CRACK)
ZURU (STAGGER)
TCH.
I MISSED...
YOU, OVER THERE... YOU JUST LAUGHED AT ME, DIDN'T YOU?
BOKIKI (CRACK)
I'VE MEMORIZED YOUR FACE. BEST WATCH YOURSELF ON YOUR WAY HOME TONIGHT.
EEK!?
DA (DASH)
DA
DA
WHAT IS WRONG WITH THIS GUY...!?

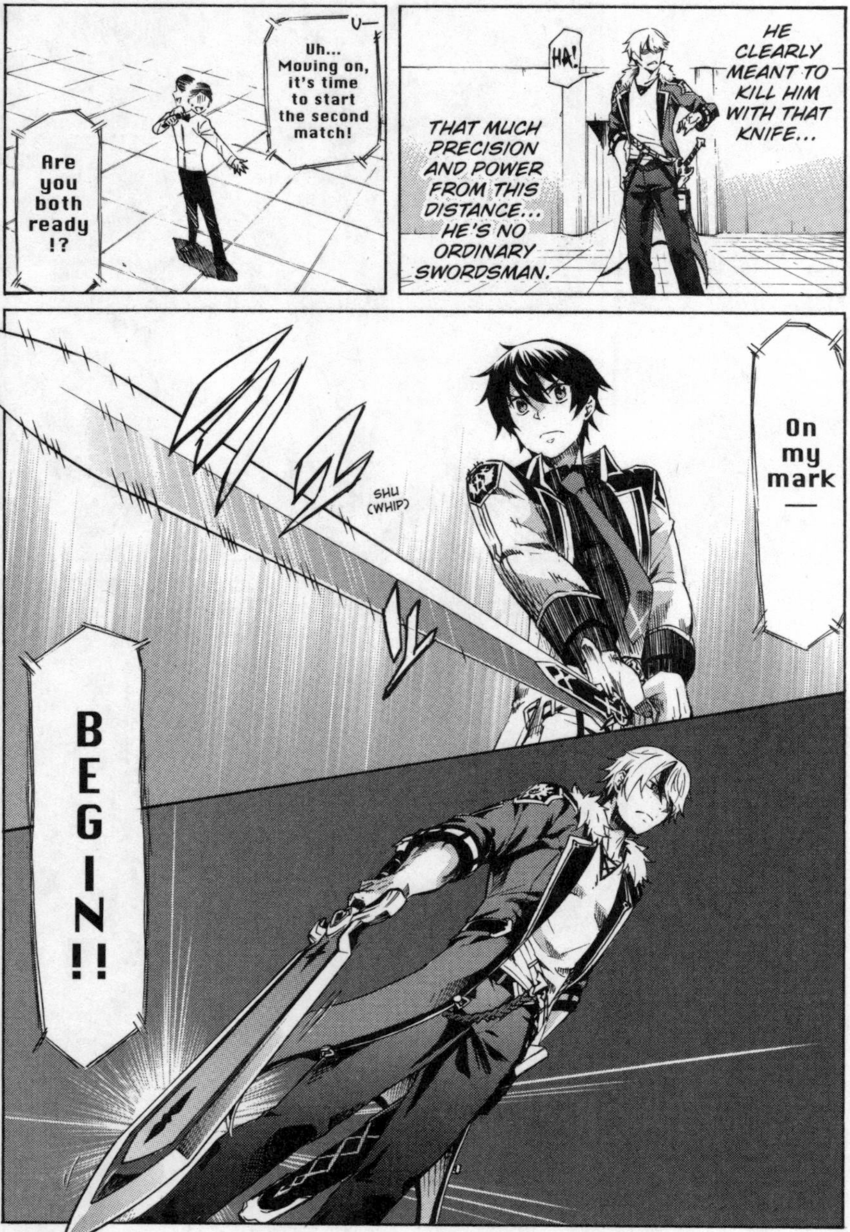
HE CLEARLY MEANT TO KILL HIM WITH THAT KNIFE...
HA!
THAT MUCH PRECISION AND POWER FROM THIS DISTANCE... HE'S NO ORDINARY SWORDSMAN.
Uh... Moving on, it's time to start the second match!
Are you both ready!?
On my mark —
SHU (WHIP)
BEGIN!!

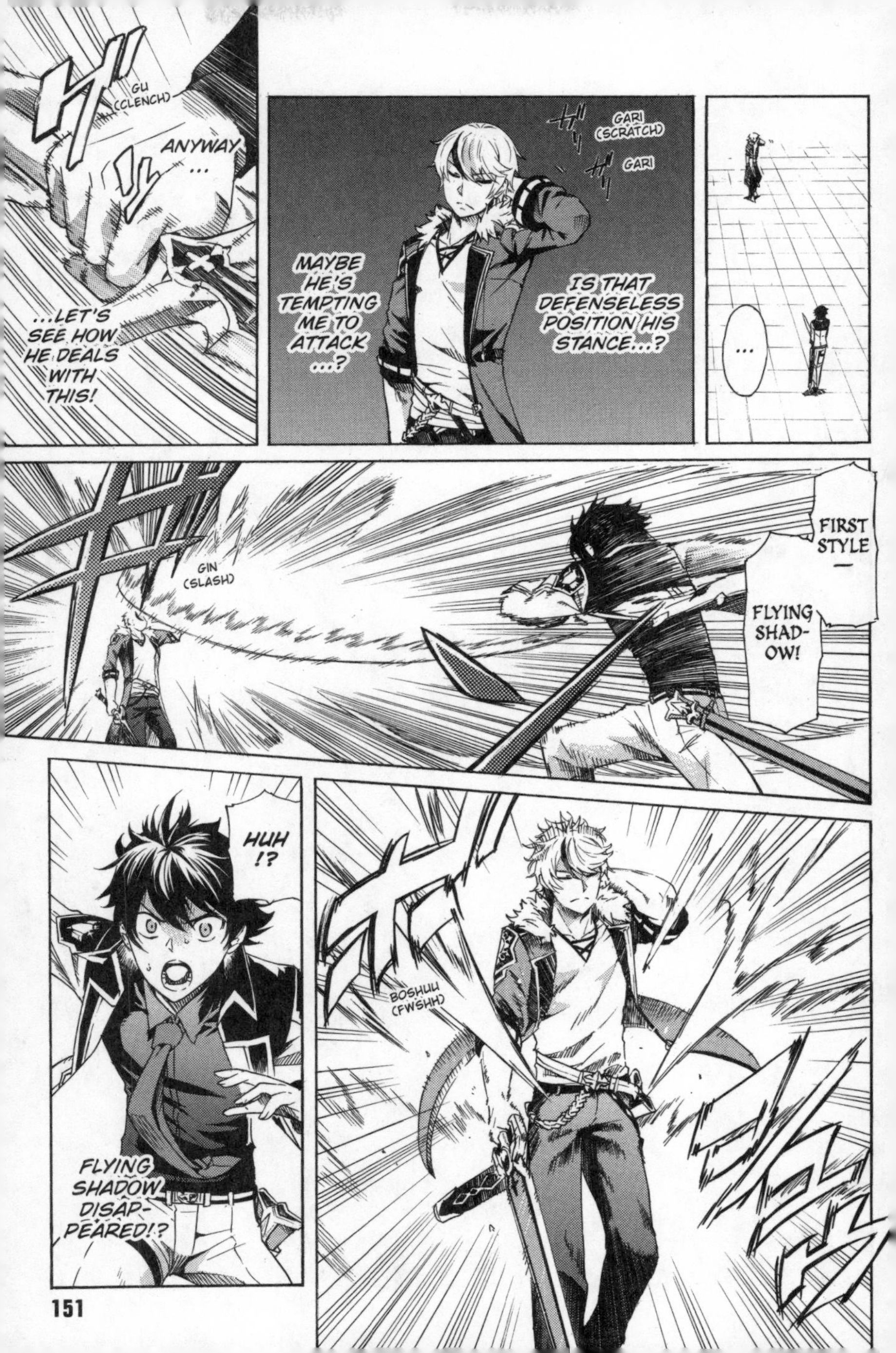
...
GARI (SCRATCH)
GARI
IS THAT DEFENSELESS POSITION HIS STANCE...?
MAYBE HE'S TEMPTING ME TO ATTACK ...?
GU (CLENCH)
ANYWAY ...
...LET'S SEE HOW HE DEALS WITH THIS!
FIRST STYLE —
FLYING SHAD-OW!
GIN (SLASH)
BOSHUU (FWSHH)
HUH !?
FLYING SHADOW DISAP-PEARED!?

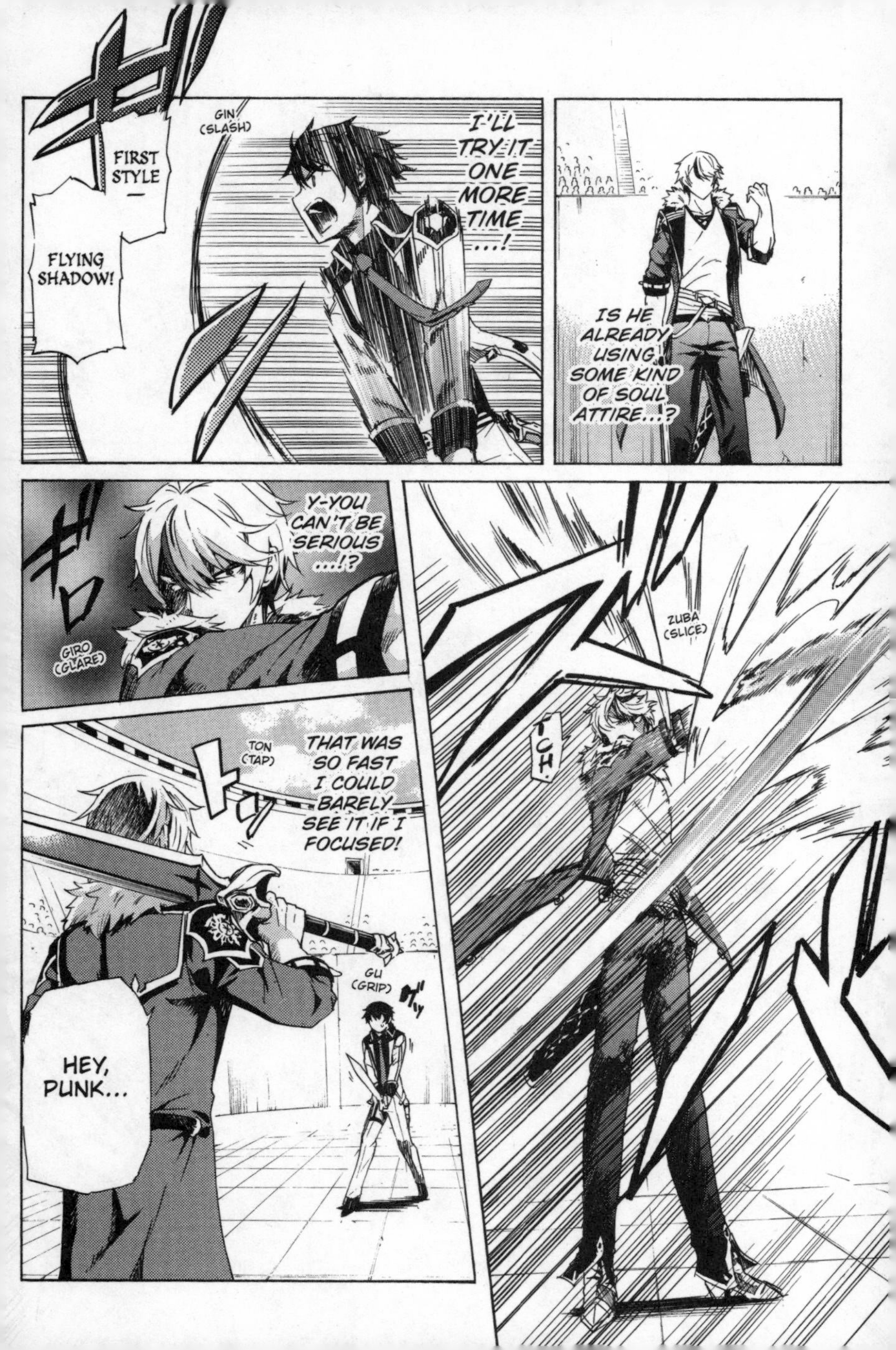
IS HE ALREADY USING SOME KIND OF SOUL ATTIRE...?
I'LL TRY IT ONE MORE TIME...!
GIN (SLASH)
FIRST STYLE —
FLYING SHADOW!
ZUBA (SLICE)
TCH.
Y-YOU CAN'T BE SERIOUS...!?
GIRO (GLARE)
THAT WAS SO FAST I COULD BARELY SEE IT IF I FOCUSED!
TON (TAP)
GU (GRIP)
HEY, PUNK...

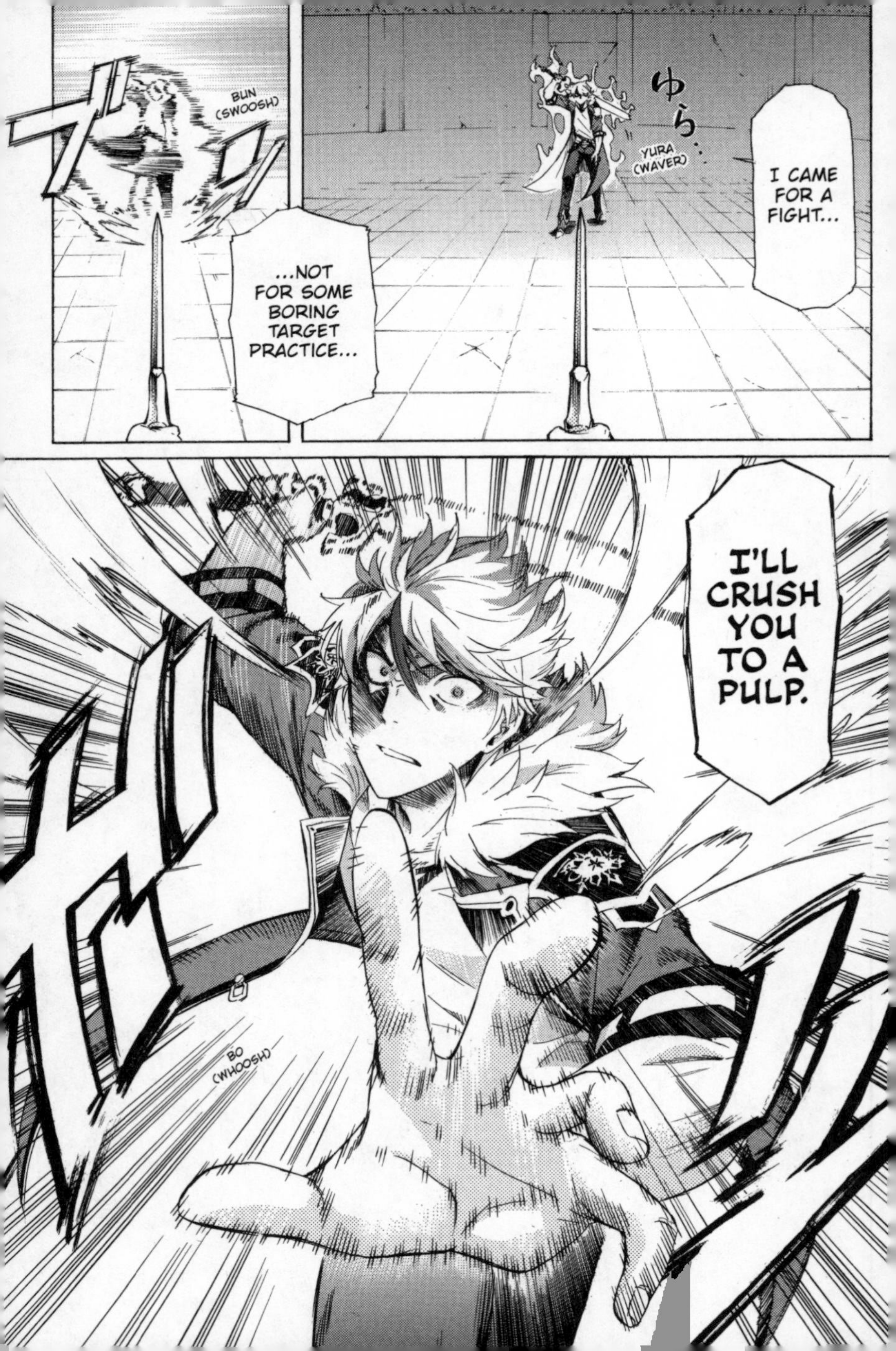
ゆら
YURA (WAVER)
I CAME FOR A FIGHT...
...NOT FOR SOME BORING TARGET PRACTICE...
BUN (SWOOSH)
I'LL CRUSH YOU TO A PULP.
BO (WHOOSH)

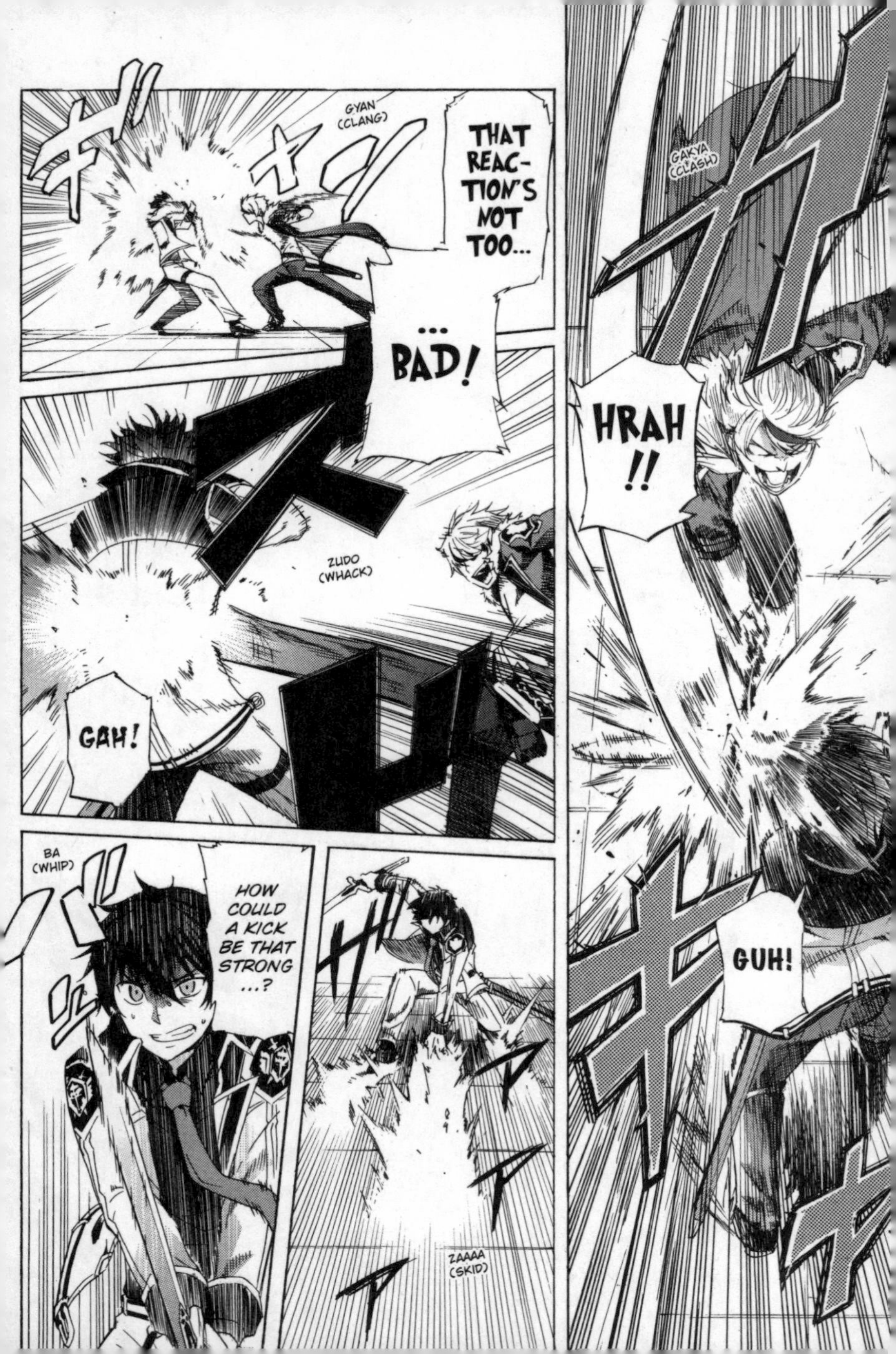
GAKYA (CLASH)
HRAH !!
GUH!
GYAN (CLANG)
THAT REACTION'S NOT TOO...
... BAD!
ZUDO (WHACK)
GAH!
ZAAAA (SKID)
BA (WHIP)
HOW COULD A KICK BE THAT STRONG ...?

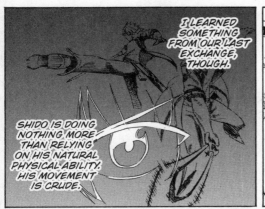

HWAH,
CRAP!
HE DOESN'T SEE ME AS A THREAT...
I LEARNED SOMETHING FROM OUR LAST EXCHANGE, THOUGH.
SHIDO IS DOING NOTHING MORE THAN RELYING ON HIS NATURAL PHYSICAL ABILITY. HIS MOVEMENT IS CRUDE.
AND ABOVE ALL— HE LACKS AN EARNEST INTEREST IN SWORDCRAFT.
I HAVE HIM BEAT IN THAT REGARD!
TON (TAP)
TON
WILL YOU QUIT STARING AT ME? YOU'RE CREEPING ME OUT...
TALENTLESS TRASH LIKE YOU COULD NEVER HOPE TO DEFEAT GREATNESS LIKE ME.
CHA (SHING)
...YOU'RE INDEED A PRODIGY, SHIDO.
...BUT...
...I AM GOING TO WIN THIS MATCH.
BIKI (BULGE)
...HUNH?

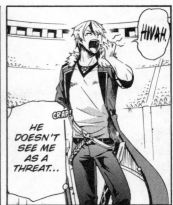

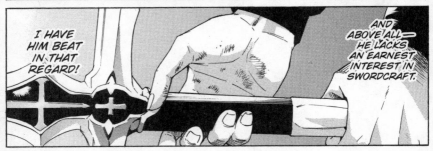

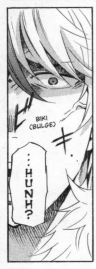

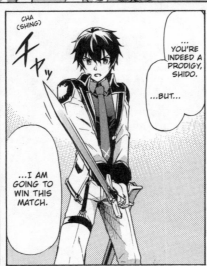

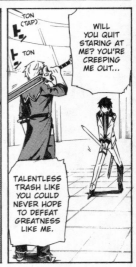

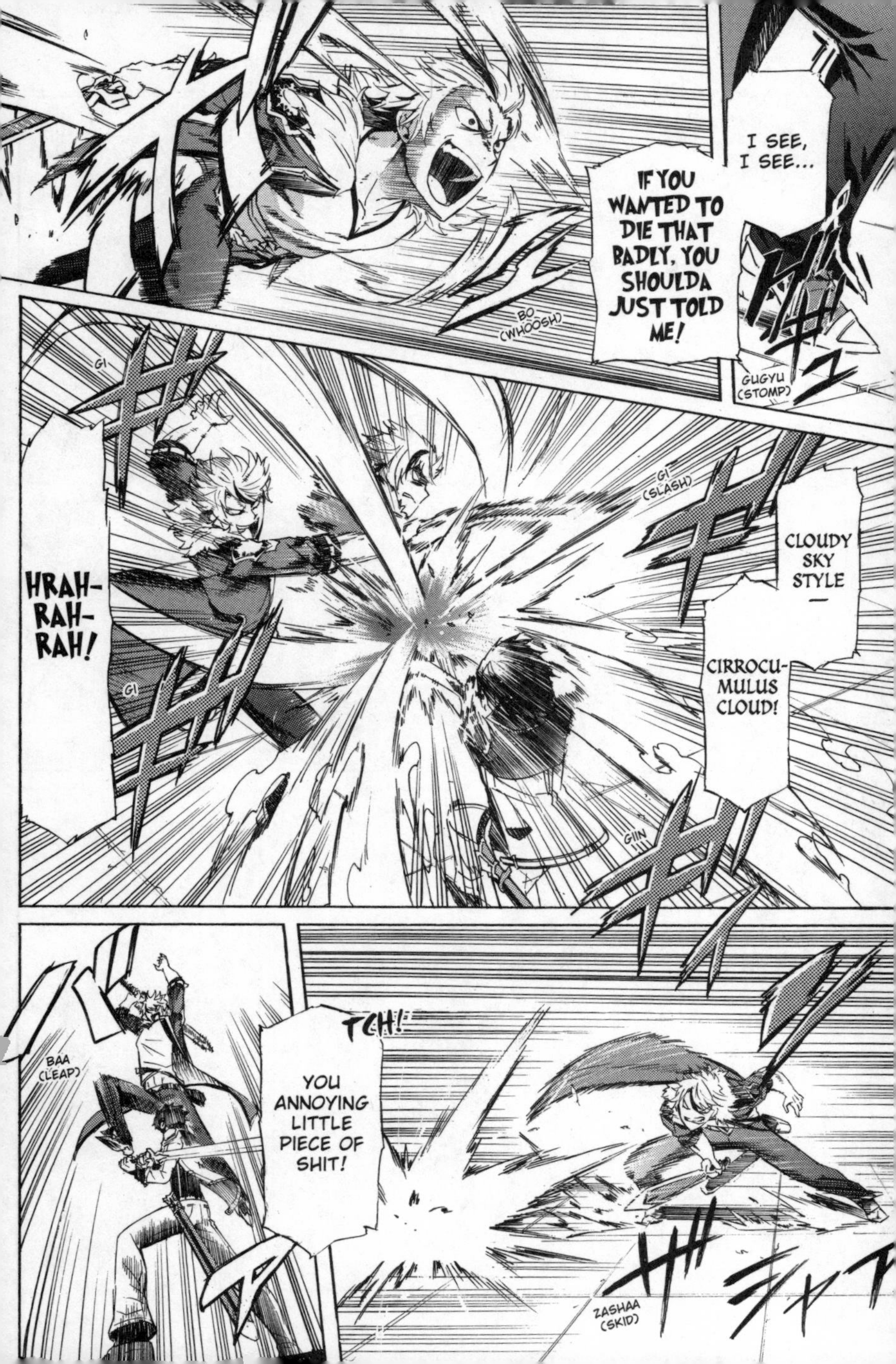
I SEE, I SEE...
GUGYU (STOMP)
IF YOU WANTED TO DIE THAT BADLY, YOU SHOULDA JUST TOLD ME!
BO (WHOOSH)
CLOUDY SKY STYLE —
GI (SLASH)
CIRROCUMULUS CLOUD!
GIIN
GI
HRAH-RAH-RAH!
GI
ZASHAA (SKID)
TCH!
YOU ANNOYING LITTLE PIECE OF SHIT!
BAA (LEAP)

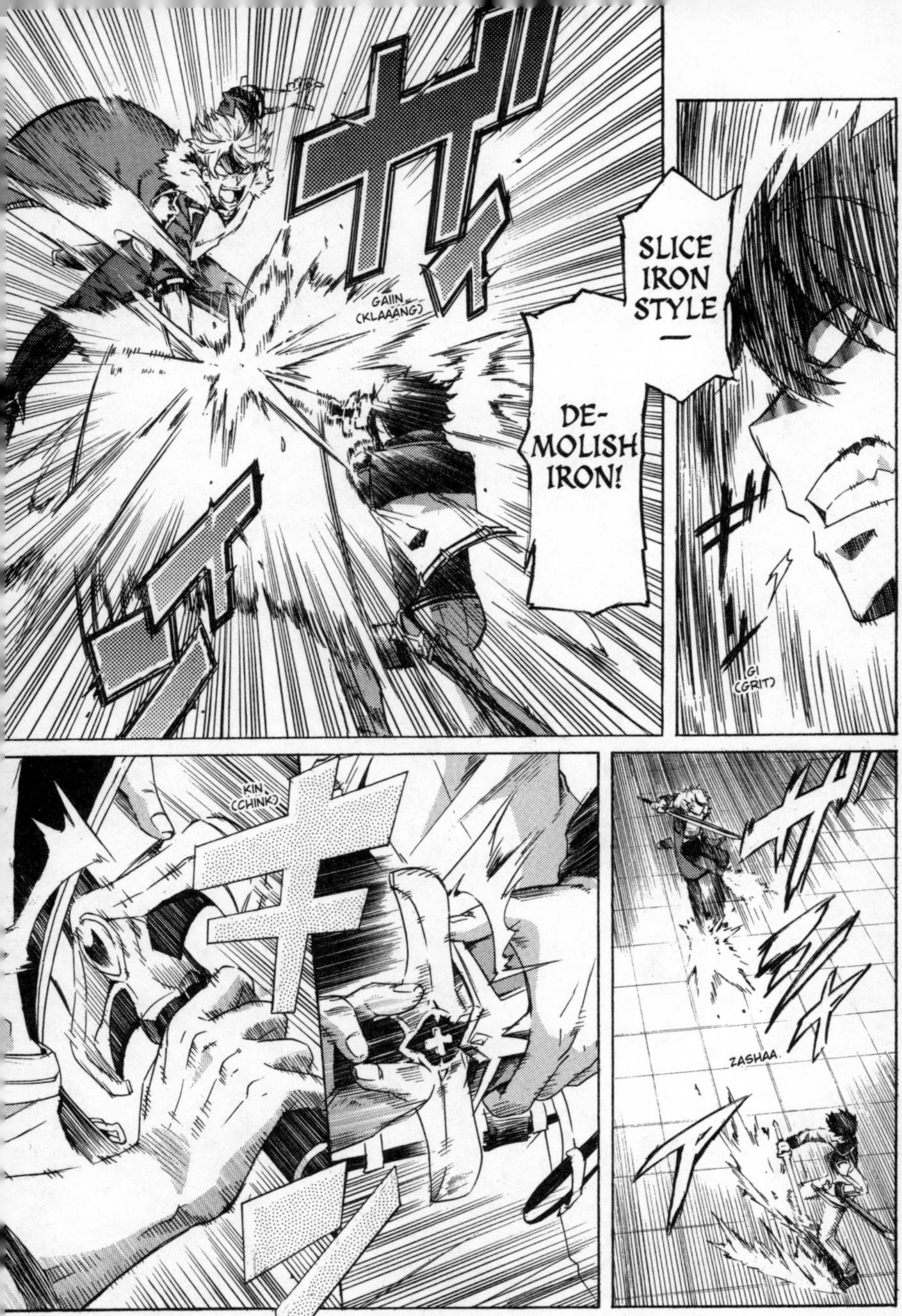
SLICE IRON STYLE —
DE-MOLISH IRON!
GI (GRIT)
GAIIN (KLAAANG)
ZASHAA.
KIN (CHINK)

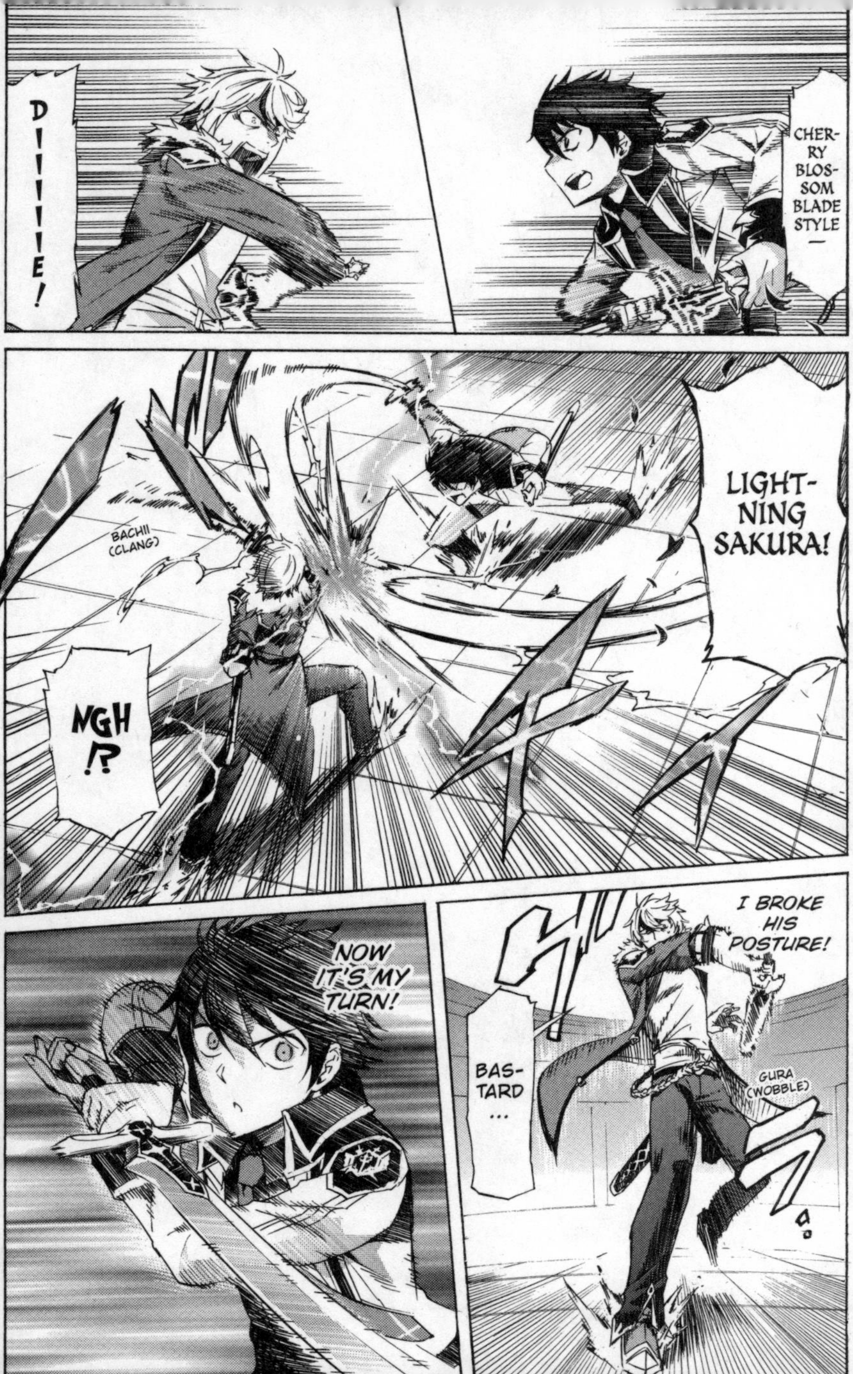
CHER-RY BLOS-SOM BLADE STYLE —
D!!!!!!E!
LIGHT-NING SAKURA!
BACHII (CLANG)
NGH !?
I BROKE HIS POSTURE!
GURA (WOBBLE)
BAS-TARD ...
NOW IT'S MY TURN!

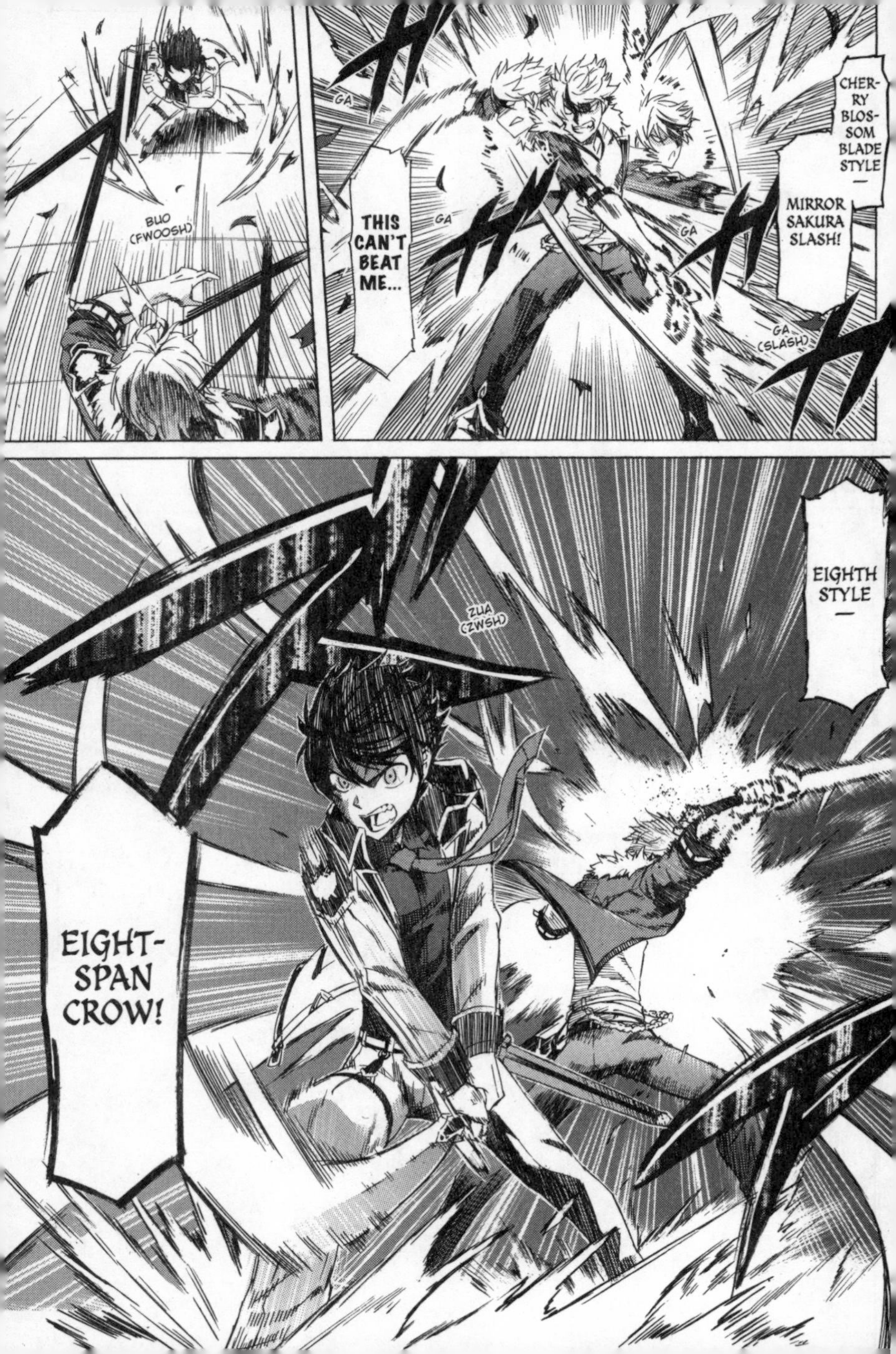
CHERRY BLOSSOM BLADE STYLE —
MIRROR SAKURA SLASH!
GA
THIS CAN'T BEAT ME...
GA
GA
GA (SLASH)
BUO (FWOOSH)
EIGHTH STYLE —
ZUA (ZWSH)
EIGHT-SPAN CROW!

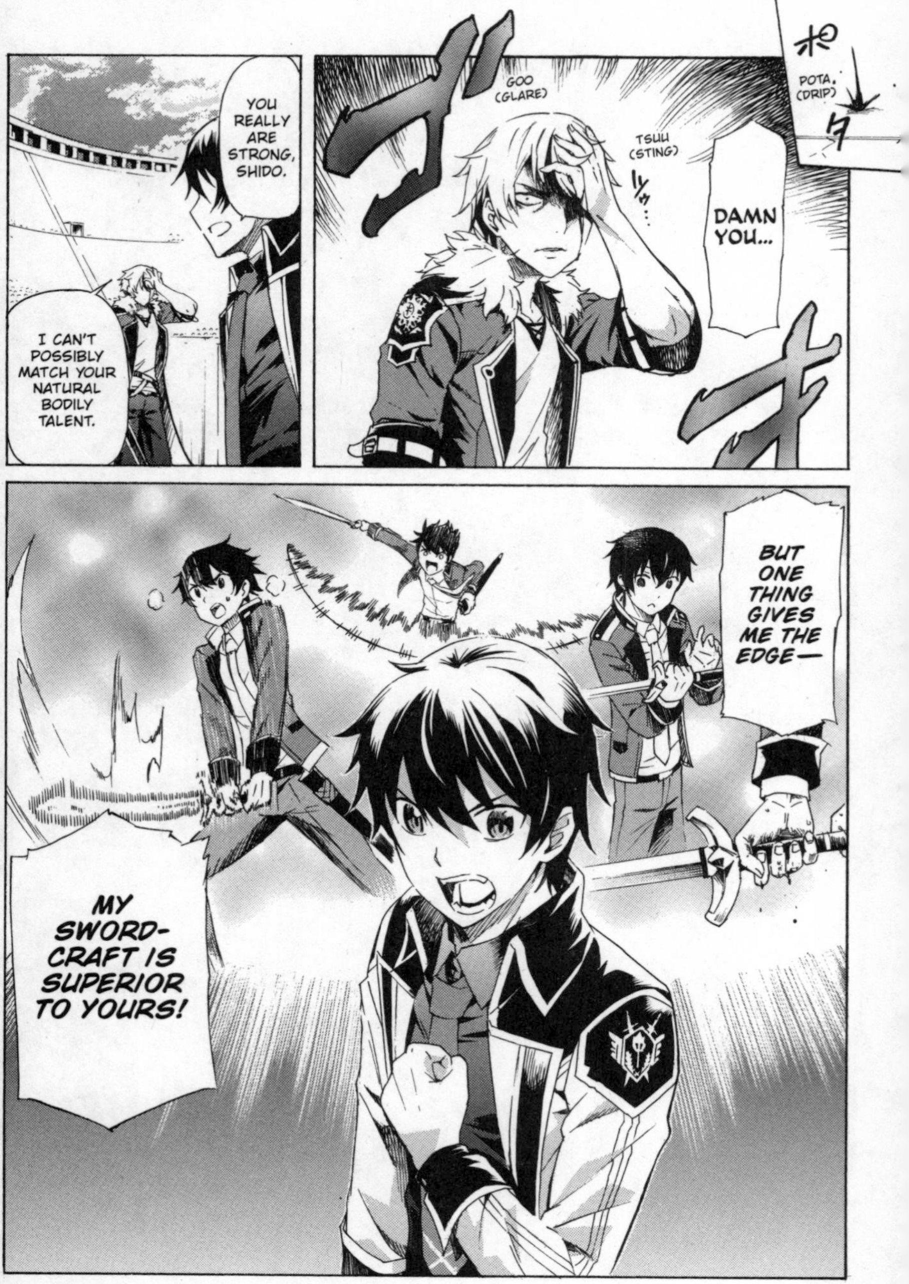
POTA (DRIP)
GOO (GLARE)
TSUU (STING)
DAMN YOU...
YOU REALLY ARE STRONG, SHIDO.
I CAN'T POSSIBLY MATCH YOUR NATURAL BODILY TALENT.
BUT ONE THING GIVES ME THE EDGE—
MY SWORD-CRAFT IS SUPERIOR TO YOURS!

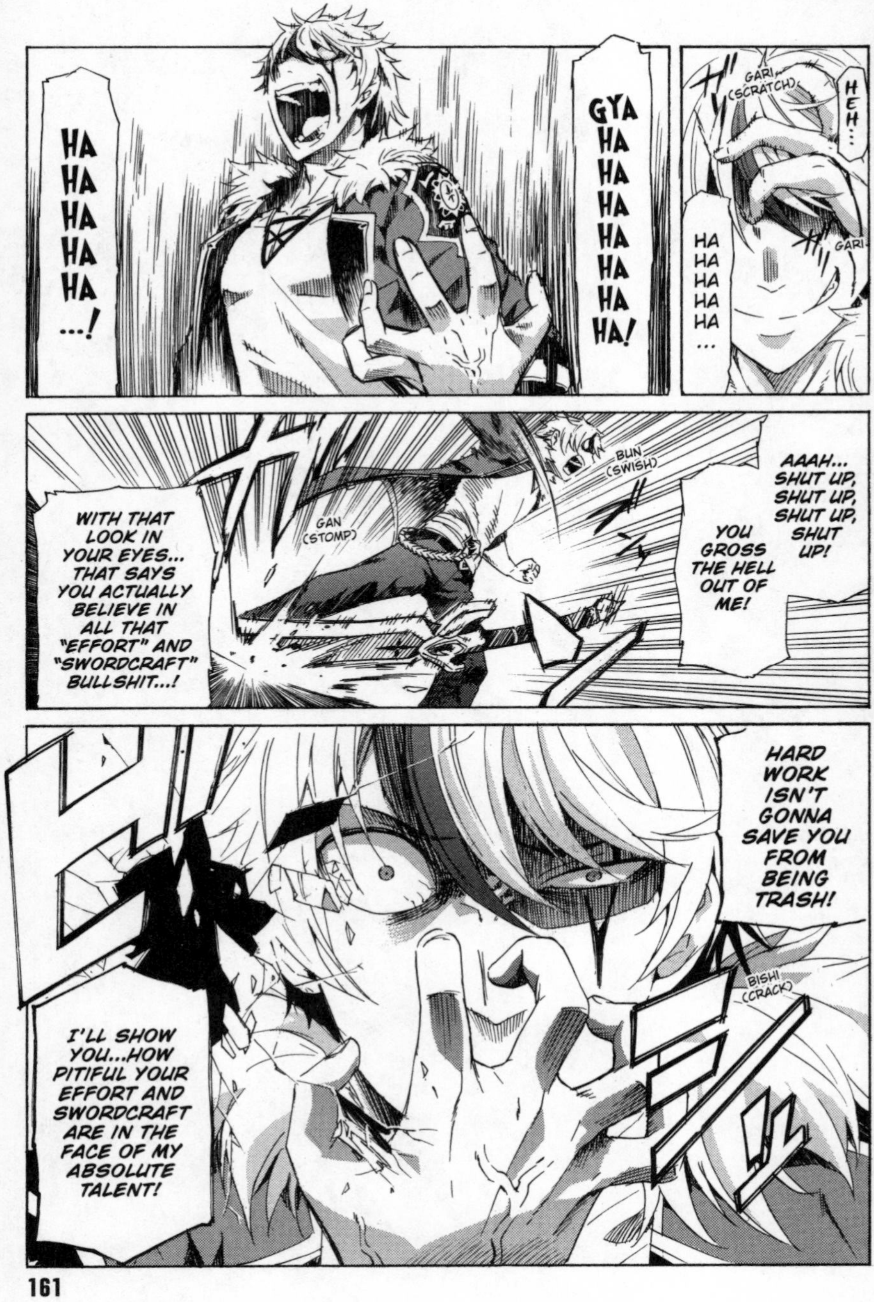
HEH...
GARI (SCRATCH)
HA HA HA HA HA ...
GARI
GYA HA HA HA HA HA HA HA HA!
HA HA HA HA HA ...!
AAAH... SHUT UP, SHUT UP, SHUT UP, SHUT UP!
YOU GROSS THE HELL OUT OF ME!
BUN (SWISH)
GAN (STOMP)
WITH THAT LOOK IN YOUR EYES... THAT SAYS YOU ACTUALLY BELIEVE IN ALL THAT "EFFORT" AND "SWORDCRAFT" BULLSHIT...!
HARD WORK ISN'T GONNA SAVE YOU FROM BEING TRASH!
BISHI (CRACK)
I'LL SHOW YOU...HOW PITIFUL YOUR EFFORT AND SWORDCRAFT ARE IN THE FACE OF MY ABSOLUTE TALENT!

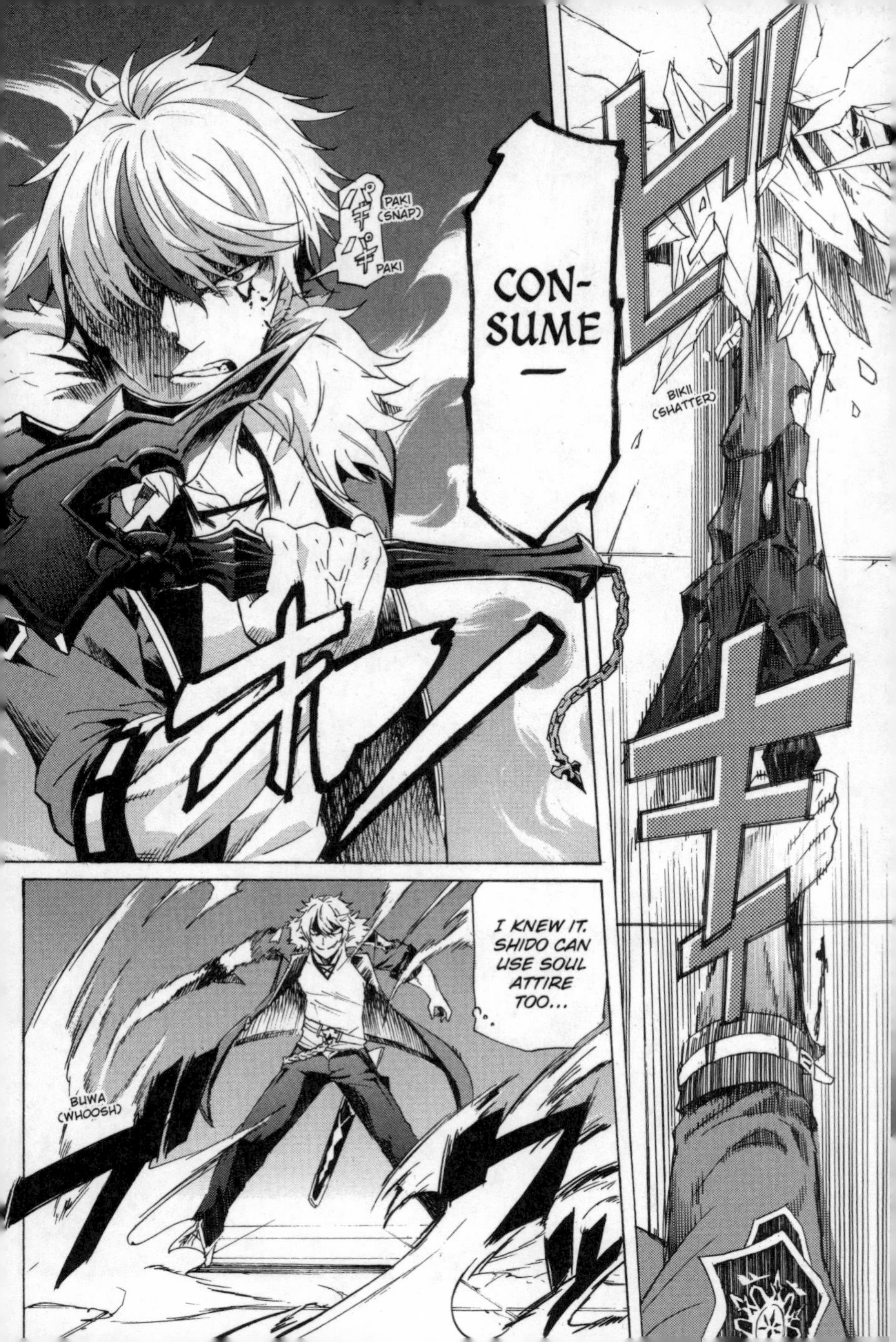
BIKII (SHATTER)
CON-SUME —
パキパキ
PAKI (SNAP) PAKI
I KNEW IT. SHIDO CAN USE SOUL ATTIRE TOO...
BUWA (WHOOSH)

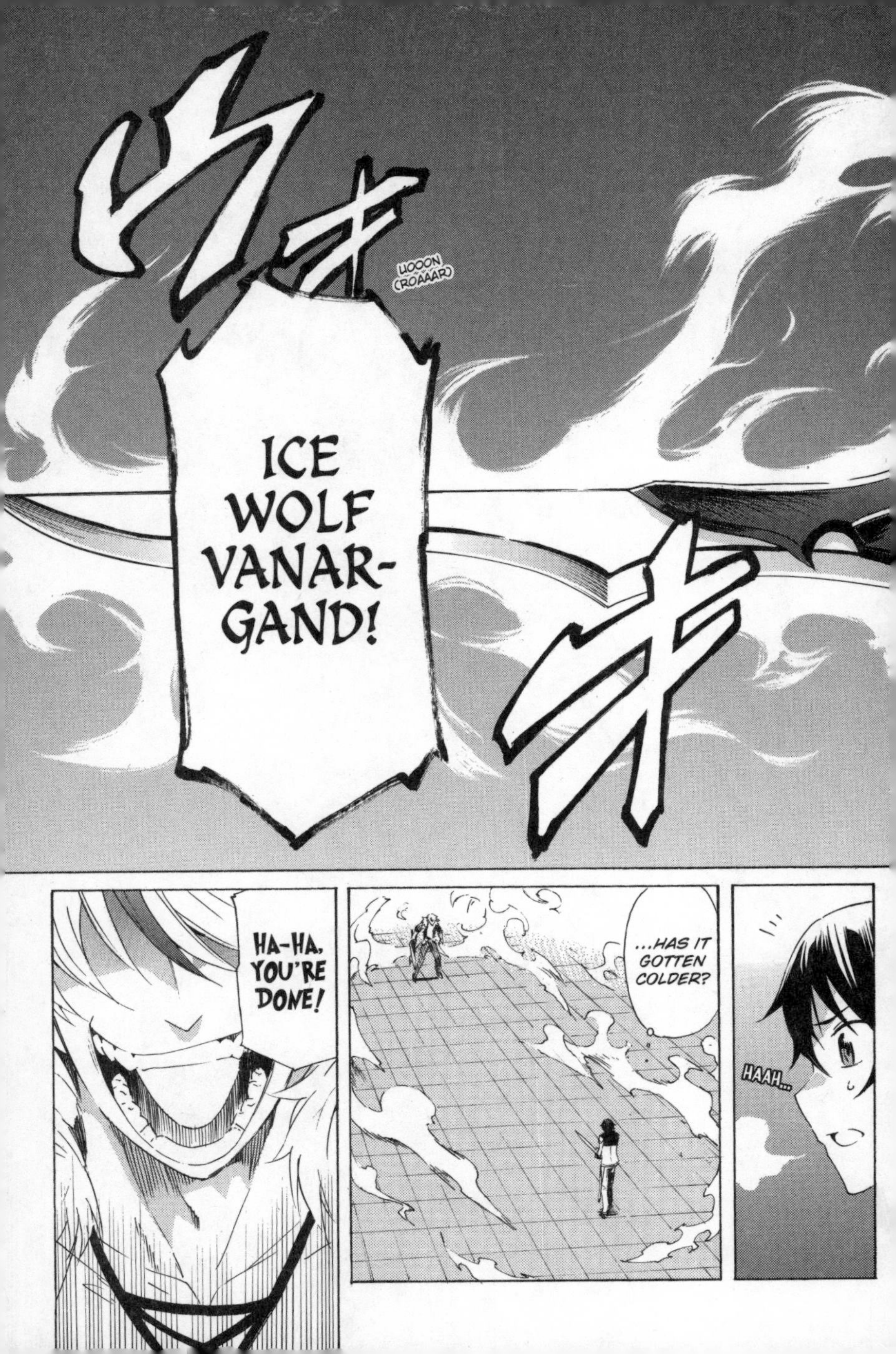
UOOON (ROAAAR)
ICE WOLF VANARGAND!
HAAH...
...HAS IT GOTTEN COLDER?
HA-HA, YOU'RE DONE!

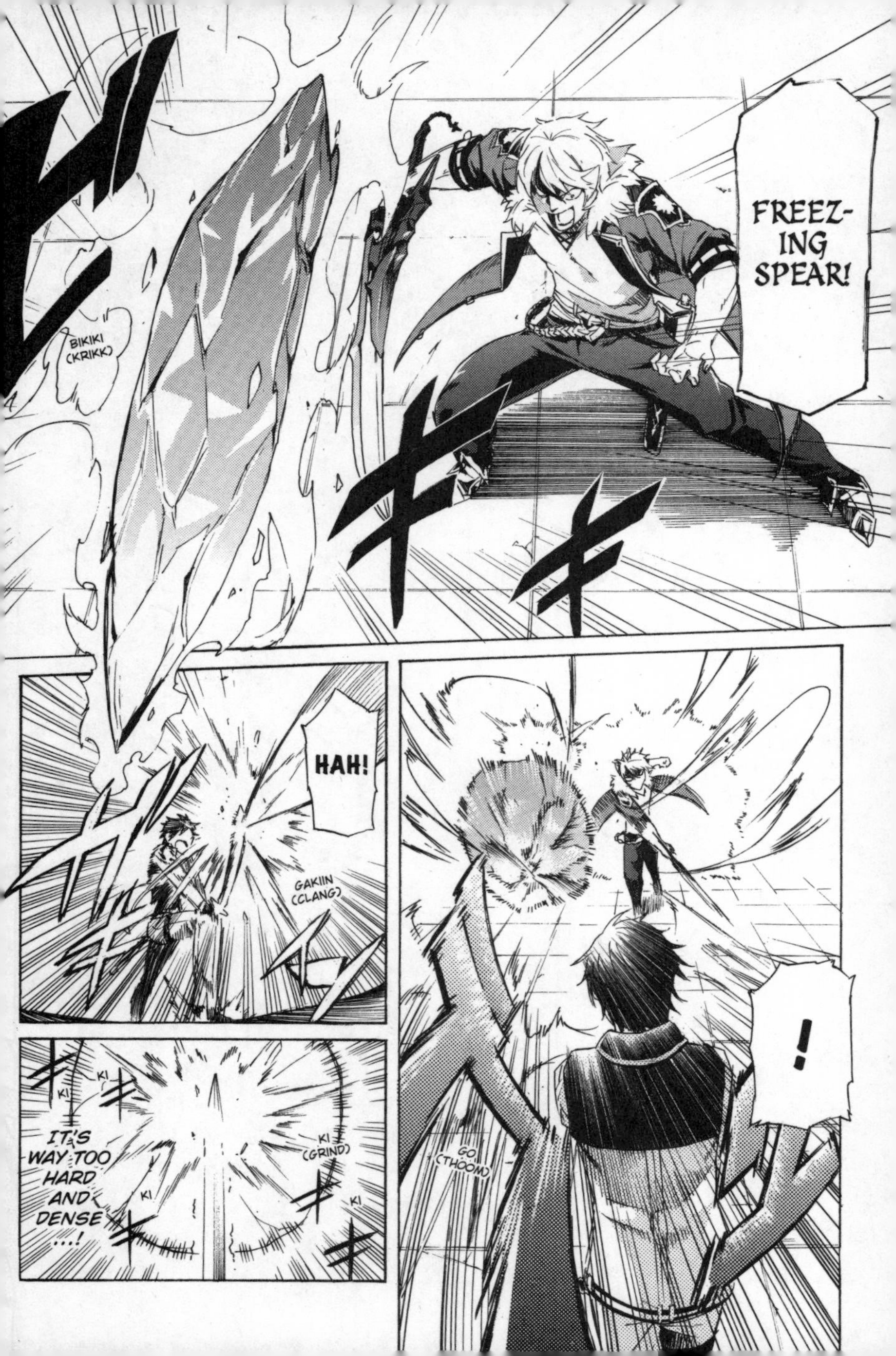
FREEZ-
ING
SPEAR!
BIKIKI
(KRIKK)
!
GO
(THOOM)
HAH!
GAKIIN
(CLANG)
KI
KI
KI
(GRIND)
IT'S
WAY TOO
HARD
AND
DENSE
....!
KI
KI

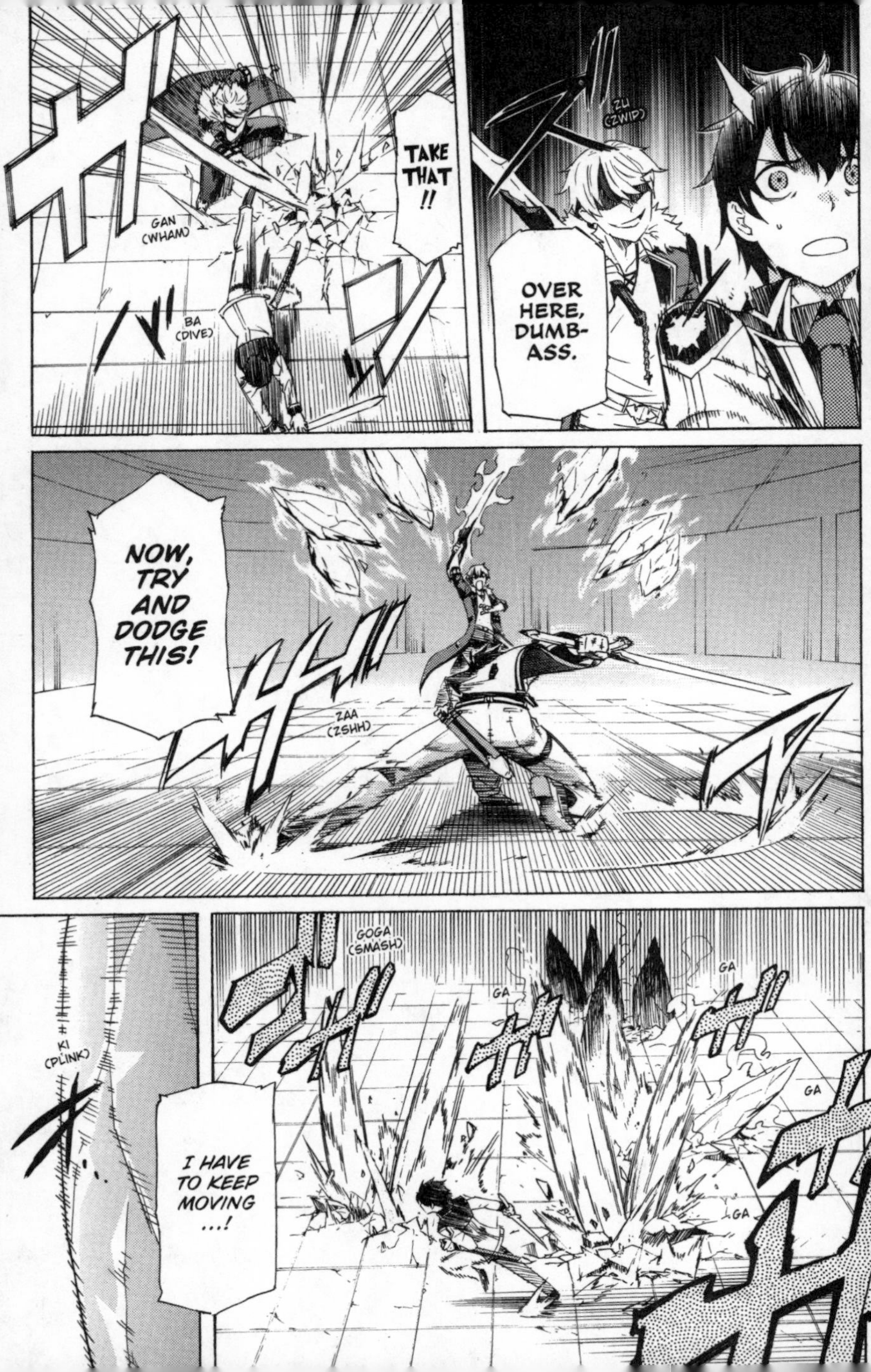
ZU
(ZWIP)
OVER HERE, DUMBASS.
TAKE THAT!!
GAN
(WHAM)
BA
(DIVE)
NOW, TRY AND DODGE THIS!
ZAA
(ZSHH)
GOGA
(SMASH)
GA
GA
GA
GA
I HAVE TO KEEP MOVING ...!
KI
(PLINK)

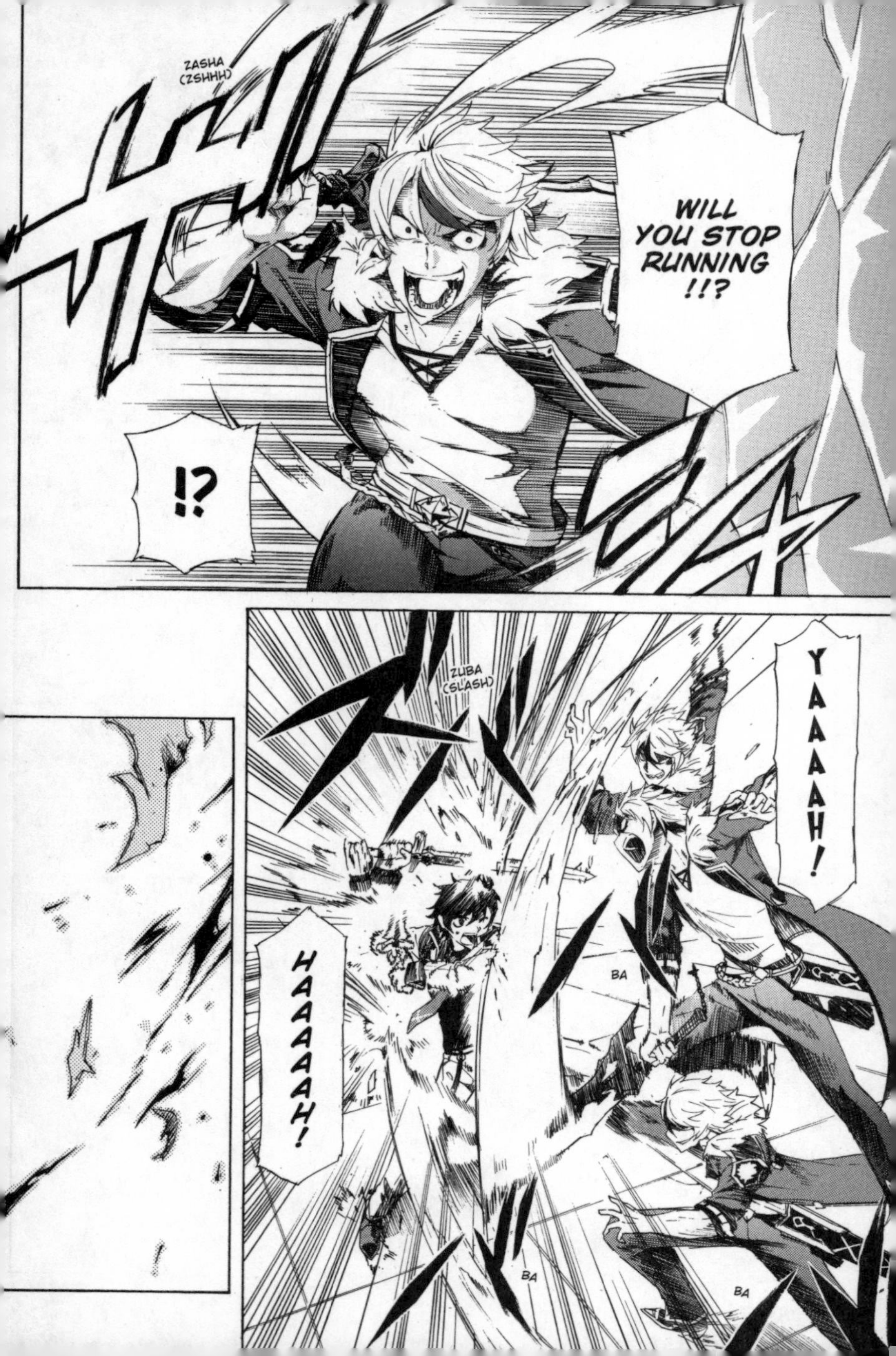
ZASHA (ZSHHH)
WILL YOU STOP RUNNING !!?
!?
YAAAAAH!
ZUBA (SLASH)
HAAAAAAH!
BA
BA
BA

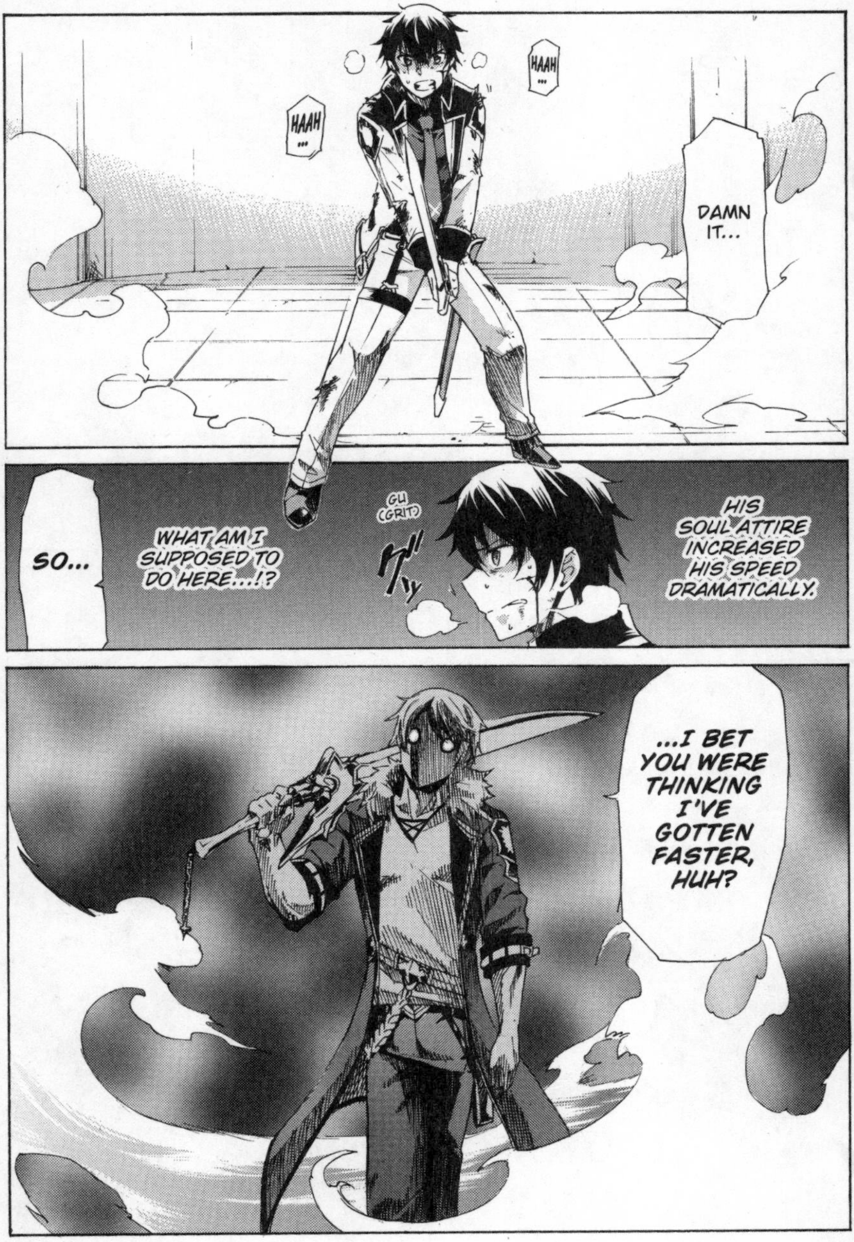
HAAH...
HAAH...
DAMN IT...
HIS SOUL ATTIRE INCREASED HIS SPEED DRAMATICALLY.
GU (GRIT)
WHAT AM I SUPPOSED TO DO HERE...!?
SO...
...I BET YOU WERE THINKING I'VE GOTTEN FASTER, HUH?

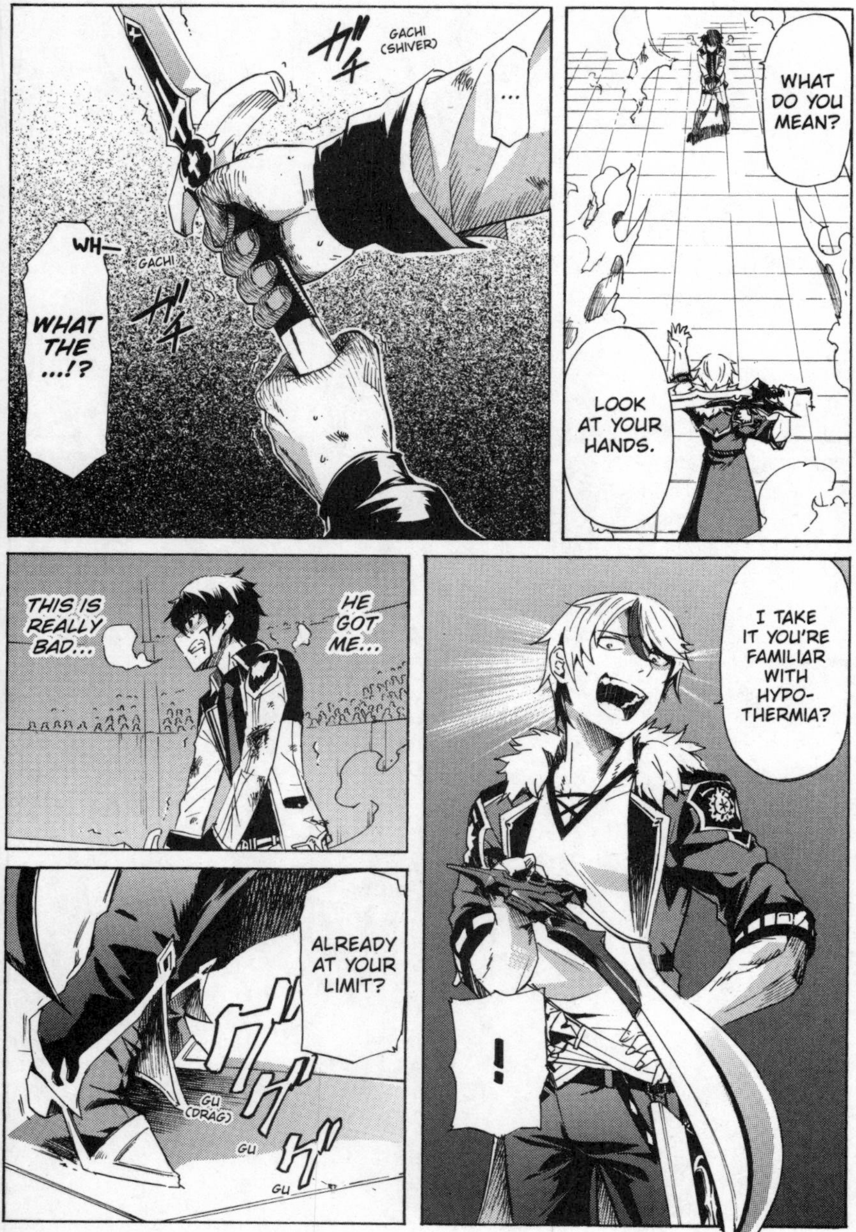
WHAT DO YOU MEAN?
LOOK AT YOUR HANDS.
GACHI (SHIVER)
...
WH—
GACHI
WHAT THE ...!?
I TAKE IT YOU'RE FAMILIAR WITH HYPO-THERMIA?
!
HE GOT ME...
THIS IS REALLY BAD...
ALREADY AT YOUR LIMIT?
GU (DRAG)
GU
GU

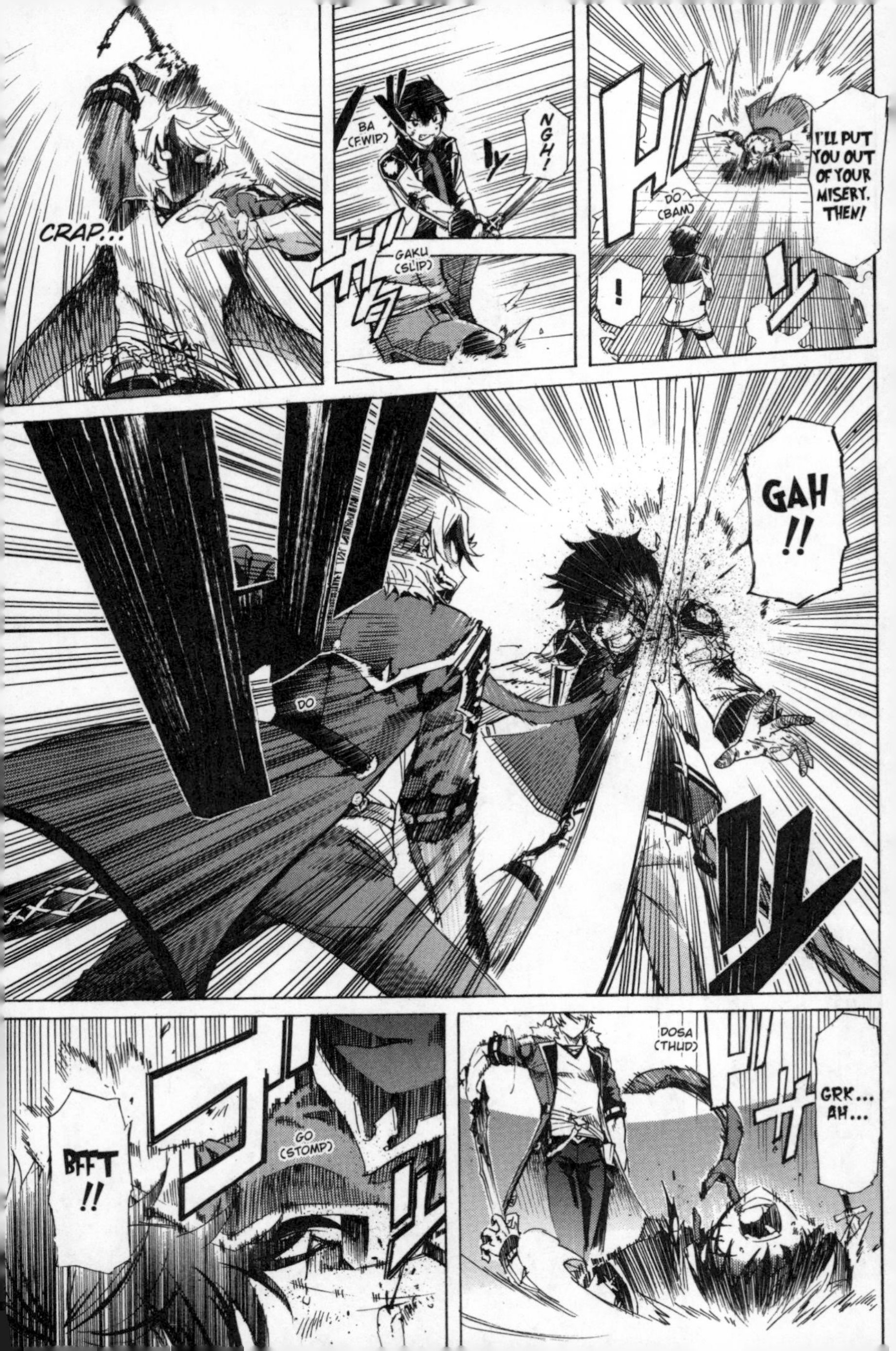
I'LL PUT YOU OUT OF YOUR MISERY, THEN!
DO (BAM)
!
NGH!
BA (F-WIP)
GAKU (SLIP)
CRAP...
GAH !!
DO
GRK... AH...
DOSA (THUD)
GO (STOMP)
BFFT !!

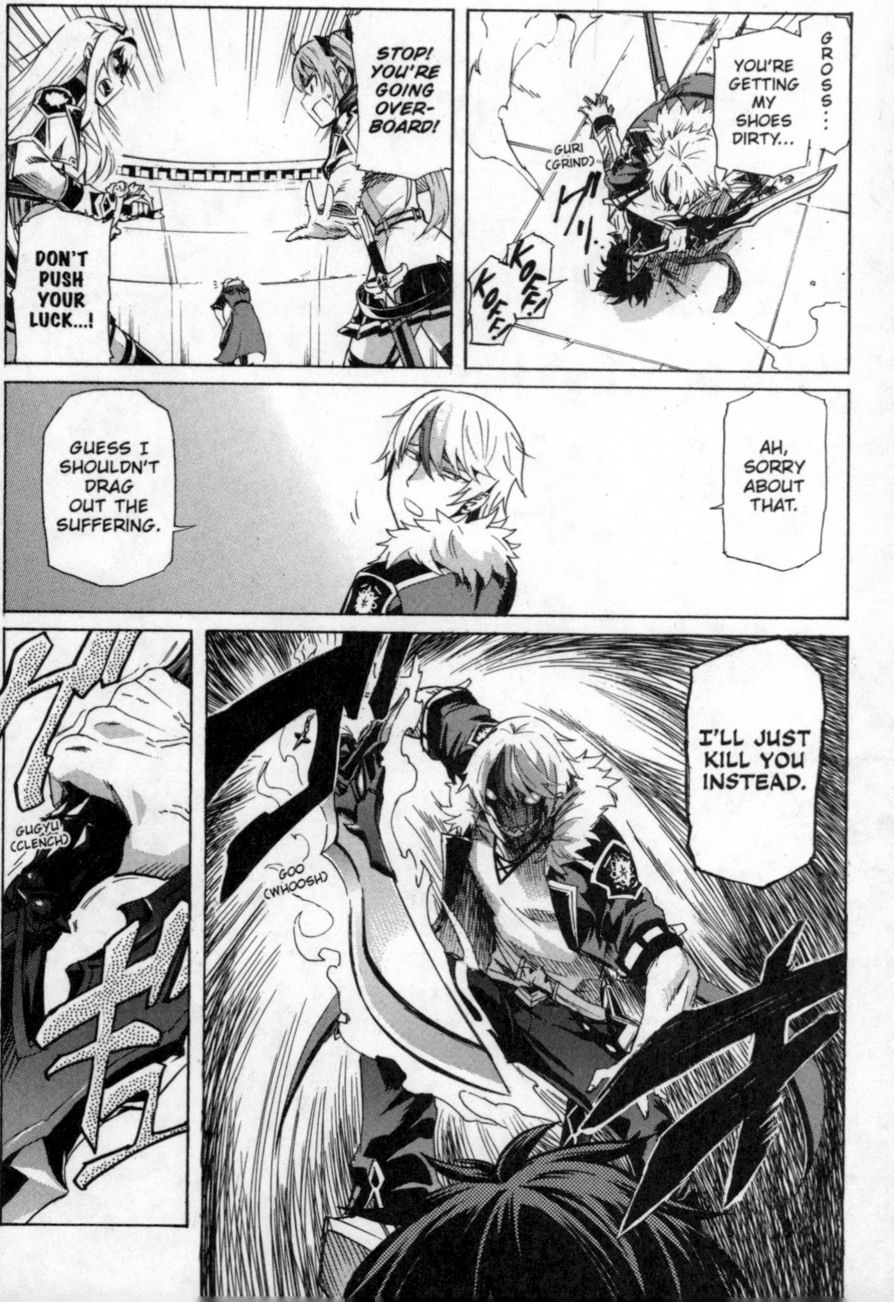
GROSS...
YOU'RE GETTING MY SHOES DIRTY...
GURI (GRIND)
KOFF! KOFF!
STOP! YOU'RE GOING OVER-BOARD!
DON'T PUSH YOUR LUCK...!
AH, SORRY ABOUT THAT.
GUESS I SHOULDN'T DRAG OUT THE SUFFERING.
I'LL JUST KILL YOU INSTEAD.
GOO (WHOOSH)
GUGYU (CLENCH)

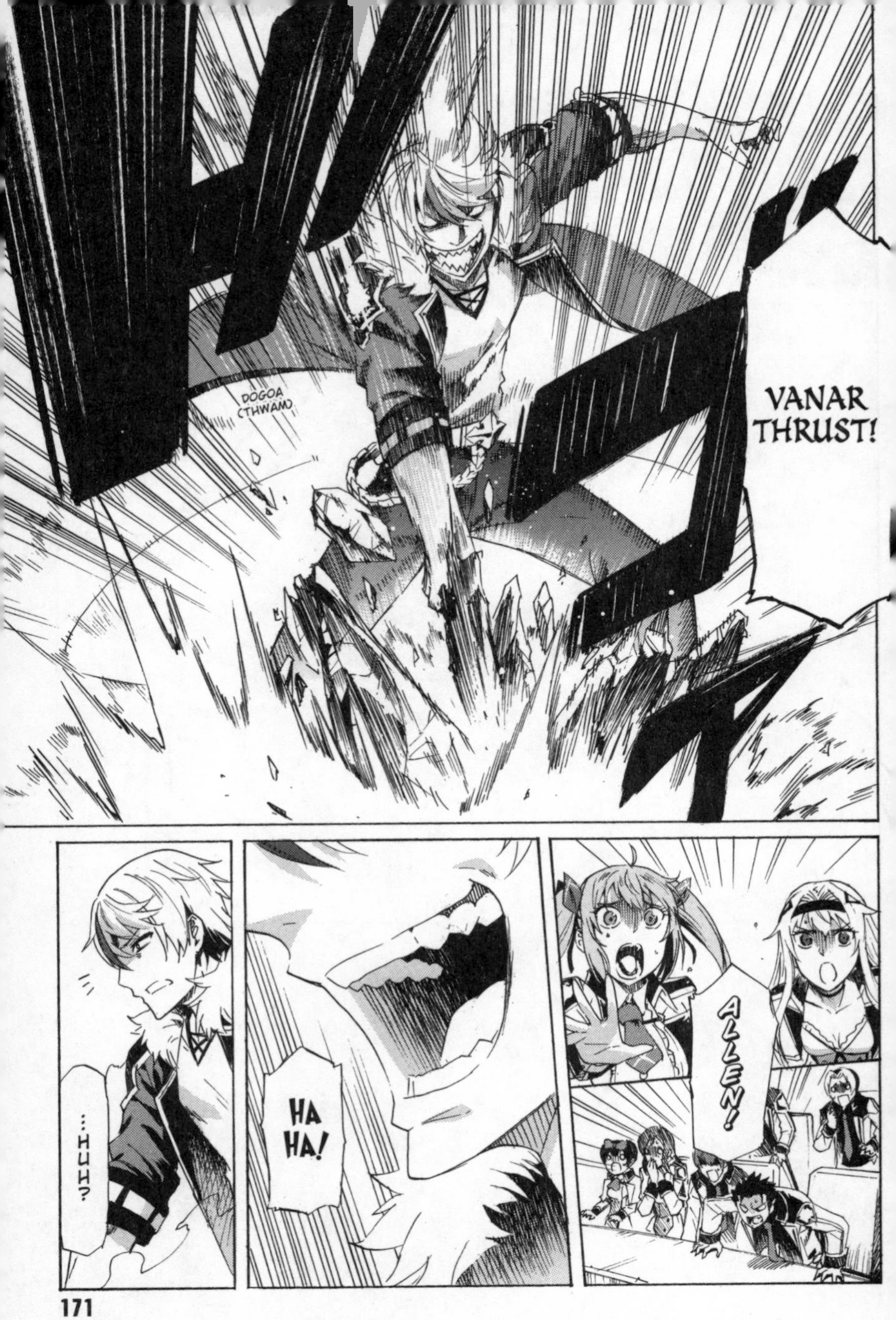
VANAR THRUST!
DOGOA (THWAM)
ALLEN!
HA HA!
...HUH?

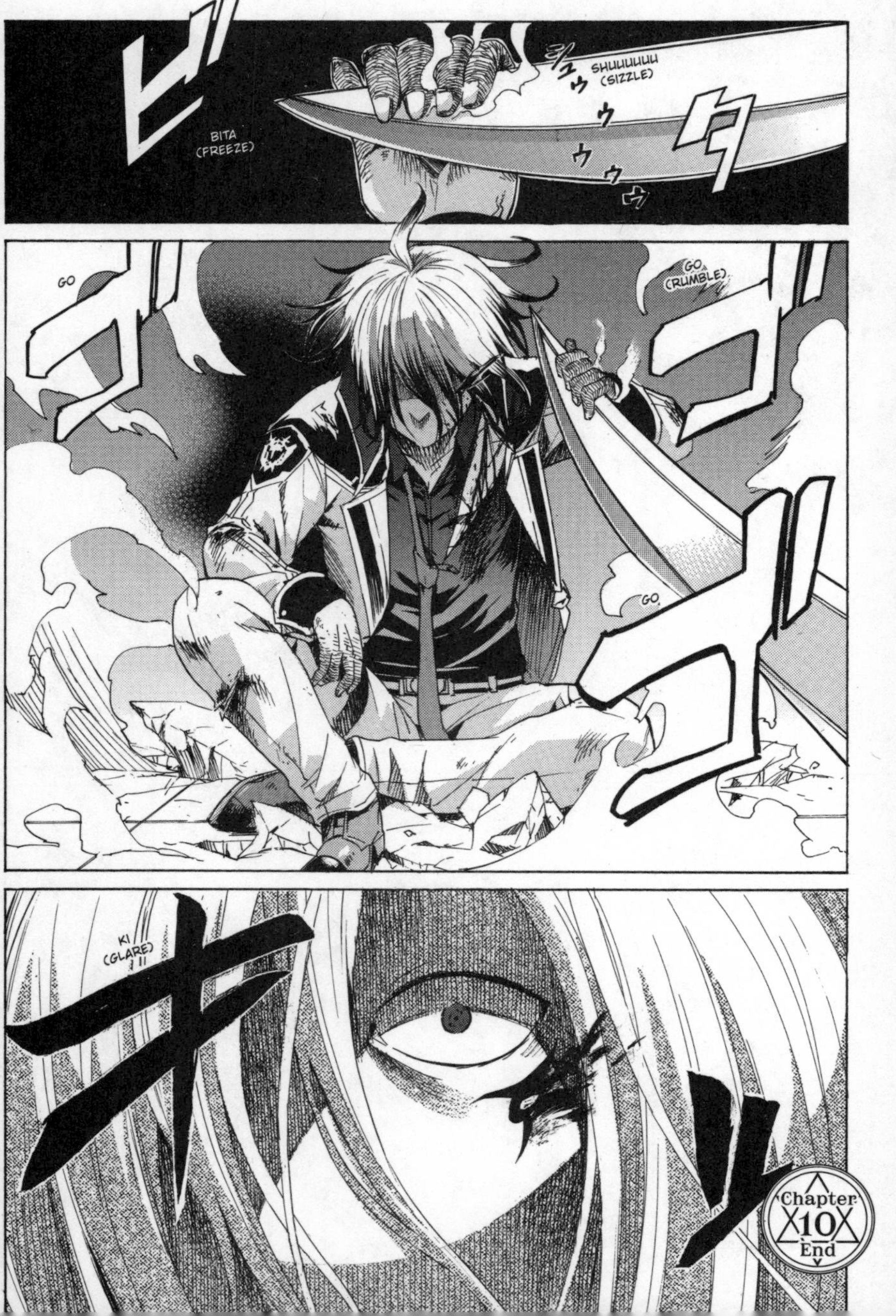
SHUUUUUU
(SIZZLE)
BITA
(FREEZE)
GO
(RUMBLE)
GO
GO
KI
(GLARE)
Chapter 10 End

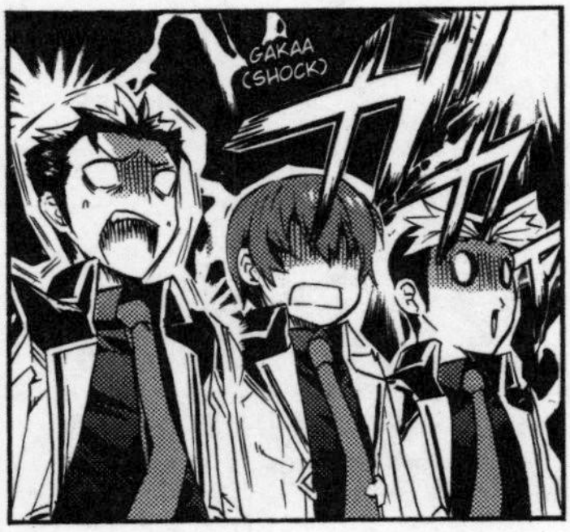
GAKAA
(SHOCK)

I KEPT PRESSING THE 100-MILLION-YEAR BUTTON AND CAME OUT ON TOP

~THE UNBEATABLE REJECT SWORDSMAN~

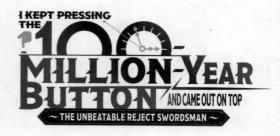

Chapter 11

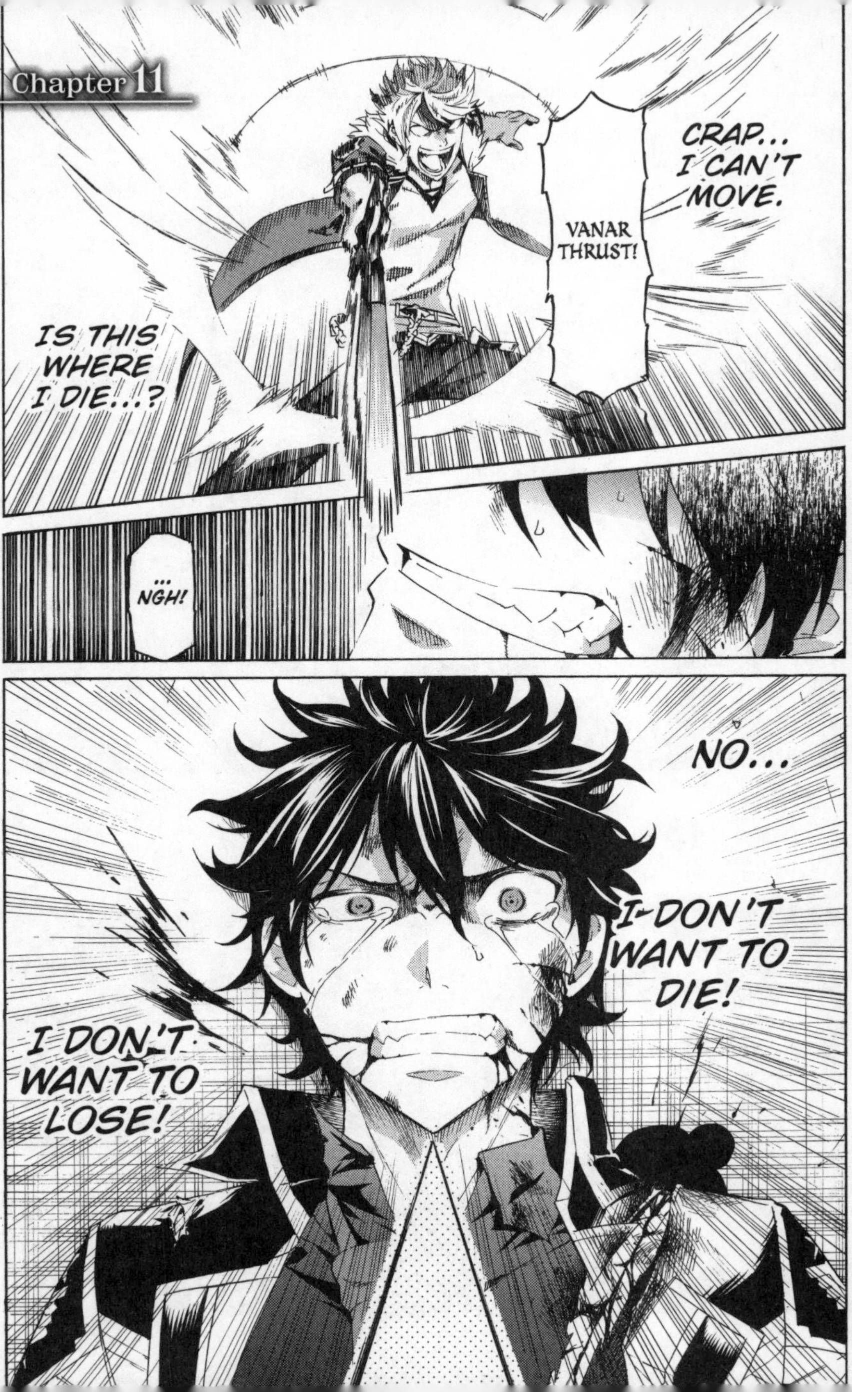
CRAP... I CAN'T MOVE.
VANAR THRUST!
IS THIS WHERE I DIE...?
...NGH!
NO...
I DON'T WANT TO DIE!
I DON'T WANT TO LOSE!

I WANT TO BEAT...

...THIS PRODIGY!

I SEE YOU'RE STILL AS SHIT AS YOU EVER WERE...ALLEN.

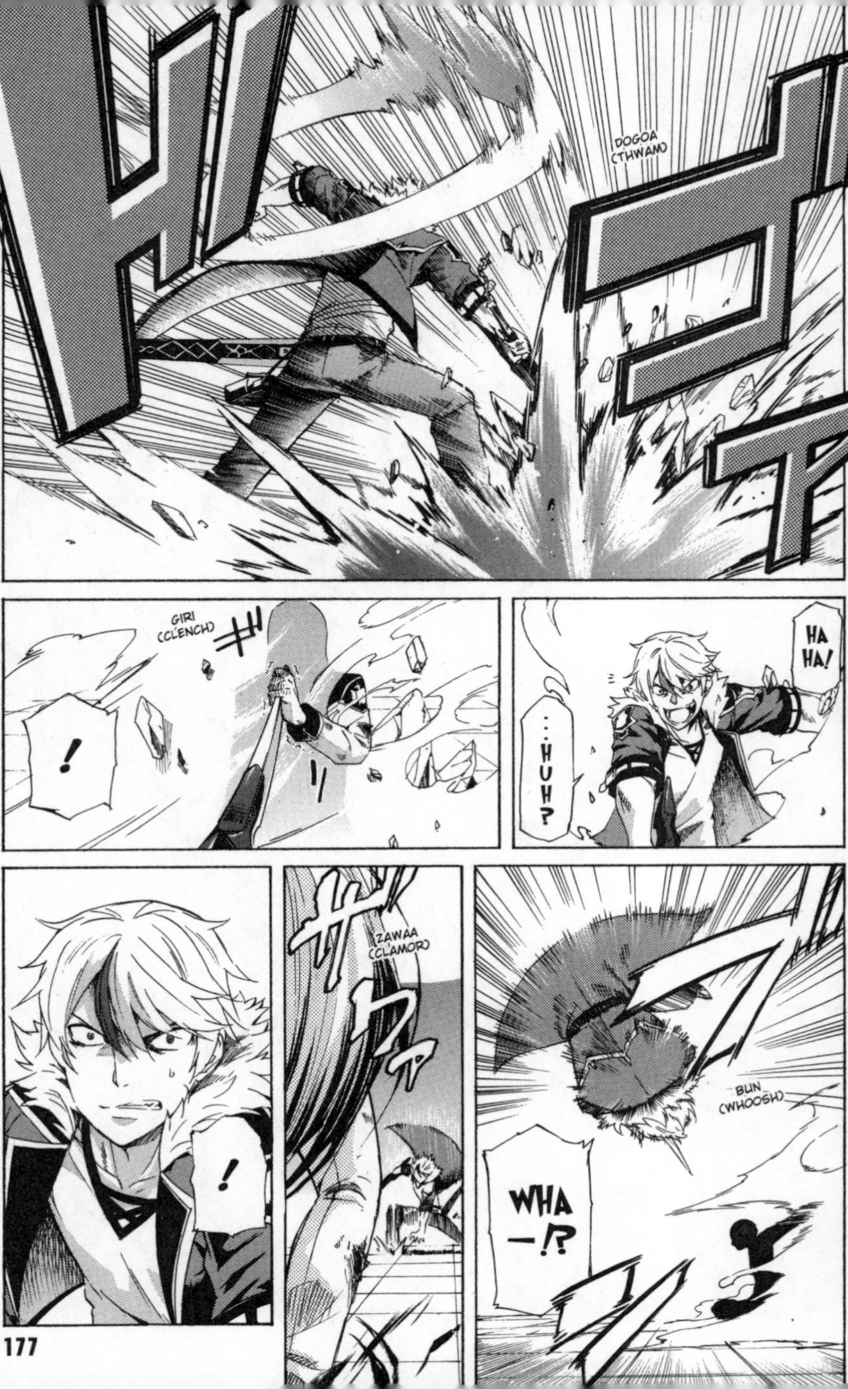
DOGOA
(THWAM)
HA HA!
...HUH?
GIRI
(CLENCH)
!
BUN
(WHOOSH)
WHA—!?
ZAWAA
(CLAMOR)
!

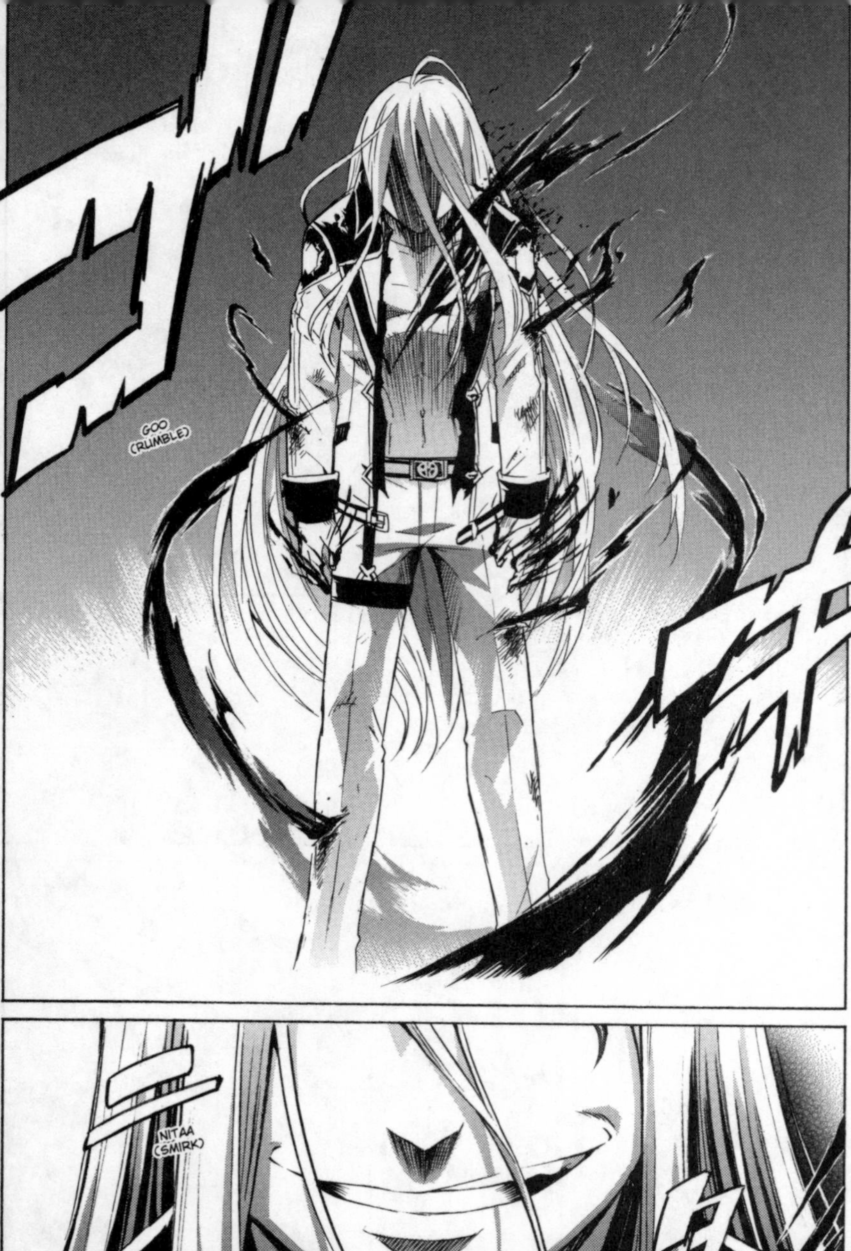
GOO
(RUMBLE)
NITAA
(SMIRK)

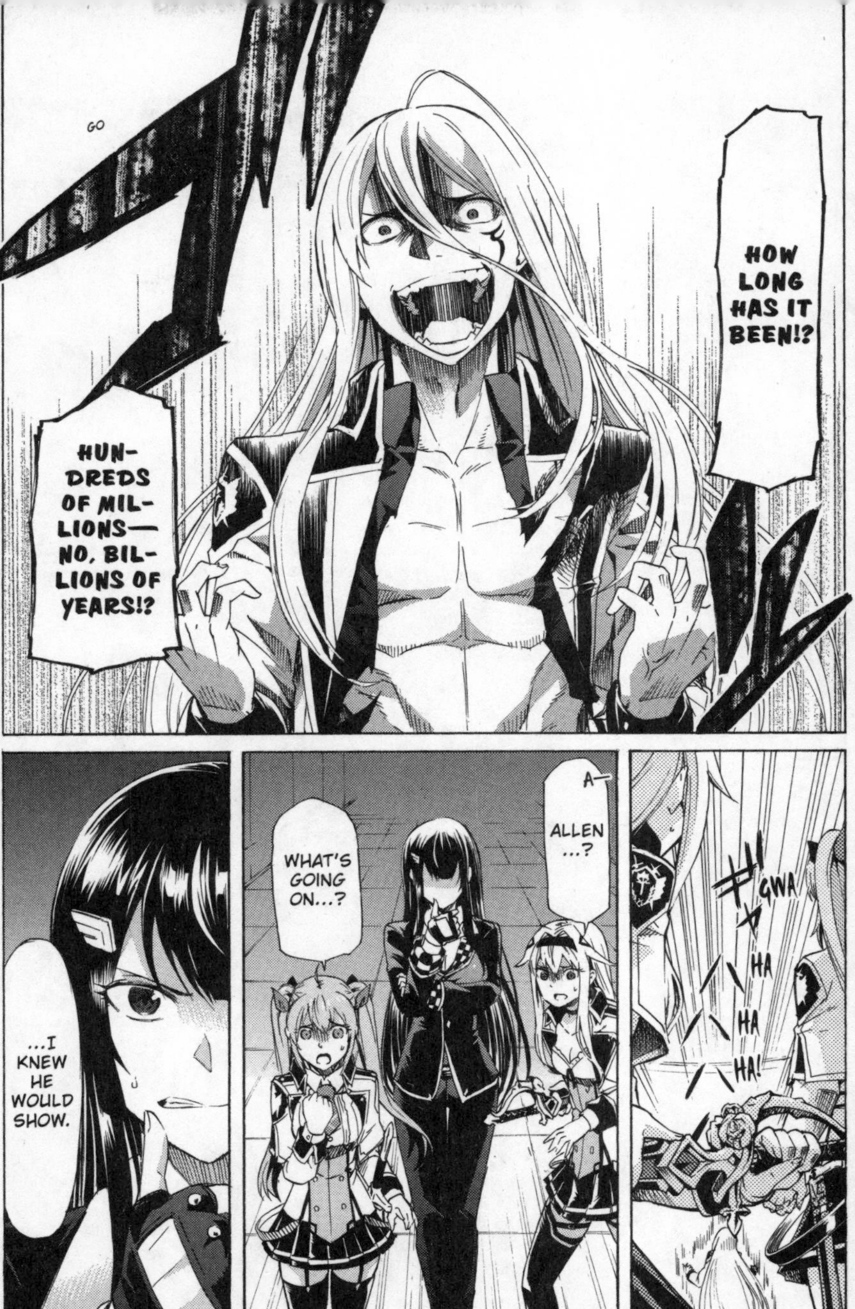
HOW LONG HAS IT BEEN!?
GO
HUN-DREDS OF MIL-LIONS— NO, BIL-LIONS OF YEARS!?
GWA HA HA HA HA!
A— ALLEN...?
WHAT'S GOING ON...?
...I KNEW HE WOULD SHOW.

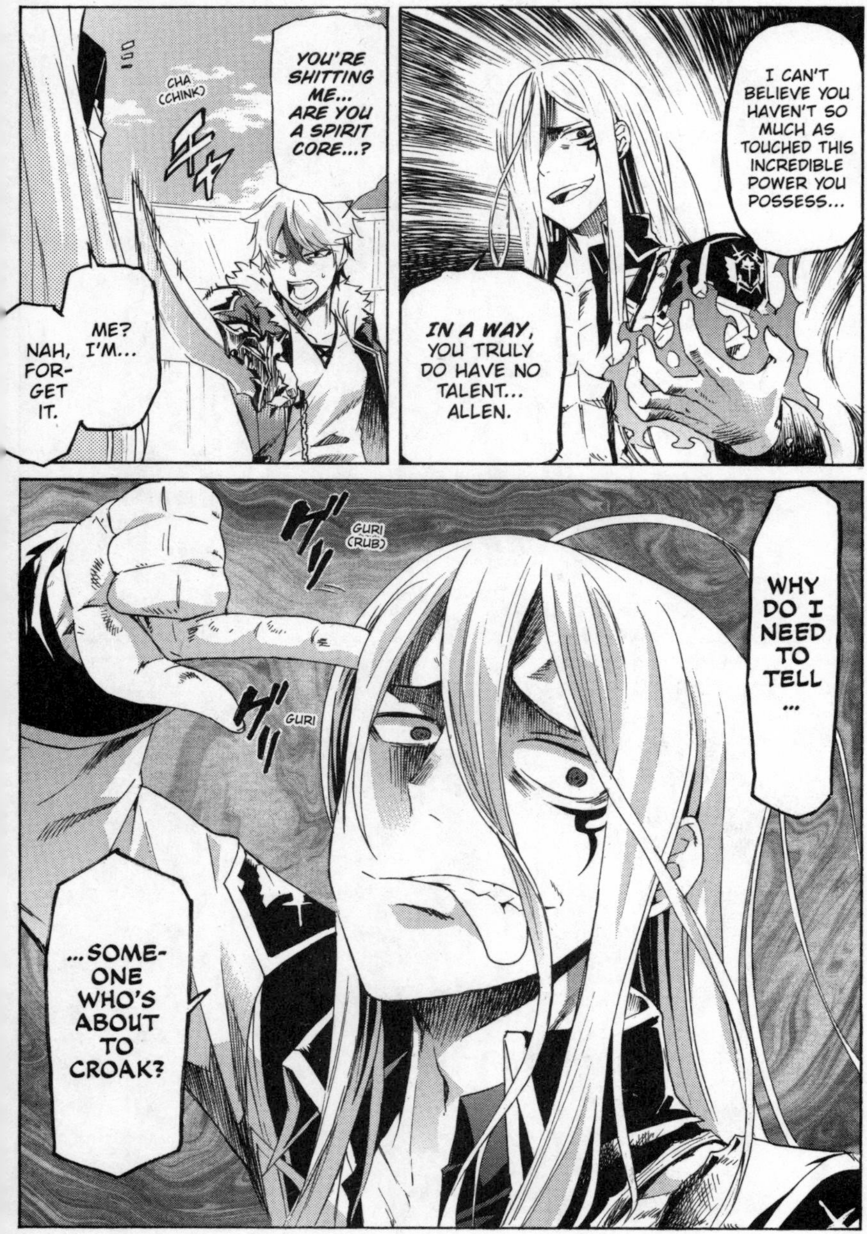
I CAN'T BELIEVE YOU HAVEN'T SO MUCH AS TOUCHED THIS INCREDIBLE POWER YOU POSSESS...
IN A WAY, YOU TRULY DO HAVE NO TALENT... ALLEN.
YOU'RE SHITTING ME... ARE YOU A SPIRIT CORE...?
CHA (CHINK)
ME? NAH, I'M... FOR-GET IT.
WHY DO I NEED TO TELL ...
GURI (RUB)
GURI
...SOME-ONE WHO'S ABOUT TO CROAK?

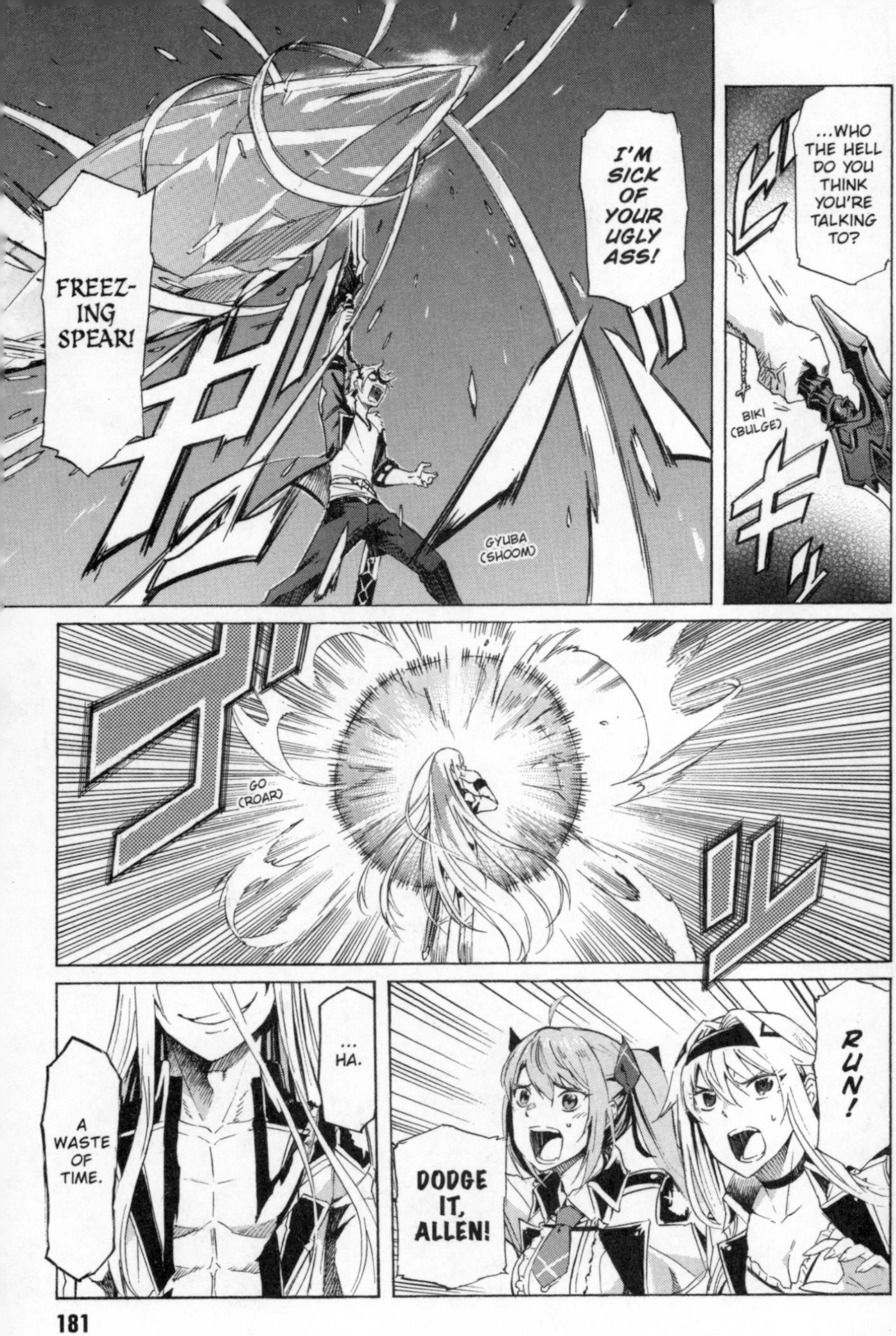
...WHO THE HELL DO YOU THINK YOU'RE TALKING TO?
BIKI (BULGE)
I'M SICK OF YOUR UGLY ASS!
FREEZ-ING SPEAR!
GYUBA (SHOOM)
GO (ROAR)
RUN!
DODGE IT, ALLEN!
... HA.
A WASTE OF TIME.

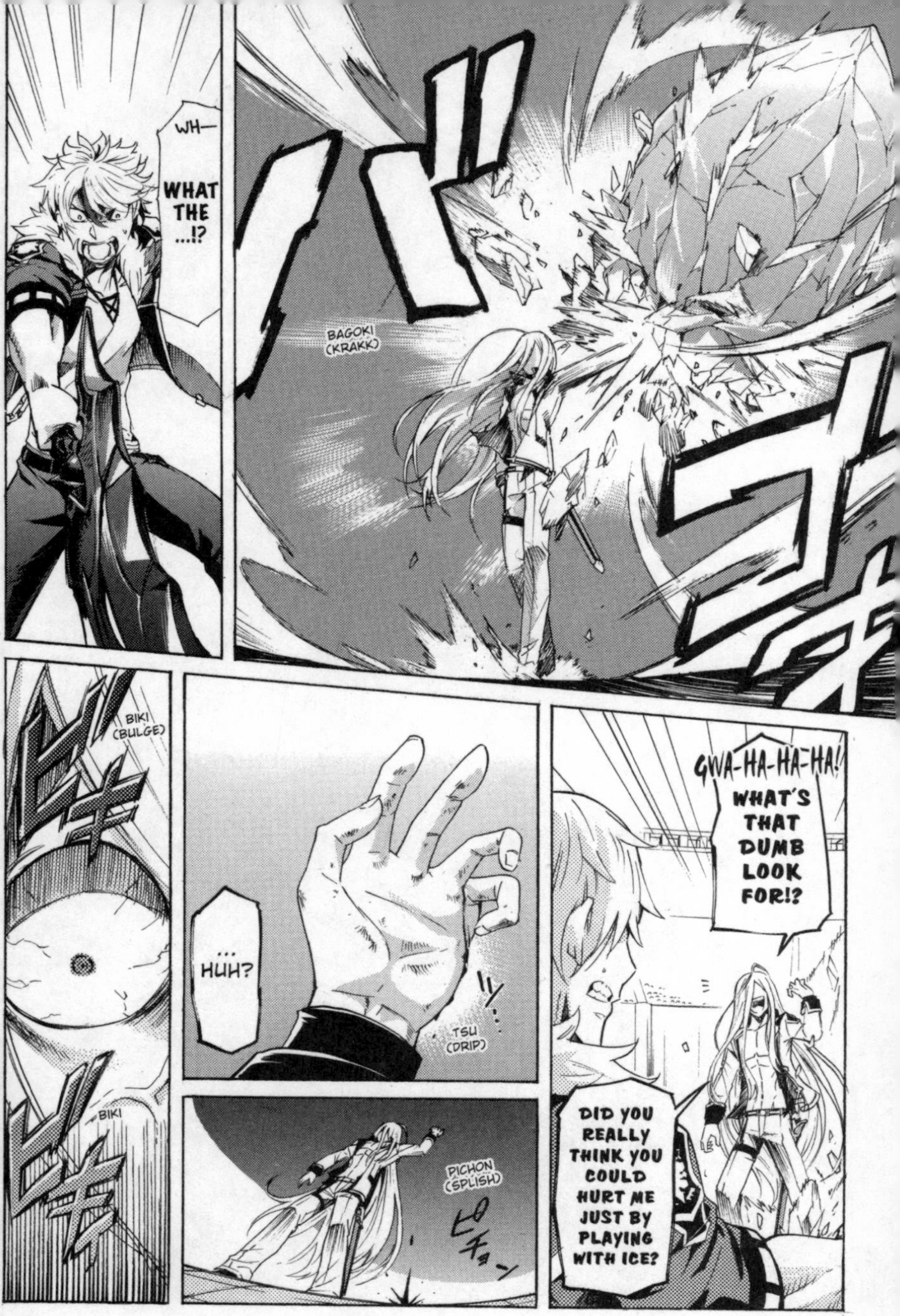
BAGOKI (KRAKK)
WH—
WHAT THE ...!?
GWA-HA-HA-HA!
WHAT'S THAT DUMB LOOK FOR!?
DID YOU REALLY THINK YOU COULD HURT ME JUST BY PLAYING WITH ICE?
... HUH?
TSU (DRIP)
PICHON (SPLISH)
BIKI (BULGE)
BIKI

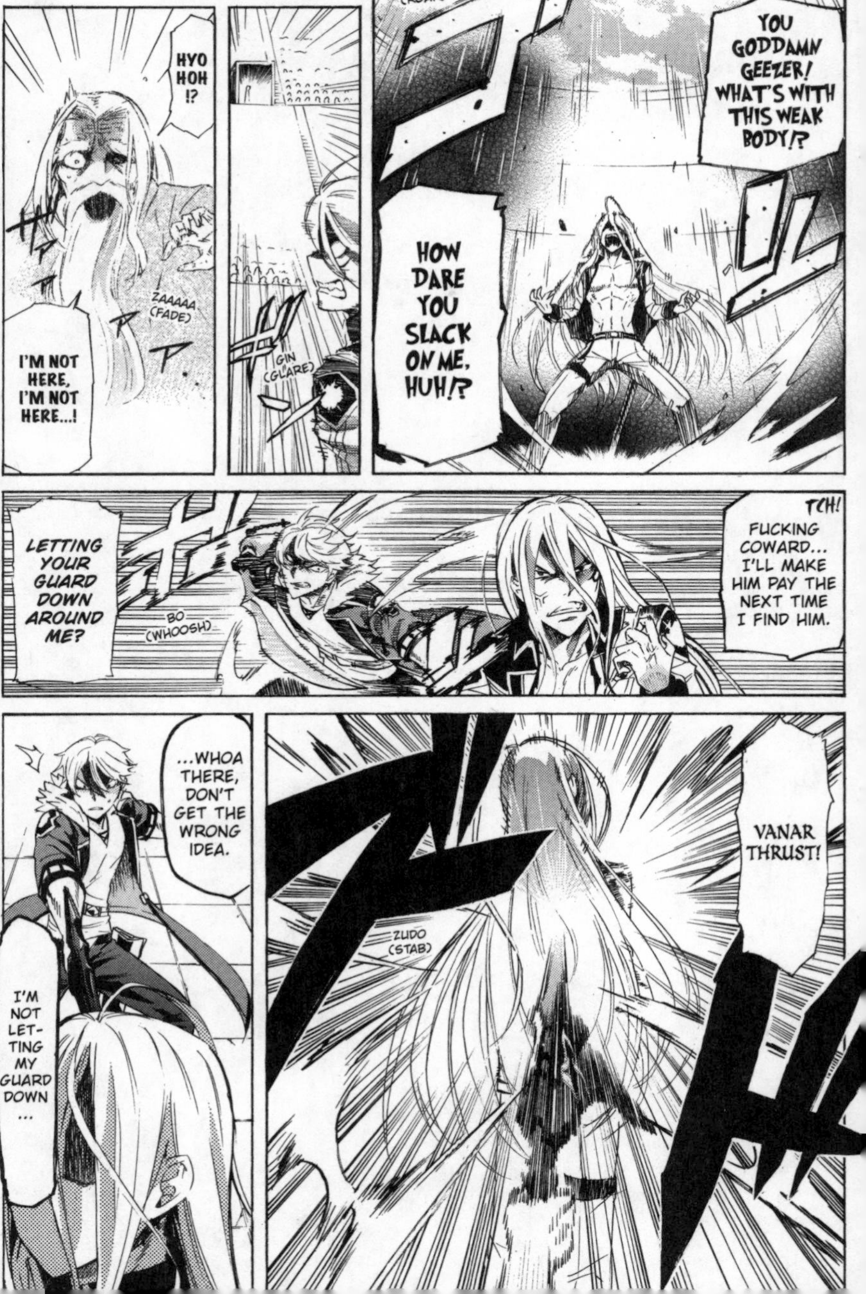
GO (ROAR)
YOU GODDAMN GEEZER! WHAT'S WITH THIS WEAK BODY!?
HOW DARE YOU SLACK ON ME, HUH!?
GIN (GLARE)
HYO HOH !?
ZAAAAA (FADE)
I'M NOT HERE, I'M NOT HERE...!
TCH! FUCKING COWARD... I'LL MAKE HIM PAY THE NEXT TIME I FIND HIM.
BO (WHOOSH)
LETTING YOUR GUARD DOWN AROUND ME?
VANAR THRUST!
ZUDO (STAB)
...WHOA THERE, DON'T GET THE WRONG IDEA.
I'M NOT LETTING MY GUARD DOWN...

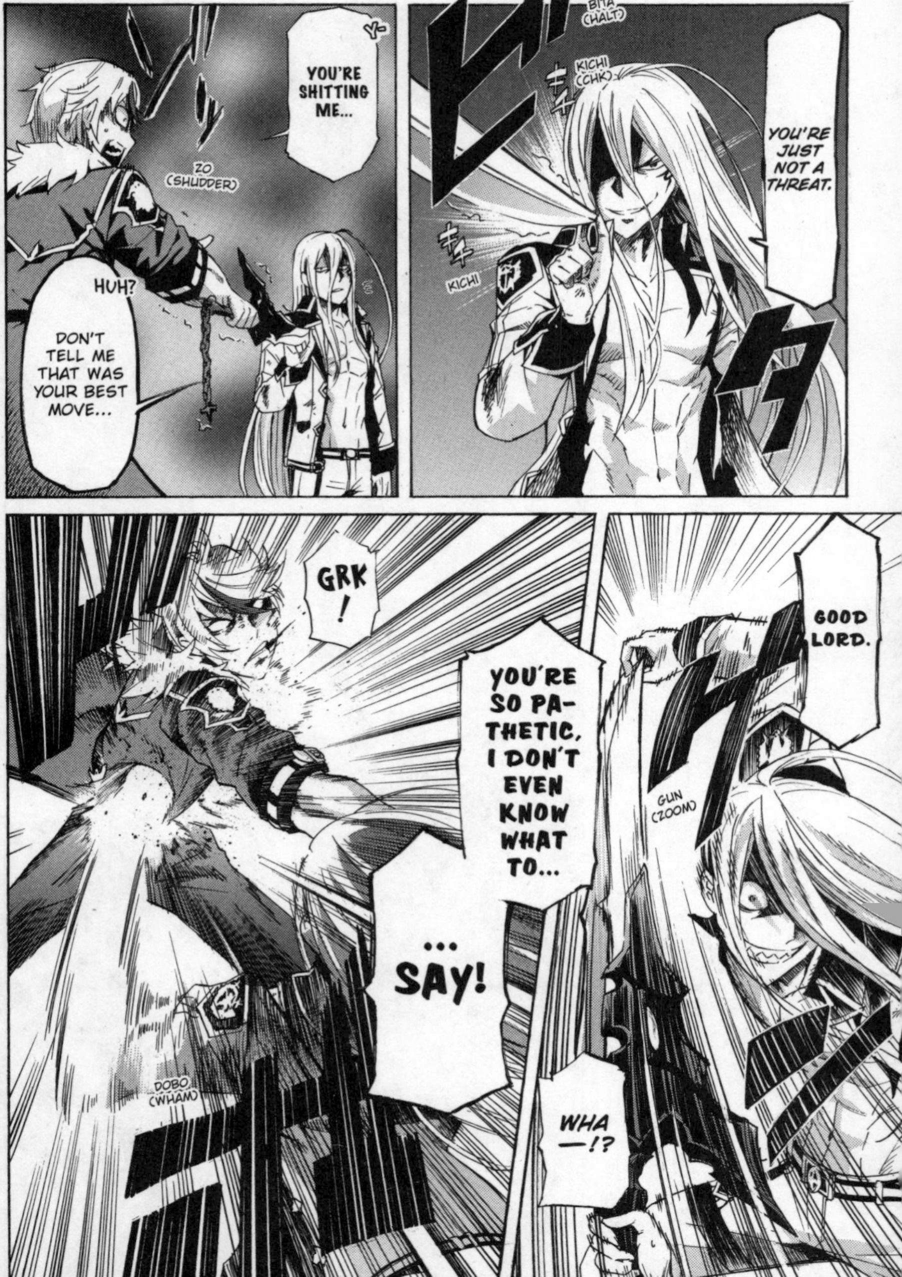
BITA (HALT)
KICHI (CHK)
YOU'RE JUST NOT A THREAT.
KICHI
Y-
YOU'RE SHITTING ME...
ZO (SHUDDER)
HUH?
DON'T TELL ME THAT WAS YOUR BEST MOVE...
GOOD LORD.
GUN (ZOOM)
WHA—!?
GRK!
YOU'RE SO PATHETIC, I DON'T EVEN KNOW WHAT TO...
...SAY!
DOBO (WHAM)

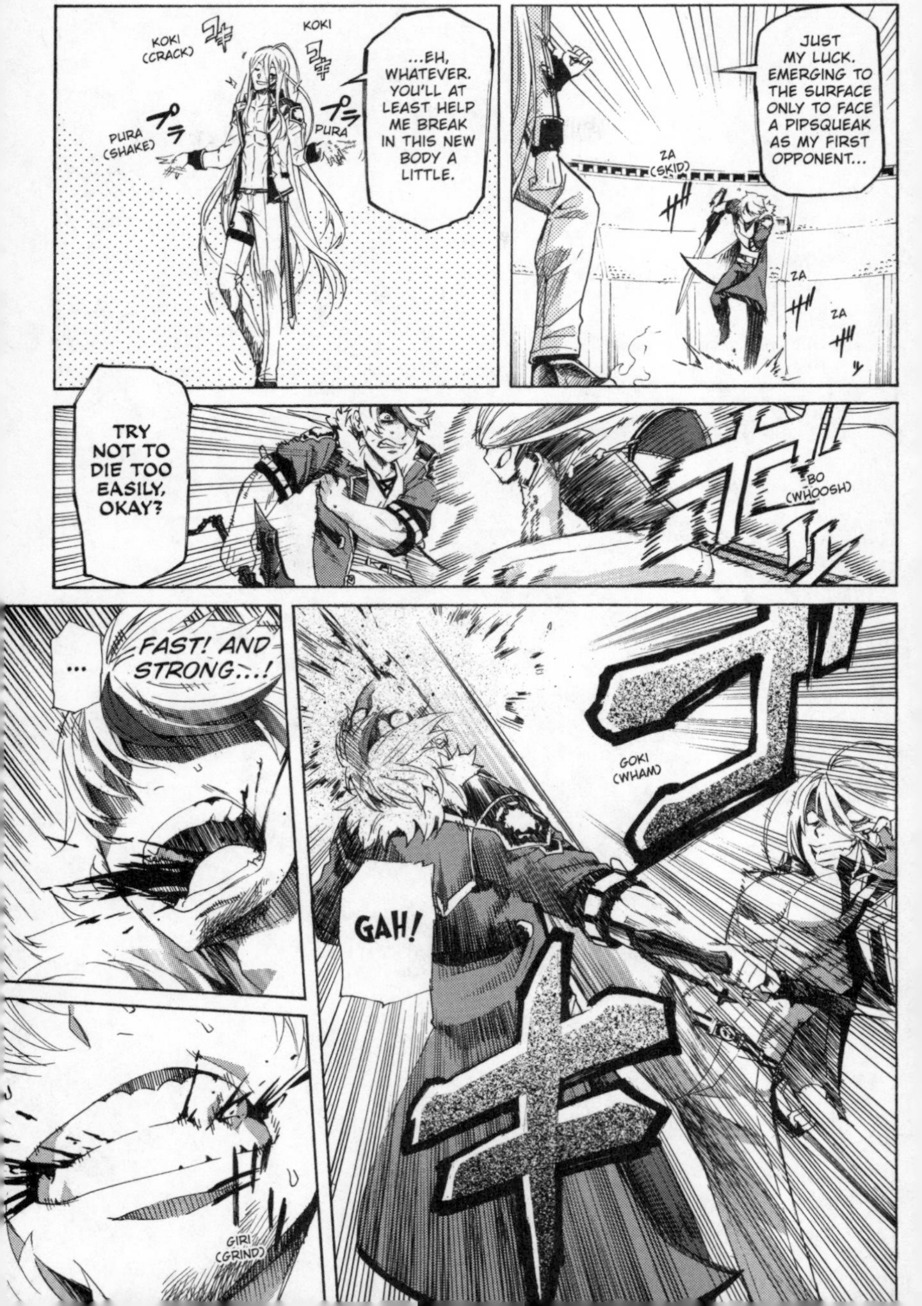

JUST MY LUCK. EMERGING TO THE SURFACE ONLY TO FACE A PIPSQUEAK AS MY FIRST OPPONENT...
ZA (SKID)
ZA
ZA
...EH, WHATEVER. YOU'LL AT LEAST HELP ME BREAK IN THIS NEW BODY A LITTLE.
KOKI
KOKI (CRACK)
PURA
PURA (SHAKE)
BO (WHOOSH)
TRY NOT TO DIE TOO EASILY, OKAY?
GOKI (WHAM)
GAH!
FAST! AND STRONG...!
...
GIRI (GRIND)

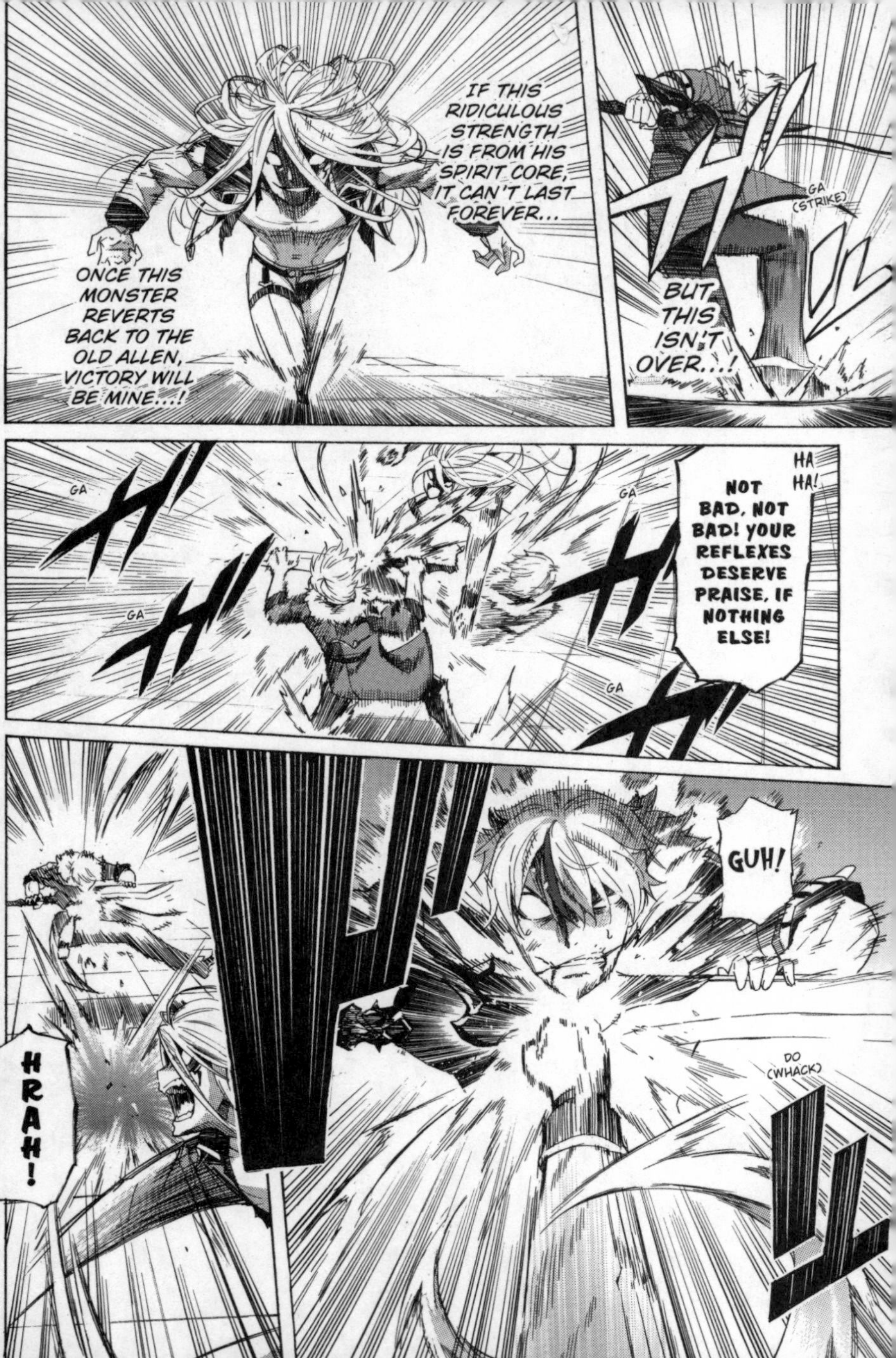
GA (STRIKE)
BUT THIS ISN'T OVER...!
IF THIS RIDICULOUS STRENGTH IS FROM HIS SPIRIT CORE, IT CAN'T LAST FOREVER...
ONCE THIS MONSTER REVERTS BACK TO THE OLD ALLEN, VICTORY WILL BE MINE...!
HA HA!
NOT BAD, NOT BAD! YOUR REFLEXES DESERVE PRAISE, IF NOTHING ELSE!
GA
GA
GA
GA
GUH!
DO (WHACK)
HRAH!

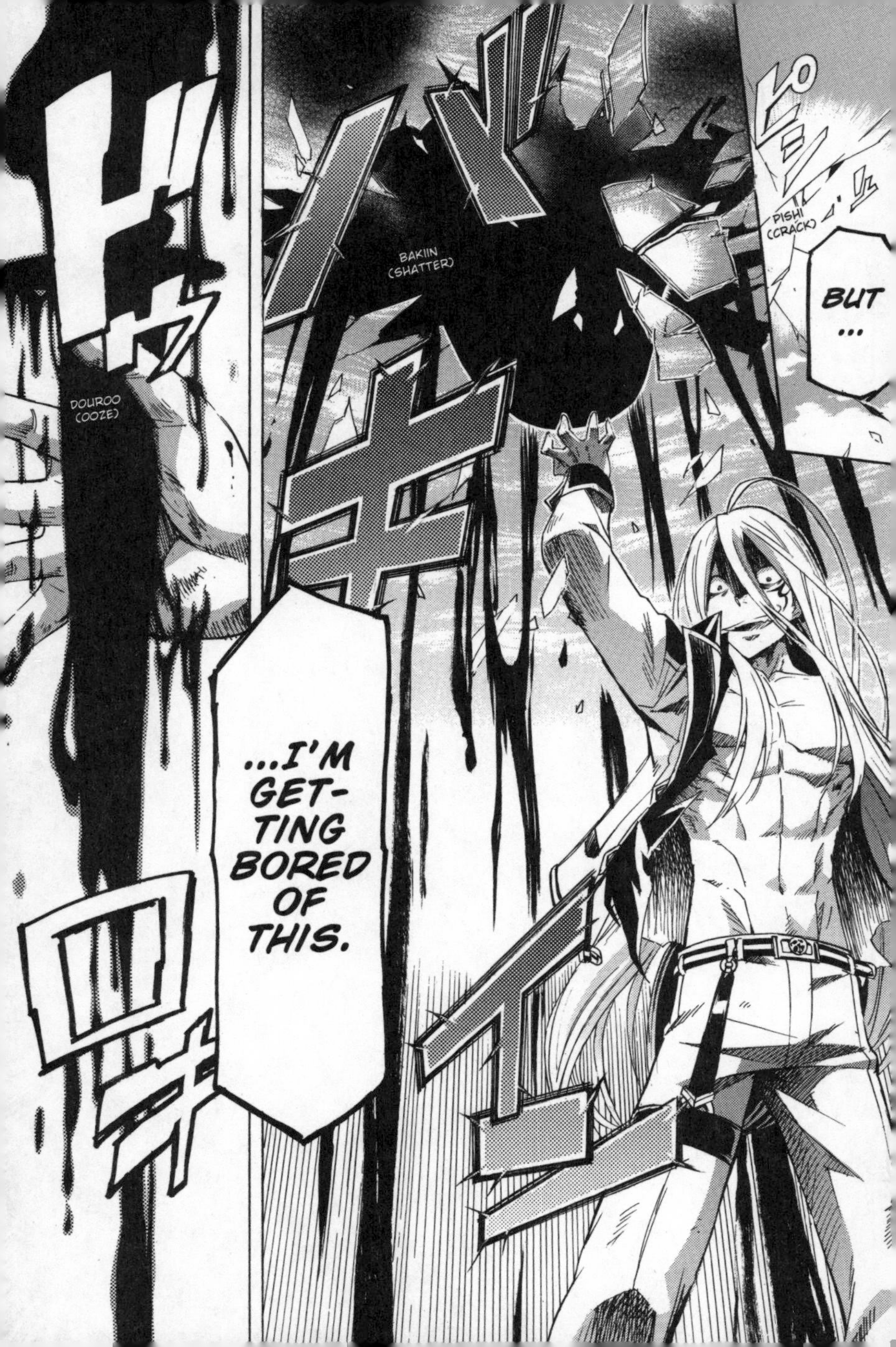
PISHI (CRACK)
BUT ...
BAKIIN (SHATTER)
...I'M GETTING BORED OF THIS.
DOUROO (OOZE)

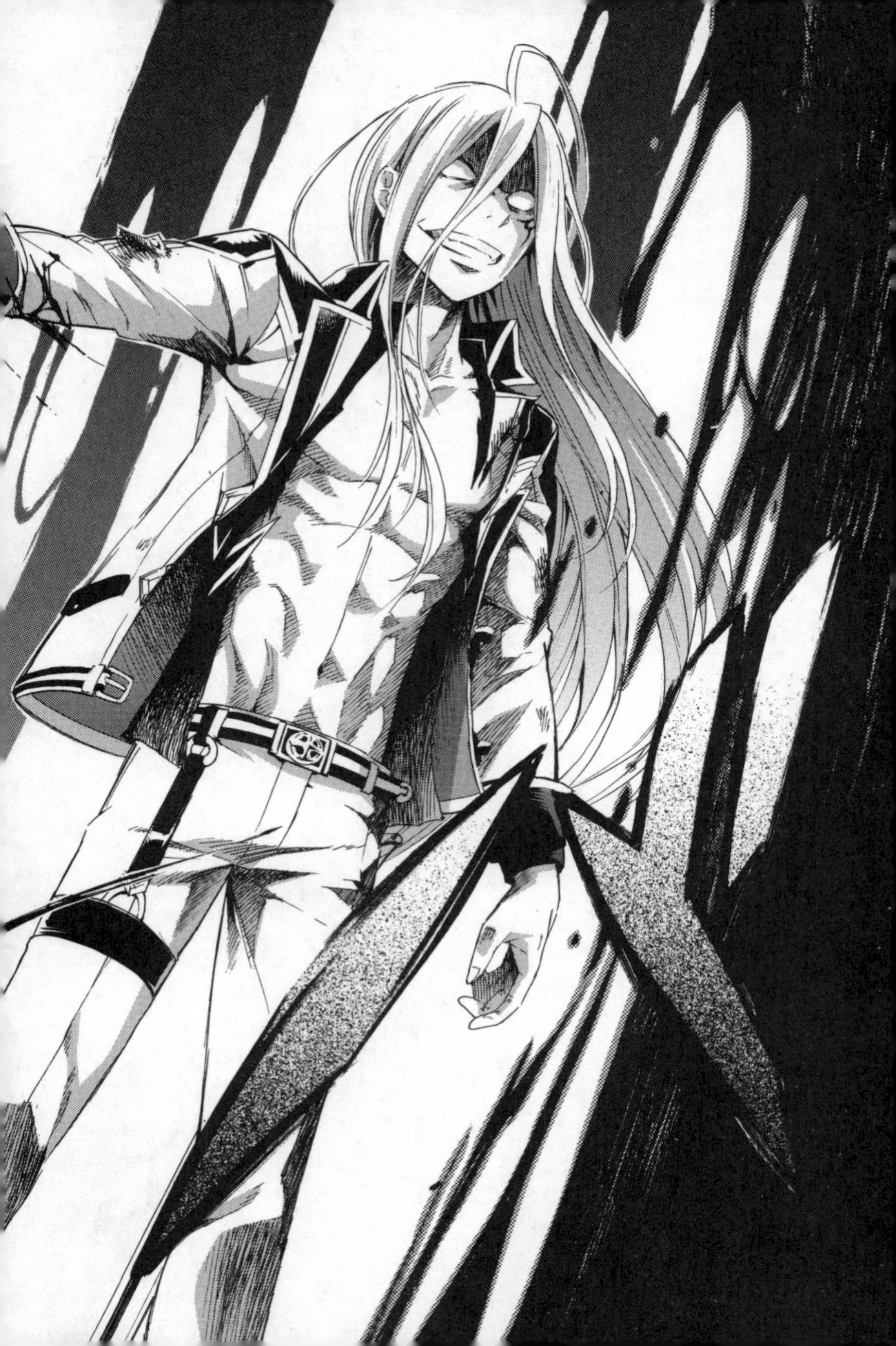

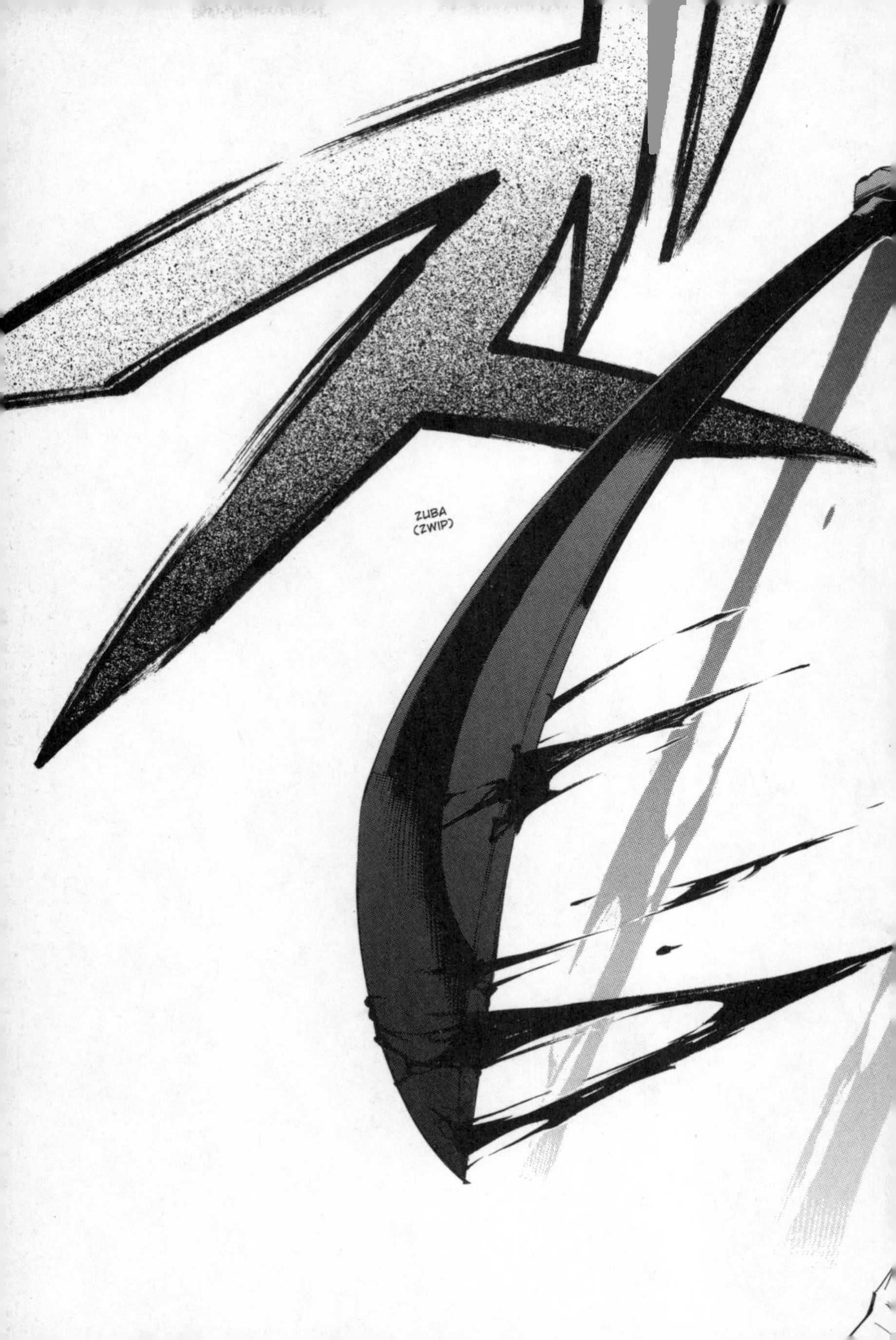
ZUBA
(ZWIP)

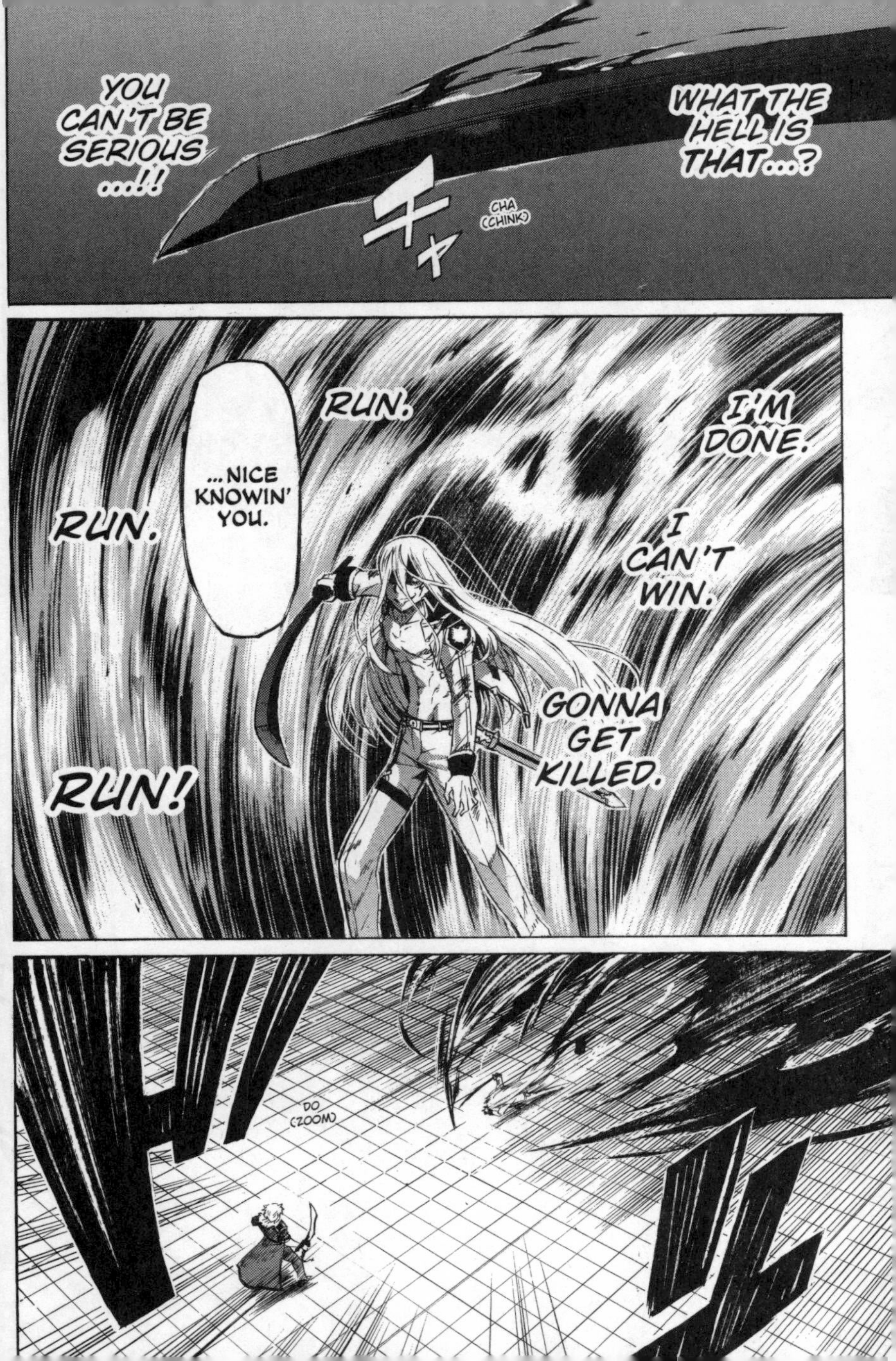
WHAT THE HELL IS THAT...?
CHA (CHINK)
YOU CAN'T BE SERIOUS ...!!
I'M DONE.
RUN.
I CAN'T WIN.
...NICE KNOWIN' YOU.
RUN.
GONNA GET KILLED.
RUN!
DO (ZOOM)

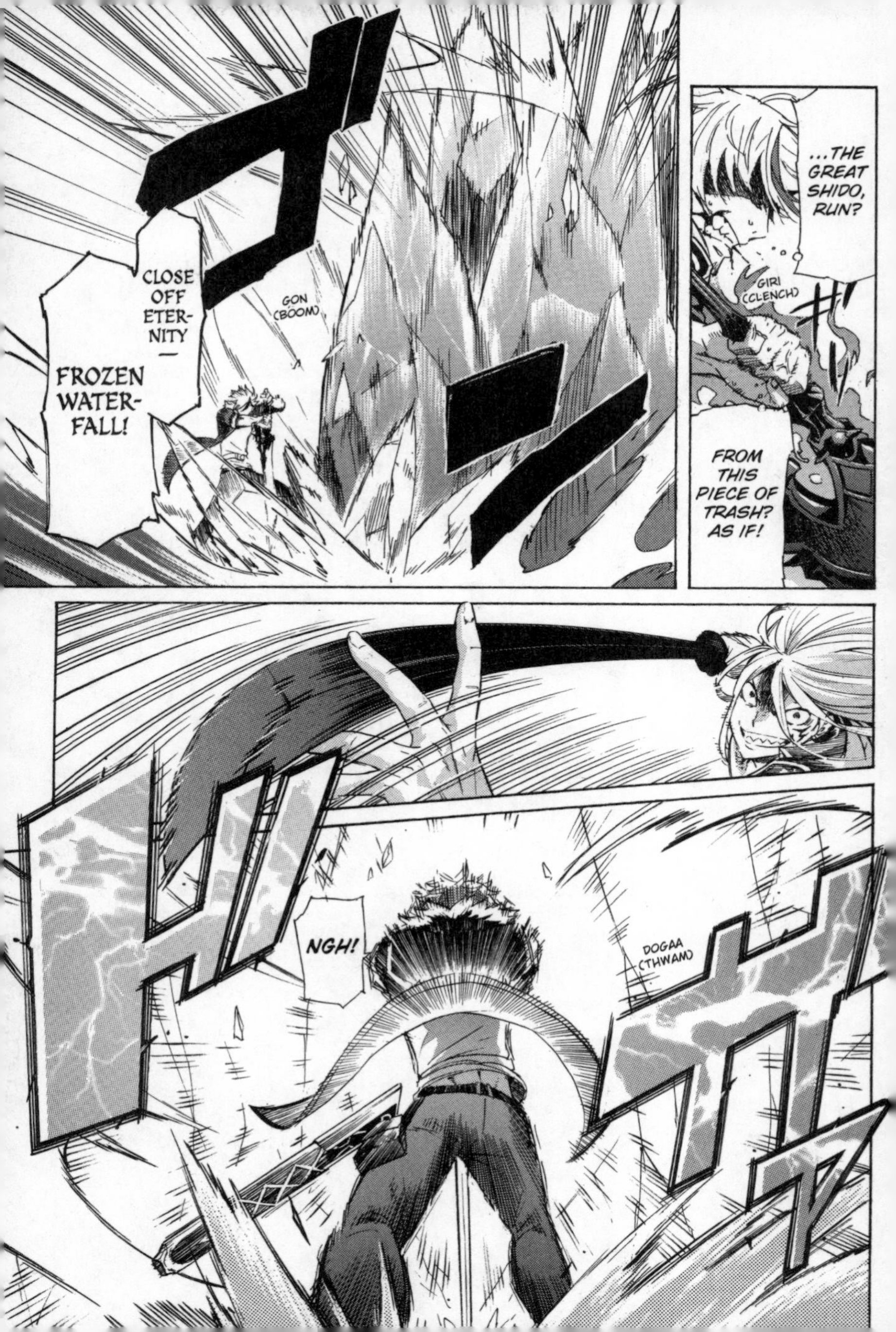
...THE GREAT SHIDO, RUN?
GIRI (CLENCH)
FROM THIS PIECE OF TRASH? AS IF!
CLOSE OFF ETER-NITY—
FROZEN WATER-FALL!
GON (BOOM)
NGH!
DOGAA (THWAM)

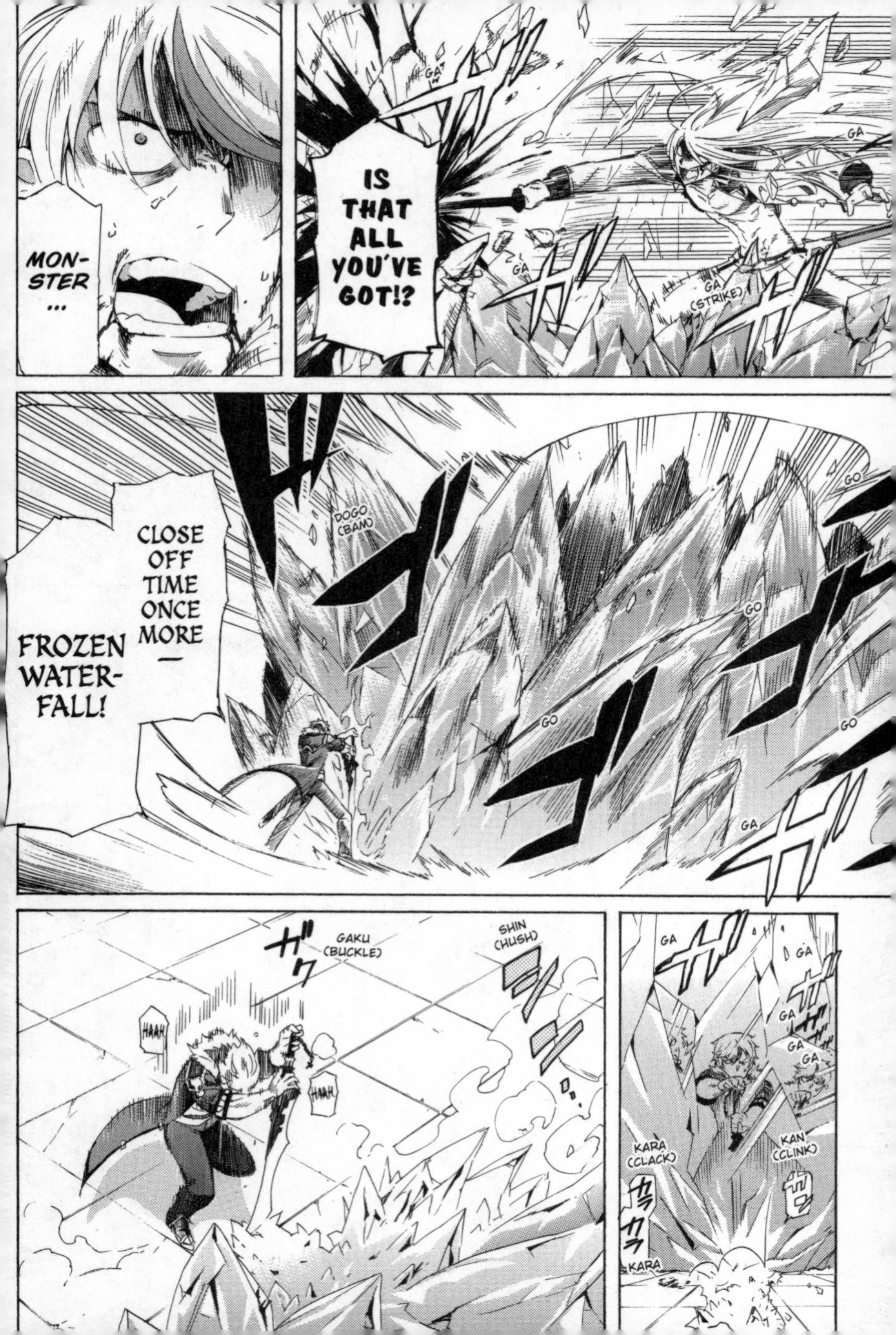
GA
GA
IS THAT ALL YOU'VE GOT!?
GA
GA (STRIKE)
MON-STER...
DOGO (BAM)
GO
CLOSE OFF TIME ONCE MORE—
FROZEN WATER-FALL!
GO
GO
GO
GA
GA
GA
GA
GA
GA
KAN (CLINK)
KARA (CLACK)
KARA
SHIN (HUSH)
GAKU (BUCKLE)
HAAH
HAAH

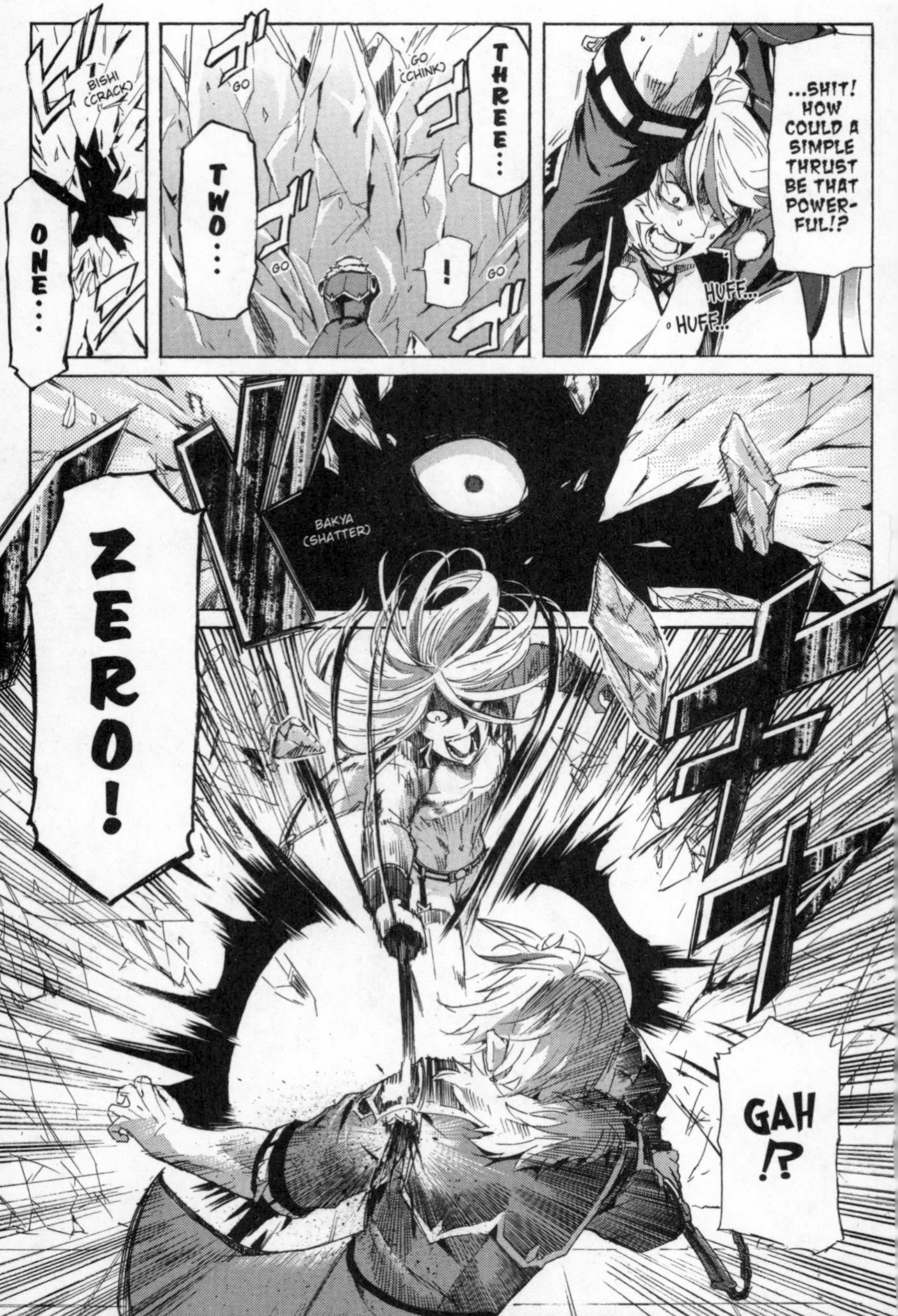
...SHIT! HOW COULD A SIMPLE THRUST BE THAT POWERFUL!?
HUFF... HUFF...
THREE...
GO (CHINK)
GO
TWO...
!
GO
GO
BISHI (CRACK)
ONE...
BAKYA (SHATTER)
ZERO!
GAH!?

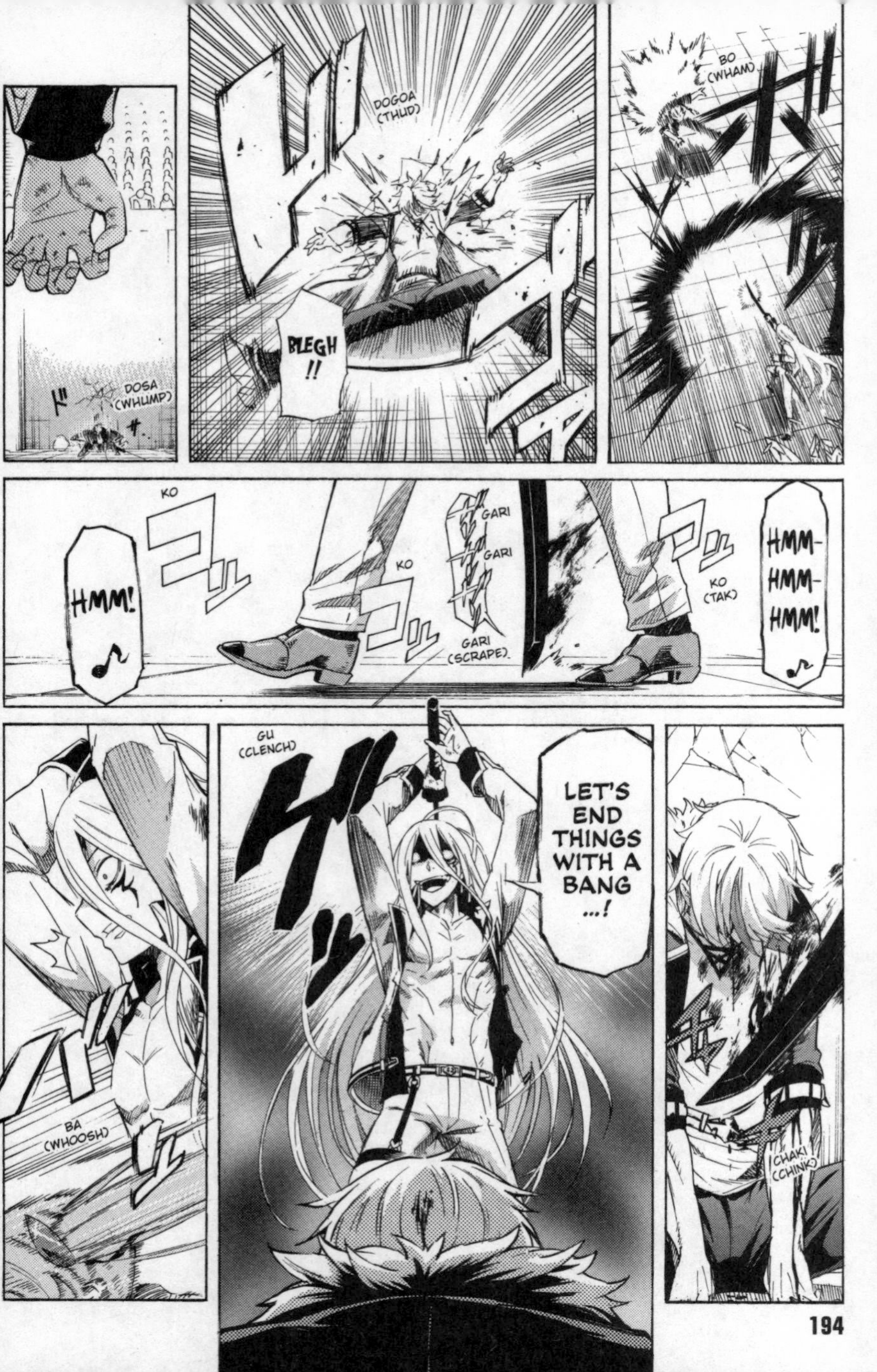
BO (WHAM)
DOGOA (THUD)
BLEGH!!
DOSA (WHUMP)
HMM-HMM-HMM! ♪
KO (TAK)
GARI
GARI
GARI (SCRAPE)
KO
KO
HMM! ♪
CHAKI (CHINK)
LET'S END THINGS WITH A BANG...!
GU (CLENCH)
BA (WHOOSH)

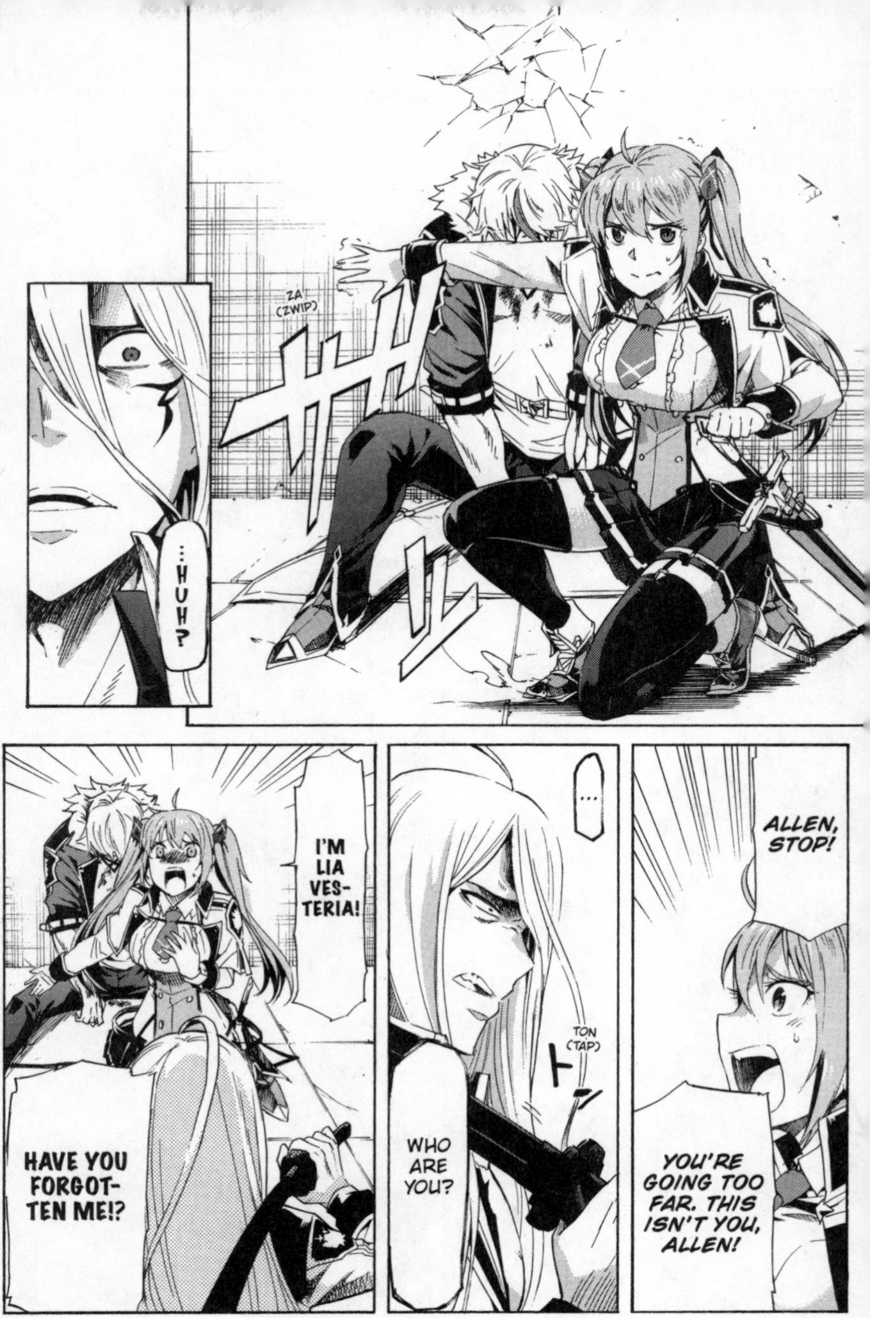
ZA (ZWIP)
...HUH?
ALLEN, STOP!
YOU'RE GOING TOO FAR. THIS ISN'T YOU, ALLEN!
...
TON (TAP)
WHO ARE YOU?
I'M LIA VES-TERIA!
HAVE YOU FORGOT-TEN ME!?

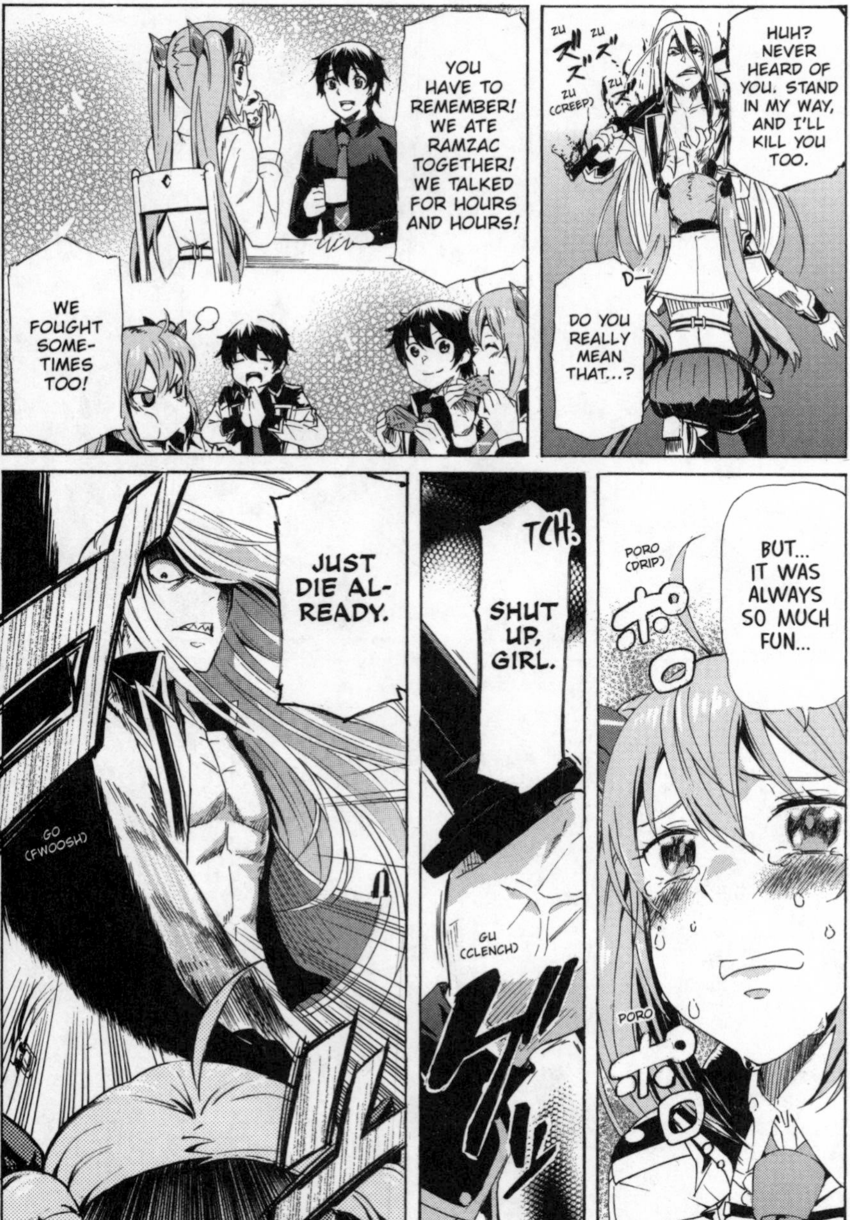
ZU ZU ZU ZU (CREEP)
HUH? NEVER HEARD OF YOU. STAND IN MY WAY, AND I'LL KILL YOU TOO.
D—
DO YOU REALLY MEAN THAT...?
YOU HAVE TO REMEMBER! WE ATE RAMZAC TOGETHER! WE TALKED FOR HOURS AND HOURS!
WE FOUGHT SOMETIMES TOO!
PORO (DRIP)
BUT... IT WAS ALWAYS SO MUCH FUN...
PORO
TCH.
SHUT UP, GIRL.
GU (CLENCH)
JUST DIE ALREADY.
GO (FWOOSH)

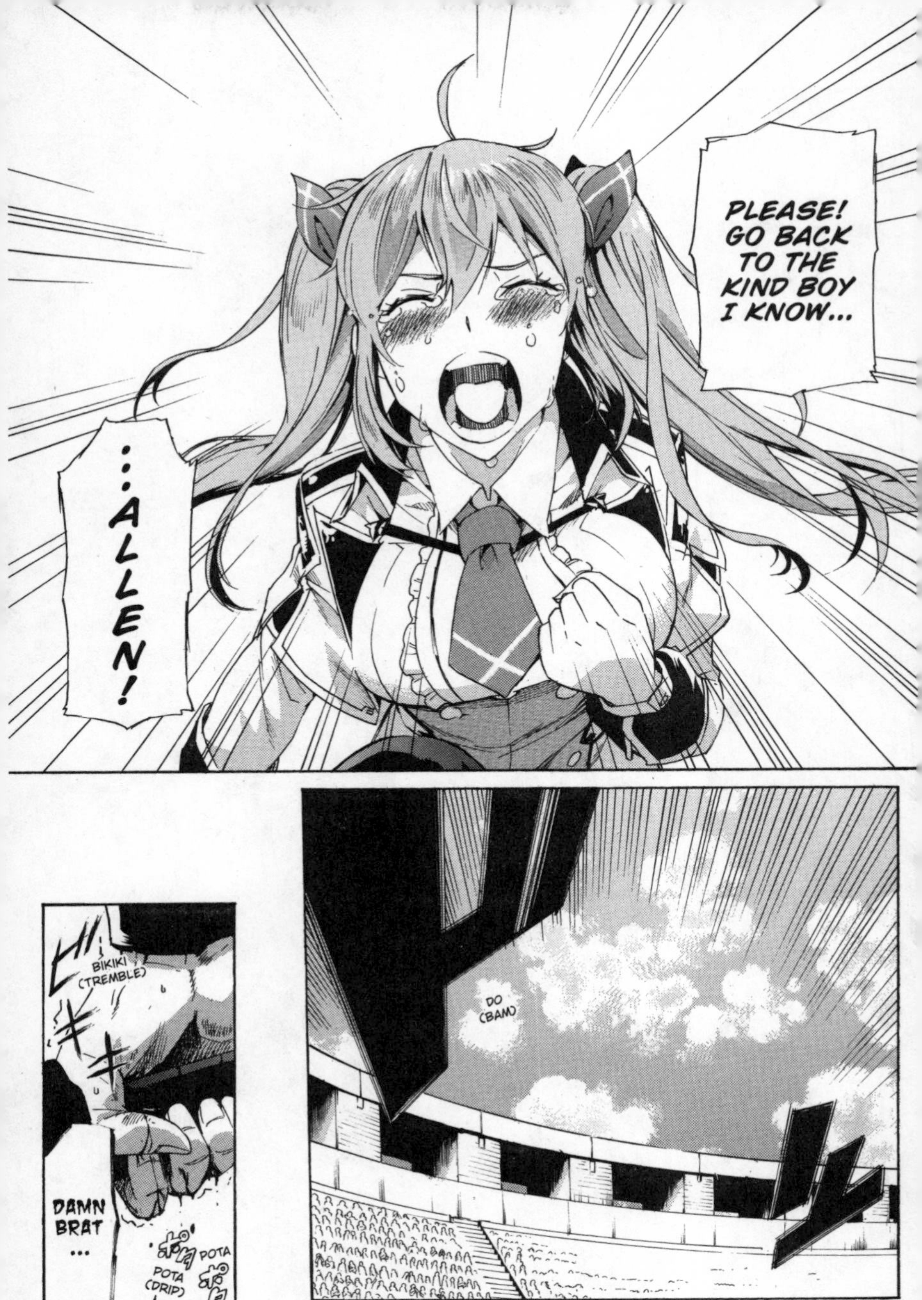
PLEASE! GO BACK TO THE KIND BOY I KNOW...
...ALLEN!
DO (BAM)
BIKIKI (TREMBLE)
DAMN BRAT ...
POTA POTA (DRIP)

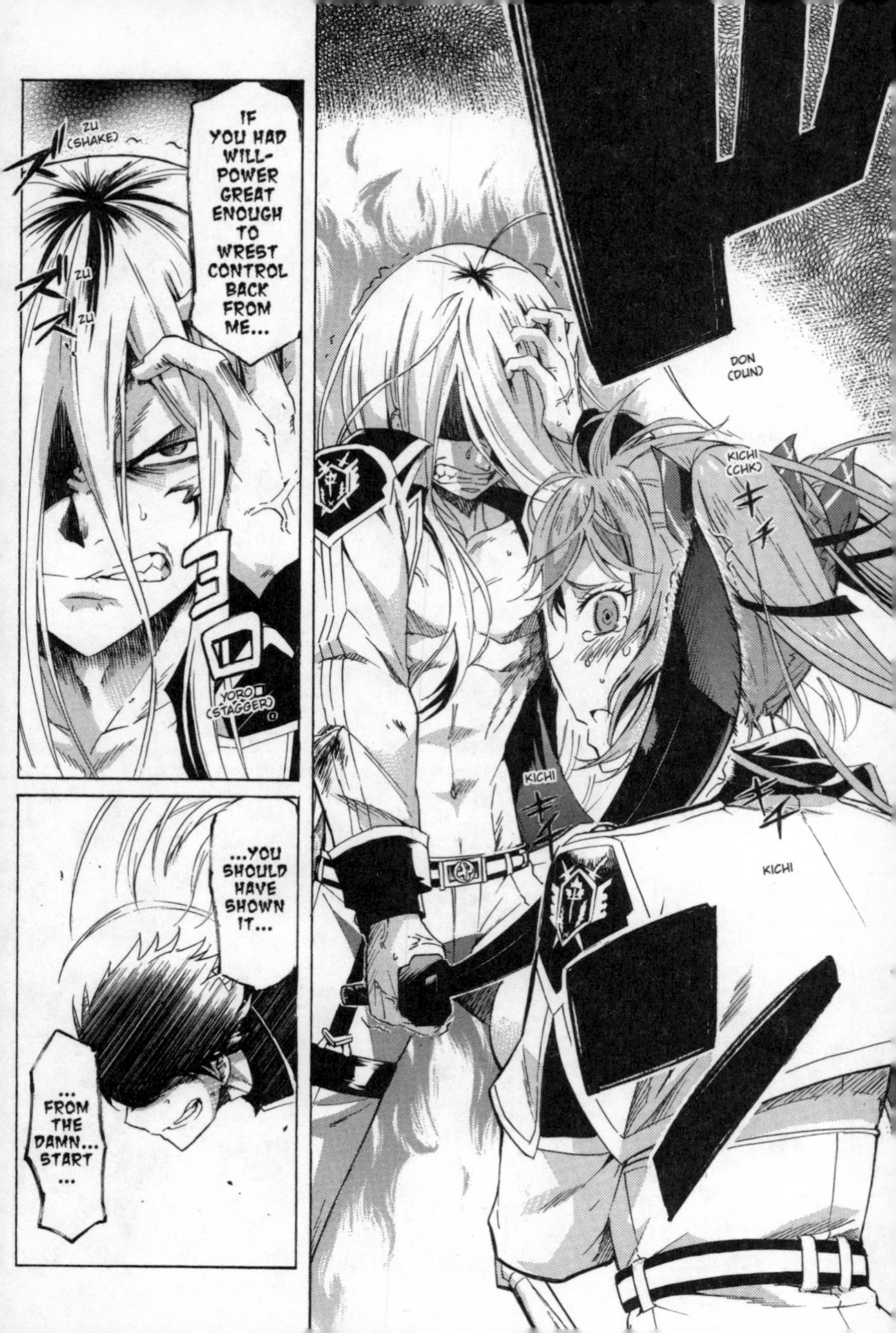
DON (DUN)
KICHI (CHK)
KICHI
KICHI
IF YOU HAD WILL-POWER GREAT ENOUGH TO WREST CONTROL BACK FROM ME...
ZU (SHAKE)
ZU
ZU
YORO (STAGGER)
...YOU SHOULD HAVE SHOWN IT...
...FROM THE DAMN... START...

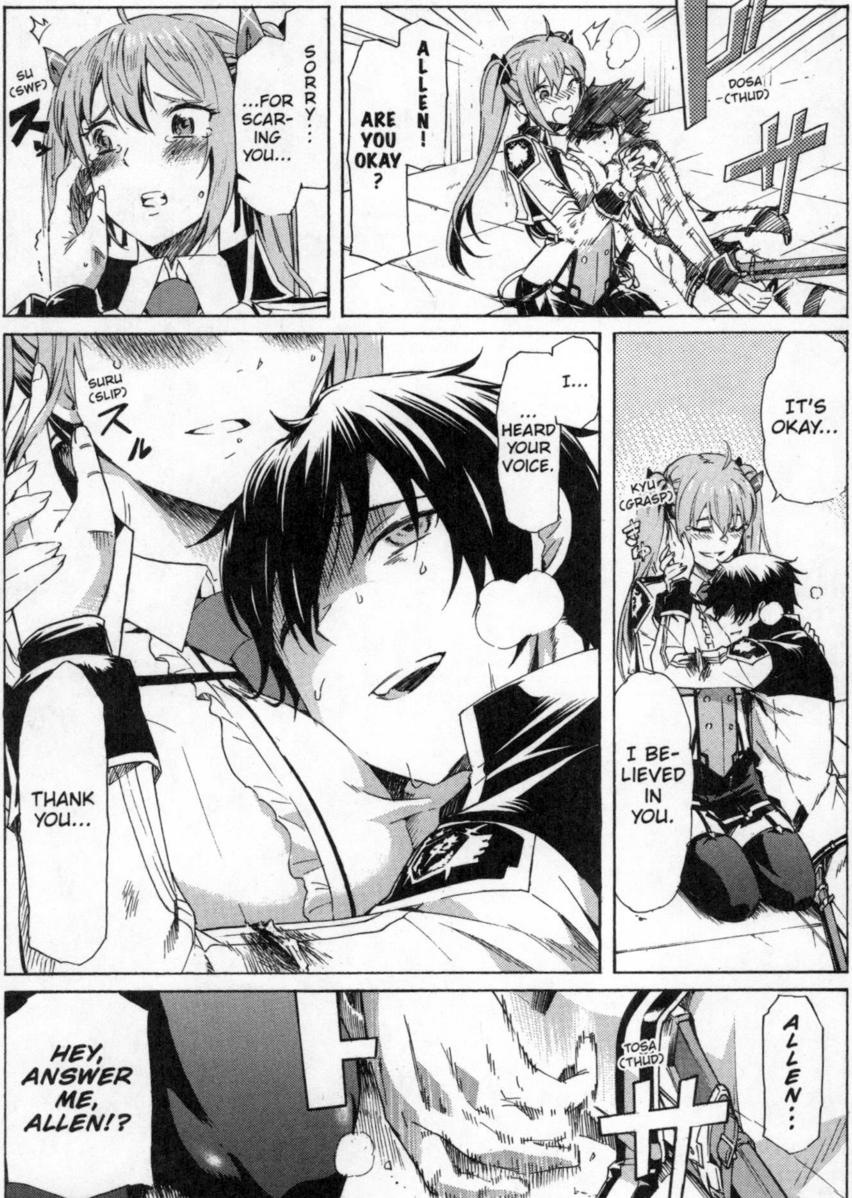
DOSA (THUD)
ALLEN! ARE YOU OKAY?
SORRY...
...FOR SCARING YOU...
SU (SWF)
IT'S OKAY...
KYU (GRASP)
I BELIEVED IN YOU.
I...
...HEARD YOUR VOICE.
SURU (SLIP)
THANK YOU...
ALLEN...
TOSA (THUD)
HEY, ANSWER ME, ALLEN!?

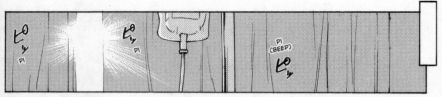

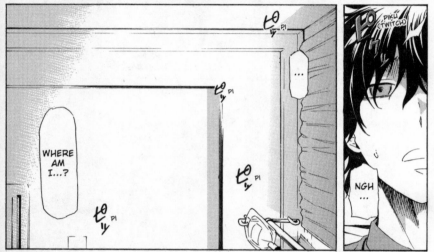

PI (BEEP)
ピッ
ピッ
PI
ピッ
PI
ピクッ
PIKU (TWITCH)
NGH ...
...
ピッ
PI
ピッ
PI
ピッ
PI
WHERE AM I...?
ピッ
PI
ググ..
GUGU (TREMBLE)
SUUU (ZZZ)
スー
SUUU
スー...

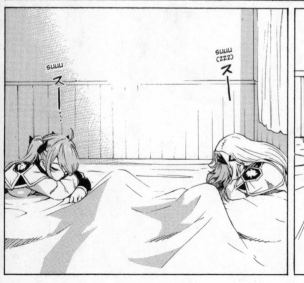

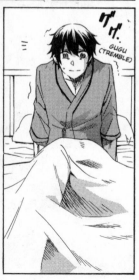

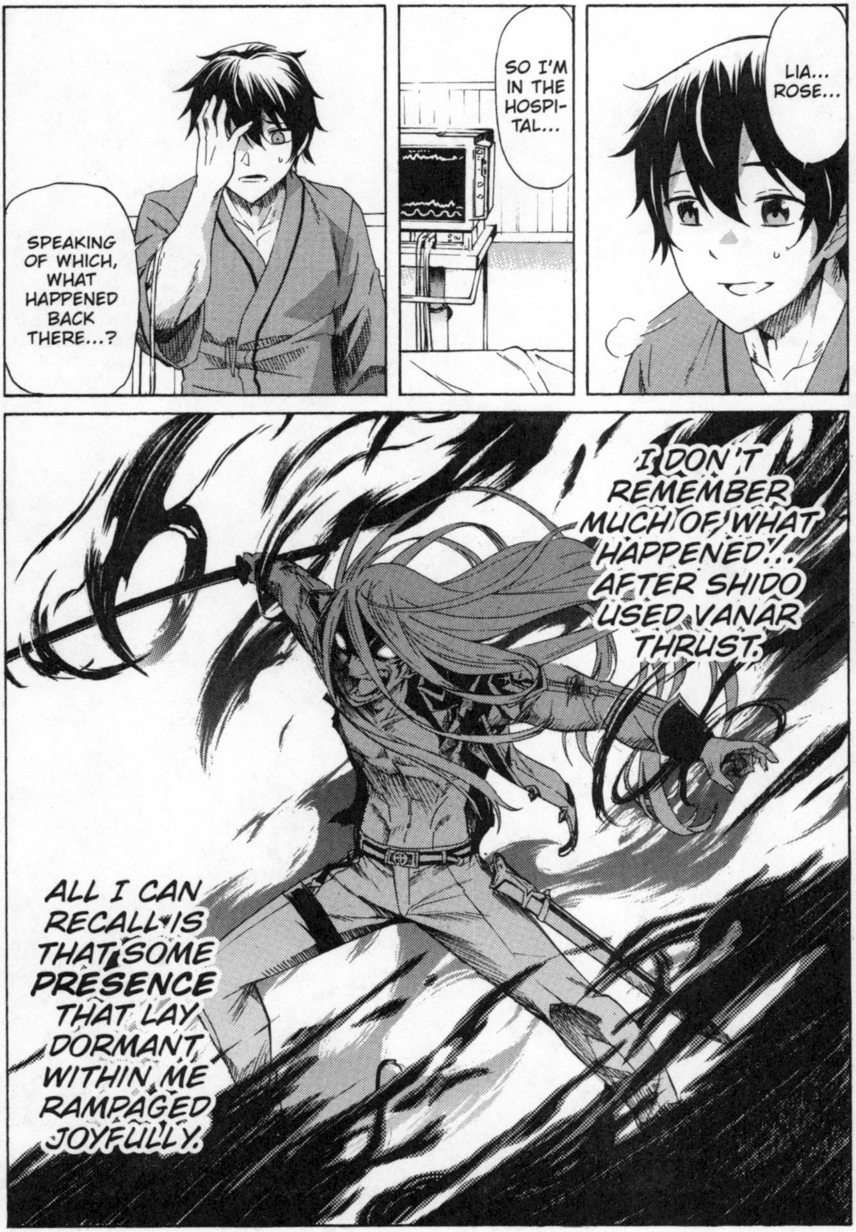
LIA... ROSE...
SO I'M IN THE HOSPITAL...
SPEAKING OF WHICH, WHAT HAPPENED BACK THERE...?
I DON'T REMEMBER MUCH OF WHAT HAPPENED... AFTER SHIDO USED VANAR THRUST.
ALL I CAN RECALL IS THAT SOME PRESENCE THAT LAY DORMANT WITHIN ME RAMPAGED JOYFULLY.

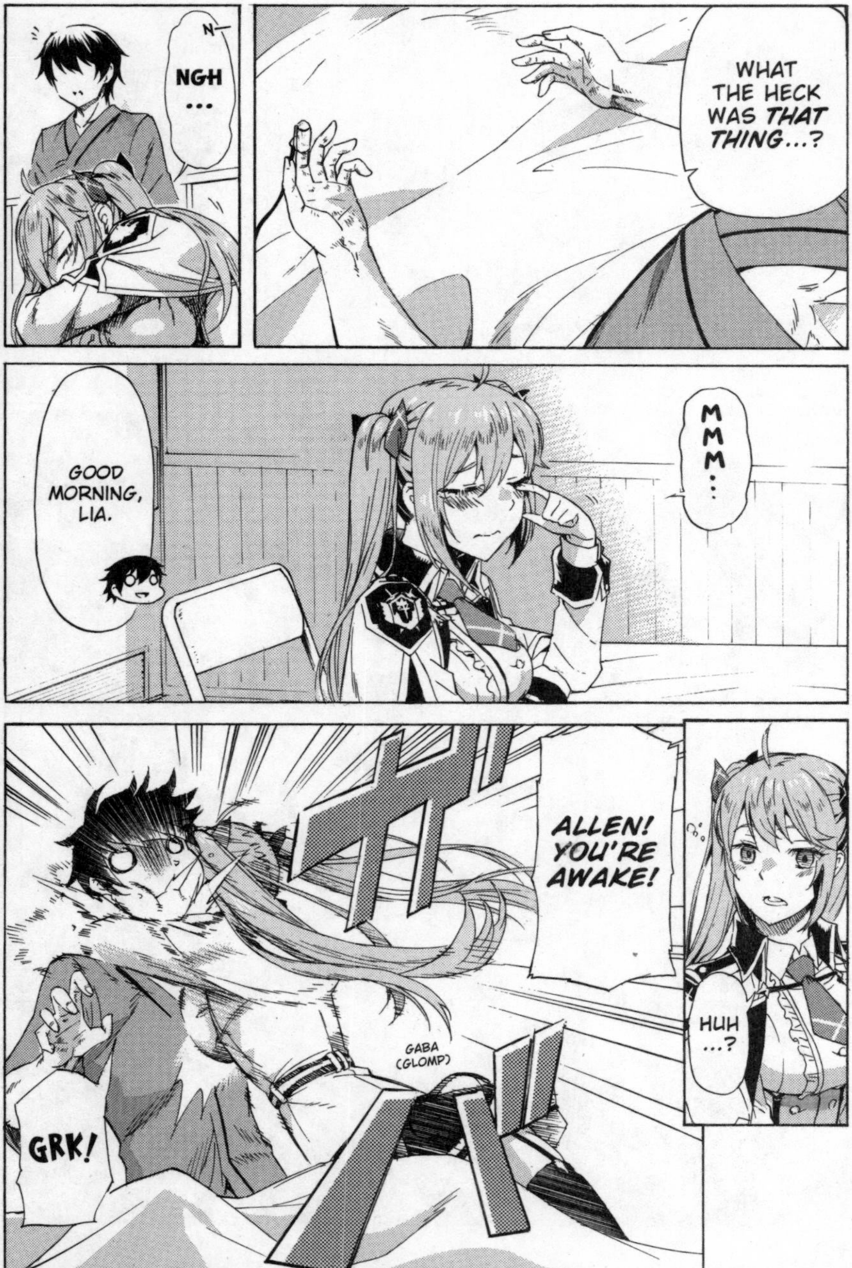
WHAT THE HECK WAS THAT THING...?
N—
NGH ...
MMM...
GOOD MORNING, LIA.
HUH ...?
ALLEN! YOU'RE AWAKE!
GABA (GLOMP)
GRK!

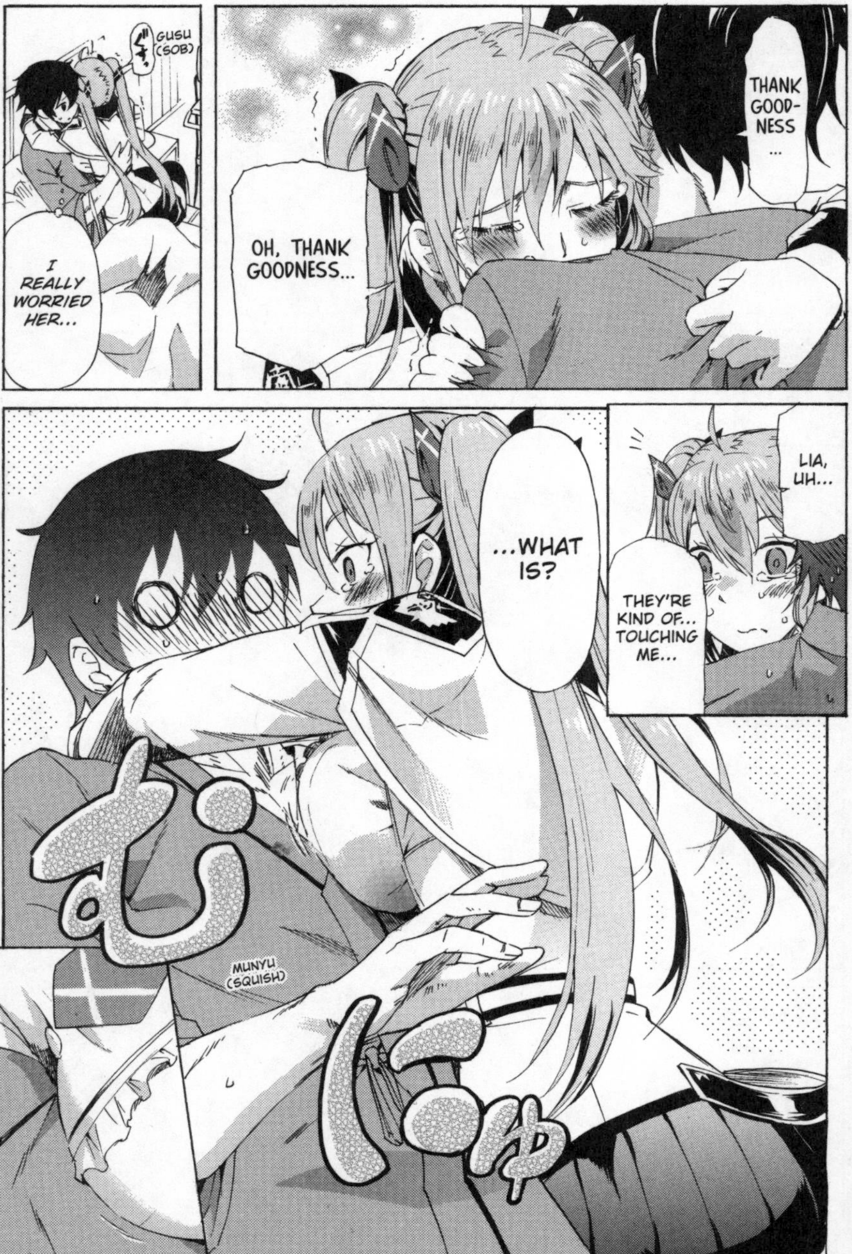
THANK GOOD- NESS ...
OH, THANK GOODNESS...
ぐすっ
GUSU (SOB)
I REALLY WORRIED HER...
LIA, UH...
THEY'RE KIND OF... TOUCHING ME...
...WHAT IS?
むにゅ
MUNYU (SQUISH)

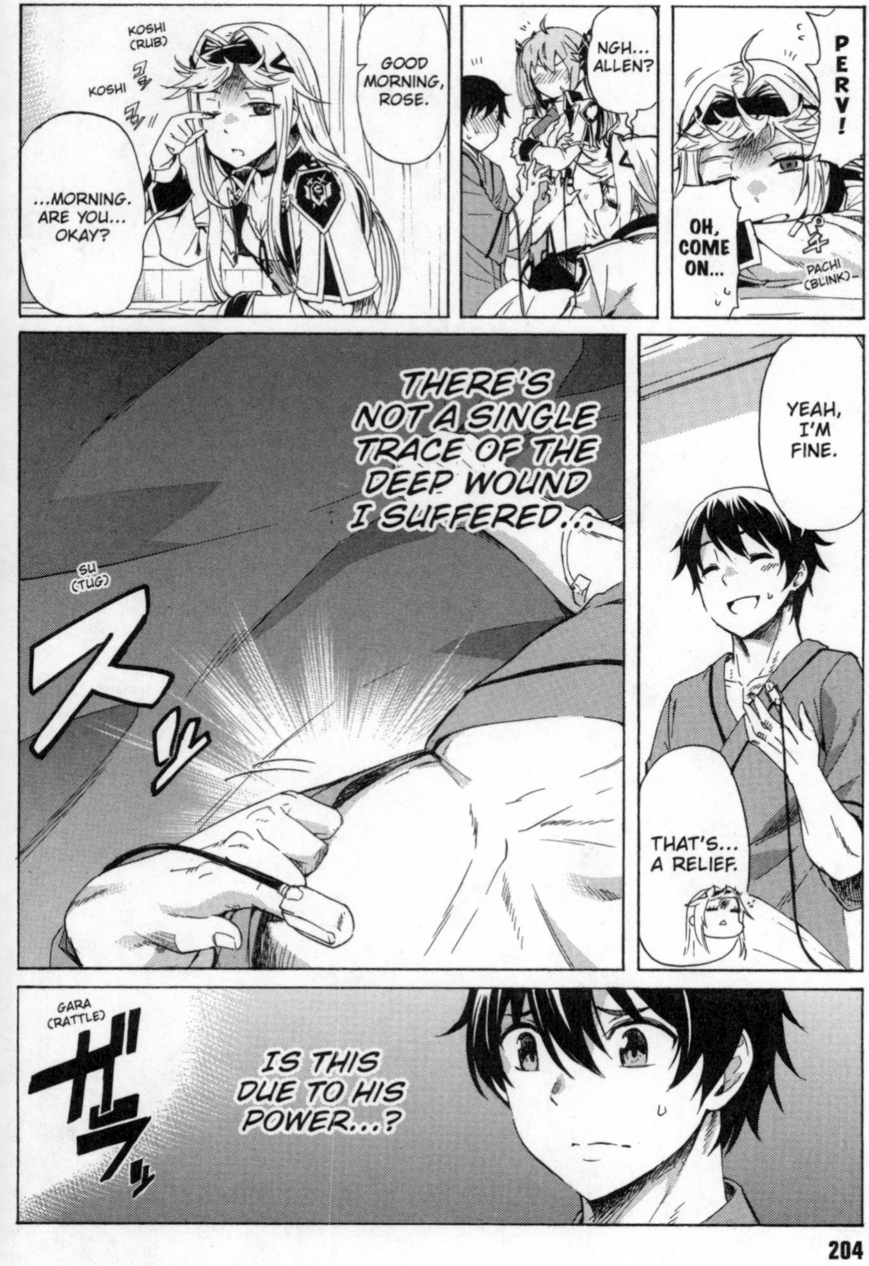
PERV!
OH, COME ON...
PACHI (BLINK)
NGH... ALLEN?
GOOD MORNING, ROSE.
KOSHI (RUB)
KOSHI
...MORNING. ARE YOU... OKAY?
YEAH, I'M FINE.
THAT'S... A RELIEF.
THERE'S NOT A SINGLE TRACE OF THE DEEP WOUND I SUFFERED...
SU (TUG)
GARA (RATTLE)
IS THIS DUE TO HIS POWER...?

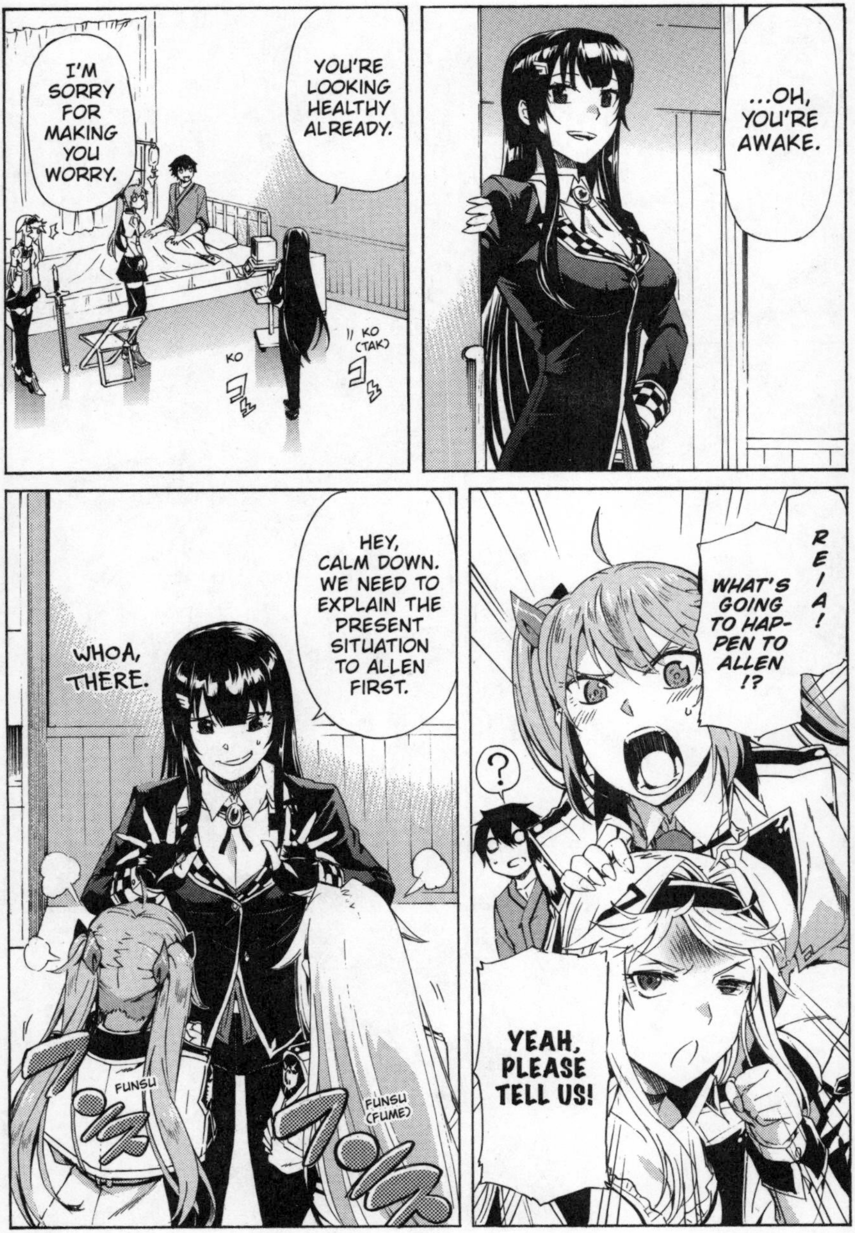
...OH, YOU'RE AWAKE.
YOU'RE LOOKING HEALTHY ALREADY.
I'M SORRY FOR MAKING YOU WORRY.
KO (TAK)
KO
REIA!
WHAT'S GOING TO HAPPEN TO ALLEN!?
?
YEAH, PLEASE TELL US!
HEY, CALM DOWN. WE NEED TO EXPLAIN THE PRESENT SITUATION TO ALLEN FIRST.
WHOA, THERE.
FUNSU (FUME)
FUNSU

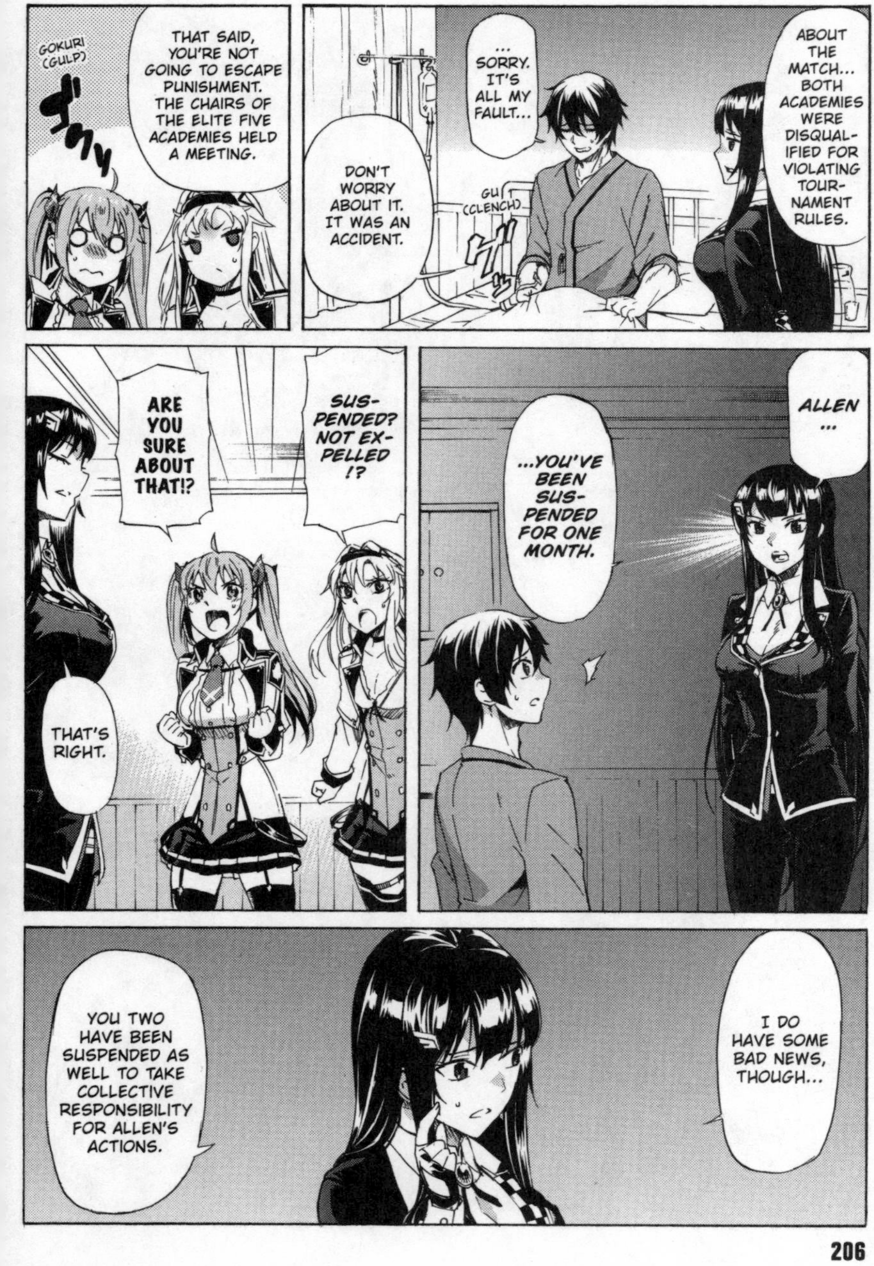
ABOUT THE MATCH... BOTH ACADEMIES WERE DISQUALIFIED FOR VIOLATING TOURNAMENT RULES.
... SORRY. IT'S ALL MY FAULT...
GU (CLENCH)
DON'T WORRY ABOUT IT. IT WAS AN ACCIDENT.
THAT SAID, YOU'RE NOT GOING TO ESCAPE PUNISHMENT. THE CHAIRS OF THE ELITE FIVE ACADEMIES HELD A MEETING.
GOKURI (GULP)
ALLEN ...
...YOU'VE BEEN SUSPENDED FOR ONE MONTH.
SUSPENDED? NOT EXPELLED!?
ARE YOU SURE ABOUT THAT!?
THAT'S RIGHT.
I DO HAVE SOME BAD NEWS, THOUGH...
YOU TWO HAVE BEEN SUSPENDED AS WELL TO TAKE COLLECTIVE RESPONSIBILITY FOR ALLEN'S ACTIONS.

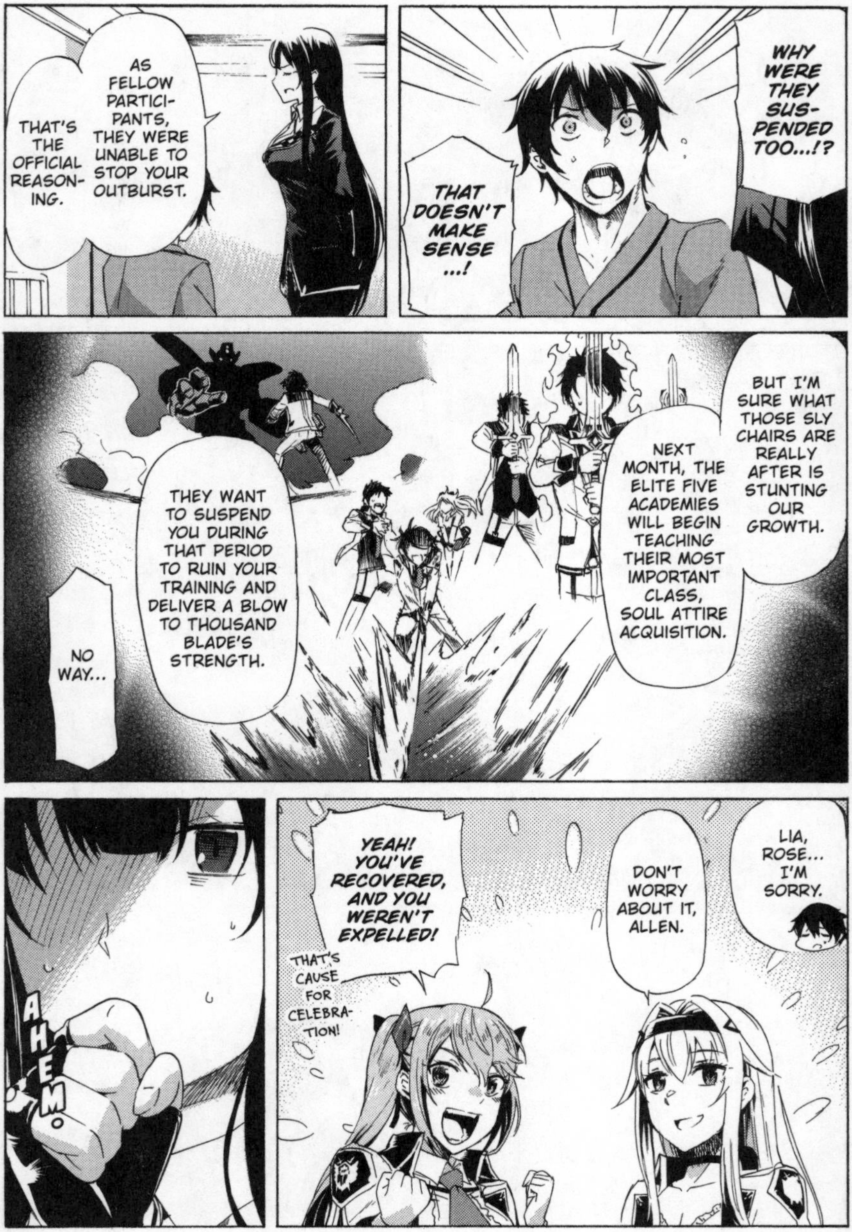
WHY WERE THEY SUS-PENDED TOO...!?
THAT DOESN'T MAKE SENSE ...!
AS FELLOW PARTICI-PANTS, THEY WERE UNABLE TO STOP YOUR OUTBURST.
THAT'S THE OFFICIAL REASON-ING.
BUT I'M SURE WHAT THOSE SLY CHAIRS ARE REALLY AFTER IS STUNTING OUR GROWTH.
NEXT MONTH, THE ELITE FIVE ACADEMIES WILL BEGIN TEACHING THEIR MOST IMPORTANT CLASS, SOUL ATTIRE ACQUISITION.
THEY WANT TO SUSPEND YOU DURING THAT PERIOD TO RUIN YOUR TRAINING AND DELIVER A BLOW TO THOUSAND BLADE'S STRENGTH.
NO WAY...
LIA, ROSE... I'M SORRY.
DON'T WORRY ABOUT IT, ALLEN.
YEAH! YOU'VE RECOVERED, AND YOU WEREN'T EXPELLED!
THAT'S CAUSE FOR CELEBRA-TION!
AHEM

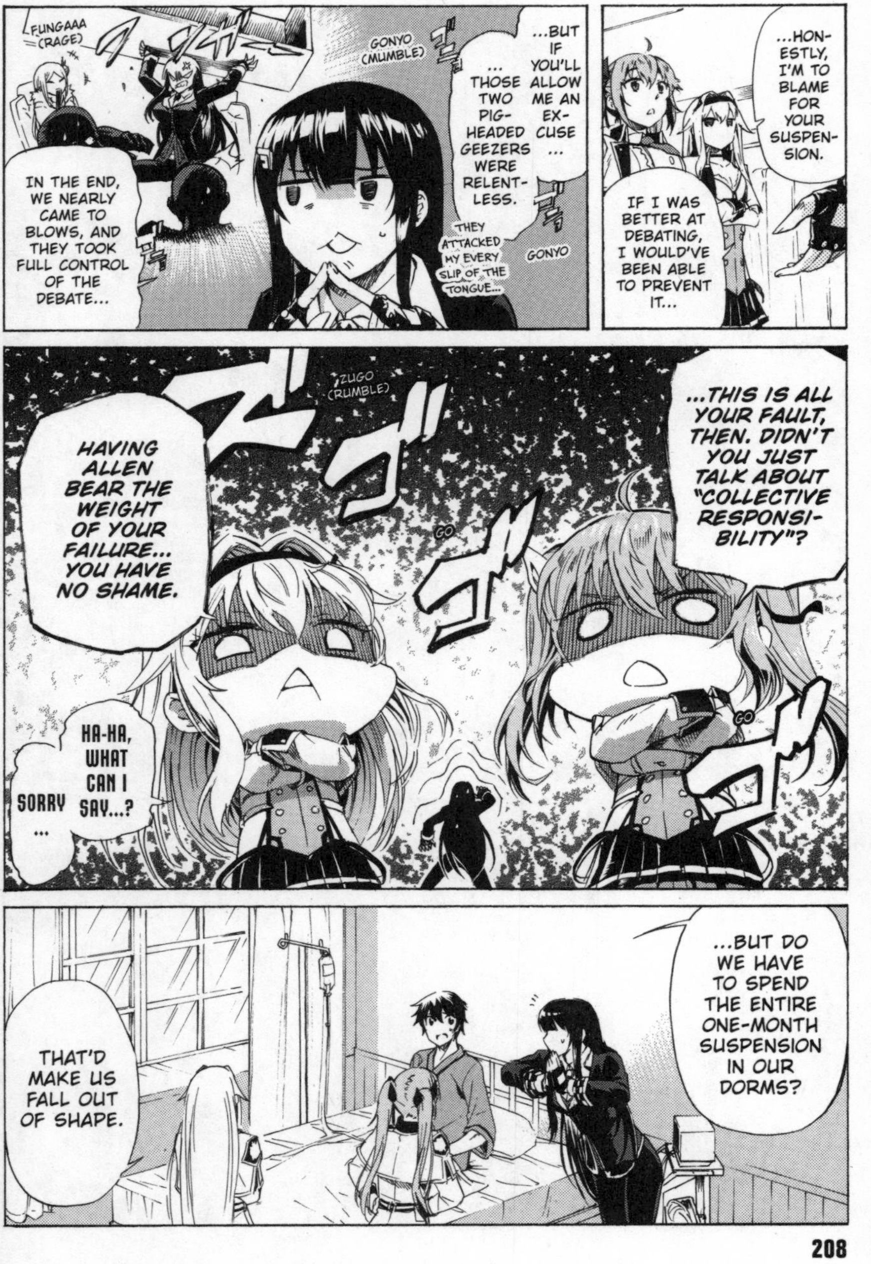
...HON-ESTLY, I'M TO BLAME FOR YOUR SUSPEN-SION.
IF I WAS BETTER AT DEBATING, I WOULD'VE BEEN ABLE TO PREVENT IT...
...BUT IF YOU'LL ALLOW ME AN EX-CUSE ...
GONYO (MUMBLE)
... THOSE TWO PIG-HEADED GEEZERS WERE RELENT-LESS.
THEY ATTACKED MY EVERY SLIP OF THE TONGUE...
GONYO
FUNGAAA (RAGE)
IN THE END, WE NEARLY CAME TO BLOWS, AND THEY TOOK FULL CONTROL OF THE DEBATE...
...THIS IS ALL YOUR FAULT, THEN. DIDN'T YOU JUST TALK ABOUT "COLLECTIVE RESPONSI-BILITY"?
ZUGO (RUMBLE)
GO
HAVING ALLEN BEAR THE WEIGHT OF YOUR FAILURE... YOU HAVE NO SHAME.
GO
HA-HA, WHAT CAN I SAY...?
SORRY ...
...BUT DO WE HAVE TO SPEND THE ENTIRE ONE-MONTH SUSPENSION IN OUR DORMS?
THAT'D MAKE US FALL OUT OF SHAPE.

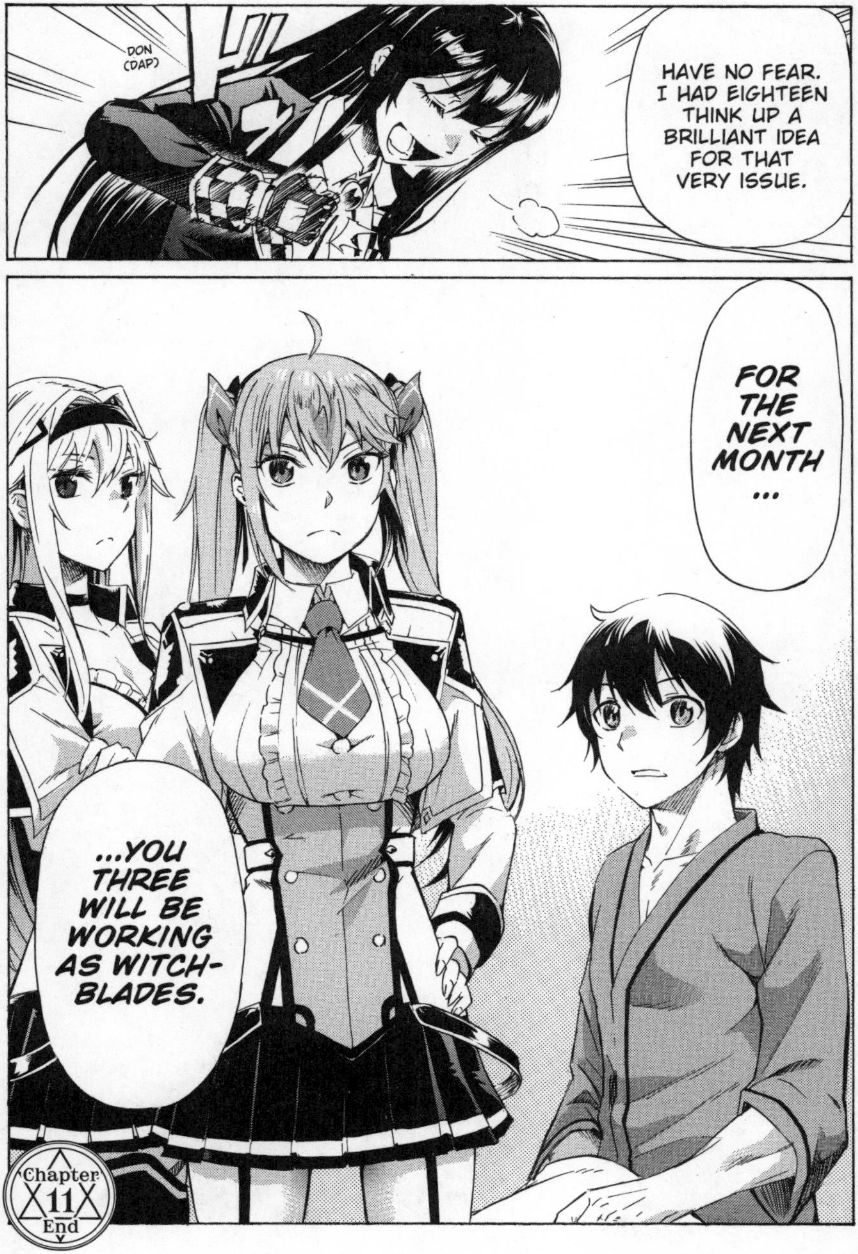
DON (DAP)
HAVE NO FEAR. I HAD EIGHTEEN THINK UP A BRILLIANT IDEA FOR THAT VERY ISSUE.
FOR THE NEXT MONTH...
...YOU THREE WILL BE WORKING AS WITCH-BLADES.
Chapter 11 End

I KEPT PRESSING THE 100-MILLION-YEAR BUTTON AND CAME OUT ON TOP

~THE UNBEATABLE REJECT SWORDSMAN~